Erotic Innocence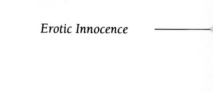

Erotic Innocence

The Culture of Child Molesting

James R. Kincaid

Duke University Press

Durham and London 1998

© 1998 Duke University Press

All rights reserved

Printed in the United States of
America on acid-free paper ∞

Typeset in Berkeley Medium by
Tseng Information Systems, Inc.

Library of Congress
Cataloging-in-Publication Data
appear on the last printed page
of this book.

For Eve Kosofsky Sedgwick ————

"In the meantime, in between
time—ain't we got fun"

Contents

Acknowledgments

Some people write good acknowledgments; others write good books. That's what an old editor of mine once let fall: wisdom acquired over the course of a long career, nothing personal. When you come to think of it, though, it takes a bigger soul to do an acknowledgments and make you believe it than to write a book and get good reviews. In order to sound sincere in acknowledgments you have to be truly generous (it can't be faked); you can get good reviews without having any heart at all. I for one have never gotten good reviews. That says it all.

But it is a bad idea to get so relaxed in writing your acknowledgments that you doze into irony, making fun of friends, kidding around, as we all do with those we love best and feel no aggression toward at all, no. I have made that mistake. At one point, I made some jokes about friends who truly had helped me a great deal, sort of, in an atmospheric way. I pretended they had helped me not at all—had, I said (all ludically) gone out of their way to offend me, mislead me, retard my labors, and salt my ground. Just joking. I remember saying that about Gerhard Joseph, N. John "Jack" Hall (who once ran for sheriff), Juliet McMaster, Rob Polhemus, W. J. T. (don't call me "Tom") Mitchell, Regina Schwartz, self-seeking old Joe Wittreich, Garrett Stewart, Gina Barreca (who really will turn on you if you cross her), Julian Markels, Uli Knoepflmacher, Hilary Schor, Phyllis Franklin, Jeffrey Robinson, that thing Joel Conarroe, and many more I now can't remember ever meeting.

To my amazement, dozens of scholars, almost all of greater stature and experience in the world than those I had so affectionately mocked, missed the irony and wrote to me letters of commiseration. I quote but two, make that three:

> I think it shows what times we live in that such as those you name can rise to where they are at. I deeply symathize with you and I hope you know better now where your trust should be placed and not in that lot again.

> I have as it happens had similar experiences with many of those who betrayed you and hate them even more than you, as their crimes against me were greater. Who is N. John Hall?

> What the hell did you expect, you simple son of a bitch?

I therefore take pains here to be free from irony and to identify clearly those who did help me and to distinguish them with clarity from those who tried but failed, those who refused, those who were willing but not asked, and those I thought about asking but decided no I wouldn't.

Those who helped (really) were the late Arthur Adrian, Sherman Alexie, Nina Auerbach (yes!), Gina Barreca (why not?), Kent Baxter, Mark Behr, Virginia Blum, Joe Boone, Leo Braudy, Les Brill, Jerry Bruns, Terry Caesar, David Cherin, Patricia Cherin, Cathy Comstock, Joel Conarroe (gasp), Lawrence Driscoll, Martha Grace Duncan, Shantanu Dutthamed, Kevin Ennis, Duncan Faherty, Keith Fitzgerald, James Fleming, Bill Germano (no matter what they say), Pamela Gilbert, John Glavin, Ron Gottesman (responsible for defects in taste), Tim Gustafson, N. John Hall (preposterous), I. B. Harrison (who merits far better company), Anne Higgonet, Al Hutter, Richard Ide, Wendy Jacobson, Heather Menzies Jones, John Jordan, Gerhard Joseph (you'll find him in the morning sun), Valerie Karno, Walter Kendrick, John Kennedy, U. C. Knoepflmacher (gotta love him), Judith Levine, Joseph Litvak, John Maclean, Peter Manning, Julian Markels, Christy Marx, Carol Mavor, Teresa McKenna, Juliet McMaster, Roland McMaster (no relation), Buck McMullen, Barry Milligan, Tania Modleski, Richard Mohr, Barry Moser, Colby Nelson, Rich Nicholls, John Nuckols, Paul Petersen, Rob Polhemus, Michael Preston, Cathy Preston, Harly Ramsey, Mike Reynolds, Adrian Richwell, J. E. Rivers, Beth Robertson, Jeffrey Robinson, Susan Scheckel, Hilary Schor (as always), Regina Schwartz, Eve Kosofsky Sedgwick (beyond all), Linda Shires,

Don Solomon, Mark Spilka, Matthew Stadler, John Stevenson, Garrett Stewart, Chris Stone, Larry Swingle (even he), Alan Thomas, Richard Tithecott, Robert Weil, Pat Winter, Julian Wolfreys.

Some will say the list is too long and, for all my preliminary noises, makes no discriminations, mixes in the distinguished with the dubious, the scholarly with the citizenry, those actively engaged in the project with those unaware that it was afloat. But that's not so. All these friends (many are friends) were involved in the same way and to the same extent, apart from a few who did more or less than the average: Eve at the top and Hall at the tail. That's the way life is.

And I will now name those who did nothing whatever or less, just as I said I would: Gerhard Joseph, Larry Swingle, N. John Hall, Gerald Bruns, Camille Paglia, W. J. T. Mitchell, Harold Bloom, and that wretch McMaster (take your pick). Some made both lists—not an error, human variability.

I should thank my Duke University Press editor, Ken Wissoker, who had the wisdom to spot this book and publish it afterward.

Beth Vesel, my dear agent and friend, got this book going not only by seeding the idea but by helping give it form and cheering for it even when it was at its most gangling and offensive. Her intelligent energies and good nature never flagged.

My immediate family deserves mention, among them my wife, Nita Moots Kincaid, and my children, who are Matthew, Anne, and Elizabeth, in order of age. I have a granddaughter, Whitney, who appeared at many points in the first version of the manuscript. One Duke reader said, "I think one mention of Kincaid's happy little granddaughter is too damn many." I would have felt more keenly my gratitude to Ken Wissoker had he told me to ignore that. Still, I must say that, little as my wife and children were willing, despite their talents, ever to come within miles of this book, I appreciate them all the same. It can't, after all, be easy to be the wife of a guy spending year after year inquiring into the subject of children and sexuality: searching out porn shops for underage material, scanning the World Wide Web for its darkest sites, eyeing the little ones in grocery stores, reading outlawed texts, and not all of them scholarly. And imagine what it would be like to be a child in such an environment and with such a patriarch. How could you have friends over or do anything but hide on parents' night? I admire them and their enduring wit. And my mother too, who blames nobody. I owe a special debt to Matt, who did the work on the illustrations that was beyond me, which amounted to all of it.

Glad-souled Eve Kosofsky Sedgwick deserves much more from me, considering all she's done and allowed and made possible, than this dedication and my loud and forever devotion; but if she got what she deserves, the wealth and heart of the whole profession would tilt dangerously toward Durham. We can't have that. I feel that a dedication and a few tasteful greeting cards now and then are about right.

This book was written with the spirit of my brother hanging out among its most incautious moments, those I love best as I loved him beyond any best.

Erotic Innocence

Introduction

I cannot say how truth may be;
I say the tale as 'twas said to me.
—Sir Walter Scott, "The Lay of the
Last Minstrel"

There are, and have been, many stories
in the culture and in other cultures
through which people examine, and
do other things to, their lives.—Adam
Phillips, *On Kissing, Tickling, and Being
Bored: Psychoanalytic Essays on the
Unexamined Life*

Our lives are stories that are being
told. The trick is to horn in on the
telling.—Anon.

Geraldo, Oprah, Sally Jessy, and many another daytime talk-show host are being flashed on the back screen, mouths flapping soundlessly. In the foreground, Morley Safer introduces an episode of *60 Minutes* (May 1, 1994) by pointing out the gulf separating his prime-time news program from the talk shows. Speaking with complacent outrage, Safer tells us, "Unspeakable things are reported, re-created, and dissected almost hourly on a strident collection of talk shows. Amidst all the noise and freakishness are the victims, the victims of the most unspeakable of crimes, childhood sexual abuse." There's a whole lot of unspeakableness going on.

Safer carefully distinguishes his after-dark show from the daytime talkers,[1] just before joining with them in speaking the unspeakable. This particular *60 Minutes* episode removes (for the first time) the muzzle on Roseanne Arnold's family.[2] Now they reveal all, refuting point by point Roseanne's claims (first made on Sally Jessy's show) that she was "very much an abused child," able to track down clear memories of molestation back to the age of six months and still going. "Utter nonsense!" say her parents, her brother, and her two sisters. Granted, Jerry Barr is a "tushy-toucher"; he freely admits that, and, as one daughter says, "The punishment ought to fit the crime," whatever that means. Anyhow, the whole family (with the one famous exception) insists that Mom is guiltless and that Jerry's mild crimes do not include doing what the crazed Roseanne said to Sally Jessy in broad daylight he did: molesting Roseanne's daughter while Mom was tying the knot (loosely) with Tom Arnold, or putting his hand down sister Stephanie's pants. Jerry may have gotten into a fight with Stephanie and pushed her down on the bed—Stephanie tells us about that—but the family is agreed, on examining the details and exploring them with us, that such things cannot reasonably be called molesting. And *60 Minutes* lays all this before us, withdraws, and leaves us to judge.

You see the point: *60 Minutes* may have been scooped on Roseanne but managed to outbid Sally Jessy for the follow-up, leaving her, Phil, and Oprah to manage as best they could with day-care scandals and satanic cults. Despite Safer's unctuous sarcasms, this bold breaking-of-the-silence surrounding child molesting is really much the same wherever you find it. And you find it in all its soft-core particularity everywhere: in cinemas, bookstores, schoolrooms, lecture halls, psychotherapists' offices, Marge's garage, Fred's hair salon, and in us. The media doesn't mind saying what cannot be said because we long to hear it; and we long to hear it because it's what we're saying too. The media is not so much a source as a friendly satellite bouncing back to us the story of child molesting we often hear, tell ourselves, and find so satisfying that we love even the echoes.

This book is a study of such storytelling: where it comes from, what forms it takes, what it does for us and to our children. Few stories in our culture right now are as popular as those of child molesting, and I wonder why this should be so. We are likely to say that the reality of sexual child abuse compels us to speak, to break the silence; but I would like to poke at that compulsion and at the connections between "the reality of sexual child abuse" and the stories we tell about it. Why do we generate these stories and not others? What rewards do they offer? Who profits from their circulation, and who pays the price?

This talk of "stories" does not mean that I regard child molesting as unreal; reality comes to us in the form of stories. When we fish for truth, for reality, for a memory, for the child within, for instructions on how to behave, for clues on the world we inhabit, we haul up a story. Look at yourself in the high-school yearbook, in the mirror, through the eyes of others, and you begin listening to stories. When we ask, "What's what?" we get back, "Once upon a time. . . ." So we understand having breakfast and having fun, doing our jobs and doing our duty, making mistakes and making love. We live and have our being within stories.

SCARED SILENT

WAYS TO SAVE OUR CHILDREN FROM ABUSE AND NEGLECT

This pamphlet, prepared by the National Committee for the Prevention of Child Abuse, was issued as a supplement to the television documentary *Scared Silent: Exposing and Ending Child Abuse,* hosted by Oprah Winfrey.

I recognize that those caught within the terrors of child molestation are likely to regard what they are telling us not as a narrative but as truth. The victimized and those accused, along with those close to them, may deplore the recasting of their pain as a story, feeling that stories have a kind of malleability denied to their experiences. Such resistance is a signal both of the depth of the pain and, I think, of the success our current story has had in selling itself as natural, as pure fact. But the commonsense notion that some hit-you-in-the-nose truths are simply *there,* plain and simple, is what allows our mainline story to pass for truth. The question, for me, is not whether truth and pain (joy and falsehood) are delivered in stories, but whether we have some choice in stories and some ability to see what our current stories are doing for us. Some stories have a very narrow focus and cause damage and confusion even as they seek to give certainty. Somewhere out there may be a healing story, of use both to us and to our children.

The particular stories that interest me here are not personal but general, a set of remarkable cultural narratives that give form to our actions and our ways of seeing children, sexuality, and transgression. These general stories are not invented by individuals but circulate like rumors or viruses. We are thus never outside these stories but always live within them, not just telling the tale but playing our parts in it. But again, why these tales and not others? And why do we tell them with such enthusiasm? Put another way: how do we know what we know about child molesting and how do we purchase our certainty?

And why, to deal openly with a vexing issue, speak of "we"? We who? I use the first-person plural to include myself, of course, but also to indicate that I am speaking of stories that blow through all of us and of locations on a map where we find ourselves without being aware that we are anyplace in particular or that where we are conditions what we see. Some geographies exact a lot from us. We are aware of that when we are on top of Everest or in Las Vegas, but I am trying to get at the commonality formed by a set of culturally and historically specific stories that we are told and tell, quite earnestly, without recognizing their source or their consequences. "We" is the we watching *60 Minutes,* protecting our children, chemically castrating "sexual predators."

But the "we" is both variable and relatively free. There are within the community a variety of views, so that sometimes my "we" may not include you (or me) but may refer only to a particularly potent or vocal (or even loony) subset of the majority view. "We" may sometimes translate as "men" or "old men" or "white men" or "heterosexuals" or "Christians" or "middle-class sorts." Sure. I am not above trying to persuade myself that I am outside this "we," and that by focusing often on its most ghoulish excesses I am, in part, demonstrating what I imagine to be my superiority to this snarling clan. I am aware, though, that these feints are both feeble and common, and that we are all implicated in a contemporary discourse on children, sexuality, and assault so mighty that it comes close to defining our moment. I trust that we can, you and me, do something with that awareness, that we (all of us) are not so eager to escape acknowledging our membership in this we-club that we skid past the point: we got ourselves into this mess and we can get ourselves out. We are not roped to paranoid conceptions of Power or to historical determinism; we need only tell different stories. We can do that.

For a long decade or so, we have been uncovering stories of sexual child abuse in the United States, discovering the alarming reach of these stories, their range and variety, only to have the pendulum swing. Suddenly, we hear that memory is suspect, that accounts of molestation that come from children are dubious, that therapists may be crooks, that Freud himself is wobbling. As we up the voltage and try to deal with the dilemma by more carefully tagging the offenders, the counterreaction grows as well. How can we locate in this bog a solid place to stand? That the stories proliferate and double back on themselves does not indicate indifference, certainly; but it may suggest that our stories are providing us with something other than solutions.

We are forever assuring ourselves that we are in denial, avoiding the issue; it takes, we say, great courage to speak out on a problem most people ignore or repress. That's an odd diagnosis, considering that these stories come at us (and from us) like killer bees. Take a look at these tales as they circulate, and two things are immediately apparent: their redundancy and their strength. When we locate a good story, which we do every week or so, we chew on it ferociously: Michael Jackson, pedophile priests, recovered memory, six-year-old molesters.

I begin with two preliminary assumptions. The first is that these stories are doing something for us: we wouldn't be telling this tale of the exploitation of the child's body if we didn't wish to have it told. The second is that what these stories do for us is keep the subject hot so we can disown it while welcoming it in the back door. These stories are not told simply to solve a problem but also to focus and restate the problem, to keep it alive and before us. If the stories we tell about child molesting were designed to enlighten us or to attack the problem, we might say, they would extinguish themselves.

Of course we all are concerned with the way our children are being abused. I think, though, that this concern for our children has to do battle with the way we tell about our concern, the way we give form to the popular story of "the child." Our storytelling has become so formulaic and so "natural" that it channels far too much of our concern into self-gratification. In the case of child molesting and its culturally approved narratives, we have stories that allow us a hard-core righteous prurience; it's a scapegoating exercise we have come to depend on. Through these stories of what monsters are doing to children, we find ourselves forced (permitted) to speak of just what it is they are doing; we take a good, long look at what they are doing. We denounce it all loudly but never have done with it, and are back denouncing it the next day, not ignoring the details. We reject this monstrous activity with such automatic indignation that the indignation comes to seem almost like pleasure.

This is a study of these stories and where they come from, of the Romantic heritage of "the child and its body" and our current reckless expenditure of this dangerous nineteenth-century inheritance. These stories seemed sweet and beneficent to Wordsworth, Dickens, and Beatrix Potter; but they have soured over time. It's not so much that they became silly and sentimental, though they may have, but that they took a turn into nightmare. These are nightmares we deal with pathologically: through disavowal, projection, and displacement. I seek here to rob these stories of at least some of their power by exposing them and their functions. What is at stake is our own honor (and health) as adults and the bodies and future of our dear children.

If the talk we are talking, then, is continuous with the problem it is addressing, if the solutions are mixed in with the dilemmas, it is time to talk about the talking. It should be clear, though, that there is no position inside the present discussions of children, sexuality, and power that will allow me to assess with easy objectivity what those discussions are doing. Still, while it is impossible to avoid common ideas altogether, since that would mean moving to Jupiter, I will try as best I can to resist the assumptions we hold most dear, suspecting that they might be cohabiting with the predicament itself.

It is for this reason that I shun the most compelling ritual gesture of all: acknowledging that of course sexual child abuse does exist, and on a very large scale. I do not deny it; I just do not want to begin the discussion in the territory left to me once I offer that disclaimer. I think, in fact, that this disclaimer is a vital part of the discourse that eroticizes the child and keeps us blind to what we are doing. It forces the discussion into channels of diagnosis and cure, mandates assumptions about what is and is not important, allows us to see some things and blinds us to others. I do not offer one more set of tips on how to determine whether or not child molesting happened. I am writing about another set of happenings: what happens to us and to our children as we tell our stories of the child and of sexuality.

It is not to the point to keep acknowledging that "molestation happens." Even the most skeptical books analyzing the current scene begin the discussion by saying, in effect, "Please don't misunderstand me; I know millions of children are sexually molested." That we feel compelled to ward off such misunderstandings suggests that our discourse has a very narrow range, a range that is conscientiously policed. Within that range, only variations on a single story can be heard, and it is this story, I believe, that walks the same beat as the molestation against which it protests. When we seek to adjust the protesting stories by removing from the plot a dubious point—recovered memory, satanic abuse, or alien abductions—we do nothing to disrupt the circuitry, only further remove from reach its generating source.

Such disclaimers seem to me custodial, ways of cleaning up little messes here and there, scouring away anomalies in or threats to our belief system so that the main narrative can go on doing its work for us. Offering judicious qualifiers and calming assurances, I can lay claim to virtue and buy a ticket for my argument on the same old bandwagon.

Lurking in the discussion so far have been some questions we don't often ask, probably for very good reason. Take the current headlines on this subject—the latest accused celebrity or day-care center trial—and ask about the source, nature, and size of the pleasures we take from such stories. What accounts for the popularity of these feverish tales about the sexuality of children and assaults on it? What is it that so magnetizes us? Why do we tell the stories we tell and not others? Those are plain questions; but we don't attend to them. We prefer others:

1. How can we spot the pedophiles and get rid of them?
2. How can we protect our children in the meantime?
3. How can we induce our children to tell us the truth, and all of it, about their sexual lives?
4. How can we get the courts to believe children who say they've been sexually molested?
5. How can we get the courts to believe adults who recover memories of being sexually molested as children?
6. How can we get ourselves to believe others when they say they remember being sexually molested years ago?
7. How can we know that people are not making these things up, misremembering?
8. How can we know that bumbling parents, cops, and (especially) therapists are not implanting false memories?

Although some of these questions seem to take revenge on other questions, they all have one thing in common: they demand the same answer: "We can't."

Perhaps that helps explain why both the standard and the backlash stories are so popular: they have about them an urgency and a self-flattering, righteous oomph. Asking these questions, I get the feeling that I care and that I'm on the right side in the vital issues of our time. Even better, these open-ended, unanswerable questions generate variations on themselves and allow us to keep them going, circulating them among ourselves without ever experiencing fatigue.

We have figured the crisis of sexual child abuse as a demonic trap, a tale of terror from which there is no escape. What we have here is an "epidemic" of child molesting, a "National Emergency,"[3] but we seem to have devised the problem as an untreatable disease. Though we have created hundreds of public and private agencies to distribute information, educate children and parents on reliable means of protection, track down the missing, and generally raise awareness, we seem to regard all that as akin to stifling an earthquake by sitting on it. We locate more pedophiles, jail them faster and longer, castrate them, track them, and where are we? Still with "a rising epidemic of child abuse," according to Secretary of Health and Human Services Donna Shalala in September 1996.[4] We have plotted the mystery story so that it can have no solution and no ending.[5]

First of all, we often speak of sexual child abuse in the passive voice —"There is a growing awareness"; "It is generally acknowledged"—as if the story had no locatable source. Second, we make the plot of child abuse unavoidable: everyone has a role. As many healing books tell us, if you have an inkling that you may have been sexually abused as a child, then you probably were and should proceed on that assumption.[6] Such inklings may be inferred from symptoms you develop, symptoms you can find out about (if not develop) by consulting any of a number of lists that will allow you to trace backward from problem to source. If you find yourself anxious or depressed, suffering from low self-esteem or overconfidence, feel uncomfortable being touched or like it too much; if your child has trouble concentrating, eats too much or too little, has fears or phobias, has noticeable changes in behavior, or is incorrigible, the cause is clear. As Roseanne, who knows, told Oprah, "When someone asks you, 'Were you sexually abused as a child?' there are only two answers: One of them is 'Yes,' and one of them is 'I don't know.' You can't say 'No.'"

You can't say no, can't write yourself out of the victim role. Worse luck, you may find yourself cast in opposition, as perpetrator. If you have children of your own or know those who do, if you are a priest, coach, baby-sitter, teacher, or someone walking down the street, you may fit the part. Once cast, you're stuck. You cannot plead incapacity for the role. As many experts tell us (and as the police know for sure), those who challenge these charges are in denial, poor risks for rehabilitation. Only the guilty plead not-guilty, so it is best not to be in denial.

The story is, in short, cagily baited, mysterious, self-perpetuating, inescapable. It is a story of monsters and purity, sunshine and darkness, of being chased by the beast and finding your feet in glue, of tunnels opening onto other tunnels, of exits leading to dead walls. Our story of child molesting is a story of nightmare, the literary territory of the Gothic. On the face of it, the Gothic is not a promising form for casting social problems. Instead of offering solutions, such tales tend to paralyze; they do not move forward but circle back to one more hopeless encounter with the demon. Why would we want that?

Gothic narratives always seem to serve a culture under stress. I do not want to draw sensational parallels to Salem, Nazi Germany, or the McCarthy-ridden 1950s; but the stark moral drama offered by our child-molesting stories does suggest the possibility of scapegoating, or at least of a cover narrative camouflaging needs so dark and urgent we want neither to face them nor to give them up.

The Gothic assumes and creates a terror so urgent it excuses the most brutal appeals. In *Dracula,* the champions of virtue pound a stake slowly through the heart of a beautiful, writhing woman (albeit a vampire), then decapitate her—and we cheer. Similarly, in 1994 the fastidious *New Yorker,* anticipating what is now a fad, ran an editorial entitled "Help for Sex Offenders,"[7] advocating "the castration option" (the magazine prefers "orchiectomy"). Any dark historical precedent for such state-managed "help" is merely a "spectre"; the idea that castration is brutal is "based on misconceptions." The procedure, the editor points out, is scarcely invasive, testicles made of soft tissue and nerve endings simply giving way to high-quality silicone balls. The *New Yorker* rhetoric might be called Orwellian Gothic: it leaves no room to protest that offering a man a choice between prison and castration is not asking him what he "wants," or that dressing up forced castration as "aid" for the sexually compulsive is genteel nightmare. Within a few years, of course, such castration talk became general and lost the need to justify itself.

Just as savage is the glee that greets the news of the suicide of those accused or convicted of sexual crimes involving children: joy at the efficiency of it all or rage that our delight in their torture has been cut short.[8] We include within the Gothic circuitry even prisoners, who are provided a role that allows them rewarding social responsibility, making the murder of jailed sex offenders not uncommon.[9] The recent translation of "sexual offenders" into "sexual predators" transforms these particular criminals into ogres, beyond redemption and with no claim on human civil rights.

We also tell ourselves that these predators are wily and numerous, which means our story will never lack for villains. We guarantee a supply by regarding almost all allegations of sexual offenses made by children as true, which means that the accused are always guilty. The famous (if fallacious) "cycle-of-abuse" notion,[10] which holds that the abused are bound to abuse others when they get the chance, means that the number of predators will increase geometrically, like werewolves.

But the Gothic answers also to more particular needs of our current culture. For one thing, it feeds the not unpleasant idea that we are in the midst of a "moral and spiritual decline," a point 76 percent of us agree with, according to a *Newsweek* poll conducted in June 1994.[11] Stark moral dramas of innocence corrupted seem to fit both conservative Golden Age myths and fundamentalist Christian patterns now finding a ready audience. Sexual child abuse allows us to brandish our own virtue by locating for us a demon, a creature harder to find since the collapse of the "evil empire." Some have suggested that the current obsession with childhood horror is a handy replacement for a hell we only pretend to find plausible.

The child-molesting Gothic story also appeals because it explains so much, explains everything. It is the semiotic shorthand that tells us to look no further: having been on either side of the child-molesting scene defines us completely. It tells us who we are. The fact that the heroine in *Forrest Gump*—and in a hundred other recent narratives— was abused by her drunk, lower-class father explains to our full satisfaction why she is suicidal, drug infested, looking for love in all the wrong places, and willing to settle for the dim-witted hero.

It is also notable that the story offers to the abused the role of the blameless victim, responsible for little and able to understand and explain his life in very satisfactory terms: mistakes and misfortunes rest at someone else's door; only the successes are his doing. Such a position seems to unite, in strange fellowship, the best parts of the Horatio Alger myth with a Calvinistic determinism. Even monsters can sometimes play the victim role in this scheme, since our story dictates that monsters are the way they are because they are or were themselves victims. This tight circle is as hard to crack as it is self-indulgent.

Finally, the Gothic draws our attention to the personal and the psychological, away from structural social problems and away from what may be more pressing pains in our culture. Casting child molesting as a major dilemma and that dilemma in purely individual and psychological terms focuses our attention on isolated horrors. It encourages us to think that what we need is more outrage and more FBI sting operations.

However it is measured, sexual child abuse is a small problem (only 14 percent of cases) compared with other forms of child abuse,[12] not to mention neglect, abandonment, inadequate nutrition, poor education, and the absence of job opportunities, a fair chance, and hope. There's a way in which we know that. And even with sexual child abuse, we do not pretend that we are getting the problem under control; quite the contrary. We know we are dramatizing the issue, making it into a spectacle. We might even know that what we are doing isn't pointing to an ending but to a continuation. But these are forms of knowing that haven't yet found themselves a story to tell, at least not one we want to hear.

You want to see an idea (a fact, even) that will never find a story? Here's one from Vern L. Bullough, a historian of sexuality: "Based on an overview of history, this author would state that adult/child and adult/adolescent sexual behavior occur less frequently now than they did in the past."[13]

Now for a blunt statement of my argument.

Our culture has enthusiastically sexualized the child while denying just as enthusiastically that it was doing any such thing. We have become so engaged with tales of childhood eroticism (molestation, incest, abduction, pornography) that we have come to take for granted the irrepressible allure of children. We allow so much power to the child's sexual appeal that we no longer question whether adults are drawn to children. We may be skeptical of the therapy industry and its ability to manufacture so easily people with recovered memories of childhood molestation; we may regard the attacks on the clergy with suspicion; we may think many of the day-care center trials are witch hunts; we may have our doubts about rings of Satan-worshipping child killers; we may know that very few children are abducted by trench-coated strangers—but one thing remains indubitable, and we are all taught to know and believe it: adults by the millions find children so enticing that they will risk anything to have sex with them. What makes such an idea plausible?

It would hardly be an overstatement to say that the subject of the child's sexuality and erotic appeal, along with our evasion of what we have done by bestowing those gifts, now structures our culture. It would not be an overstatement to say that the way we are handling the subject is ripping apart our young people. I do not deny that we are also talking sincerely about detection and danger. We worry about the poor, hurt children. But we worry also about maintaining the particular erotic vision of children that is putting them at risk in the first place.

Is the erotic appeal of children really such a mystery to us? Is pedophilia really so "unspeakable"? Why is it that the figures given for abused children keep climbing without arousing suspicion? Why is it that we now include in our pool of likely child molesters not just misfit middle-aged males but distinguished grandparents, gymnastics coaches, priests, women, teenagers, and, most recently, children themselves. While we maintain the monstrous and perverse criminality of the act, we also move to make it universal and inevitable.

We have made children lovable, which is fine, but we have also failed to make it clear to ourselves just what that means. What is our loving to consist of? And what is it in the child that we are to desire to love? What are the forms of the desirable in our culture?

We see children as, among other things, sweet, innocent, vacant, smooth-skinned, spontaneous, and mischievous. We construct the desirable as, among other things, sweet, innocent, vacant, smooth-skinned, spontaneous, and mischievous. There's more to how we see the child, and more to how we construct what is sexually desirable — but not much more. To the extent that we learn to see "the child" and "the erotic" as coincident, we are in trouble. So are the children.

How did we get ourselves into such a fix? One way to put it is that the development of the modern child and modern ideas on sexuality grew up over the last two centuries hand-in-hand, and they have remained close friends.[14]

The Romantic idealization of the child — "Mighty Prophet, Seer

Blessed!"—was meant as a poetic figure, a metaphor, but it soon developed a quite literal, material base. For the Romantic poets, the child packaged a whole host of qualities that could be made into a poetics and a politics: the child was everything the sophisticated adult was not, everything the rational man of the Enlightenment was not. The child was gifted with spontaneity, imaginative quickness, and a closeness to God; but that's as far as its positive attributes went. More prominent were the negatives, the things not there. The child was figured as *free of* adult corruptions; *not yet burdened with* the weight of responsibility, mortality, and sexuality; *liberated from* "the light of common day."

This new thing, the modern child, was deployed as a political and philosophical agent, a weapon to assault what had been taken as virtues: adulthood, sophistication, rational moderation, judicious adjustment to the ways of the world. The child was used to deny these virtues, to eliminate them and substitute in their place a set of inversions: innocence, purity, emptiness. Childhood, to a large extent, came to be in our culture a coordinate set of *have nots,* of negations: the child was the one who *did not have.* Its liberty was a negative attribute, however much prized, as was its innocence and purity. What is purity, anyhow? Ivory soap used to say it was 99.44 percent pure, leaving one to suppose that there was 0.56 percent of substance there in the foam, and 99.44 percent of—nothing at all?

As for innocence: at one point a theological trope, in the nineteenth century it became more and more firmly attached to this world and to this world's sexuality. It was, further, a characteristic that outran any simple physical manifestation: innocence became a fulcrum for the post-Romantic ambiguous construction of sexuality and sexual behavior. On the one hand, innocence was valued deeply and guarded by criminal statutes (albeit often bendable ones); on the other hand, innocence was a consumer product, an article to possess, as a promise to the righteous and the reward to the dutiful. It came to you in heaven or in marriage, a prize. We were trained to adore and covet it, to preserve and despoil it, to speak of it in hushed tones and in bawdy songs.

Freud (or the usual way he is read and allowed to operate) did little to disrupt this historical pattern. In sexualizing the infant and then making sexuality merely "latent" in the slightly older child, Freud, by this now-you-see-it-now-you-don't, smoothed the way for our contemporary crisis. By conceiving of infancy in terms of stark sexual drives, Freud put the essential connection so directly as almost to threaten it: If we posit openly that children are activated by sexual energy, the evasive screens necessary for eroticizing them disappear; that is, it is necessary that they be "innocent and pure" if they are to be alluring and also give adults the sentimental stories of denial and projection we find indispensable. But Freud carefully protected our main story by driving under cover the sexuality he had just implanted, thereby giving us cake without calories: the child is both sexual and pure. Freud upset no applecarts; he provided a useful and dangerous way of telling one story and living another. The latent child, empty of the sexuality by which he had earlier been defined, is haunted by an absence, by an amputation that may seem to leave the child incomplete, unnatural.

The same goes for purity, of course, another empty figure that allows the admirer to read just about anything into its vacancy. The constructions of modern "woman" and modern "child" are very largely evacuations, the ruthless distribution of eviction notices. Correspondingly, the instructions we receive on what to regard as sexually arousing tell us to look for (and often create) this emptiness, to discover the erotic in that which is most susceptible to inscription, the blank page.

The consequences of this insistence on an empty innocence are often perilous, especially when they are reduced to commonplaces, so that what at first seemed odd becomes obvious. Take, for instance, the assertion that children's accusations of molesting must necessarily be true, an assertion based on the belief that innocence is incapable of inventing ideas of that sort: "How could a child her age *know* of such things? She could scarcely make them up!" Such a view renders guilty anyone accused until innocence is proved, as Lillian Hellman knew when she wrote these lines for *The Children's Hour*.[15]

Another example: the cry that child molesting is worse than murder has been heard so often it has become a tired slogan, self-evident and vapid. Certainly it is better to take the child's life than its virtue, we feel, and we needn't waste time saying it. The 1993 siege of the Branch Davidian complex in Waco, Texas, was initiated and then justified through stories of child molesting, suggesting that eighty-one deaths can be outweighed by violated innocence.[16] But if we teach ourselves to regard the loss of innocence as more calamitous than the loss of life, whose needs are we seeing to? Who is it wants the innocence and who the life? Ask any child. Are we defining the child's innocence in the way older societies defined women's virginity?

> When lovely woman stoops to folly
> And finds too late that men betray
> What charm can sooth her melancholy?
> What art can wash her guilt away?
> The only art her guilt to cover,
> To hide her shame from every eye,
> To give repentance to her lover,
> And wring his bosom, is—to die.[17]

Do we feel that a defiled child is of no use to us and might as well be dead?

We seem stuck with a vacant child that is both marginal and central to our lives: easily disposed of, abused, neglected, abandoned; and yet idealized, treasured, adored. The eroticizing of empty innocence seems to have left us ashamed and transfixed, unable to change and unable to resist the cultural directives that instruct us to long for children precisely in reference to what they do not have.

Bodies are made to conform to this set of cultural demands. Heathcliff and Cathy (aged twelve) are symbols of titanic passion; Shirley Temple was enticing until she reached puberty, and instantly became a Republican frump; Rick Schroder lost our interest when he stopped calling himself "Ricky"; Macaulay Culkin soon teetered over the brink of unerotic oblivion; Tom Sawyer's later adventures do not interest us. On a recent talk show, Schroder put it bluntly: "You go through puberty, and you're no longer desired."[18] Baby-smooth skin is capable of inciting desire; unsmooth, or contoured skin is not: is this because flatness is innately more titillating than texture, or because flatness signifies nothing at all and thus doesn't interfere with our projections? In the same way, desirable faces must be blank, drained of color; big eyes round and expressionless; hair blond or colorless; waists, hips, feet, and minds small. The physical makeup

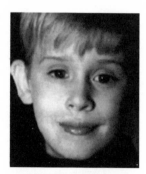

Compare the large eyes, generally narrow chins, high cheekbones, and empty come-hither expressions. Pictured are Alicia Silverstone, Betty Boop, Macaulay Culkin, Jay North, Elijah Wood, Winona Ryder, Sandra Bullock, Ricky Schroder, Shirley Temple, Buster Brown, Demi Moore, Marilyn Monroe, and Patty McCormack.

of the child has been translated into mainstream images of the sexually and materially alluring. A recent study of ideal desirability using a computer program called FacePrints found that "the ideal 25-year-old woman . . . had a 14-year-old's abundant lips and an 11-year-old's delicate jaw," that small lower face providing also the prominent eyes and cheekbones of children.[19] We are told to look like children if we can and for as long as we can, to pine for that look.[20]

This imaginative dwarfing of cute adults into children suggests the extent to which "the child" is both a fetish and a flexible construction that is, to a large extent, independent of outside standards like age. Adolescents are stuffed back into childhood when it serves our purposes, as it often does when we are talking of molestation or crime. Victims of crime as old as eighteen or nineteen can be thought of as children, whereas perpetrators as young as six can be thought of

18   Erotic Innocence

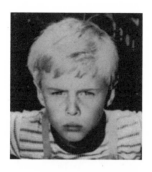

and treated as adults. Such analogical playing with categories follows our needs. For instance, thinking of an eighteen-year-old molestation victim as a child allows us to create a composite image that gives us innocence as well as sexual capacity. The child is functional, a malleable part of our discourse rather than a fixed stage; "the child" is a product of ways of perceiving, not something that is *there*.

And we perceive what we want to, what we desire. It bears repeating: both men and women rate "younger-looking faces and faces with 'babylike' features" tops on the "physical attractiveness" scale.[21] Compare the waif or schoolgirl images in fashion magazines with actual waifs in playgrounds and homes. Line up the images of kids from television sitcoms against the centerfolds in *Hustler* or *Penthouse*. Compare Culkin, the young Jay North, Patty McCormack, Shirley Temple, Elijah Wood, and Ricky Schroder with Marilyn Monroe, Alicia Silverstone, Demi Moore, Winona Ryder, and Sandra Bullock. They all look like cartoon characters: Buster Brown or Betty Boop—images vacated so we can write our passion there.

It is worth noting that these hollow child images not only focus and allow desire but also erase various social and political complications, performing essential cultural work that is not simply erotic. By formulating the image of the alluring child as bleached, bourgeois, and androgynous, these stories mystify material reality and render nearly invisible—certainly irrelevant—questions we might raise about race, class, and even gender. Such categories are scrubbed away in the idealized child, laved and snuggled into a Grade-A homogeneity.

When poor children are allowed to play this part, as they sometimes are, they are helped into the class above them; boys and girls leave difference behind and meld together; children of color find themselves blanched to ungodly sallowness. In all our stories, there is but one erotic child, and its name is Purity: without color, station, or gender.

Fourteen-year-olds used to win beauty contests held for adults. Now we hold child-molesting trials. There is no direct connection between those two facts—other issues, events, and needs intervene—but there are, I submit, links between desire and our attempts to regulate and deny it through legal spectacle. More is involved; our compassion and pity play a part, hardly qualified even if some of that pity has been for ourselves. But it is still true that the trials feed the talk, and that talk is more important than we have yet allowed ourselves to see. The trials don't have to do it by themselves, of course: films, television movies and sitcoms, the newspapers, advertising, and sensational best-sellers all tell us there are terrors everywhere about us, a multi-billion-dollar kiddie porn industry, and a vast network of pedophiles.

Or so we say. As everyone who has inquired and all police agencies know, the "kiddie porn industry," if it exists at all in this country, is a puny cottage industry. But we pay the FBI to conduct stings and tell ourselves that vast porn rings exist. Missing children are missing more than 99 percent of the time because they have run away or been spirited off in a custody battle. But we put up posters, look at milk cartons, and imagine an abductor on every block. The talk feeds the desire, which in turn feeds the talk—and the need to blame somebody else. We are instructed by our cultural heritage to crave that which is forbidden, a crisis we face by not facing it, by writing self-righteous doublespeak that demands both lavish public spectacle and constant guilt-denying projections onto scapegoats.

A country that regards children as erotic and also regards an erotic response to children not merely as criminal but as criminally unimaginable has a problem on its hands. It is to our credit that we maintain the tension and try to find stories that might somehow protect the children from what we conjure up as a barely corraled lust eager to feed on everyone under fifteen. The trouble is that these stories of protection are also stories of incitement; the denials are always affirmations. The stories we tell of the monsters are also stories of home and family (our home and our family), and when we speak of the unspeakable, we keep the speaking going.

For all the pleasure it offers, this talk has some effects we might consider undesirable. Since I have much to say about that sort of thing later, I'll make do here with a list:

1. It directs our attention away from more pressing ills.
2. It allows us to continue eroticizing children while denying we are doing any such thing.
3. It creates the sexualized child we pretend we are sanitizing.
4. It projects onto others a whole host of failures we may be experiencing as parents and as a culture.
5. It attacks working mothers most viciously.
6. It raises such fears of touching that any form of intimacy may seem hardly worth the risk.
7. It gives the police and policing agencies Godlike power.

A corrective and skeptical counterstory has, of course, been developing—what traditionalists call a "backlash"—and we like to think we see things now with a clarity that is perhaps not unflinching but growing in sharpness and focus. But turning the accuser into the accused, swapping villain and victim, does not, when you look at it, seem like a radical transformation. The Gothic game stays basically as it was; everyone just switches sides: the accused now deserves sympathy and the accuser condemnation. The primary discourse sticks, fueled now by a rejuvenated energy serving the same old needs.

Under the new dispensation, we expand the list of perils facing children to include bumbling rescuers—psychiatrists, therapists, and social workers—carefully restricting our analysis so that others (the culture at large, you and me) are not implicated. Our admission costs us nothing. As Freud saw so clearly, the idea of childhood trauma (being sexually molested) provides a self-sustaining explanation for present miseries: it is simple; it invokes and justifies self-pity; it gives absolution. Many of us have good reason to recall past traumas.

The recent shift in focus away from recovered memory to the erratic functioning of memory and its ability to give us not only what is somehow *there* but also what we want to be there is, in a general way, a rediscovering of what Freud told us about memory nearly a century ago. But why do we want to tell these stories about "false" memory? Why are we telling stories that throw doubt on the accuracy of recovered memories and on the competence of professionals who assist in resurrecting them? What needs can such skeptical, revisionist stories be serving?

What if we said memory was itself a storytelling agency, a collection of narratives we can call on for various purposes. Everything in our past, everything lodged in memory, is available to us as a story (an almost infinitely rearrangeable story). We generally assume, despite what we secretly know, that anything coming from memory is authentic, since that channel (the conduits carrying material from memory to consciousness) has been invested with authority: it tells the truth.

Hence it is no surprise that we believe it when our memory tells us we were victims or perpetrators of sexual molestation. I believe memory will make the story of child sexuality available to nearly anyone in this culture, not because *it happened* (though it may have) but because all our memories are riddled through with this story of the powerful eroticism of the child. It is a story we all hold in memory; we cannot be of this time and place and be free of it. Our memories store not only personal but also cultural stories, that is, and it is an easy step to make the cultural into the personal in quite literal ways. Some cultures (the Irish, for instance) make this mandatory. And note how easily family legends (the stories of a small subculture) become "memories," even if they happened to somebody else or to no one: our memories give to all of us cute things said, exciting adventures, intolerable grievances cobbled together from various stories, none of which need ever have been "true" about anybody or anything. Our most dramatic and inescapable modern legend of this sort features the erotic child, its allure and travails. We all have that in memory, ready to take on the form of a persuasive narrative—really of several narratives, depending on our needs.

We do not, in fact, need trauma to provide us with horrors to recover. Nightmares come from sources often far darker and more complex than trauma, as Freud saw when he sought out the alien region of the unconscious as a territory at least as likely as any direct assault on innocence to yield pain. Our attempt to reinvest trauma with this kind of authority (and to beat up on Freud for "abandoning" it) is an attempt to displace both the unconscious and the imagination, which hold powers so strong we have not begun to uncover them. Again, it's not to the point to say that attacks do happen, attacks so simple in their brutality as to replay in life the fierce logic of horror stories and melodrama. Consider another horror: our current means of investigating the problem and, behind that, of understanding what that problem is, will never stop the assaults or allow us to understand much of what is going on.

For one thing, it's a matter not of whether it *happened* but of whether we are induced to search our memory for the story of it happening. The distinction between what happened and what didn't is precisely the one that is not available to us. And that is the one fueling the current activity and the talk. We can never know, and we direct our energies to knowing. We vow not to stop talking until we find out, and we focus on what can never be found out.

This protects not only the discourse on the erotic child but even the form that discourse takes, a form that changes little. We still search for villains, whether it be the molester or (just as good for our purposes) the one who "lies" about being molested, or the psychoanalyst or therapist who directed the retrieval of false memories. In any case, we protect the fundamental idea (and our fundamental need to believe) that child molesting is a clearly defined, discernible, marginal activity engaged in by others who can be (along with their acts) identified and punished, maybe even eliminated altogether. If we can find this villain (and we always do), we can tell ourselves that it happened, that we had no part in causing it, and that all will be well if we continue on our present course of dealing with the child molesters, their victims, and those who only think they're victims. The way we pretend to deal with that is to keep talking the same old talk.

We are caught within a trap, but I think it is fair to us all to say that we wish we weren't, wish we were not forced to wallow in one more trial, watch one more disgusting movie, hear Oprah-Ricki-Geraldo once again being righteous, unfurl our own virtue, warn our children about the dangers of touching. The talk that allows us so easily to escape our position within this dilemma also, if paradoxically, springs from our desire to locate that position. We do want to do something to help—or at least stop hurting. It is a sign also of our distress that so many children are being wounded, at least partly by our desperation. We really would like to stop it.

The analysis I am offering hopes to be more than a cynical scalding of our psychic hypocrisies. If we are trapped by stories, we can perhaps startle those stories out of currency. What if we tried the effect of outrageous, impossible stories? Saying, "Yes, we all feel the attractiveness of children" does not make it true or mandate sexual activity with children, but it certainly relocates the talk. And that's the point: tease the storytelling into a new territory, find new possibilities.

I believe we can locate the energies now being directed to denial and employ them for a far more productive and easy loving and protecting of children. Even facing up to where our history has landed us would be a promising beginning. The children are not faring well right now, and it may be that we're protecting, denying, anesthetizing, and scaring them nearly to death.

We might try to manage without stark essentialist ideas of sexuality and sexual behavior, see what might be done by positing a *range* of erotic feelings within and toward children. Rather than assuming that such feelings exist in only two forms—not at all or out of control—perhaps we could learn something of their differences, manner of expression, and effects, allowing them a complex and dynamic relativity.

It's important to be plain about this and not to try to counter erotic attraction to children with nothing stronger than nostalgia and talk about how sweet children are. For one thing, nostalgia and sweetness are not antidotes to eroticism but ingredients of it; for another, they are trifles. I believe most adults in our culture feel some measure of erotic attraction to children and the childlike; I do not know how it could be otherwise. I propose, first, that as long as these feelings are denied and projected as outrage, nothing will happen. Second, I suggest that just about all of us, looking what is what in the face, will not find ourselves compelled to have sex with children. I think our present procedures have wildly exaggerated the extent of our present dilemma; after all, if most of us were molested as children, then our parents must be a uniformly vile group, whose abused children (us) are doomed (according to current wisdom) to molest in turn; which means that, past and present, we are a culture of monsters, rendering child abuse trials arbitrary, even superfluous. We might look at the way children and eroticism have been constructed for us in order to see whether the problems involved in accepting these things are not much smaller than those that afflict us when we displace them.

I do not pretend that the form of speaking I am promoting will easily give us some permanent truth, that it is risk-free, or that it escapes the trap of scapegoating porn-speak I have tried to avoid. Maybe this is just another way of keeping the talk going—the same old cruel, cowardly talk that hurts us and the children, that will hurt them much more than it hurts us.

But maybe not. At least the questions I am asking do not take a form that guarantees that they cannot be answered, that simply generates more self-satisfied storytelling. If we are to get anywhere, we need to find better questions, and I do not think we can find them within the realm of the cozy and self-protecting. Our heritage is a complicated and distressing one, but it need not be figured as a double bind. Enormous changes can come by shifting the way we see problems, by looking through a differently focused lens.

It is my belief that an understanding of the history of this dilemma and a shift in our focus will cause us not only to *see* differently but to *know* differently. From altered forms of knowing can come new actions and new feelings about the actions we take. In this case, I think we can find a happy paradox: by locating the problems within our common heritage—that is to say, within ourselves (and giving up on the monsters)—we will find it in our hearts (and in the way we see the problem) to be easier on ourselves and, consequently, easier on our children. It comes natural to us to be generous to ourselves. That generosity will lower the voltage, shifting the child into a new field of vision, and us into a lower gear.

That sounds like a conclusion (overdue) to this introduction, but it's too mellifluous, I think, too dominated by happy thoughts and winning smiles. I don't really think familiar storytelling habits will be given up so easily. They do so much for us, or we think they do, that we will hardly move away from them without a boost, or a kick. In fact, I suspect something like a scandal is needed.

Scandals are powerful traps, capable of snapping shut on the most confident social myths. The *Oxford English Dictionary* roots the word in the idea of a snare or ambush, says it is believed to be from the Indogermanic *skand,* "to spring or leap." Early on, scandal meant to cause perplexity of conscience, to hinder the reception of faith or obedience to Divine Law, to present a stumbling block. Scandal is, then, a trap sprung on the main bullies of any culture: faith, law, and submission to them. Scandal is the enemy of cultural hegemony; it is the offense that frees us from piety; it is the gross material fact that thumbs its nose at all metaphysical officialdom. We are drawn to scandal by our desire to trip up the cultural censors, by a dream of escaping culture or transforming it. Compliance, we sense, will get us nowhere, great as the rewards for compliance may be.

Take the most banal of all scandals, political scandal—and ask yourself what draws you to it. Why are the erotic doings of, say, President Clinton so much more interesting than his policies? Not, I suggest, because he is himself erotic; like most politicians, where he is, eros is not. Let me assume, then, that what draws us to scandal is the energy and promise of scandal itself, not the particulars of any one scandal. It's the offense that matters, that holds out promise, gives us hope.

The offensive may maul us into an awareness of where we are and what anchors us there. Sufficient rudeness, clamorous boorishness, can hope to force the politeness police to explain themselves. The rules we are obeying now and the grammar of our discourse seem natural to us, their naturalness being protected all along by silence, by the illusion that they aren't rules at all. It may be that we can bust something that needs to be busted by using the disruptive pressure of simple nose thumbing, pies in the face, or an assertion that we make erotic children bloom like dandelions. Scandal might lead us not to cynicism but to new lands.

If scandal is one shape in which resistance and hope might appear,[22] there are others too, just as there are many besides myself who have grown tired of the same old story, skeptical of its authority and its power to do good, who wonder about other tales that might have parts more lively and happy for the children and, not incidentally, for ourselves. It is to these friends that I address this book and its appeals.

1. Trapped in the Story

When you get hit with an allegation
that you're a pervert and a child molester, what do you do? —Jerry Barr
(Roseanne's father)

I never got a chance to tell my story.
No one ever said, "What happened?"
—Mary Baxter[1]

I am tenderly aware that not a few of the assertions made in the Introduction rest on the fact that they've been presented in English sentences. Without support, and soon, they'll die. Even so, reinforcements won't arrive until this short chapter does its job, which is to show how our culture's commanding story about child molesting works when it goes into action. It is the simplest story; and, like most simple things, intolerant and relentless: it recognizes no other stories and claims for itself absolute truth. It is ferociously pious and thus has the force of dogma. Resist it at your peril—though it is healthier to resist than to swim in it.

We like to think there are innumerable sides to any story. Not to this one. It has an outside, where those of us who tell it can stand, and an inside, occupied by those about whom it is told, the actors caught in the story. Those inside are enmeshed in a script with nothing but bad parts, a contest-story in which everyone loses, the accused and the accusers. There are two main roles, monster and victim—both unrewarding—along with supporting parts for police, judges, juries, therapists, parents, friends, journalists, and lawyers.

Because this is a Gothic story, the rigid parts allotted by our culture to those doomed to play them out demand acting so shrill that Bette Davis would have turned them down. Those within child-molesting dramas become intensely isolated, caged by their parts and denied any view outside them: the scripts constitute total reality. When asked, as they sometimes are, why their enemies are acting as they are (or have), participants invariably say, "I don't know." Of course they don't. Motivation is not a big issue when the story is about angels and ghouls.

When the drama becomes strained and its fictional nature starts to show through, we play it at a higher pitch, show our confidence in the standard story by having it screamed at us. Those caught in that blare find their voices absorbed into headlines that do not ask for a response: "Student Tells of Sex Encounters"; "Teacher Sex Trial Goes to Jury."[2] Just past the headlines, there in the very first paragraph, is a caricature of a life: "A high school teacher had sex with a student at a mountain getaway, in the school teacher's prop room and in her class-room office to compensate for the love and approval she never got from her mother, according to court testimony Monday."[3] That's what happened to Mary Baxter, a teacher at Van Buren High, in a Los Angeles suburb, and to Alan Hoyt, her seventeen-year-old accuser.

Once embedded in the cultural narrative, both sides bitterly protest the fact that no one seems especially interested in their story, that they have become anonymous and somehow utterly predictable, subject to implanted emotions and expectations alien to them. Mrs. Baxter is most eloquent on this point. She grants that her attorney wanted simply to hit the high spots, and even understands "why you would want to believe the accuser, for otherwise no one gets caught and you create an environment where true victims are afraid to come forward." All the same, she remains baffled and frustrated. "I never," she says, "got a chance to tell my story—never did, not even during the trial. No one ever said, 'What happened?'"[4] The fact that Mary Baxter is uncommonly thoughtful and articulate only makes matters worse for her: she has a complex and modulated story to tell, but she is forced into a monotonously single-toned, crudely rudimentary plot.

As, in a very different way, is her accuser. A smart and active older adolescent is shrunk into a child, a generic "essence-of-child," by this cultural story, remolded as passive, innocent, and guileless. His actual age, activities, particularities are melted away to fit our needs. Alan's sexual activity in particular is fashioned as unwilled, forced onto him or drawn from him "unnaturally." Thus, while sex is, of course, the center of the drama and of our interest, it is also made to seem freak-ish and shocking, providing us with a safety screen. We need never acknowledge our own part in creating this erotic spectacle, since the eros is both displaced onto the actors and made oddly hallucinatory, just as Alan's slippage from adolescent into child is both essential and misty.

Before we vanish into the mist ourselves, perhaps we should look at both principals in a way that does a little justice to their human variability and mysteriousness before they merge into the stereotypes of the child-molesting trial we have before us.

Alan Hoyt, first of all, is probably, despite his youth, nearly as complex as anyone in this drama. In the fall of 1992 he was sixteen and, at least on the surface, zinging along: doing well in his classes and with the girls, happier at home, connected to a Big Brother, working with a therapist he liked, off the drugs that had been making things tough for him (LSD and pot) and onto Prozac, which was helping. Earlier (in June) his mother had arranged for therapy, worried that his behavior—"he lies, he is manipulative"—was linked to deeper problems.[5] Possibly those problems had to do with drugs, with feeling unloved, with being molested by his father as an infant,[6] and with being sixteen. Anyhow, as school started he seemed to be making progress in carving out a position for himself, one both safe and productive. He was deliberately trying to reorder his life and expand his interests, acquiring, among other things, a subscription to the L.A. Philharmonic. As his junior year opened, "things were," his mother says, "going much better,"[7] partly because he had found creative outlets in literature and drama classes and an unusually receptive and gifted teacher.

Mary Baxter was teaching both Alan's AP literature class and the drama class that was part of the blooming theater arts and theater history program she had established. Attractive, witty, and dexterous, she had the sort of energy that seems always to be going outward, engaged with the person before her. Elected Van Buren High School Teacher of the Year in 1991, she was at a fine point in her life: she and her husband, married for eight years, had decided the year before that things were so propitious they could proceed with two important plans: Dolph Baxter could begin full-time Ph.D. work, and they could start a family. Mary Baxter sailed happily into the fall term.

That Alan was in love with her is hardly a bombshell,[8] and it was only a matter of time (a very short time) before he confided in her—

not his love but his troubles. Nor was she surprised at this over-flow: "When you teach drama it all comes out, including the horrible stories. I usually found myself knowing more about the kids than I really wanted to; but it was vital that kids felt they could be open with me." "OK," I say, "but what about kids falling in love with you?" "Yeah-yeah," she says wryly. "I'm not conceited, but that's not uncommon with high-school boys and their teachers—I could list many. I'm one of many teachers—perhaps nearly all teachers—forced to deal with that issue, and it usually isn't, for any of us, that big a deal." "And Alan?" "I don't know if I'd say 'in love'—but a crush." (I would say "in love"; but I wasn't there.) "Later on," she adds ominously, "I think he was obsessed."[9]

That's one possibility: Alan became obsessed with Mrs. Baxter, entered into a fantasy projection that we all recognize (remember), and didn't know how to stop it. That would explain why Alan exploded when, in January, Mrs. Baxter told her students she was pregnant. Feeling betrayed, perhaps, and fearing that his fantasy place was being usurped by the husband, he tried to reclaim his imaginary position by declaring, among other things, that the baby was his. But there are other possibilities, as we shall see: Alan was in big trouble at school and may have concocted the charges to deflect attention away from his plagiarism and onto more sensational matters. He may have wanted to replay in another arena a terrible but necessary drama he could not enact with the real demon in his life, his father. He may have had no deliberate plan at all, may have simply fallen into a course of events that seized the initiative from him. And it may all have happened as he said. I suppose it is clear that I don't think it did; but for our purposes actual events are less important than the power of the cultural narrative, which now takes over and renders historical truth irrelevant in the face of the "truth" mandated by the way our culture wants to see these things.

Two complex and articulate people, Mary Baxter and Alan Hoyt, are complex no longer, really now are rendered mute. The official plot speaks through them, does not allow them to do anything impromptu or out of character. Let's look at one example, the "drama log," a homework assignment that entered the stack of supplementary sheriff's reports very late in the game, on November 17, 1993 (the case began in late May). Detective Julia Pausch, author of this report, says that at that meeting Alan "told us that he had found an entry in his drama log from school that he thought would be helpful in proving the allegations against Mrs. Baxter." Pausch, who from the start saw her duty as gathering "proof" rather than investigating, treats the material with her customary quasi-literate solemnity: "I read the paper and saw that Alan wrote an entry on 11-25-92. There was a notation written below it [from Mrs. Baxter], saying, 'Peachy. How are you? Doncha Love Thanksgiving?'"

There are, in fact, more entries than just this one, though the eye of Detective Pausch located the one that could be twisted into use at the trial. There are ten entries in all, stretching from September 15 to December 3, mostly involving Alan's claims to increased knowledge about Greek ("which I had known little to nothing about") and Roman theater (despite being "confused w/ all the weird names"), to greater confidence about his role in an upcoming play (*Tom Jones*), to various acting techniques he has mastered. For me, this is a weary stretch of reading indeed, and I marvel at Mrs. Baxter not only examining so much (representative, I suppose) self-centered blab—"This week I learned a tremendous amount about the audition process"—but summoning the enthusiasm to comment on it. Those comments, granted, are not lengthy, usually amounting to a hearty "Good!" though now and then whole sentences are heroically added: "Re: Western [his role]—I've seen tremendous growth. More will come this week." It seems to me, in other words, a highly conscientious pedagogical performance, one I would not be up to but can applaud.

But Pausch and, a short time later, the prosecution did not see it that way, interpreting the comment on Thanksgiving as an erotic nudge from teacher to student, a smutty response suited for the *Penthouse* "Forum." By this later date, Alan had located the most elaborate of his sexual encounters with Mrs. Baxter on the day after Thanksgiving, making "Doncha Love Thanksgiving" transparently (for Pausch) a way of reliving (reinciting?) the ardor of the Friday before. There's no way to catch the full flavor of this interpretive act without slogging over the whole Sahara of the drama log, but perhaps you can get a sniff from an excerpt written the week after Thanksgiving vacation:

11-25-92 The Play is Finally over! *I* think *My Best* Performance was opening Night—Though All Nights Went Very Well. I Learned To Use Pre-Performance Fear & Anxiety To Your Benefit. I Learned A Little About Roman Theater This Week Too! How Are You? ☺

Peachy. How are you? ☺
Doncha Love Thanksgiving?

The prosecution later seemed unable to decide which was more offensive: that a teacher would refer to what they figured was sex or that a teacher (of English!) would write "Doncha."

In Dickens's *Pickwick Papers,* the incriminating evidence in a breach-of-promise suit brought against the hero by his landlady is a note he sent her while on the road, warning her of his arrival: "Dear Mrs. B.—Chops and Tomata Sauce. Yours, Pickwick." To the unwary, this looks like a dinner order, but the prosecution knows better and hopes the jury will too, will see that the very "covert, sly, underhanded" language is "far more conclusive" than anything direct could be, since it is evident that this coded message was "intended at the time, by Pickwick, to mislead and delude any third parties into whose hands it might fall." Having said this, the prosecutor need only read the message again for its meaning to be clear as day: "Gentlemen, what does this mean? Chops and Tomata sauce! Yours, Pickwick! Chops! Gracious heavens! and Tomata sauce! Gentlemen!"[10]

Doncha! Gracious heavens! *Love!* What can this mean? *Thanksgiving!* Now, really!

Under the conditions of our culture's master narrative of child molesting, nothing is without meaning, and all meanings are sinister. An indifferent action, an action meaning what it seems to mean, is unthinkable. And so it is with characters: everyone is either impossibly devious or impossibly naive. Mary Baxter is either "a troubled, unhappily married woman willing to 'seek love anywhere,'" a diabolical fiend who "preyed on an impressionable young student in order to satisfy her need for affection,"[11] or a persecuted saint; Alan Hoyt is either a helpless child or "a manipulative, trouble-making student."[12] Where is there such a world as this, where such inhabitants?

The Story

As it turned out, Mary Baxter was charged with only one misdemeanor count, oral copulation with a minor, his allegations of other forms of sex being irrelevant, since the other forms of sex he mentioned were not against the law—not at the time anyhow; sexual intercourse with boys aged fourteen to seventeen was not officially prohibited until a year after the alleged affair ended. The reduced charge, however, scarcely worked to her advantage, since it focused on what to many is the more salacious sexual activity and also allowed the drooling *Glendale News-Press* to insert in its daily account of the trial a reminder that prosecutors had no doubt that intercourse took place (and very often) but were barred from raising that issue by the fact (ironic) that the bill outlawing sex with boys under eighteen (sponsored by Glendale's own state senator, Newton Russell) didn't go into effect until January 1, 1994. This allowed the prosecution to try Mrs. Baxter on charges that were never addressed and thus could not be refuted. Of course, the accused in such cases can always do as little to refute such charges as accusers can to substantiate them, and that allows us to write virtually any story we like, the one we like being, every time, a variation on the same tale.

In our case, the story is this: Alan Hoyt, in the fall of 1992, was enrolled in Mary Baxter's classes in AP English lit and drama. We already know that. Through these classes he became involved in the fall production of *Tom Jones* and the spring's *Romeo and Juliet,* both unluckily charged plays, the former dealing, even worse luck, with a young man pursued by older women. During rehearsals for *Tom Jones,* in which Alan played the middling-important role of Squire Western, he began, along with other students, staying after rehearsal and, especially in the week preceding Halloween, talking to his teacher about difficult personal problems, including those stemming from the incest. These wrenching conversations, filled with high emotion and tears, were not unusual, says Mrs. Baxter, given the way theatrical experience (and empathetic presence) works on young people. Still, Alan's pain was fierce: he spoke, she says, of being raped by his father, of anger he did not know what to do with, of a drug problem, of a life he regarded generally as "a big stinking mess."[13] Mrs. Baxter directed Alan to the school counseling program, but he said he had tried it, found it wanting, and was already involved in successful private therapy, needing now only to talk.

At this point, Mrs. Baxter made what she told me was "the mistake of my life," though at the time it seemed banal: having heard that writing a letter to the abusive parent could be therapeutic, she mentioned to Alan that it might help both his psychic health and, not incidentally, his acting: "I was being very selfish, looking for a way to keep him from being absurdly angry on stage." It was a suggestion he took up at once. She told him further that she could "kind of understand his anger," having been abused herself as a child, though not sexually. He wrote his letter, showed it to Mrs. Baxter the next day, and then suggested she write one too, which she, as a sign of trust, agreed to do. The following day, these letters (written with no intent of sending them) were exchanged, Alan taking Mary's, writing on it "Do Not Mail," and retrieving his own as well, for use by his therapist—and, as it turned out, the prosecutors, who read out the choicest parts in court, parts in which Mary tried, she said, excessive language in a futile attempt to tap her anger, parts in which she complained to her mother about being made to feel hurt and unlovely.

In November, then, we have the play itself, which as we read in the drama log, went smoothly enough. According to Mary Baxter, nothing else of note happened that month, although she did give Alan a couple of music tapes (one classical, one of old standards, sung mostly by Ella Fitzgerald) to facilitate his attempts to enculture himself. According to Alan, somewhere about November 10 they began having sex (genital, with him on top, apart from the one oral encounter) in her office, in the prop room, in Mary's car (driver's side), outside on the ground (in the Angeles National Forest), and several times on that all-stops-out mountain cabin encounter the day after Thanksgiving.[14]

In December, Alan's mother gave Mary a Christmas gift and invited her and her husband to go to the San Gabriel Civic Opera's performance of The Nutcracker. Mary went, accompanying Alan, his mother, and his sister, and taking along the young daughter of a friend, Dolph Baxter choosing to give it a miss: "Not only was it The Nutcracker, but the San Gabriel Civic, for God's sake!" In return, Mary gave Alan a book (having given other students gifts as well), The Little Prince, inscribed "Unconditionally," a reference, she says, to her assurance to Alan that despite his earlier rocky experiences, she loved her students without conditions (though she comments now that had she known, she would have attached a qualifier about the effect being dragged into court could have on the "unconditional").

In January, Alan invited Mary to go to an L.A. Philharmonic program on his subscription, his usual companion being unable to attend. Alan said it was on this date (January 9) that they last had sex and that he decided it was time to end it all. Mary says he took off his shoes during the performance and embarrassed her by being a little slovenly; otherwise, it was an important concert to her only because she had a chance to hear Corigliano's First Symphony, *The AIDS Symphony*, which she connected to the recent death of a friend. Also in January, Alan went off antidepressants — "And we all felt that!" Mary says. More important, perhaps, he suffered what he may have taken as a double-barreled betrayal: expecting to be cast as Romeo in the play, he had to make do with the part of Mercutio; and he heard for the first time that Mrs. Baxter was going to have a baby in August. Alan's account is that she had told him of this in December, along with the news that he was the father.

Both accounts agree that relations between the two deteriorated throughout the winter and spring, rehearsals being so stormy that Alan came to be directed by proxy, through student directors. In April–May Alan contracted mononucleosis; became convinced, apparently, that Mrs. Baxter was giving him unfair grades; wrote a letter to the principal complaining about that (and about the way Mrs. Baxter was promoting "female supremacy" in the classroom); and plagiarized a paper for Mrs. Baxter on the playwright Ionesco. Mrs. Baxter learned about the letter of complaint during a discussion with her principal about her fall maternity leave and agreed that a special meeting with Alan to discuss the letter should be arranged, as it was, for May 26.

Meanwhile, unbeknownst to Mrs. Baxter, Alan scheduled on May 23 a double session with his therapist for the twenty-fifth. On the twenty-fourth, Alan's mother elicited from him a full disclosure of the alleged affair. She accompanied him to the double session with the therapist, who, when informed, did what she was by law required to do; she called the cops. The timing of all this seems suspicious, I know, but waive that. On the twenty-sixth, then, expecting to discuss Alan's academic problems, Mrs. Baxter, along with her department chair, entered the principal's office to be confronted by the Hoyts (mother and son), the therapist, and the charges. Mrs. Baxter left, called her husband, and returned to her classes.

On June 18, she and her attorney met with Detective Pausch. Mary Baxter reconstructs the opening of that interview as follows:

> *Pausch:* You know you don't have to do this interview and that we can stop at any time if you don't feel well.
> *Baxter:* Okay.
> *Pausch:* Do you understand the charges against you?
> *Baxter:* Yes.
> *Pausch:* How do you respond?
> *Baxter:* They're not true.
> *Pausch:* Well, I don't believe you. He says that between either October or November and January you had sex with him, and I believe him.

Later in the interview, according to Detective Pausch's own report, Pausch told Mrs. Baxter that "things don't look good," that she was busy "gathering proof" against her, and that Mrs. Baxter was "an actress." Pausch's animus spills over in her description of Mrs. Baxter's manner during the interview: "Throughout my interview with Mrs. Baxter, she remained very calm. She answered my questions deliberately, with very long narrative answers. She would sit in her chair and rub her pregnant abdomen with great affection. Mrs. Baxter was very composed despite the serious and embarrassing nature of the allegations against her." Detective Pausch closed her report with a sneer: Mrs. Baxter's lawyer "handed me a stack of papers," "statements about what a great teacher she is, and how Alan Hoyt is a troubled liar." [15]

The rest of the summer was empty; the teacher's union to which Mrs. Baxter appealed disappeared, though her principal and fellow teachers offered strong support. That summer (1993) the Baxters' child, Philip, was born; the next day, Mary was served with a subpoena. Throughout the fall and winter, the district attorney's office tried to force the Baxters to have blood tests made on the baby to get evidence on his paternity, a procedure the Baxters both found "sickening" and invasive, and steadfastly refused. The judge in the case eventually upheld the Baxters' refusal, declaring the tests a violation of the child's civil rights and also irrelevant to the charge (which was, after all, "oral copulation").

The trial lasted from March 3 to March 18, 1994, and ended in acquittal. But the drama is far from over. In May, Mary Baxter received a summons informing her that Alan Hoyt, through his mother, was naming her, her principal, and the school district in a civil suit, asking for damages on seven causes of action ranging from malpractice to childhood sexual abuse to negligence to battery to infliction of emotional distress. That suit lingers on today, more than three years later, along with the possibility of a countersuit. In August 1994, Mrs. Baxter was forced to appear before the state Committee on Credentials in Sacramento. In September, she was informed, without any explanation, that the committee had declined to renew her teaching credentials.

That's the story, and it's a common one, common and ugly and, in my view, devised to minister to interests that have nothing to do with justice. After all, who wins? Who is the better for this turmoil? What principles are served? I think only the story gains, the story and the ghostly cultural psychodrama it is devised to enact. In the case before us, I think everyone involved, even Detective Pausch, is telling what she or he takes to be the truth, "truth" having been usurped by the demands of the roles they have been forced into. Because of that, I want to spend the rest of this chapter analyzing not questions of guilt or innocence, which the story itself assigns, but rather what seem to me a few curious, especially vulnerable points in this particular story.

What Sort of Sex Did You Say It Was?

Cases like the one I described above do not seem to excite in us high demands for logical consistency or even plausibility. It may be that our prurient interest is so high we are willing to forgive a fair amount of haziness, contradiction, and plain nonsense. In this case, common sense often took quite a beating, which says no more than that our master story requires a whopping investment.

For instance, though insisting he broke off the sex business on January 9, Hoyt was always blurry on when the affair started and how often it was consummated. In the original sheriff's report he estimated twenty-five encounters, but later changed his guess to "approximately 5 times a week,"[16] which would yield between forty and sixty. Hey, who's counting? We also will pass over Hoyt's account of the inauguration of the physical business: "He said that the first time he and Mrs. Baxter kissed they were sitting in her car and it just sort of 'happened.'"[17] That this sounds like a mixture of fantasy and teen romance novels might not rule out its truthfulness, since perhaps (I wouldn't know) actuality can be a blend of fantasy and teen romances. We might also choose to be deaf to the testimony of two students at the trial who said they were usually around when the auditorium closed, watched Mrs. Baxter drive off alone, and even walked home with Alan Hoyt.

But how do we conceive of the locations for these bouts? "Alan told me," Pausch says, "the majority of their sexual encounters took place in the Angeles Crest [sic] Forest, either in the suspect's car or outside the car." Actually, it's the Angeles National Forest, the Angeles Crest Highway being the best way to get into it. One supposes (and Hoyt's courtroom testimony confirms) that he was claiming he and Mrs. Baxter traveled up the highway and into the forest, where they would sometimes stay in the car, sometimes get out.

There are problems either way. Putting aside the fact that this road and area are frequently patrolled by police on the prowl (why?) for teenagers making out in cars, rendering it a terribly indiscreet choice, going up there near midnight in these months and getting out of the car, much less taking off any clothes, would have been most uncomfortable. At nearby Mount Wilson, the average temperature in November was thirty-nine degrees, and it got worse: thirty-five in December and thirty-two in January. Staying inside the car would have improved things, but not much, if Hoyt's testimony is to be believed. He said in court that they had sex on the driver's side, defendant on the bottom; but there is less than twelve inches of clearance between the steering wheel and the seat. Maybe it's possible—for lindy champions—but it sounds so pinched that it would hardly be worth the trip.

And then there's the car Alan Hoyt testified to being in more than twenty-five times and which he insisted to the bitter end was a blue two-door Japanese-made compact—heroic consistency, considering that anyone who looked could see that it was a dark gray Volkswagen with four doors.

Our Little Mountain Hideaway

It is odd how some details are given meaning in these cases and others are ignored—or is it? Somehow it doesn't seem germane that the plaintiff had no idea what kind of a car he was in as he (so he says) went at it night after night, or how the freezing cold militated against his pleasure; it only matters, perhaps, that he's focusing our attention in the right area, giving us the details that do matter. And those are the details that contribute to the hard-core story being demanded by prosecutors, press, and public. It's extremely difficult for a defendant to relocate details from this hypercharged sexual conspiratorial context back into a mundane, it-doesn't-mean-much-of-anything world. Once inside the story, it's the story that decides which meanings will count, not the human participants being tumbled around. If someone says something happened, you simply cannot say, "Yeah, so what?" even if that's a good response. "Yeah, so what?" will get you into big trouble.

Even worse, when the story takes to inventing scenes out of whole cloth, simply to make itself play better, there's not a lot that can be done to resist. For instance, in the Baxter trial, there's the mountain cabin, quite obviously less a lonely, romantic chalet than an overused, bustling family getaway; but "obvious" just didn't matter.

The cabin owned by Mary Baxter's family is in Wrightwood, a couple of hours from the valley, up in the mountains—the mountains playing so prominent a part in this story that it sometimes sounds like *Heidi*. The cabin isn't mentioned in Alan Hoyt's first report to the police, but when Detective Pausch arrived on June 11 he had recalled a trip to this cabin with Mrs. Baxter, right after Thanksgiving, for eleven hours of the usual, and had prepared a detailed diagram of the cabin. In addition to the diagram, Hoyt provided supporting details:

there were other cabins around, the street was paved, the land sloped up, and there was a general store not far away. All of this strikes me as purely generic for a mountain town, but I'm not Detective Pausch, who saw that it was all highly significant, emphasizing the fact that this particular mountain land really did slope, just as Alan said.

On August 9, Detective Pausch filed a report of a visit she made with Alan "to locate the cabin where Alan had sexual intercourse with the suspect." No namby-pamby "allegedly" here. Alan was indeed able to point out the general store, though Pausch scrupulously notes in her report that it seemed more like a "market" to her—but then she wasn't in the same state of mind that must have possessed Alan just after Thanksgiving. They found the cabin, though, and spied in through some of the many glass windows, not having a key: "I saw," Pausch says, "that the interior of the cabin matched the diagram Alan had drawn in June." And to this she testified in court the following March.

Mrs. Baxter says there was no trip, ever. She had talked on several occasions with the play casts about the cabin, in reference to a possible retreat there, like those she had managed with cast members and parents the year before. She had drawn diagrams of the cottage on the board and discussed its location—"Take the road until you hit the cabin with the tree growing through the balcony." So its site was no mystery, nor are its insides hidden from those (Alan, say) who, like Detective Pausch, have "stood on the rear porch and looked inside the cabin through the glass." At least not all its insides are hidden. But several startling things are not visible to peepers: some rooms, unusual architectural features, and furnishings so eye-catching only those who haven't seen them (or have merely peeked in from outside) could miss. Everything visible from the outside is in the diagram, as Detective Pausch notes; but there's nothing there that can be seen only from the inside, where Alan claims to have been. It's a detail that escapes detectives who see through the eyes of plaintiffs and a public that journeys to places already convinced that they are viewing landmarks of criminal sexuality.

Such complicating details are so annoying that we have learned to make them not exist. Which leads us to the tattoo on Mrs. Baxter that Alan never saw, but the jury did, and also every interested trial follower, in the mind's eye. At the Wrightwood cabin (not to mention the scores of other occasions he claimed), Alan saw Mrs. Baxter naked "in all her glory," as the defense attorney put it.[18] But he missed the tattoo, a tattoo there since 1990, when Mary and her husband celebrated their fifth wedding anniversary by—what else?—getting matching tattoos. Faced with an embarrassing detail they could not make disappear, the prosecution insisted that the tattoos, which they did not deny existed NOW, did not exist THEN, that the devious Baxters had rushed out and got themselves stuck after the fact. Experts were consulted on both sides, a defense dermatologist said the tattoo looked about five years old, all right; a prosecution expert, not a dermatologist but an actual tattooist from Hollywood (where they know what they're doing), said he could date tattoos within two years and proceeded to date this one within eight months. What's important is that the *Glendale News-Press* got to gibber on about the tattoo, tell us how the jury actually saw it (did the *Glendale News-Press?*) and how it was "a red, heart-shaped tattoo on her right thigh."[19] I don't know if the jury peeked at Dolph's tattoo as well. I think they should have.

Do You Have a Degree in Psychology?

Mrs. Baxter gave Alan tapes (two) of classical and old standard music, a book (*The Little Prince*), went with his family to a ballet (amateurish), with him to the L.A. Philharmonic (he slouched), and traded letters with him in an attempt to initiate a therapeutic anger. She talked with him and tried to help him, partly because that's what she does and partly, we remember, so he might be a slightly more credible actor. There was a play going on during all this time, and Mrs. Baxter is a drama teacher. But it's her excellence as a teacher that, arguably, got her into trouble. The above list of gifts and events constitutes pretty much the whole of the evidence offered by the prosecution. And what is it evidence of? Seduction or effective teaching? To some, the letter business might make Mrs. Baxter guilty of temporary excessive zeal in promoting pop psychology, but it seems to me to be the sort of action that, as Jane Austen says, only the outcome can prove right or wrong.

Mrs. Baxter was Teacher of the Year only a year or two earlier, and it was, at least in part, as a teacher that she was put on trial. Why did the newspaper remind us in almost every issue of her award: as a gesture of fairness or as a form of sarcasm and a way of focusing our scapegoating fury? This teacher-of-the-year can be made to stand as a convenient target for our culture's resentment of pedagogues and its delight in humiliating them. Especially now, we seem willing to see teachers as predators, enemies of the family and deadly rivals for our control over children. Perhaps teachers like Mrs. Baxter, rare teachers of enthusiasm and compassion, make the best targets because they insult our heedlessness as regards children.

So, Mrs. Baxter was grilled by Pausch on whether her degrees really are, as they do not seem to be, in psychology. If not, the implication is, why was she talking to "the child" at all? Mrs. Baxter told me, "I knew all I could do was listen. After all, a lot of kids want to talk— and do talk, if you'll listen. I did tell him to go to Outreach, but he said he'd been there and didn't find it helpful, was seeing a therapist, and that talking to me meant a lot to him." As Ado Annie sings in *Oklahoma,* "Whatcha gonna do, spit in his eye?"

Probably so. The story, in any case, allows us, once we have located an approved target, to attack her as much as we like. Here's the *Glendale News-Press* giving us our sadistic due: "Baxter sobbed" as the D.A. read the letter to the jury; she often "bitterly wept"; and when asked why she gave him the letter, "'I wanted to show him that I trusted him,' she testified, her face turning red and her eyes dampening." [20]

Young Men and Bananas

Which brings us to bananas, a part of the prosecution's case given heavy play by the *Glendale News-Press,* which knows evidence when it sees it. In the case of the bananas, the prosecution even had what it pointedly did not have for any other part of its tale, a witness, a student and friend of Hoyt's named Fred Daley, who was able to testify, quite without hesitation, that during lunchtime a group of students would, you know, have lunch in Mrs. Baxter's, like, classroom, and she would eat her lunch there too, and when, you know, she ate a banana, "we would make eyes at her" and Alan would, like, make these lewd noises.[21] Others would make these noises too and sometimes rude comments, as jokes, you know. Fred often made "a joke" of his own,[22] asking the defendant to have his baby. She mostly just ignored him, but finally, in weariness, told him to cut it out. After numerous requests, he did.

But we're straying from the bananas, which were made available for high-school wit by the play the class was rehearsing, *Tom Jones,* specifically by a famous scene in which Mrs. Waters tries to employ lascivious and slurpy eating to seduce the hero. It's a scene that became famous following the 1963 film and was titillatingly uproarious to these high-school boys after Mrs. Baxter demonstrated to the students playing the part how to do it. Finally, from boredom more than embarrassment, she moved her lunch spot to the faculty lounge to escape their hilarity. She dealt with matters like this by feigning amusement, inattention, or annoyance, very seldom the latter: "They were," she says with resignation, "horny boys who didn't have anywhere else to turn,"[23] except to such wildly excessive displacements, in Mrs. Baxter's view as harmless as they were witless.

Alan was often an instigator of the banana fun, Fred Daley and Mrs. Baxter say; but he was overtly sexual in many circumstances—including a classroom reading of *The Crucible*—not, for most, an irresistibly arousing play. Detective Pausch affected surprise that Mrs. Baxter had not, at the very first banana episode, marched Alan to the principal's office and set into motion the discipline-and-punish machinery.[24] Doubtless feeling that she could hardly be trotting all the boys and several girls up and down the halls every five minutes, Mrs. Baxter replied that she maintained, on principle, an open classroom, and that a trip to the principal's office was just what Alan, given his problems, did not need. After all, "though Alan was ill-behaved, he was certainly no worse than most high-school boys."[25]

Once inside the story, the calflike blunderings of adolescents everywhere are forgotten. We somehow fail to recall the giddy idiocy that stemmed from nothing more than horniness and managed to get itself expressed only indirectly: in public, in a burbling crowd; and then only because we were sure it would never be put to the test. We could then giggle and say obscene things precisely because all we'd ever have to do was say them. Mrs. Baxter was too wise and experienced a teacher not to know this: "I couldn't be too mad at Alan—or any of them. I'm sure we all remember being in high school." Unhappily, that is just what the story does not remember, not at all.

Bleeding the Baby

The story makes possible certain social barbarisms we would otherwise flinch from. For months before the trial began, the prosecution battled to conduct genetic tests on the Baxters' baby to see if Alan was the father as he claimed to be. The *Glendale News-Press* told us all about it, quoting the deputy district attorney running things, one Anne Hennigan, as saying, "We believe in fact there is a high likelihood that (the victim) is the father of the child."[26] This is interesting. What does "we believe in fact" mean? What does "fact" have to do with it? Also, who is calling the plaintiff "the victim"? Since the word appears in parentheses, it seems as if it is the reporter, Amy Koval, who, here and elsewhere, has little doubt about who is victimizing whom. Koval is quick to remind readers, when she can, that the baby "was born approximately nine months after the start of the alleged affair,"[27] never pausing to consider that the "start" was as "alleged" as the "affair" and that the plaintiff could count.

When the judge ruled that any such testing was a civil rights violation,[28] the prosecution tried to subpoena Mr. Baxter and the baby, Philip, to appear in court as "exhibits." Mr. Baxter is, as Detective Pausch reported right off the bat, "half Asian" (Dolph Baxter says it usually came out as "part Oriental"); and the prosecution wanted the jury to have a look at Mr. Baxter and the baby together and see for themselves. The judge quickly vetoed that spectacle.

A Foolish Consistency Is a Real Hobgoblin

But he allowed us other you-can-hardly-believe-it's-happening-before-your-eyes displays, including the daring high-wire performance of Deputy D.A. Hennigan, summing up with an argument that focused (I swear) on the very implausibility of Alan Hoyt's story and its highly variable quality, on the way it shifted and swayed to meet new circumstances. That Alan changed his story now and then, and often chose a version that slid between the improbable and the unbelievable, indicated, she said, that he was telling the truth. Had he been inventing stories, they would have been (at least some of them) coherent, in accord with the facts. Alan, she said, was a smart young man and could easily come up with a narrative that would *seem* true, were he lying; that he came up with stories that did *not* seem true indicated, Hennigan said, that true is what they were. By that measure, the world is flat, my next-door neighbor is a satanic priestess, I am ravishing to behold, and the cat drank up the last of the gin.

What's Our Role?

But sneering at others should not protect us from exploring the pleasures we take from these trials, the requirements we place on those reporting them, the way they are designed so skillfully to grab our attention, to play directly to what we want to see and hear. The allowance of disguised voyeurism in this trial, though it probably did not exceed the usual quota, was great enough to satisfy any trench-coated frequenter of bushes. The charge of oral copulation was bolstered by talk about "threshold issues," namely, sexual intercourse. Amy Koval managed to insert this legally irrelevant issue into virtually every single article, usually by way of mentioning that it was irrelevant, though it soon wouldn't be, thanks to Senator Newton Russell, R-Glendale—blah, blah, blah. But Koval didn't originate this sort of porn; she was doing as she was told, giving us what we ask for—like that bit on the tattoo, the heart tattoo, small, right there on the thigh.

Once the trial ended, Ms. Koval searched for material in other events to supply us with what we long for. On April 18, for instance, she got another front-page story: "Nude girl, 15, hospitalized after kidnapping attempt." Clothed, she would have been page 34, tops.

When Does It End?

It ends with the acquittal on March 18—only it doesn't. The *News-Press* gave a single nippy sentence to the innocent verdict and then was immediately off and running: "But most jurors after two days of deliberations thought the teacher and the teenage boy did have sexual intercourse between November 1992 and January 1993, one year before the law made it illegal." The next column repeats the point: "Baxter was tried on the oral copulation charge—not statutory rape—because there wasn't a law against sexual intercourse." But what about those jurors, the "majority," who persuaded themselves of the accused's guilt of a crime she had neither been charged with nor defended herself against? A single juror identified as "Connie" says "the majority" of the jurors were convinced that sex was in the air, Connie's view apparently being plenty good enough for Amy Koval.

As if that weren't enough, the paper provided a second, inset column, "Despite Verdict, Baxter's Future Unclear," in which Koval repeats this prattle about the majority view and raises the specter of the state Commission on Teacher Credentials hearing, though she is mum about (discreet Amy) the looming civil suit.

Naive citizens might think an acquittal would buy them something in the way of exoneration, or at least peace. But the fact is that after acquittal the pornographic fun lingers on. In this case, the state commission refused to reinstate Ms. Baxter, apparently feeling that when there's a whiff of smoke in a Glendale courtroom, they'd better assume a firestorm. So there are likely appeals there, along with the civil suit, which might drag on into the next millennium. We know that it will and that our transmitters from the *Glendale News-Press* will be there for us. Amy's our friend.

Who Wins?

After the trial, Sophia Hoyt told the paper she was "in shock," adding that "she wasn't sure if the outcome was worth the experience of coming to court and exposing the details of her family life." She's very shrewd in divining that it's exactly those details we want exposed. The more the better. But why should it be "worth it" to her and to her son?

To Mrs. Baxter, winning was certainly a terrible loss. She speaks of the irony of the defeated plaintiffs actually being able to take a good measure of control over her life, of the horror of these months of charges and hectoring and, worst of all, silence. But she does not hate Alan Hoyt, says she can't even muster revenge fantasies. When she's pressed on that point, she smiles, "No, I'm not going to go down that road. There's no coming back." But she seems absolutely resolute about one point: she will never teach high school again: "I'm leaving teaching. I couldn't ever be the kind of teacher it would take to be safe. Maybe college, though." There's a shimmer there at the end, a little glow of hope. But it's a great sadness when we force out of teaching those willing and best able to teach.

But *we* win. We ought to acknowledge it openly. We have tortured Alan Hoyt and Mary Baxter, made them compete for the role of Purity in a sadistic morality play in which both purity and its enemies are so highly eroticized that they cannot escape. That Mary Baxter is aware of the Kafkaesque trap and that Alan Hoyt may be as well is beside the point: their awareness buys them nothing.

We become so arrogant that we even seize a bit part in the play and manage to get ourselves mentioned in the paper. Here we are, in a side column headlined "Van Buren High Trial Draws Curious." (The curious: that's us.) Ms. Koval thinks we are drawn there because "at stake is the 31-year-old woman's dignity and teaching career, now teetering on the brink of extinction," but that's only part of it. Shhhh. Here's where we come in: we are the group who "showed up to listen to a portion of sexually graphic testimony, suppressing giggles until they dashed from the courtroom." When asked our opinion of the matter, our leader, his finger on our pulse, says, "Some say she did, some say she didn't."[29] It really doesn't matter, just so long as we can go on saying stuff. Know what I mean?

2. Inventing the Child—and Sexuality

Give a little love to a child, and you
get a great deal back.—John Ruskin

Children are about as sweet as coral
snakes and as innocent as hogs in
rutting season.—My uncle Raymond

We are the world,
We are the children,
We are the ones
To make a better day.
—Michael Jackson and Lionel Richie

I'm not the first to announce that both the child and modern sexuality came into being only about two hundred years ago, but it isn't often noted that, in the excitement of getting these two new products on the market, they got mixed together. One somehow got implanted in the other, and it shouldn't have happened. Despite the loud official protestations about children's innocence, our Victorian ancestors managed to make their concept of the erotic depend on the child, just as their idea of the child was based on their notions of sexual attraction. We've been living, not so happily, with the results of their bungling ever since.

The New Child

Those with an interest in last century's invention of sexuality can consult Michel Foucault; I'll concentrate on the fabrication of the modern child, the other half of our problem. According to a fascinating and controversial group of historical constructionists, led by Phillipe Ariès, little that looks anything like our "child" existed before the seventeenth century, the modern concept of children and that social and biological category not really flowering until the eighteenth century. Before that there were, of course, little people; but the difference between them and bigger ones was not sharply marked and was largely, when it was noted at all, a difference set in economic terms: a child stopped being a child when it entered the labor force, often as early as age five or six.[1]

Now this thesis is not uncontested,[2] but if we think of it as illuminating modern ways of seeing rather than as offering a confident description of the past, the idea of the invented child can be useful. It is not, in other words, a matter of what children *were* or were not in the past but of how we view that past, what we are able to spot there with our modern lenses. From that perspective we can watch as the modern child takes shape, divorcing itself from the adult gradually until it is very nearly an alien, unknowable and not quite real.

The Romantic child, formulated at the end of the eighteenth century, was injected with a host of qualities—naturalness, innocence, downright divinity—that could then be celebrated. But for writers such as Rousseau and Blake, "the child" was also a potent political and philosophical weapon against skeptical and secular rationalism. Their child was a beacon for the man, not an alien; a reprimand to our corruption, certainly, and our superior in many ways, but not a stranger. "The Child is father of the Man," and we never cut that cord, no matter how far we might journey from our celestial home.[3]

That link, however, was dissolved later in the century, as this new child developed into a distinct species. Strange, mysterious, and ungraspable, the truly modern child was and is both radiant and oddly repellant, the object of fawning and not-so-secret resentment.

Blessed Innocence

As I mentioned in the Introduction, this Romantic child was largely figured as an inversion of Enlightenment virtues and was thus strangely hollow right from the start: *un*corrupted, *un*sophisticated, *un*enlightened. The child was without a lot of things, things it was better off without, presumably, but still oddly dispossessed and eviscerated, without much substance. As we have slowly succumbed to the collective illusion that the child is a biological category, we have still managed to hold that category open so that we can construe it any way we like. We have, according to the needs of history and our own whim, made children savages and sinners, but we have also maintained their innocence, a quality we seem to need much more than they do.

Innocence is a lot like the air in your tires: there's not a lot you can do with it but lose it. Besides, it doesn't amount to much in the first place. Innocence makes you vulnerable, badly in need of protection, which is one reason adults like it to be in others. It is also very close to natural immodesty, which is another. Originally, for the Romantics, innocence was connected not only to God but to active sympathies and primal love; but in the course of the nineteenth century it gravitated more and more toward a passive nullity, a pure point strangely connected to its opposite, depravity.

Innocence was such a pure conception in the nineteenth century that we may be struck with the difference between the adored literary child—little Alice or Oliver Twist or Ragged Dick—and the chimney sweeps dying of cancer of the scrotum, the factory children being mutilated, cast-off kids being left to wander the streets and peddle their bodies. We should not be surprised, of course, since we have likewise elevated the idea of innocence into the stratosphere and haven't far to look for similar contrasts between tender protestations and brutal actuality. Perhaps there's something about the way we have idealized "the child" that makes us indifferent to most children, even those whose misery and devastation strike our eyes. Or perhaps we have so saturated the idea of innocence with erotic appeal that we idealize to avoid facing what we have done.

Erotic Innocence

According to traditional figurings of marriage as the joining of virgins, the hoarding of innocence was promoted and secured by the promise of wild dissipation—a save-and-squander economical model. It's no wonder that innocence itself pulsed with sexual attraction. It may be that this cultural model has now been so weakened by the sexual revolution and changing patterns of sexual behavior that it's been all but abandoned. It may also be, however, that the sexual revolution has made us cling even more desperately to the old glowing myths surrounding innocence and to attach that idea of innocence all the more hysterically to our children. Faced with the growing ease of access and frequency of sexual activity among young people and the manifest failure of traditional teaching, we may well have shifted innocence more decisively backward, onto younger and yet younger people. Along with innocence, we have loaded them with all its sexual allure.

If so, we have aggravated a problem that was there from the beginning: eroticizing a product that was marketed as eros-free. That was not the definition of the child at first; but as time went on, the idea of innocence and the idea of "the child" became dominated by sexuality—negative sexuality, of course, but sexuality all the same. Innocence was filed down to mean little more than virginity coupled with ignorance; the child was, therefore, that which was innocent: the species incapable of practicing or inciting sex. The irony is not hard to miss: defining something entirely as a negation brings irresistibly before us that which we're trying to banish. It's like the surefire alchemical recipe for turning lead into gold: just add water and don't think of the word *rhinoceros*.

Freud and the Latent Child

The child had thus been fully sexualized long before the advent of Freud, who, as I've said, did little but oil the mechanisms we were developing to deal with sexualized innocence, to eroticize the child and deny we were doing so. We were, in fact, discovering the benefits of taking the position that a sexualized child was a mystery to us, and a monstrosity too, since we, in accord with our very nature, regarded the child as something holy or at least precious in the way an expensive vase or a new car is precious—something to look at, not paw.

Freud's insistence on the polymorphous perversity of infants certainly was a scandal, a flat rejection of the doctrine of the asexuality of children: "All the feelings which a child [i.e., an infant] has towards its parents and those who look after it," he says, "pass by an easy transition into the wishes which give expression to the child's sexual impulsions." He insists that tiny children want to kiss and touch, to examine genitals, to watch loved ones "perform their intimate excretory functions"; in short, they fuse their feelings with their "sexual intentions" and focus these "sexual trends" onto the person they love.[4]

In one way, that line is truly distressing, but Freud gives us ample recompense: when the Oedipus complex kicks in, the infant's enormous sexual firepower "succumbs . . . from the beginning of the period of latency onwards to a wave of repression. Such of it as is left over shows itself as a purely affectionate emotional tie, relating to the same people, but no longer to be described as 'sexual.'"[5]

This is as curious as it is convenient. The child's sexual motor is still humming, but it is now "inhibited in its aims" and takes substitute paths, expressing itself "as a purely affectionate emotional tie." What changes is the outlet, the way it appears—or maybe just the way it is "described": even if sex is the root, it is "no longer to be described as 'sexual.'" The linguistic obligation is withdrawn: we can have the sex without calling it that. Freud first roots the idea of "the child" unmistakably in erotic ground, then tells us not to worry, since it's not really operating out of this ground at all until puberty; and even if it is (as it is),[6] we needn't acknowledge it: if the child is feeling "purely affectionate emotional" feelings, then we are too, *purely* affectionate emotional ones. Affectionate emotional ties are, of course, part of our response to children, but how do we understand this emphasis on purity? Why does Freud feel the need for such absolutism, and why might we welcome that cleansing qualification?

And what do we, the heirs of Freud, do when latent children manifest, as they do daily, anything but latency? We respond with enlightened bewilderment. The experts at *Child* advise us "to do whatever you feel most comfortable with, keeping in mind what's considered acceptable by society, and being sensitive to your child's feelings." Even if I didn't have to gauge social acceptability and my child's feelings, whatever they might be, I still wouldn't know what made me "comfortable." *Child* is, however, always ready with details. Playing doctor "is normal." Good. However, *Child* continues, "if kids are playing this game excessively, stop the activity in a calm and nonjudgmental way. Be particularly vigilant if grade-school kids are playing with their younger siblings." Stop it? Be vigilant? What happened to "calm"? And if your child is not teaming up with another but is touching him/herself? Again, "teach kids that this behavior is okay . . . but . . . if your child is doing it excessively, mention it to your pediatrician."[7] In other words, the latent child's sexual behavior should be treated with serenity rising quickly to panic as normal fades to deviant. Relax and then phone the authorities. Thanks, Freud.

Freud did tap into one feature of the Romantic child that really was latent: its power. Though innocence had been pumped into the child in an effort to pump everything else out, other, more threatening conceptions of children were still around, complicating the vacuously pure ideal. Among these were notions of the child as primitive, as embodying a natural form reaching back to an earlier and more authentic stage of the species: the child as savage, noble but raw. Related uneasily to this model was the idea of natural depravity, a savagery altogether ignoble. But let's deal first with the happier conception: the admirable child of nature and of natural energy.

This savage child usually appears in the softened form of the moderately naughty child, often in trouble but never malicious. In England, the rebellious heroines of Charlotte Brontë tap into this mythology, as do a host of boy heroes from Tom Brown to Tom Swift. The American version is best known through Alcott's Little Women, Twain's Tom Sawyer and Huck Finn, and Peck's Bad Boy. Modern versions are legion, from the Little Rascals through the Katzenjammer Kids, Little Iodine, and the nearly sadistic (but sweetsy) home-alone Macaulay Culkin.

The energy in these figures would seem to work against the erotic emptiness of the child described above, the hollow child whose innocence allowed for the inscription of all forms of desire. But these naughty figures are strangely innocent too, protected by their ignorance and their "primitive" status from bearing any real responsibility for their misdeeds. Even when they are punished, as they often are, the punishment goes no further than a little carnal whipping. Leslie Fiedler has it right when he calls these figures, boys and girls alike, good-bad boys. Their actions never cause us to doubt that their hearts are pure: they are, as much as a *Playboy* centerfold, empty inside and thus idealized, conventionally erotic figures.

But they do exercise over us a strange fascination, these wild children, a fascination related to the fact that they resist the taming we so relentlessly try to apply. Insofar as the child is disobedient, he or she recalls, however dimly, the dream of savagery, the dream of that untrammeled sexuality lurking, Freud says, behind the child. The disobedient child gives the lie to the joke of "latency," suggests that sexual energy is never far from the surface of the child. Adults typically incite the very disobedience they pretend to abhor, punish what they promote. The naughty child recalls for us, down deep, the truly wild child; and the wild child does so many things for us: puts us in touch with our most stirring nostalgic fantasies of what we might have been, might have come from. Beyond this, the wild child seems to resist all, and in so doing, allow all. We see in the wild child something of ourselves and something that also mocks us, shows us what we've lost or repudiated: our fully sexualized youth.

Thus we are disturbed and angered by the wild child, a figure of energized innocence that lies at the heart of our modern dilemma. Because this wild child is crucial to our discussion, I would like to interrupt the argumentative flow I have gurgling along with what is (there's no disguising it) a not-all-that-short discussion of the most famous of these natural manufactures.

The Wild Boy of Aveyron

Perhaps no child was ever loved more ardently or more fruitlessly than Victor, a boy trapped in 1799 by hunters in the district of Aveyron in southern France. The naked boy was found outside a forest and seized by three "sportsmen" as he tried to climb a tree to escape. Taken to a nearby house, he seems to have been treated kindly enough, but kept trying to break free of his captors, once managing to escape for a whole week. But he was retaken, and as word of this curiosity got out, orders were given, and he was carted to Paris so that sightseers might gawk and scientists probe. Neither meant any harm, but at least one came to "condemn the sterile and inhuman curiosity of the men who first tore him from his innocent and happy life."[8]

This is, of course, the voice of the medical man who took charge of the boy, named him Victor, and pored over him with a mighty curiosity of his own. Jean-Marc-Gaspard Itard, only twenty-five at the time and earnestly ambitious, not surprisingly viewed the wild boy's arrival as a chance to clinch a career. But it was not just that. He was determined from the start to admire Victor and even to love him: "to treat him kindly and to exercise great consideration for his tastes and inclinations."[9]

Victor represented for Itard and for the new revolutionary government a brilliant opportunity to confirm the doctrines so vital to the democracy then being established. The new France was, after all, a state relying for its authority on the ideology of freedom and its ability to civilize the "natural." Victor's liberty had seemed absolute, an exemplary symbol of man in an uncorrupted and barbaric state— just waiting for Reason. That it was not really "man" but "boy" made it all the better. The progressive new democracies (our own as much as the French) placed the new "child" at the center of their creed, just as the imposing bourgeois family organized itself around this same image. The child represented the new world: the focus on the future, the confidence in the power of education, the fervent belief in the goodness of the tutored human heart.

The little boy, probably about eleven years old, arrived in Paris looking savage enough, and certainly not noble. He was, Itard says, "disgustingly dirty," covered with scars and gashes, and terrified; when he wasn't loping like a beast, he was crouching and swaying back and forth as "animals in the menagerie" do, grunting, snorting, and trying to bite or scratch anyone who came near. Worst of all, he was utterly "indifferent to everything," not what one would hope for from an innocent who had been drinking in God's wisdom. He wasn't even loving, Itard says: he "showed no sort of affection to those who attended him."[10] It may seem odd that Itard would say such a thing, would expect this hunted boy to emerge from his cage brimming with fondness for his jailers. But Romantic children are always expected to be loving, right from the start. Itard, the scientist and rationalist, is mocking Romantic expectations here.

But he turns out to be a closet Romantic himself, immediately taking to the boy and deciding there is a rational and affectionate creature inside this "animal" after all. The scientist is filled with contempt for the mobs who "saw [Victor] without observing him [and] passed judgment on him without knowing him," and for those who wanted to institutionalize him, "as if society had the right to tear a child away from a free and innocent life, and send him to die of boredom in an institution."[11] Notice that Itard is very busy distinguishing himself from the herds of those who don't notice (i.e., love) the boy, from a callous "society," and from a "curiosity" that is merely "sterile." Victor thus defines Itard—not only elevates him but tells him what he is, a caring scientist. This sense of being made special, of actually receiving an individual identity, is a gift given by the modern child, whether that child likes it or not: the family or the adult protector commonly assumes the role of being the only helper, the only one who understands, the only lover. Partly for that reason, children inevitably feel trapped, and adults betrayed.

But for now Itard has Victor all to himself, Victor with his "fine and velvety skin," his voice of great "sweetness," and his "naturally sweet character." Despite the cursed tests he feels he must run, Itard finds time to love the boy, to see and feel those moments that draw from Victor "cries of delight": "a ray of sun reflected upon a mirror in his room and turning about on the ceiling, a glass of water let fall drop by drop from a certain height upon his finger tips while he was in the bath." Itard merges ecstatically into Victor's joy. He admires Victor's determined distaste for gourmet food and for all strong drink, his heart-stirring attachment to things that are bare and free: "It is near the window with his eyes turned toward the country that our drinker stands, as if in this moment of happiness this child of nature tries to unite the only two good things which have survived the loss of his liberty—a drink of limpid water and the sight of sun and country."[12]

Itard is somehow never more moved, nor, to me, so moving, as when he is filtering his esteem for the child of nature through a gummy screen of sadness. As with Peter Pan or Wonderland's Alice, the child's liberty is never so valued as when it is about to disappear and can be imprisoned in nostalgia. That Itard is by now the chief instrument of the boy's poignant "loss of liberty"—why doesn't he just let him go?—seems never to occur to him; he is equipped with the convenient blindness to the obvious granted to parents, teachers, and all us mooners-over-loss.

Itard is not the villain here: there is no villain. Itard, in fact, sees Victor as not simply a sentimental icon but a pain in the neck, a humorous companion, and a bore. Victor sometimes annoys him or embarrasses him, as when he follows his noble-savage instincts with visitors who have overstayed their welcome: "He offers to each of them, without mistake, cane, gloves and hat, pushes them gently towards the door, which he closes impetuously upon them."[13] Itard is most eloquent when he allows to soak into his reflections about Victor some dark currents of regret, shame, and pride at being a knowledge-producing servant of the new state.

He often detests the tests he performs on Victor, hating the fits of anger that overtake the boy and, even more, the sadness,

> the profound state of moroseness into which my young pupil always falls when, in the course of our lessons, after struggling in vain with the whole power of his attention against some new difficulty, he realizes the impossibility of overcoming it. It is on such occasions, imbued with the feeling of his impotence, and touched perhaps with the uselessness of my efforts, that I have seen him moisten with his tears the characters which are so un-intelligible to him, although he has not been provoked by any word of reproach, threat or punishment.[14]

Itard's sense that Victor is hurt most deeply not by his own failure but by his beloved teacher's is remarkable. The scientist may be indulging in wild empathetic projection here or in simple selfishness—but he may be right.

Even Victor's punishments, resulting mostly from scientific controls on the experiments rather than discipline, seem to pain the boy most deeply when he feels he has somehow injured Itard. Of course, this ability to instill guilt has always empowered the punishers, but Victor seems heartbreakingly susceptible. Itard at one point holds him upside down outside a window, pointing downward toward a "chasm," a ghastly punishment that scares Victor horribly. But this torture seems almost benign compared with the cold experimental punishments doled out randomly to discover if the boy has any sense of justice (he certainly does) and to determine the point at which he will realize that blows with a ruler are no longer fun and games but expressions of painful disapproval:

> Tears rolled down from under [the] bandage over his eyes. I has-tened to raise it, but . . . he persisted in keeping his eyes closed

although freed of the bandage. I cannot describe how unhappy he looked with his eyes thus closed and with tears escaping from them every now and then. Oh! how ready I was on this occasion, as on many others, to give up my self-imposed task.[15]

But Itard doesn't, of course, perhaps because he feels tied to his duties (even if they are "self-imposed"), but also because his attachment to Victor runs deeper than duty ever goes:

When I go to the house in the evening just after he has gone to bed, his first movement is to sit up for me to embrace him, then to draw me to him by seizing my arm and making me sit upon his bed, after which he usually takes my hand, carries it to his eyes, his forehead, the back of his head, and holds it with his upon these parts for a very long time. At other times he gets up with bursts of laughter and comes beside me to caress my knees in his own way which consists of feeling them, rubbing them firmly in all directions for some minutes, and then sometimes in laying his lips to them two or three times. People may say what they like, but I will confess that I lend myself without ceremony to all this childish play.[16]

People may say what they like, but Itard will say what he likes too, even if his language in describing it—"I lend myself without cere-mony"—suddenly becomes awkward and self-conscious. We can bet that Itard is not "lending" anything. At such times, he wants nothing in return from the affectionate child.

One wishes this love story had the happy ending François Truffaut could not keep himself from adding to his movie. In fact, dreary fact, Itard soon left Victor to his fate, a future that did not include any fur-ther contact with Itard. His second official report, written five years after the first, admits to "results much below . . . expectations,"[17] but we must wonder if his desertion was prompted by Victor's illiteracy or by his puberty, more exactly, his adolescence and then dull adult-hood. Victor ceased to be mesmerizing; Itard probably wondered how that magic boy vanished. That's the melancholy wonder expressed by everyone who has watched anticipation turn to tedium. After all, who wants an affectionate thirty-nine-year-old slobbering all over his knees? Where have all the flowers gone? Victor died at age forty, alone and mute, still delighted by water and sun.

As a brief, but not uplifting, coda, I cite the case of Genie, another wild child, this time from a modern version of the woods: an attic in a Los Angeles suburb where she was imprisoned, without human contact, until she was discovered in 1970 at age thirteen.[18] Like Victor, Genie was a sensation. She attracted attention that turned into fascination, that turned into love—which lasted as long as she was adorable. Then nothing. Genie was dropped by the scientists and abandoned to foster parents, one of whom beat her for vomiting. She was no longer adorable, wouldn't smile or open her mouth for fear of being beaten.[19]

There have been many wild children. Linnaeus in 1735 mentioned ten instances from 1544 to 1731, eight girls and two boys; and later there were uncovered a number of "wolf-children." There was once a bear-boy of Lithuania. I wonder if he missed the bears when humans stopped finding him attractive, left him to live as best he could and die alone. I don't think the bears would have done that to him, shunned him because he was no longer cute.

The American Dream Child

Victor's story, or sentimentalized versions of it, entered into Western popular mythology in the nineteenth century as a way of keeping alive the image of the child of power, somehow in contact with sources of primal energy (not excluding sexual energy) adults would like both to deny and to claim as our own. This child, then, strikes us as both valuable and dangerous, familiar and very strange. We are never sure whether to worship this child or spank it. The key point is that this Romantic child has become central to the way we structure our world of desire. He reappears throughout the nineteenth century and the twentieth as Bomba and Tarzan and a host of other savage children. He is also domesticated, in a variety of middle-class imps, leading to a parade of mischief makers, recyclings of Kim and Buster Brown.

Our own distinctive national spin on romanticism's wild child of power is also cute, in need of taming, and discardable after use—but adds the charged issue of class. America's adorable bad kids are often poor and ask for more, ask for a special allowance of care from their adult admirers but also a willingness to enter treacherous waters. This child might offer an appealing image of innocence-in-need, a figure crying out for our hugs and comfort; but he might also be asking for money and offering in return some stinging social criticism. I'm thinking of Huckleberry Finn here, of course, our most gifted child satirist. But ordinarily, this child from "the lower orders" is a little less threatening: think of Tom Sawyer and Topsy or Hawthorne's Pearl, the Dead End Kids or the Little Rascals. These children are sliding fast toward bourgeois accommodation, though they carry some of the appeal of distance: the erotic strangeness of the poor, who are imbued in sexual fantasy with raw power and helplessness.

At their most benign, they still cry for our aid with something of a snarl, a point illustrated most clearly, I think, in the boy heroes of Horatio Alger. Although the phrase "a Horatio Alger story" often signifies our national myth of rugged independence, fables of wild success achieved through the application of hyper-Protestant virtues, the actual novels tap into a more potent legend: of how boys are helpless and beautiful, how they depend not so much on fine inner qualities to attain success as on fine outer qualities to attract responsive adult gentlemen who will more or less hand them their success (which in fact is pretty moderate) on a platter.[20]

Take, for instance, two of Alger's roaringly popular novels, *Ragged Dick* and *Mark the Match Boy*. The titles seem to speak for themselves, and most of us can imagine that we have read them without going to the trouble of doing so. Actually, they're not so agonizing to read, and they don't turn out to be much like what we had imagined. Ragged Dick, the more appealing of the two heroes (Mark being something of a sniveler in the Oliver Twist line), is a paradigm of the good kid who's had bad breaks, the survivor who retains genteel feelings, the tough punk who is good-hearted and good-looking: "decidedly good-looking," Alger says; "in spite of his dirt and rags there was something about Dick that was attractive."[21] That "something" that so beguiles Alger and his readers is a beauty that is more than skin-deep, that is tied to Dick's very faults. Not at all "a model boy," Dick swears, plays tricks on the innocent (clergymen especially), gambles, smokes, lies—"I knowed a young man once who waited six hours for a chance to cross [Broadway], and at last got run over by an omnibus, leaving

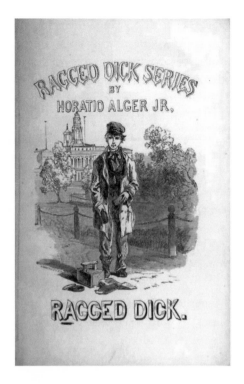

The original frontispiece of
a fetching Dick, not all that
ragged.

a widder and a large family of orphan children"—and is, ominously, extravagant. On the other hand (and it's a big, open hand), Dick is good to younger boys, never "mean," always "frank and straight-forward," downright "noble," "manly and self-reliant."[22] As it turns out, he needn't be so self-reliant as all that, because others (most of all Alger) are anxious to help him.

Alger feels so kindly toward Dick and all his other heroes that he often forgets to subject them to a harsh Protestant morality—or any morality at all, which may be why the books were so popular. Now and then (but very seldom) he inserts little homilies on smoking or theatergoing, and he sometimes remembers to send the boys to Sunday school; but his heart's not in such things.

These are surprisingly naturalistic stories, filled with details of the lives of street children and with compassion for their plight. Alger himself may or may not have had suspicions of pederasty shadowing his life,[23] but it is clear that he cared for these boys and that he understood the fierce world in which they struggled. He hammers at us with his knowledge of the economic squeeze crushing the bootblacks, the paper kids, the match boys and girls. They lived a hard life made even harder by the absence of any protection whatever; if they sickened or became unable to compete, they died. Further, in order to escape the horrors of a future without a safety net, these children needed to get a "position," which meant, in New York, clerking in a store (a job with a future and, more vital, protection). But there was a catch. The beginning salaries for clerks were low, even lower than the earnings of street kids, so one generally had to have some savings to struggle through the months or years until the raises started coming, not to mention getting together the good clothes it took to obtain such positions in the first place. In order to escape, these children, who ranged in age from maybe five to eighteen, needed to be almost inhumanly self-denying and frugal, shunning even the cheap pleasures that made their lives partly livable. That's why Dick's initial extravagance, even his sweet-hearted generosity, is so perilous. In Alger's world, you save not to find righteousness but to escape from the streets; and the only way to do that is to squeeze a toe onto the lower rung of the mercantile bureaucracy. Alger's warnings about such things as the theater and smoking are not appeals to piety; they are not evil but expensive. His homilies offer tips on survival, not salvation.

Alger was so moved by the plight of these children, so anxious to help them, that even in his novels he could hardly wait to give them a hand. So much the worse for his novels, we might think, since the suspense he does manage to inject never lasts for more than a couple of pages. Alger has such a low threshold for fretting that he gets his boys out from behind eight balls about as fast as he rolls these before them, opening for them the arms of some kindly old gent ready to shower a handsome, dirty-faced lad with gratitude and goods. If these boys help a person from the country cross the street, the tourist is sure to show maniacal gratitude. Let them take a ride on a ferry, and a child belonging to a wealthy fellow (who can't swim) is sure to topple overboard—and you know the rest.

Those favored by fortune and by Alger get what they get (which, incidentally, is never fame and fortune but just lower-middle-class security) because they are pretty and lucky. Alger may have felt he was inculcating a Protestant ethic, but he seems to have exploited instead a pedophilic fairy tale, a narrative that runs at least as deep in America as Puritanism. It's not hard work that brings success but being cute, cute in the presence of susceptible adults.

This Alger/American child, deeply eroticized as it is, departs from the pure and passive child of heaven imaged by Wordsworth, the Romantics, and the greeting-card people. Alger's child is much closer to the wild child of nature. His heroes have about them a primal integrity, an independent power, and at least a rudimentary complexity: a capacity to read society on their own terms, to lie and speak ironically, to make independent decisions, to tell us to go jump in the lake. They need our help, but they stand on their own feet too and won't accept just any boost. They are choosy. They keep their distance, refuse to be sucked into sentimentality or into us. When Alger wants to create a perfectly comfy ending, as he does for Mark the Match Boy, he unites him with a man "whose great object in life is to study his happiness."[24] But although they may live happily ever after, this is not a marriage, the adult being held at bay, always providing for, "studying," the happiness of the child, making do with nothing better than, let's face it, voyeurism.

Remember that these novels, while participating in the formation of a cultural reality, are also fantasies, adult projections onto an erotic field they are at the same time framing. These are powerful fantasies that tell us what a child is, what we are, and what connections between us are possible. As fantasies go, however, they might seem pretty skinny, providing satisfactions as gaunt as they are uncertain. The loved child is rescued, pampered, always the sole object in the adult's viewfinder; and the adult gets in return a lot of photo opportunities and barely a thank-you besides. As a result, as this fantasy developed and took hold, the eroticism it offered became entwined with a resentment, a resentment (as we shall see in chapter 5) that could offer its own rewards but recognized the complexity of the child and our own ambivalent attitude toward it.

Independent Children

Thinking of "the child" as complex and independent, as a *species,* also made it a distant and exotic being, which heightened its attractiveness, but at some cost: the cost of remoteness, one of the reasons we feel all dewy about "the child" even as we whale away on the kids around us. The child we have inherited from the Victorians is both inside us and distant from us, a repository of nostalgia and a hope for the future, weak and powerful, alluring and revolting.

One oddity of this "child" is that it has seized hold of the power to define *us*. It's not just child molesters who are specified by their relationship to children; most of us are. This becomes clearest (and most painful) as we examine the manufacture in the nineteenth century of "the parent," an entity dependent on and subordinate to the preexisting (although also recently fabricated) "child." This "parent," a comic and wobbly idea, has been aiming ever since, lately with desperation, to assert what it manifestly does not possess: sovereign power.

Organizations spring up, Of the People being one example, to declare that parents exist as people and not just in the minds of their children. Of the People "aims to give parents more muscle" by having inserted into state constitutions a forlorn declaration: "The right of parents to direct the upbringing and education of their children shall not be infringed,"[25] as if they had once, in some mythical long-ago, possessed such power and had been robbed of it by liberal politicians.

Nevertheless, we don't stop pretending that we're the primary reality, not the child. One man buys up the paintings of serial killer John Wayne Gacy and destroys them so as to affirm the power of parents: "We're going to burn all the pictures and try to get the attention of parents to watch their kids so this never happens again"; "Young people have to be watched—so there's never another Gacy."[26] It's not entirely clear to me what parents are to be watching for— the reincarnation of Gacy or one of his victims, nor do I understand how a holocaust of paintings can give us the ability to control the future. Of course, I may simply be speaking sourly from my own impotence, cursed as I am with children who never heeded a thing I said or burned. I feel more in sympathy with Jeffrey Dahmer's father, whose agonizing *A Father's Story* shows us the fiction of "the parent" dissolving before our eyes.[27] And *that* we do not want to see.

Generally we do not have to see it; our culture is doing all it can to bolster the parental myth. We are bucked up by newspaper and magazine articles telling us that parents exist, are even important.

Anthony Wolf has written a book that assures us of "the power that parents have over children because of their children's automatic love and attachment to them," and chides us because "we do not always appreciate our power."[28] This used to be called reverse psychology: telling a loser he didn't realize how unbeatable he was. It was a shabby strategy then, and it is now. Penelope Leach, Ph.D., tells us in *Child* "How to Make Your Child Want to Be Good,"[29] a neat trick the truly effective parent is, Oz-like, able to manage by way of something called "positive discipline," a nice phrase and maybe a nice thing; I wouldn't know. Adults are even willing to have a go at hopelessly arduous tasks in order to believe in "the parent": "If you pressure your child too much, you may get a submissive but dispirited child; if you don't press hard enough, you may get an undisciplined one."[30] Here's a double bind so tight you'd think we'd say to hell with it. That we don't speaks to how much we need "the parent."

As long as we keep pretending parents exist independent of children, we can load on the parents powers, responsibilities, and rights. We don't acknowledge that these powers, responsibilities, and rights are sneakily sexualized, but now and then that fact worms its way out. In Kentucky, for instance, where parents and children have a long tradition of complex relations, a man of twenty-two married a girl of thirteen a month after he had gotten her pregnant. He was convicted of statutory rape, Kentucky assuming that those under sixteen cannot consent to sex unless they are married. The girl's new husband protested that it made no sense (and was unconstitutional) for the same act to transform itself from criminal to blessed because of a ceremony. The judge, nettled, responded that it might be nonsense but it was certainly constitutional, since it wasn't the religious ceremony that was at issue but the rights of parents to dispose of their children's bodies, children under sixteen requiring parental consent before experiencing marriage and then sex.

The Child Within

The subordinate and relational product, "the parent," thus testifies to the complexity of the problem and the weakness of simple responses to it. The child we have inherited in this century is a very intricate construction that demands a modulated, generally contradictory response.

Lately, however, we seem in our panic to have regressed, to have deluded ourselves into thinking that we can go back to a rudimentary child, a child whose simplicity is absolute. We are drawn to this Romantic child by a deep escapist nostalgia and an eroticism so privatized, enclosed, and fantasy laden that we make Horatio Alger seem the image of health. Right now we are busy re-creating Lewis Carroll's "child of the pure unclouded brow," the healing child within. This child rechurns our cultural curds, innocence and purity, into a modern snack food we can ingest and use to nourish, excuse, and explain ourselves. This is the child whose identity we steal and can then "find" and use to create the happy time we deserved all along.

The idealization of the prepubescent child and its location within the sad adult is not simply fuel for therapists and best-selling self-helpers; one sees it all over our culture, perhaps most pointedly in films such as *Stand by Me,* Rob Reiner's 1986 adaptation of Stephen King's goose-bumpy erotic story "The Body." This film offers as its capstone sentiment the idea that "nothing that happens after you're twelve matters very much,"[31] which makes sense only if nothing vital happens after you're older than twelve because you never are. As the child-within-the-adult-narrator (Richard Dreyfuss) says at the end, "I never had any friends later on like the ones I had when I was twelve. Jesus, does anybody?" This child-as-inner-dweller idea seems to form the basis of the reversal films: *Big* (1988), *Vice-Versa* (1988), *Like Father Like Son* (1988), the earlier (prescient) *Freaky Friday* (1976), and variants such as *Jack* (1996), in which the child within emerges, often to exact vengeance.

But usually we have that child under control; the problem is that it is lost, like the children on milk cartons. We must find that inner child and attend to its needs. This fantasy has been around for some time, popularized in therapy at least as early as 1963 with Hugh Missildine's *Your Inner Child of the Past,* but receiving an enormous boost from John Bradshaw's 1990 *Homecoming.*[32] According to Bradshaw's powerful model, each of us has a positive "wonder child" and a negative wounded child. The first is "vulnerable, childlike, spontaneous, and creative"; the other is "selfish, childish, and resists emotional and intellectual growth."[33] The trick is to heal the second to liberate the first, this wounded child causing us untold problems. Now the first child, "the wonder child," is nowhere more wonderful than in somehow staying put for all those years, never growing up, patiently waiting for us to get in touch. This is the perfectly good child, the child who remains loyal, not like the unruly wounded one, who badly needs a beating ("healing") and some very tough love.

In order to circumvent the bad child and contact the wonder child, we write letters, first as a gentle adult wanting to adopt a child (not just any child, of course, but our own child-self) and then as the answering inner child, who writes back with the nondominant hand, unleashing the wonder. Then we regress, find, re-parent, comfort, cuddle, and begin to heal. We listen to that child, get to know it, understand that it is insecure, has a "desperate need to be loved," and likes getting presents: "A good way to identify and care for your inner child is to buy a stuffed animal or doll for her."[34]

This sort of thing has become a staple of the healing industry and the whole culture of child molesting. Ellen Bass and Laura Davis feature "making contact with the child within" as a vital part of their fourteen-part program: "Getting in touch with the child within can help you feel compassion for yourself, more anger at your abuser, and greater intimacy with others."[35] And Mike Lew's *Victims No Longer: Men Recovering from Incest and Other Sexual Child Abuse* chortlingly cites a button, "It's Never Too Late to Have a Happy Childhood," glossing it approvingly: "While you can't change the past, you can forge a new perspective on it that will allow you to have a happier adulthood."[36]

We can "forge" a good many things, no doubt, and certainly we can rearrange the past to give us what we think we want. Still, this manipulation of the child within and of our general heritage is not without its perils, especially if we persist in imagining that we can play with these metaphors so literally, can make concrete our wildest and most selfish fantasies. What about the children outside us? What are we doing with them while we buy teddy bears for and drop love notes to the child in our solar plexus?

We commonly live in and through our children and then hate ourselves for doing so—or, more exactly, project that hatred onto others. Little League parents are despised by others, especially other Little League parents; ditto stage mothers, football fathers, Macaulay Culkin's greedy parents, and the mother and father of little Jessica Dubrow, the seven-year-old pilot killed in a cross-country attempt in April 1996. "Twisted Mom Brainwashed Little Pilot," howled the *National Enquirer; Time,* more judiciously, asked on its cover, "Who Killed Jessica?"[37] Which of us does not adore that inner child, indulge it sometimes, and give it what we never had—but now, through this child, perhaps can?

What is it we are loving, really, and what are we seeking to recover? The child's love, Freud asserts, is "boundless," demanding everything, which is attractive enough as an idea; but Freud also reminds us that the child's desire is infinite, has no concrete aim, and is thus always doomed to frustration. In seeking to recover the child, we seek the inexhaustible, the ecstatic, and we refuse to accept any limits; but ironically, the child we want to love us in return has no interest in "us" and wants the same oceanic love-without-end. We return to impossible erotic fantasies, ardently sexualizing our children and sentencing them to feel the full force of our childish disappointments.

3. Myths of Protection, Acts of Exposure

Dese are de conditions dat prevail.
—Jimmy Durante

Understandably, serial child molesters provoke the utmost in fear, outrage and concern. However, once a suspect is caught or the attacks cease, we tend to return to a misplaced optimism about the safety of our children. The fact is that monsters prey on children . . . with alarming frequency, and constant vigilance is demanded.—*Los Angeles Times* editorial, February 2, 1995

In Rob Reiner's 1994 bomb *North*, we see on a billboard an image of young Elijah Wood as the Coppertone child, his bathing trunks being first pulled down and then jerked back up by a mechanical dog. *Time* tells us the Coppertone child has become a paradigm for fashion, as "thin and winsome" models pose with "underpants on the way off." [1] Not only do we read our adult desires back onto the blushing child, there's a crude allegory of cultural practice here as well, an emblem of vigorous duplicity: we uncover what we shield, censure what we enjoy. [2] We get away with this double-dealing through a series of clever feints folded into a master story of evil and innocence: it's someone else pulling down the trunks, putting the children at risk; we're busy re-covering the child, comforting him, and denouncing the dog. To sustain this fantasy, we regard the dangers as both ubiquitous and inhuman, demonic. This dehumanizing runs so deep that it seems natural and inevitable. If we don't get the monster, convicts or the pressure of our condemnation will: "Molester Found Dead in Orange County Cell." [3]

Doing away with demons is only one part of the job; the other is providing them. The reserve of trench-coated misfit homosexuals has been pretty much drained, so we now hear that our average pedophile is gentle, heterosexual, married, without a criminal record, conservative, moralistic, perhaps as likely to be a woman as a man, and possibly a child himself. [4] That certainly expands the range of possible suspects. We deploy ballooning myths of infiltration that allow us to position predators not only as coaches, priests, and choir directors but as dentists, realtors, and second-graders. Some, "in the hope of deflecting attention from themselves . . . have moved to the forefront of the anti-abuse lobby . . . as might be expected."[5] We would expect this only if we had taught ourselves to believe that, like yesterday's Communists, pedophiles are everywhere and nowhere, so well disguised that the person who gives the least indication of being one most probably is.

Parents have become popular, often chief, suspects. Shielded by the trust they bear and by a portly tradition of sentimentality, they are also especially vulnerable when the shield is lowered. Roseanne provides a model onslaught:

> I believe that once your dad molests you you can kill him, and it ought to be legal. . . . By God, why shouldn't it be legal? All the mothers that let it go on, they just need to be taken off the earth. . . . Every kid getting abused out there has a right to kill their parents. Get a gun and kill them. And every woman: Kill him, man. This is a war against children.[6]

Roseanne's blunderbuss firings make the rest of us seem moderate, although one notices that as a rule, talk on this point varies little in content or tone.[7] Even generic stand-up comics drop into self-righteous cant when addressing (why do they?) this topic: At the 1994 "Comic Relief" (for AIDS) show, broadcast on HBO January 15, comics from Whoopi Goldberg to Paul Rodriguez got steely-eyed and firm-jawed ("But seriously, folks") when being dull and predictable on child abuse. Dennis Miller, billing himself as an intellectual, out-did even Roseanne: "If you ever get to a place in your life where you want to fuck or murder a kid, forget prison—just kill yourself, take one for the team."

I guess we all get a boost from such talk, even if it is stolen from warm-up-the-lynch-mob harangues. Our myth of protection gives us permission to inflate ourselves with outrage and then blow it out. *Time* runs a full page on NAMBLA (North American Man-Boy Love Association), working itself up to the point where it seems to believe that this subminuscule group threatens the very fabric of our traditional way of . . .—"no society interested in its own preservation can allow such conduct"[8]—leaving unclear whether the doomsday conduct in question is sex with children or the publication of a newsletter.

Ann Landers joins the hunt, printing letters such as the one about a Montreal judge who sentenced a man convicted of sexually assaulting his stepdaughter to twenty-three months: "Dear Ann: Where is justice? Where is decency? What kind of judges are sitting on the benches in Montreal, Canada? Do you have the courage to print this?" Ann does, agreeing with the reader from Port Charlotte, Florida (where citizens are on guard against lapses in Montreal), that "this sort of 'justice' is outrageous."[9] The *Los Angeles Times* editorial printed as a lead-in to this chapter says that the "alarming frequency" with which "monsters prey on children" makes any optimism "misplaced," a dangerous relaxation of the "constant vigilance" we must maintain.[10]

How did we get to the point where what may well be rational people like Ann Landers, Up-in-Arms-in-Port-Charlotte, and *L.A. Times* editorialists are willing, without knowing a thing, not simply to form judgments but to issue them as wake-up calls? I think such blaring is authorized by the set of interlocking assurances that I have been calling our national "myth of protection." That myth, in turn, rests on a common perception of the problem we face and of the roots of that problem. In order to act like this, we need first to believe that an emergency is upon us and that this emergency springs from an Evil so intransigent that it must be countered with an equally implacable Virtue.

The Problem

In 1990, the U.S. Advisory Board on Child Abuse and Neglect "surveyed the state of child protection in the United States" and in its first recommendation urged "each citizen to recognize that a serious emergency related to the maltreatment of children exists within American society and to join with all other citizens in resolving that its continued existence is intolerable." Regarding the magnitude of the problem as "stunning" and increasing "at a breathtaking rate," with our system "on the verge of *collapse*,"[11] the board seemed to feel that declaring a national emergency and employing an unflinching rhetoric would bring us to the right linguistic home. Congress passed two Missing Children Acts (in 1982 and 1984) and held extensive hearings in 1983, but that was just the start.

The crisis talk took off from this point and soon developed into an accepted mode of speaking. Since it had no apparent effect on the statistics on child maltreatment, which continued to climb rapidly, I think we can assume that this talk about epidemics, crises, and collapse was serving needs other than the immediately practical. On the one hand, it made us feel enlightened:

> Until recently, accusations of sexual abuse originating from children were interpreted either as maliciousness or . . . fantasy. . . . The major contributors to this lack of recognition of the problem were the secrecy surrounding the abuse and the denial of its existence once it was disclosed. While the secrecy and denial still prevail, professionals . . . have . . . become sensitized . . . are increasingly likely to believe in children . . . awareness heightened . . . procedures improved . . . increased clarity of thought.[12]

This increased clarity of thought is not to be found just anywhere:

> The unprecedented emergence of child sexual abuse . . . is a disaster played in slow motion. It is a nightmare of exposure, fear, confusion, helplessness, and paralysis. The scream won't come out and the flight reflexes are petrified. The nightmare is made all the more Kafkaesque by the legions of spectators who serenely pass by as if nothing is happening.[13]

It is the necessary warm-up to terror in monster movies: people just won't wake up to the fact that the monsters are coming, are already here. The reason: they don't want to face it, so "they go into denial about it," so much so that "it is frightening to realize how widespread sexual abuse is in our society and yet how strong the denial of it is."[14] "Denial" is, of course, a heavy club with which people who think something is so can beat those who don't. But the idea that people who ignore or dispute us are afflicted with some sort of condition (*in denial: in* shock, *in* the grips of a delusion, *insane*) allows us also to perpetuate the problem. We insist the situation is hopeless because, as the National Committee to Prevent Child Abuse (NCPCA) puts it, "the sexual abuse of children is something most people neither talk about nor believe."[15] Amidst the jabbering, the committee detects silence. Assured that it has the floor, the committee can issue sneering pamphlets ("Think you know something about child abuse?"),[16] glowing with the certainty that its lost cause will remain lost, that it (and we) may fight on in perpetuity, with no risk of winning.

It's true that our enthusiasm for broadcasting our enlightenment outran itself. In the heady early eighties, things got a little oversublime, *Reader's Digest* suggesting that thousands of missing children are murdered each year (it's closer to one hundred) and Representative Paul Simon of Illinois proclaiming confidently, "The most conservative estimate is that 50,000 young people disappear each year because of stranger kidnapping"[17] (actually it's two to three hundred). In 1985, the Center for Missing and Exploited Children said there were between four thousand and twenty thousand stranger kidnappings every year, a figure soon bloated to fifty thousand by the media, although the FBI that year investigated only fifty-three cases.[18] The issue is not that we jacked things up, but that we felt the need to do so.

And still do. We get word from overseas that in Berlin the molestation rate among contemporary schoolchildren is 80 percent, and in England 90 percent of women reported childhood sexual abuse.[19] In this country, we keep up: "It's pretty common—several percent of boys and girls get molested by fathers or stepfathers, several dozen percent get molested by other adults, and practically every child gets molested by other children."[20] Being more specific, Lloyd Demause suggests "40 percent for girls and 30 percent for boys," hastily adding that they "are only a portion of the hidden true incidence rates."[21] This "hidden true" rate allows us to factor in a multiple: "These figures are seen by researchers as only a fraction of the actual cases of abuse."[22] The U.S. Department of Health and Human Services, surveying the studies on child sexual abuse, reports that "rates for victimization for females range from 6 to 62 percent," for males, "from 3 to 24 percent."[23]

That's a pretty good range, even without throwing in the hidden-true multiplier, a wild range that reflects our uncertainty about what we mean by "a child," an exploitative age difference, and "sexual abuse." We have expanded the category of sexual abuse to include issues that would have been regarded three decades ago as nuisances or nothing: a wide variety of touching, some of it at least ambiguous; suggestive language; exhibitionism that used to be passed off as casual; and voyeurism. This last abuse, "in which an adult watches a child undress, bathe, or use the bathroom," may seem harmless, says the NCPCA, difficult for adults to regard as abuse at all; but children will know it is: "Children oftentimes can tell that 'something is funny' if you ask them." They will know that the adult is receiving "sexual gratification" from looking on.[24] The "intention of the abuser" is becoming more and more central in differentiating what is sexual abuse from what isn't, even when this means "that children can be abused without being aware of it (for instance, in some forms of voyeurism)."[25]

We constantly expand definitions, partly because we suppose we have grown more sensitive to less obvious offenses and more subtle victimizations, partly because the expansions feed the alarming discourse. By adding "intent" to the law we have greatly increased the possibilities for sexual interpretation: in California (our bellwether), for instance, the state high court overturned seven appeals court rulings on "lewd and lascivious" touchings of children under fourteen. The appeals court had defined such criminal touches as those "inherently sexual . . . by the nature of the act or the area touched." The high court moved the focus from the act and area to the mind of the toucher, to "any touching of an underage child with the intent of arousing the sexual desires of either the perpetrator or the child."[26] How can *any* touching be clearly and unequivocally legal under such a ruling? Won't it be necessary to discuss each and every touch, weighing the possibilities, dissecting the erotic experience of both the adult and the child?

Douglas J. Besharov and Jacob W. Dembosky call such expansion of categories "definitional creep" and show how Health and Human Services director Donna Shalala's recent crisis-mongering announcement —"a rising epidemic of child abuse"—is based entirely on making the definitions, like the ooze in *The Blob,* cover more and more territory. Shalala claims "child abuse and neglect nearly doubled in the U.S. between 1968 and 1993," and "the number of 'serious cases' . . . quadrupled," while cases being investigated declined. What Shalala finds "shameful and startling," the authors find to be a case of flawed methodology. For example, 55 percent of the increase is accounted for by a brand-new category, "endangered children"; the rest, the authors say, almost certainly is from increased sensitivity among social workers and a greater readiness to report abuse, especially "emotional abuse," marking another huge jump in Shalala's figures. As for the explosion in "serious cases," the authors point to a corresponding decline in "moderate cases."[27]

In our carefree play with these figures and our fascination with these studies, we commonly ignore details that don't fit, bury them in footnotes or ignore them altogether. For instance, these studies tell us that many missing children are not really missing—their "caretakers did not know where they were"; that a large number of runaways are really throwaways; that, contrary to the mythology, older children (fourteen to seventeen) are at much greater risk of stranger abduction homicide, and that the total number of these is between 52 and 158, not several thousand; that sexual abuse is only one of five operative motives for child abduction ("exaggerated" by "public fears"), according to the U.S. Department of Justice; that no evidence exists to show that stranger kidnappings are higher now than they've ever been; that runaway rates may have gone down.[28]

Perhaps nowhere is our ability to mold reality more striking than in our narrowing of the general category of "child abuse" into the realm of sexuality. Statistics compiled by the National Committee to Prevent Child Abuse show that of just under three million reports to child protective agencies in 1993, 11 percent were for suspected sexual abuse, ranking a little higher than "other," but far below physical abuse (30 percent) and neglect (47 percent). The percentage of missing children connected to sexual abuse is even smaller, less than 1 percent, with up to 575,000 runaways and throwaways, but 200–300 kidnappings and 3,200–4,600 abductions, not all of which, of course, were sexually motivated.[29] On May 31, 1994, CBS ran a special, *Break the Silence*, in which twenty-nine children told stories of abuse; half of the stories and most of the discussion were devoted to sexual abuse, an emphasis aimed clearly at our interest and not at the problem.

The murder of children receives less attention unless it is associated with abduction; but garden variety murder is becoming more and more frequent, even among tiny children. Since 1950, murder rates for minority children under age four have quadrupled; they have doubled for white children in the same age group. The raw numbers are just as stark: about 8.8 homicides per 100,000 for minority children; 2.4 per 100,000 for white children.[30] Judging by our discourse, attacks on lives interest us far less than attacks on innocence.

It is we who forge the tie between child abuse generally and sexual activity or sexual attraction; the facts don't lead us in that direction, our needs do: that's a blunt statement of the argument we've been testing.

There are a few corollaries to this main proposition, a few myths-on-wheels that, despite the backlash and vigorous refutation, keep rolling along.

1. False allegations are a rare problem or a nonproblem. Children have such an immediate and direct relationship to experience and speak such a transparent language that it is safe to say they never lie about sexual contact with adults, even if they don't understand it. When they do "lie," it is commonly to minimize the importance of the whole thing. Oprah's *Scared Silent* puts it this way: "It is extremely rare for children to lie, particularly about sexual abuse."[31] I wonder where these candid children can be found? Joyce Brothers, not usually a friend to skepticism, says that "often, children lie to parents in an attempt to please them."[32] I would add (from experience in both roles) that children also lie to please themselves, to make things rosy, to save their skins, to make the story more interesting, to protect a friend or sibling, to get a friend or sibling in trouble, and for the hell of it. I would say that children, like adults, speak always in complex contexts, among them the frantic atmosphere of child abuse talk, which hangs heavy over all of them. We do children no favor, in the long or short run, by insisting that their world and motivations are impossibly simple.

2. Children commonly deny that sexual abuse happened, such denial being the usual response to sexual abuse and therefore an indication that it has occurred. On the other hand, if a child does say it happened, it happened. We know, of course, that a child may say it didn't happen, then say it did, then say it didn't. This is called the "child sexual abuse accommodation syndrome."[33] In layman's terms, CSAA syndrome amounts to a way of understanding retractions not as retractions but as confirmations of the original accusation. In sum, accusations are always to be believed, denials never, except when the denial is, as it must be, really an accusation.

3. There is a cycle of abuse going on, almost all present abusers having been abused themselves as children and now abusing because of that. We know that is true because convicted abusers, when asked if they were abused as children, say they were; and when asked if that's why they abused, say, "Yes, it was." This is a sad business—not that it quite excuses the abusers, but it means that "child sexual abuse may be increasing of its own accord." "As the number of victims increase[s], so does the population of future abusers, and because many abusers have more than one victim, the sexual abuse of children threatens to become an upward spiral."[34]

Never mind that Dr. Joyce Brothers estimates that only one-third of victims grow up to abuse,[35] and that other scientists as reliable as Dr. Brothers suggest that there may be an inverse effect (abused children growing up to be repulsed by the idea). Our myth of protection feeds on this "upward spiral" in the population of pedophiles.

4. What's lacking now in our battle to protect is adequate publicity. Despite centers and their pamphlets; movies and television shows; congressional hearings; milk cartons, grocery bags, and billboards; computer bulletin boards; and MTV, the danger is not being spoken. There's work to be done, but hopeful signs here and there too. Take James Chin, who opened a restaurant in Hollywood called Duck Heaven. Mr. Chin considered Pig Heaven, liked the name himself, but figured some people would be offended by "pig," sensed that "Chicken Heaven doesn't sound so good," and settled on "Duck." The important point is that he's printing photos of missing youth on his takeout menus, changing them every three months: "It's a matter of sacrificing some space," he says, "but it's worth it."[36]

The Enemy—Who Is S/He?

We know that those we are protecting children from aren't wearing identification badges. Despite what we once thought, they don't all look like Caliban or Quasimodo; we now know they may look like Orrin Hatch or Sir Richard Attenborough, Tina Turner, or Aunt Bee. They are not skulking outcasts but mainliners, not frenzied but calm, not violent but gentle—young and old, male and female, rich and poor, abled and challenged, religious and rational, all colors and all cultures.

As pedophiles have multiplied (and hidden themselves), we have reconstituted and extended the range of their activity. Most pointedly to boy victims—"sexual molestation of boys is much more common than we once thought"[37]—and to female perpetrators, who "are a great deal more prevalent than is typically thought," abusing to an extent "far greater than anyone ever suspected."[38] The *Eureka!* quality of these pronouncements, the exhilaration attendant on making these important "discoveries," drowns out those, like David Finkelhor, who point out that we have no evidence to support such claims.[39] I have, without looking hard, uncovered a dozen similar breakthroughs, all supporting the idea that viewing child sexual exploitation not as a "gender issue" but as a "human issue" marks an advance,[40] because "once we are open to the fact that adults, both male and female, are sexually abusing large numbers of children every year, we will be better able to provide comfort and treatment to the victims and offenders."[41] Swelling these categories, targeting every human as potential pedophile and/or victim, gives zing to protecting.

By this means we also pry open more titillating stories. Here are examples—only two, but good ones. Women prison guards guilty of "visually raping [male prisoners'] nude bodies as they shower" were foiled by Citizens against Sexual Exploitation of Men in California Prisons and a state senator, who saw to it that "modesty screens" were erected.[42] And there's Kelly Brown, wife of Hemet High football coach Randy, pleading guilty to having sex with one of her husband's players, then seventeen, who agreed to it, said the prosecution, "to please the coach, not to let the coach down." The coach pleaded guilty to soliciting a second player, who, less willing to please the coach, let him down by refusing. Kelly Brown pleaded guilty to conspiracy and to "oral copulation on a minor," oral copulation being the tilted focus here, as it was at Valley High (see chapter 1), simply because that's what is against the law—or was then. Even the coach, never really suspected of having sex with anybody (on the team), was charged with oral copulation. But it's Kelly Brown who took center stage, the woman as molester. Her attorney tried to argue that the case was "about human frailty," but it was really about evil, the jury felt, the failure to protect children.[43]

It's not just gender expansion that is extending our range, but the electronic age as well. Internet erotica, still nearly uncensorable, can only be countered, *Time* says, by parachuting directly into such newsgroups as "alt.sex" and "alt.binaries.pictures.erotica" with messages like "YOU WILL ALL BURN IN HELL."[44] The demons are not always sent packing by such reminders, however; they infiltrate even national security systems to store and distribute their porn. The Lawrence Livermore National Laboratory computers, for example, were found to contain, along with the usual classified material, more than a thousand erotic images.[45]

Most net-regulation talk centers on kiddie porn, that and the use of cyberspace by pedophiles to find kids. The kiddie porn is seldom home-grown; it pours in from abroad, especially from Japan, our sometime economic rival and now the international king of perversion, according to the *New York Times*, what with its "disturbing national obsession with schoolgirls as sexual objects."[46] Lewd displays of children for passive voyeurism are bad enough, but we worry more about the internet as an agency for active criminal aggression: "Too often parents let kids while away hours in their rooms assuming that nothing more dangerous than Nintendo target shooting is on the screen," says *Newsweek*. In fact, "though no one actually knows how many pedophiles are on line," the numbers are, *Newsweek* lets us assume, not small.

What's worse, "in the battle against electronic pedophiles, the police are technologically outgunned." They don't know much about computers (pedophiles are smarter), and their equipment is "inadequate" (pedophiles are richer), so it's up to us to save figures like the little boy *Newsweek* runs in its cartoon illustrating the new danger.[47] The *Newsweek* boy is shown trying to type away at a computer which has arms extending outward from the screen, ready to snare the child and pull him in. The demons who emerged from the television set in *Poltergeist* to suck in children have oozed into cyberspace. And into prime-time plots: *New York Undercover* on January 11, 1996, gave us, according to my guide, the following: "Lt. Cooper's young daughter meets her internet correspondent, who turns out to be a pedophile. (Repeat.)"

The capture is almost an embrace.

Realizing the severity of the battle at home and abroad, we spread our protective net not just from coast to coast but across the oceans. We run features, with pictures, on child prostitutes in Nepal and street children in Brazil.[48] We are told that we are "Widening the War on Child Sex," as the headline puts it, the subheading telling us further that although south Asia's "vice trade" once flourished, "now, the U.S. and European 'consumer' countries are joining the battle to keep men from seeking young prostitutes overseas," in Thailand and the Philippines particularly.[49] It's a losing battle. Other countries in the world not only compete with us in vice; they have distressing customs. Lloyd Demause, an expert, tells us that although child molestation is practically universal in the West, "the incidence in countries outside the West is likely to be much higher . . . the use of children for the emotional needs of adults is far more accepted . . . widespread incestuous acts [exist] along with other child abuse."[50] He conducts a tour, beginning with a glance at Latin America and Europe, where things are not good, before hustling us off to the main show in the Middle and Far East: India "provides a veritable Galapagos" of incest, where "boys as well as girls are reported as being masturbated and raped by the men in the family"; the same is true for China, we can be sure, although "exactly what happens in Chinese family beds has not yet been much investigated," a word to the wise graduate student in search of a project; Japan claims that it hardly has a problem, a claim Demause finds laughable, a sure sign of "denial"; the rest of the

Far East, hurrying along, "follows the pattern of India and China"; while "the sexual use of children in the Middle East," moving even faster (we dawdled in India), "is probably as widespread as in the Far East."[51] There you have it, a planetwide cry for our protective stories.

When those in need of protection turn out to be headstrong, middle-class high-school kids seeking money and lots of it, we tend to blame it on permissiveness, liberal politicians, relativism, and the decline in corporal punishment. "Girls Who Offer Sex Upset Japan," the front page of the *Los Angeles Times* tells us on September 30, 1996, making it clear that we are upset right along with the beleaguered Japanese, who are wringing their hands over the more than 2,200 telephone clubs active across the country, employing, the Japanese PTA says, as many as 25 percent of high-school girls in the country, at least now and then, when the need for prom dresses or new contacts comes up.

Somewhat annoyingly, there has been a rebound, an unwelcome echo: other countries are claiming they need to protect themselves from us. Charges of stealing children to sell them, use them sexually, or harvest their organs have erupted in Guatemala and have led to beatings of American tourists (one for patting the head of a boy she had photographed) and widespread stories of what Americans are doing to children in Brazil, Argentina, Colombia, Honduras, and Mexico.[52] But perhaps this is the inevitable negative consequence of the successful push to publicize the danger posed by our mutual enemies.

But When It Does Happen?

When monster stories do turn up, which they do rarely but always spectacularly, our horror and sympathetic outrage quickly outrun all bounds, move almost at once from pain into the pleasure of feeding the story. The arrest in August 1996 of Marc Dutroux in a small village in Belgium sparked an international orgy of lascivious indignation. Dutroux led police to a cell where he had kept and molested for several months two girls (twelve and fourteen years old), then showed them the graves of two eight-year-olds he had kidnapped, kept for eight months of sexual abuse, and then allowed to starve. This is pain

The "missing" are clearly
identified with the "abducted."

out of Dante, but I do not want to concede that the size of this pain justifies our easy outrage. It does not. Our fuming is self-indulgent and gratuitous, feeding only our determination to ignore what we have done.

When presented with Marc Dutroux and his poor victims, we remove all restraints on our language: "A Country Awash in Horror," says my local paper; "OUTRAGE," screams the cover of *Time* in type that quivers. We then make Dutroux emblematic, the tip of the iceberg. Reuters immediately reports that "the abductions are believed to be related to an alleged child pornography ring." This believed-to-be alleged local ring is bloated into "Children for Sale," "the booming child-sex market." "For," Reuters points out, "if it can happen in a rural village in a country as benign as Belgium, surely it can happen anywhere. And it does." The German paper *Stern* runs a cover picture of a beautiful child stamped "Vermisst" and claims that "10,000 Kinder verschwinden jedes Jahr in Deutschland." "Wo Sind Unsere Kinder?" it asks. "Mit Der Pedophiles!" is, we know, the answer. Papers depending entirely on the wire services or without local news to report (yet) splice together whole pages out of events in Belgium, an arrest in Austria, and the idea that Southeast Asia is the world child sex

Myths of Protection, Acts of Exposure   87

center. When the magistrate in Belgium was pulled off the Dutroux case after attending a rally for the prosecution, my local paper said this was a case of the letter of the law winning out over the feelings of right-thinking people.

Time concludes its coverage by quoting Save the Children's Edda Ivan-Smith: "We've actually got to take a step back and protect our children, both as parents and as societies." Since we're already stationed at Protecting Headquarters, it's not clear to me where we would step to. Maybe we need to move forward and stop protecting ourselves.[53]

The Enemy: What Is It?

The "pedophile" is the place where a host of current revulsions are relieved; it is perhaps our most frequented cultural and linguistic toilet. The central figure in our drama of child molesting has been pried free from medical and psychological explanations and is now subject only to moral ones. That liberation has made possible our manufacture of this particular cultural demon: not only do we not have to ask what place this figure has in our culture; we don't even have to ask what makes it tick. It is our Iago, driven by "motiveless malignity."

Pedophiles have not really been, as we like to say, "othered," or marginalized; they have been removed from the species, rendered unknowable. At a party I was attending and enjoying recently, a local wit (albeit a physician) I had just met announced that two activities were absolutely baffling to him: military service and child molesting. People (not all, not I nor Mrs. K) laughed, clearly because the witticism collapsed the difference between the presumably comprehensible (wanting to go into the military) and the agreed-upon incomprehensible (wanting to have sex with children). I think we've come to agree that pedophiles are best regarded as inexplicable.

"Why Do They Do Those Terrible Things?" *Time* recently asked in a reassuring and bulky column telling us that we don't know and can't know why they do it. "For most adults," the article begins, "the very idea of considering children as sexual objects is an unfathomable deviancy." Not only do we not feel that attraction; the very idea of someone entertaining it is "unfathomable"; we cannot dig that deep.

The experts consulted by *Time* are no different from "most adults," saying things like, "There's much we don't know." What they do know amounts to variations on nothing, a few clichés that apply to everyone alive: "pedophiles are looking for affection"; "pedophilia . . . may have at its root some childhood sexual trauma." At the end, we learn what we knew all along: "It never goes away. It's not a matter of curing somebody."[54]

It's nothing to do with us. Not in our wildest dreams . . . why do they do those terrible things . . . the very idea!

The Enemy: What to Do with It

We have already done a good deal to lessen the distinction between accusations of child sexual abuse and convictions. Just as it is easy to believe a child unless he is recanting, it's not easy for the accused to be believed unless he or she is confessing. Further, as Lawrence Wright points out, a suspect who confesses is "usually given a 'safe to be at large' evaluation and let out of jail after a day or two," the confession suggesting that s/he is facing the truth and therefore might be helped; but an insistence on innocence, not being "cooperative," means the suspect is "in denial" and therefore must be "sent to a state institution for evaluation and . . . a likely prison sentence."[55] We seem to feel that those admitting guilt are at least being honest, and those maintaining innocence are either lying or delusional. Since being charged is so close to being guilty in the public mind, California voters in 1994 passed overwhelmingly a proposition (189) billed as the "Keep Sexual Predators off Our Streets" law, which allows judges to deny bail to anyone charged with felony sexual assault, whether or not that person has a prior record.

Once in jail, convicted or not, the fast-growing population of predators presents us with more problems, since, despite the scantiness of the evidence, we have come to believe treatment is hopeless. What treatment exists usually amounts to aversion therapy, often in conjunction with behavior modification monitored by a penile ring (a "plethysmograph") hooked to a computer. A technician observes responses, usually to erotic pictures, and then administers shocks, blows, or "olfactory therapy" (cat urine, rotten meat).[56] The *Wall Street*

Journal, apparently annoyed even at this paltry effort, tells it all in its headline: "Treating Sex Offenders Becomes an Industry, but Does It Work?" The answer is not hard to guess: despite the "thriving new industry," "there is little evidence that the therapy really works."[57] Actually, according to the *Charlotte (N.C.) Observer,* many therapy experts agree that "there's only one way to treat child rapists: Keep them locked up."[58]

There are, of course, other ways of approaching the problem, a popular one being cited by Ann Landers in response to a letter from a wife wondering whether to wait—"five years is a long time"—for her husband, "Dan," imprisoned for child molesting, when he "might never be cured." Ann assures the writer that her husband "does indeed have an illness. It is called pedophilia." She says she "checked with a sex therapist" about a cure and learned that Dan's condition could be treated by "a drug that will reduce his sexual urges drastically. . . . This drug, of course, will put an end to any sexual activity with you, also. It's a tough call."[59] By September 1996, California had instituted mandatory weekly injections of Depo-Provera into repeat child molesters, and first-time offenders too if the judge so ordered. The "chemical castration" measure passed overwhelmingly in the state legislature, although Democrats succeeded in getting the term "chemical castration" changed officially to "hormonal suppression treatment." The bill also allows offenders to choose surgical castration, such a choice attracting those most anxious to show they are not in denial. Despite opposition from the ACLU, there was wide acceptance of the argument offered by the bill's sponsor that the activity would free "thousands of California children" from "the psychological nightmare of forced molestation." "We have set the stage for America," he continued elsewhere, "and we hope you are listening."[60]

Such treatment edges close to the final solution, calling to mind what is always round the corner and shows itself from time to time—on Sally Jessy Raphael's show, for instance, here in a conversation with Ed from the ACLU and Gary, a registered sex offender:

> *3rd Audience Member:* I'd just like to say to Gary . . . you should be out here and show your face to these people, and also, I think they should cut it off, and you won't have the feeling anymore to do this again.

Sally: By the way, there are countries, Ed, you should know, where it is almost mandatory. Castration is almost mandatory for sex offenders, countries in this world. I'm not suggesting it. I'm merely—
Ed: There are countries that cut off the hands of burglars.
Sally: Exactly.

As the show winds down, considering finally the number of prisons it will take to house all these predators, fixed or not, the castration treatment comes to seem too liberal:

Sally: I don't know how you—I don't know how you build prisons for all those people.
Kathi: Well, the state of Washington executed two sex offenders this year.[61] [Curtain]

Punishment makes a better showing than treatment. In addition to the three-strikes bills now in effect in most states, some also have one-strike laws aimed at those convicted of rape or child molesting, like California's, which can mandate twenty-five years to life for a first offense. Governor Pete Wilson, in signing the law, said, "If I had my way, we would have LWOP—life without possibility of parole."[62] Beyond sentencing, we have various keeping-track and warning schemes for those who are released: library records, a special 900 hot line giving out names of forty thousand child molesters, registration requirements that now apply in (as of September 1995) forty-six states, and, in Washington, a program that is the mother of all scarlet letterings.

The Washington Community Protection Act, enacted in 1990, created a Center for Sexual Predators, which determines whether those deemed "dangerous" will, in fact, be set free after the sentence is served. Anyone sent there has to prove he (or she) is no longer a "sexual predator," a condition the Washington State Psychiatric Association does not even recognize but which the state assumes it can cure. The author of the bill admits that keeping people locked up indefinitely, regardless of their sentence, wouldn't be "fair—*if* we were punishing," but claims this isn't punishment at all but "treatment" offered to guarantee "public safety." Alan Dershowitz points out that being confined against one's will might feel a lot like punishment, that the committee deciding who is and is not a "sexual predator" is made up of amateurs, and that there is no evidence to suggest that anyone on the planet can predict which prior offenders will commit new crimes.[63] Aside from that . . .

California courts have ruled too that sex offenders who have served their time can be held in a mental institution if they are deemed "likely to commit another sex crime."[64] It is not necessary that they be *currently* dangerous, only prone to repeat. As current wisdom holds that child molesters are not only prone but certain to repeat, all sentences would seem to be life sentences, and we are jailing people for crimes we think they are *going to* commit. The governor's response to this is, "Vicious convicted sexual predators cannot be allowed to roam the streets."[65]

The Supreme Court has agreed, upholding what the *Los Angeles Times* calls "the new wave of state laws aimed at keeping so-called sexual predators behind bars indefinitely." Clarence Thomas, speaking for the majority, pointed out that "even though they may be involuntarily confined . . . persons confined under this act are [not] being punished." The ACLU, hardly appreciating the force of that logic, argued in a losing cause that mental hospitals were being used as prisons and that psychiatry was hardly a predictive science.[66]

Let's say one of these catch-as-catch-can review boards somehow allows a former sex offender to leave at the end of his regular sentence. Troubles are only starting to rain down: the freed ex-offender must not only register but is also subject to "public notification," which may range from door-to-door warnings of his neighbors to posters on telephone poles. According to one free-but-hounded man, Alan Groome, "It's safe in an institution. You don't got people handing flyers door to door on you saying, 'Hey, this guy's a sex offender.'" Groome was finally driven from the state by a law echoing the tribal edict on Oedipus, the exiling of the unclean. Such banishings do not make neighboring states happy, and they act to increase dramatically the isolation and fantasy-supported loneliness that may exacerbate the sexual desire causing the problems.[67] Still, like castration, such actions answer to basic impulses, recalling the days of blood sacrifice, branding, and exile.

The highly popular "Megan's Law" and its spin-offs have resulted in a nearly nationwide set of tracking and holding regulations. It will indeed be nationwide now that the courts have upheld President Clinton's view: "We respect people's rights," he says, "but there's no right greater than a parent's right to raise a child in safety and love"[68] — a remarkable sentence, that; one version of "right" (constitutional) slides right into another (sentimental). In California, the register of "sex offenders in the area" (i.e., those released from prison) is available to anyone visiting the police station. It provides photos, physical descriptions, and known locations whose accuracy is ensured by laws requiring timely reporting of any change of address. For those too busy to visit, there is a 900 hot line; for ten dollars you can learn whether "up to two individuals" are registered as child molesters. I don't know if they run specials.

Even better, one can click onto www.childmolester.com to find listings of offenders by state and county; there, one can also view the history of each, the court disposition, and, where allowed by law, the "most current photo." Another site, www.sexoffenders.net, allows the curious to locate listed Californians by city of residence and, in the case of those classified as "high risk offenders," by name. Those without personal computers can visit the local county fair (here at least) and check (I'm not making this up) at a "Protect You and Your Family" booth ("TAKE THE TIME . . . CHECK IT OUT!"). No charge. Worried that too few were logging on and fewer still were visiting police stations in search of this registry, our State Attorney General, Dan Lungren, figured he'd catch lots of people moving between the sheep barn and the Vegematic demonstration. I think he has. These registries are apparently spreading to Germany, where the model used to locate Nazi war criminals may be adapted for this purpose; and to playgrounds, where, at least in San Mateo, California, anyone working with children in any volunteer capacity is fingerprinted.[69]

All of this activity erodes boundaries between authorized and unauthorized justice systems, so that the responsibility both for awareness *and* for punishing comes to include the medical profession, social workers, you and me. The results are predictable. Here are two typical stories, appearing side-by-side in the *San Francisco Examiner* on August 8, 1977: "3 women charged with revenge kidnap, rape" and "Pair held for torture of teen rape suspect" (p. A–12). In the first, three women in Delaware, Ohio broke into the home of a convicted child molester, wrestled him to the floor, tied him up, shaved his head and pubic hair, raped him with a cucumber, wrote "I am a child molester" with black markers "on several parts of his body," and dumped him naked (with a blanket) seventy miles from home. In the second, a Thibodaux, Louisiana teenager suspected of molesting a boy was kidnapped by the boy's father and a friend, who drove him to a swamp and there "sexually brutalized, punched and whipped [him] with a tennis racket." Then stringing the teenager up with a rope so that only the tips of his toes touched the ground, the men beat him some more and threw rocks at him, abandoning their activity and their dangling victim when the headlights of a passing car scared them off. The wife of the torturer-in-chief said afterward, "My husband is not a violent person."

Maybe not. Our ferocity is, after all, a necessary part of the demonic story we are telling. If we construct a demon as the enemy, then we lock ourselves into a war story that asks of us two things: that we choose the cruelest weapons from our stock, and that we lose. We have no choice but to combat demons, and we can never get rid of them. That's the point. The pedophile is something more than a scapegoat for us; it does more than siphon off and bottle dark desires and fears the culture cannot otherwise contain. Our pedophile handles those chores, certainly, but not so well that these desires and fears are expelled. We need to torture pedophiles as if they were scapegoats, but we need always to make sure the torture isn't fatal— not to the breed, anyhow.

Wait a Minute

This pedophile we have manufactured to castrate, track, and hound may be a very useful device for us, but he is largely a bugbear. A different, less fanciful portrayal of this figure might make us hesitate, allow us to see that our glee is misplaced.

For instance, both the castrating and Megan Lawing of released sex offenders is commonly (and successfully) justified by the argument that predators cannot be cured and simply are what they are—child molesters—once and forever. It is their unchanging essence. My own governor, Pete Wilson, proclaimed in September 1996, while signing into law a sweeping chemical castration bill, that child molesters "have a drive to do what they do. As long as they have that drive, they'll keep doing it—unless we do something first." He backed up this plain-as-day logic by offering the fact that "three out of four will commit a new offense or parole violation within two years." "Simply false!" says Frank E. Zimring, professor of law and director of the Earl Warren Legal Institute at UC Berkeley. The actual rate is 26 percent, and that figure includes many small "technical violations such as failure to register." This 26 percent recidivism, by the way, is very low, "less than half the rate reported for burglars and robbers released in 1991 and lower than for any other of the major crime categories."[70] If we take all this to heart, we may regain some measure of proportion, even composure.

Myths of Protection

Every bit as hyperbolic as our construction of the enemy are the assurances we trade back and forth about how much child defending we are doing. To protect the innocence of children we hold congressional hearings, put their faces on milk cartons and menus, found multiple centers, and speak out. Marc Klaas, Polly's father, advises all parents to rear their children "as if there were a molester living in their neighborhood";[71] and we do. We do so much in the way of patrolling the frontiers of innocence that there can be no doubt about our dedication or about our ingenuity in finding new safeguards. Here are a few of the other things we do:

1. We censor: we rate movies and records, cleanse the airways, and put some things on late at night. The internet presents problems for censors, problems that are delightful for some and vexing for others. Attempts to legislate have been so far baldly unconstitutional, so we have turned to helpers like *Time*'s "A Parents' Guide to Sex on the Net,"[72] which probably serves the same ends as the clergyman's marking objectionable passages in a book so young readers would skip them. But President Clinton appears with V-chip in hand, playing Holden Caulfield, *Time* says, saving innocence just in the nick.[73] In addition, there is a variety of software available with names like "Cybersitter" and "Net Nanny," and the television world has buckled

under to pressure and moved to regulate itself (and boost ratings) by labeling.

2. We train older children at school about sex, one popular program, Sex Respect, teaching them to avoid it altogether, and another, the New Jersey model, using the classroom to show how noncoital sex (mutual masturbation, full body massage) can be just as good as intercourse. Sex Respect, developed under the Reagan administration, has a text and course materials, although its author, Kelly Mast, says it's not these things that reach the kids but "the Holy Spirit": it's not an educational matter but a "war against sin." Teaching, among other things, how AIDS is spread through French kissing, Sex Respect relies a lot on T-shirts (I'M WORTH WAITING FOR), buttons (STOP AT THE LIPS), a *Chastity Challenge* video, and chants: "Do the right thing and wait for the ring!" "Pet your dog, not your date!" "Don't be a louse, wait for your spouse!"[74] New Jersey teens, on the other hand, are advised to save only a smidgen for the spouse, what the program's founder calls "this narrow little thing called intercourse."[75] The programs may seem very different, but both assume that a combination of knowledge and coercion will control or at least modify sexual behavior—very dubious assumptions, it seems, since neither program has had any measurable effect on what teens are doing.

3. With younger children we use antimolestation education:

a. Good touch–bad touch, the difference being explained variously in terms of location, duration, or effect. Location is commonly defined in reference to "private parts" or those parts covered by a bathing suit. That's sometimes, depending on the suit, a lot of privacy. Duration means "too long," as in it's OK to be patted on the fanny gently, but "if someone pats you too long on the fanny, then that is bad touch,"[76] which probably leaves the confused right where they started. Effect means trusting your "funny feelings": "the little voice," "the alarm," "the Uh-Oh feeling," "goosebumps."[77]

b. How to make a scene, which assumes children need to be taught this skill, and that they're reluctant to employ it. Some programs instill a special "safety yell,"[78] and others tell children not only that "kicking is a good idea" but that "scraping down the shin and stomping on the stranger's foot are also good ideas."[79]

c. Learning to distinguish between good secrets, which should be honored, and bad secrets, which should be told at once. The difference is that the good secret makes you "feel good when you tell it," and the bad secret is "scary."[80] Such advice may guide the child about which secrets to accept, but seems counterproductive as to which ones to spill.

Other lessons are taught too, but these provide a fair sample. We also circulate tips on techniques, Dr. Brothers, for instance, mentioning "role-playing with children, asking them what they'd do in a variety of dangerous situations."[81] Rather rugged theater, it seems to me, but not as unsettling as some popular activity books such as *What Every Kid Should Know about Sexual Abuse*.[82] In addition to coloring in the molester, children learn from the book that "sometimes, touching makes people feel bad or upset. This kind of touching is called ABUSE" (p. 2), a definition loose enough to ensure that every reader is inside the fold. They hear further that "all kinds of people can be victims of sexual abuse—especially young people like you" (p. 3); that you can't tell who sexual abusers might be by looking at them; that they are probably not strangers but "PEOPLE THAT YOU KNOW—and even like or love" (pp. 8, 10); and that you should turn them in at once since that will be "helping" them (p. 14).

Perhaps we should not be surprised if a package of terror and mendacity acts as an education in anxiety, confusion, distrust, and exactly the wrong kind of empowerment: "My child told her brother that she would tell the police he touched her where he shouldn't if she couldn't see a particular TV program," one parent claimed.[83]

4. We patronize antikidnapping clinics, often in the form of self-defense classes for kids. There's one here in my town, which I inquired into (saying I wanted to enroll Whitney, my little granddaughter, a shameless lie). Al (not his real name) told me kids tend to let adults get too close to them and have to be taught "target denial," that is, how to escape people "within the sick society of child abductors." To this end, Al told me, "we have people dressed up and we grab the kids," who "learn how to escape and make the right kind of scene, as well as where on the body to strike." Al says his school "turns the amperage up." I asked him if this dressing up and grabbing might not frighten the children a little. "Good question, Jim," he said, in the tone of an auto mechanic speaking to someone pretending to know what

Anti-Kidnapping Clinic

- How to Get Away
- How to Attract Attention
- How to foil Abduction from the Start
- How to Escape Molestation or Child Abuse
- How to be Prepared for a Violent Attack, Physically and Mentally

Children ages 6 and up. Parents are encouraged to participate as a team with their child to support learning drills which can be practiced over and over at home.

LOS ANGELES COUNTY & CITY OF PASADENA
PARKS AND RECREATION

Self-Defense *and* Safety Awareness Education

Teaching Boys and Girls Since 1987

Only $4.00 Per Lesson
Pay Weekly

Promoting Self-Esteem and Self-Confidence!

All Children and Teens Should Learn to Defend Themselves!

"Safety Awareness" slides into terror.

a voltage regulator is, "good question. You see we don't do it from a fear factor; we do it from an awareness factor."[84]

5. We make April National Child Abuse Prevention Month, and Nickelodeon runs a show titled *Stranger Danger.* Other television specials and thousands of magazine articles such as "Missing Children: The Ultimate Nightmare" (*Parents,* April 1994) or "Child Abductions: What a Mom Must Know" (*McCalls,* March 1994) spread the word.

6. We encourage American business to turn its expertise in this direction, and it does: videos, alarms, books and games, safety kits, fingerprinting sets, photo registration services, and dolls: anatomically correct or incorrect; nippled or nippleless; with attached or interchangeable male and female sex organs; all races, creeds, and colors; with movable tongues; "senior-citizen models" available; cir-

cumcised or uncircumcised "exchangeable penises"; velcro fasteners; washable.[85]

One enterprising association, CHILD Team: The Family Protection Network, runs such alluring full-page ads that I again used Whitney as a front to explain my interest. "Concerned," the "team" says in their literature and on the phone, "about the widespread incidence of child abduction in this country" and determined to do something about this "terrifying problem," they charge $250 per year. For that, they register your child and stand ready, if your child is missing, to make "your very own Child Team investigator . . . go to work immediately" in a manner "reserved exclusively to our discretion." The police and media are alerted, a reward "may be offered," and "customary" (but not "extraordinary") expenses are covered, whatever that may mean. In any case, they promise to think about the missing child relentlessly: "IF YOUR CHILD WERE MISSING, YOU'D THINK ABOUT IT EVERY MINUTE —SAME WITH US," says their headline. "With the Child Team behind you," you have "the added sense of security knowing that you'd be doing everything you could to ensure your child's safety." This is artfully devised to say just the opposite: parents who don't come up with the $250 are offering their children to abductors on a platter.

7. We exercise vigilance. In a long *Child* article entitled "What Police Wish Every Parent Knew,"[86] "law enforcement experts share their most effective strategies to prevent kidnappings, abuse, and more." More? What police, at least those talking to *Child,* clearly wish is for parents to be Argus-eyed. The very fact that only 100 out of 50 million children in this country are kidnapped each year does not mean we can relax, says Ernie Allen, president of the National Center for Missing and Exploited Children. Strangers are not much of a danger, true, which simply means, he says, that warning kids about strangers (while essential) is not enough, is "grossly inadequate." We can never abandon our lookout towers and peepholes.

"Your best weapon in the fight to keep your children safe is your watchfulness, law-enforcement experts advise." This gives us something to do, defines us by assuring us that a watcher's work is never done. We should begin by educating: "Teach about Sex Abuse Before They Understand Sex." After they absorb all that—learn that "something," never mind what, can be abused—we can turn our attention to "Assessing [Our] Child's Vulnerability." We do that by making sure the child forms no ties with other adults, no good ties, at least—" 'If a situation seems too good to be true, it probably *is*,' says Lieutenant Bill Walsh"—and spying: "Don't be ashamed to eavesdrop on your child's half of a telephone conversation." By comparison, Claudius let Hamlet run free.

8. We tell stories about the unprotected, ranging from children stripped to children murdered. Sally Jessy airs "My Child Was Searched" (March 14, 1994), detailing (and that's the word for it) how fourteen-year-old Amanda was forced to take part in her school's drive to find out who stole forty-one dollars in Spanish class, and how twelve-year-old Bobby was humiliated on a field trip. Amanda says, "I had to pull up my bra so she [the nurse] could feel inside the cups" and then "pull down my underwear," which means, Sally Jessy tells us, her "panties." Bobby was made to pull down his underwear: "So I pulled down my boxer shorts and I lifted up my groins," which is just the start: "The teacher asked him to lift up your groins, bend over, pull apart your cheeks, jump up and down, to see if the money will fall out." "Fall out of his rectum," Bobby's mother adds. "Out of his rectum?" Sally says, perhaps thinking we had missed that point. Bobby's mother protests that four hundred dollars "wouldn't fit" in such a place. We then pass on to other instances, to experts, and to talk about the posttraumatic disorder now afflicting both children. The audience seems to agree that this is an issue that reflects, as one member says, "the condition of society," which is not the condition we want.

At the other end of the scale, at least at the start, are such things as the abduction of twelve-year-old Polly Klaas from a slumber party at her mother's house in Petaluma, California, on October 1, 1993. She and her friends were playing a board game at the time. An agonizing search for the child went on for two months until Richard Allen Davis, who was arrested for parole violation on November 30, confessed to the abduction and murder of the girl and led police to the body. This horror generated the usual tasteless drooling; *People,* for instance, ran a long (for it) story that emphasized the irony of it all,[87] and others followed suit. But something even worse happened: since Polly's confessed killer was on parole at the time, he, and really she, became an argument for three-strikes hysteria. My own congressman, David Drier, lost little time in issuing a letter, dated December 31, 1993: "The shocking death of Polly Klaas reinforces the need for a *tough* anti-crime bill. That includes an effective and believable death penalty, increased penalties for gang violence, an end to parole for serious offenses, prison construction instead of early release and mandatory minimum sentences. Illegal immigration is also a crime." This howl was perhaps in harmony with the general mood.

Any discussion of protecting children would be incomplete without a glance at the considerable energy we direct toward serving ourselves. In fact, it could be argued that within the last decade or two, since we've spotted the child within, we've decided to begin our charity at home, to first look after the adult, who is really, deep down, the injured child. We've concocted lists of symptoms that prove we too are children, mistreated and alluring. These symptoms, drawn from here and there, include compulsive sexual activity or disinclination to sex (I suffer from both), overachievement and underachievement, eating disorders, substance abuse, negative body image, anxiety attacks, anger, guilt, insomnia, confusing sex with intimacy, compliant behavior or bullying behavior, minimizing, exaggerating, rationalizing, denying, self-mutilating, splitting, being a control freak, carelessness, spacing out, being superalert, lying, gambling, becoming religious, forgetfulness. If you don't check off at least three of these symptoms, I'd say you're a bore.

One reflex of our obsessive focus on protection is to saturate children with a sexual discourse that inevitably links children, sexuality, and erotic appeal. Worse, such notice as we take of our sexualized kids carefully separates us from the problem. A particularly hypocritical ABC *Primetime Live* episode (May 10, 1995) featuring an "innocence lost" examination of "Kids and Sex," blamed our problems with kids, sex, and who knows what all on the media—though not on *Primetime Live*. Asking "Is Your Kid a Sexual Time Bomb?" the program hid some cameras and caught kids four to ten years old talking about being sexy, "big boobs," and having babies. The adults interviewed, four schoolteachers, assured us that this sort of talk was never heard before about 1985 and that we had better do something about it fast, perhaps get Diane Sawyer to express dismay on *Primetime Live*. Such bunkum may work to distract us from our own responsibility in the production of the erotic child. Our excited insistence on the sexiness of children permits us to believe the figures we generate on the incidence of child molesting, figures indicating that most of the population is pedophilic and that the condition is incurable. Would that make any sense if we were not involved in this industry?

Exposing the Children

Our fundamental dilemma is that those protecting the child and those exposing it play for the same team. Eroticizing exists in symbiotic relation with sanitizing, and the veiling and the exposing exist in an encircling doublespeak. Since most of the rest of this book is devoted to an examination of the techniques we have evolved for eroticizing the child in such a way as to screen from ourselves what we are doing, I'll deal with only a few obvious points here, places where the child is put on display most blatantly. As Richard Mohr points out in a superb and acidic essay, "The Pedophilia of Everyday Life," our culture is saturated with "pedophilic images," which are "surprisingly common" given that we "careen from hysteria to hysteria over the possible sexiness of children." Mohr points to advertising and movies; *Newsweek* notices how supersexy Saturday morning bubblegum television is.[88] Childhood allure is everywhere on display.

Parenthood provides the best excuse for direct exhibiting, compelling us to attend thousands of public spectacles per child: sports, dramatic galas, music, dancing, parades, awards ceremonies. All children must pretend to have gained some kind of competence; and we must go along. Both sides pretty much know this is a whopper, but it's mandatory for kids to present themselves to public view as a rite, however humiliating, of growing up. My son was in a sixth-grade play (three acts, not a comedy); my youngest daughter played in a junior-high orchestra with a full string section (two-hour concert, no intermission); my older daughter's first-grade choir did "Songs of America" for ninety minutes straight (with gestures—*down* in the vallllllll-leeeeee, valley so *low-hoh*). I was worse. I played football, loathed it, on each play doing everything I could not to suffer, which meant running away (quasi discreetly) from the hurting. My mother and father observed every excruciating down, as mortified as I. None of us had a choice in the matter.

Those who do have a choice can find children who devote nearly all their short lives to making themselves worthy to be scrutinized: pre-teen tennis players and gymnasts, for instance; models, movie stars, and, at fairs and swap meets throughout the land, beauty contests: "Little Miss Maid of Cotton," "Sweet Niblet," "Missy Mississippi," "Little Queen of Honey." They all exist, I am told (all but one, which I made up), samples of the titles pinned on thousands of children each year. There are now more than 250 national beauty pageants, with more coming, the fastest growing being for the eight-and-under gorgeous. That's national: there are (my guess) 730,000 local contests just for babies and primary-schoolers. At least half a million contestants are under twelve, officials estimate, and it's a $5 billion a year industry, say other officials.[89]

Life ran a special (April 1994) on the "Queen of Queens" beauty pageant, which reaches down to infants, though *Life*'s emphasis was on eleven-year-old Blaire Ashley Pancake, daughter (I'm not making this up) of Dr. Bruce and Debbie Pancake. Blaire is good at what she does, having won ninety beauty contests, including "Little Miss Hollywood Babes." Her pictures make her look—am I sounding like Humbert Humbert?—glamorous. Not "pretty," exactly, but more like Zsa Zsa Gabor or Sharon Stone, both of whom, come to think of it, look much like eleven-year-old Blaire Pancake, which is probably the point. Blaire sounds like an expert on makeup and admits to wearing fake nails and a fake tooth (covering a missing baby tooth), though she and her parents wax indignant when asked about the mutterings (dark sour grapes) among rival parents about plastic surgery (Dr. Bruce's profession) and hair extension. Anyhow, it's not, with Blaire, a matter of parts but of the whole: "Blaire loves the stage," says her pageant coordinator, Tony. "She becomes . . . Blaire! A total package!" Blaire practices for interviews ("What's your secret weapon?" "When people have problems I try to help them."), but her consultants usually avoid contests with interviews, since they know (and Blaire agrees) that this star's package does not include interesting talk: "She's got a blah personality," her mother says, "like me." But who cares? She looks

Blaire, piling years on herself cosmetically, looks alarmingly like actresses in their thirties, who slice years away by the same means.

like a million, *Life* obligingly not only giving us pictures but describing her appearance when she "unself-consciously strips down to her panties."[90]

Just as obliging are fashion designers, who not only feature childlike clothes but kids in them: "More children are modeling than ever before. Does your little one have what it takes?"[91] These designers dress little girls as adults, undress teens (Brooke Shields's "There is nothing between me and my jeans"), and disguise adult women as little girls: the waif look and the pixie cut and Kate Moss and baby-doll looks and little-girl braids and Shirley Temple dos had a long run (several weeks at least), leading to a longer run for the schoolgirl look, "unmitigated eroticism à la Lolita," says *Time*.[92] Though some designers protest that all this is a way to "make fun of women by dressing them as children," the "naughty schoolgirl" look, "somewhat more innocent than that found in a child-porn magazine, but suggestive of it," is "nowadays what women seem to want." Unlike Freud, *Time* knows what women want. Of course, by the time you read this, the schoolgirl look will be an old joke, but it will have been replaced by something like it, since that is how our culture doles out women's allowance for desire.

This double-dealing that dresses the erotic woman as a child can approach the shameless, stimulating even a rage for what *Newsweek* termed "the color of Barbie," not just pink but cute pink, itsy-bitsy pink, "cotton-candy pink, bubble-gum pink."[93] The pink that sank out of sight in the seventies as feminists persuasively connected it with ornamental, submissive, and childish seductiveness, came back. Anne Hollander, identified by *Newsweek* as " 'Sex and Suits' author," says women now have the power to look like children: "We don't have to be scared to look like little girls that don't have any power, because we *do* have power." What does it mean for these powerful and assured women to overcome their fear of appearing as "little girls"? Are these girls well served by being so clearly identified with the enticing? Are these cute adult Barbies pinking up the scene even a little concerned about borrowing the sex appeal of nine-year-olds? "We *do* have power," but who is supplying the hot pink sex power, grammar-school kids?

Newsweek suggests that this obsession with cute is so extreme that it amounts to cultural arrested development: Elizabeth Taylor in her early twenties was asked to look thirtyish; Sandra Bullock at age thirty-one is asked to look pigtaily sweet, maybe thirteen.[94] Kids, arguably, ghost the national obsession with underpants, a possibility heightened by Calvin Klein's bold use of young and even younger-looking models in peek-a-boo, I-see-your-undies ads. Sultry kids simulating age fourteen were used, and Klein was accused of kiddie porn. He dropped the ads but got what he wanted; so did we. Klein, after all, only slightly extended the astonishing power of the Kate Moss look: *Newsweek* reports a London clinic saying that one of its "sickest patients," an anorexic girl of fifteen, five feet seven inches tall and weighing ninety-eight pounds, "was courted by two modeling reps."[95]

And there's photography, of course, professional and amateur. Though some states have instituted laws restricting home snaps of naked children,[96] we keep reaching for the camera when our children are both naked and cute, defining a moment we want to preserve, and sometimes show to others—and in the case of Sally Mann, publish

Try looking at the Calvin Klein ads without focusing on the underpants.

and exhibit. Mann's famous photographs of her three young children have aroused considerable controversy, partly because "the extraordinary care taken in rendering the flesh, including the attention paid to incipient sexual characteristics, is not accidental. By the cropping and 'burning in' of detail, Mann presents obsessive—not casual or clinical—examination of her young children's nakedness."[97] One art critic has praised her photos "because they beautifully demonstrate that being pure and innocent has nothing to do with being sexless,"[98] a point that seems to me self-evident but seems to Sally Mann ridiculous and abhorrent: "I think [she says] childhood sexuality is an oxymoron," a statement one may regard as a common-place, a wise view, a rationalization, or a haggard disavowal that clouds the issue.[99] However you regard Mann's work, it raises to consciousness for a flicker our need to peek at what we are hiding: the unsexed and sexualized bodies of children.

It's another matter with children who aren't cute to begin with: poor children and most children of color, fat and skinny and diseased children, and children who are simply plain. It's the same with children who have stopped being children, who misplace childhood along about (exactly at) puberty, at which point we drop the camera, start screaming at them, search their rooms for drugs, and long for the day they'll leave home. When the construction of adolescence is forced on them, they become officially eroticized on their own account and thus lose all erotic interest for the rest of us.

Those who enrapture and then weary us, changing overnight from fascinators to pests, illustrate this most dramatically. Many will not be deeply moved by the plight of ex–child stars; but these kids who devote their entire childhoods (every day, every day) to displaying themselves to us do have sad tales to tell. Paul Petersen, an original Mousketeer and later "Jeff" on *The Donna Reed Show,* is an eloquent writer and spokesperson for the hundreds of children used and discarded in this business, and he has begun an active and far-reaching support and lobbying group, A Minor Consideration. Though some of these exploited people blame greed—Jay North told me he thought it wouldn't hurt if they took all agents, producers, and stage parents, put them in a bag with rocks, and dropped them in the Mindanao Deep—Petersen understands the issue as a cultural problem, involving money, certainly, but stronger needs too. He told me that children in such positions become quickly aware of the intense sexual interest (general and quite specific) directed their way and find some way to respond to it. And to its disappearance a few years later—along with the calls, the money, and the attention.[100]

But what about the yearly half million or so throwaways, runaways, neglected and beaten and starved children? What about those denied health care, education, a house, attention of any kind? Those shunned or killed? A few years ago there was, I'll admit, considerable publicity about a parent who drove her little boys into a lake in a locked car, and another who threw her baby into a yard for pit bulls to eat; but unspectacular child killings have little chance of competing with allegations of satanic abuse or the latest day-care scandal.

Two thousand children are killed every year, and more than 140,000 are seriously injured;[101] even more are cast away: children without any home at all represent the fastest-growing distressed population in this country.[102] One-fourth of U.S. children live "below the poverty line," with an estimated 10,000 dying every year "as a direct result of poverty."[103] Nine out of every 1,000 American babies never reach their first birthday, a world ranking of twentieth, which is better than the thirty-first we get in low birthweight babies (finishing behind Turkey and Iran). Sixty percent of our two-year-olds are not immunized; 8.3 million U.S. children have no insurance coverage at all; 22,000 infants are abandoned yearly in hospitals; the rate of adolescent suicide has tripled since 1960; teenagers are five times more likely to be crime victims than adults over thirty-five; and among the new syndromes is shaken baby syndrome, "the most common cause of death in children under a year."[104] As a recent Carnegie Corporation study says, what we have is a "quiet crisis."[105]

Can we ever be forgiven for all that quiet, or, on the other hand, for all the drowning-out noises we make about dilemmas that titillate us and deflect attention from the terror, a terror all the consuming talk about child molesting allows us to visit on the bodies and minds of our children?

Children suffer and die, and we tell ourselves we're protecting them with milk cartons, say-no comic books, undying vigilance against child lovers, and no-touch day care. This last innovation gives us, we might say, our protection story in its purest form and in action— nobody touches, no one sits on a lap, no comforts, no hugs. As one expert said on NPR, "I think a lot of schools are making the decision to protect themselves, you know, and I think that it's really too bad." On the same program another expert said that untouched children have defective immune systems and "much more illness": "We know children need touch to grow."[106] That being so, I think that the first expert was justified in saying that no touching is "really too bad." I think it should make us wonder who we care about and want to protect. We are anxious to have desirable children, but we seem reluctant to tend to them. Sometimes we seem not even to love them or to take note of their suffering.

Not all children are truly adorable children, dream children. None are. And we might be asking whether our cuddling of fantasy cute kids, kids with sticky kisses and fistfuls of dandelions, is what other kids need, the kids who flock around us in the flesh. Ina J. Hughes's poem defines them as the kids "who never get dessert, who have no safe blankets to drag behind them, who watch their parents watch them die, who can't find any bread to eat, who don't have any rooms to clean up, whose pictures aren't on anybody's dresser."[107] It's not just a class issue, though it is that, or an issue of racial and cultural bigotry, and it is that too; it's also an issue of a destructive psychic drama we have inherited and cannot find a way to escape. I am sure we all want to, would like to give up the virtuous glibness about protection that is ripping our children to shreds.

4. Home Alone with the Adorable Child

Blessings on thee, little man,
Barefoot boy, with cheek of tan!
With thy turned-up pantaloons,
And thy merry whistled tunes;
With thy red lip, redder still,
Kissed by strawberries on the hill!
—John Greenleaf Whittier,
"The Barefoot Boy"

I said to her, "And bring the poor little
child. God bless the poor little child,"
I said to your sister, "there's room
for *him* at the forge!"—Joe in *Great
Expectations*

I can see the judges' eyes
As they handed you the prize:
I bet you made the cutest bow!
Oh you musta been a beautiful baby,
'Cause Baby look at you now!
—Song: "You Must Have Been a
Beautiful Baby"

I didn't need a shove,
Cause I just fell in love
With your pretty baby face!
—Song: "Baby Face"

My cousin's children are adorable, a point established at the last family reunion. My own children were adorable too until they got to be fourteen, at which stage not even Shirley Temple was adorable. I was especially adorable myself as a child. No one has ever said so—not even my mother—and photos of me from that period are alarming; but photos are a dead thing and I know what I know. What I know is that just about all American children are, in our mythology, adorable.

Our culture demands that the official child be that way; it is mashed into our heritage, literary and otherwise. Even tough kids. Here's Huck Finn being adorable:

> Pray for me! I reckoned if she [Mary Jane Wilks] knowed me she'd take a job that was more nearer her size. But I bet she done it, just the same. . . . She had the grit to pray for Judas if she took the notion—there warn't no backdown to her, I judge. You may say what you want to, but in my opinion she had more sand in her than any girl I ever see; in my opinion she was just full of sand.[1]

And Holden Caulfield:

> Anyway, I keep picturing all these little kids playing some game in this big field of rye and all. Thousands of little kids, and nobody's around—nobody big, I mean—except me. And I'm standing on the edge of some crazy cliff.[2]

Here's Shirley Temple in *Poor Little Rich Girl,* singing to Daddy:

I love to hug and kiss you—
Marry me and let me be your wife!
In every dream I caress you . . .

Here's Macaulay Culkin in *Home Alone,* wearing only a towel:

I took a shower washing every body part with actual soap, including every major crevice.

We are required to find these things adorable. Sometimes, and I'm
thinking not just of my cousin's children here, this mandated rapture
can be a heavy burden. We may sometimes snarl, that snarl being the
subject of the next chapter. This one deals with this culture's swoon
before the adorable child.

This adorable child is both the center of and the best excuse for our
wish-fulfillment fantasies about our own being, our memories, our
longings, our losses, and our arousals. According to this tradition, the
child is not simply radiant but disarmingly cunning, unexpected—in
a word, cute. No matter how drearily predictable and pig-iron limited
in scope and ability actual children may be, we find their ideal form
majestic. Certainly Christian iconography of cute babies is vital here
and has a lot to answer for; but the religious tradition was given a
secular and sexual twist in the eighteenth century by the tendency of
sentimental philosophy to value the helpless, that capable of arousing
our tears. Children, both holy and pathetic, became a domesticated
icon. Even Christian art by the nineteenth century tended to conflate
the diminutive with the sacred, Millais's famous *Christ in the House
of His Parents,* for instance, making Our Lord look very much like
Bobby Brady.

In Victorian culture, as I've said, this erotic idealizing of children
was caught by writers such as Lewis Carroll and J. M. Barrie, who
drove into our cultural foundations the images of two children frozen
forever before they could betray us by growing up. "All children, except one, grow up," wrote Barrie in the process of showing us how to
find that one; and Carroll devised "magic words" he hoped would mes-
merize his dream child and "hold [her] fast."[3] Alice and Peter Pan are
what Holden Caulfield hopes to catch before they fall from that field of

rye, and what we all want to hold onto—in memory or on film. Adoration always seems to be a plunge into a psychic deep freeze, which is why kids are especially adorable when they are still: the sleeping child or, for the Victorians, the child in the coffin, stilled forever.

Perhaps the erotics of adoration work best when we can calm our fears about children leaving us, about losing our child within. We need somehow to collar and hold the child, the memory, to keep it where it is, available anytime for viewing and reviewing. Comic strips, advertising, and television have always been full of children, all useful to us but none so useful as the movie children we skillfully manufacture and consume.

We are always noticing with surprise and affected annoyance that the market is overrun by kid movies that are not for kids: child actors playing to adult audiences. Maybe it has not been ever thus, but kids have been sashaying before us for at least sixty years without much pretense that their peers would be interested. *The Little Colonel* did not appeal to five-year-olds, any more than *Shane* or *A Perfect World* played to second-graders.

Graham Greene found himself the subject of a lawsuit for speculating on the motives of "middle-aged men and clergymen" who flocked to see *Wee Willie Winkie* and its star, Shirley Temple, an eight-year-old with, he said, "an oddly precocious body," strangely "voluptuous," slyly practicing on eager audiences an adult "coquetry" in movies Greene regarded as "interestingly decadent."[4] Greene was very blunt, calling her "a fancy little piece," "a complete totsy" remarkably able to twitch her "well-developed little rump" and practice a "sidelong, searching coquetry" "with the mature suggestiveness of a Dietrich." Her "dimpled depravity," he continued (clearly enjoying himself), elicits excited "gasps" "from her antique audience," an audience able to pant after the "well shaped and desirable little body" because the same movie that elicits this erotic longing also provides the means for denying it: "the safety curtain of story and dialogue drops between their intelligence and their desire."[5] This is talk as brilliant as it is dangerous to let loose, though a later Shirley Temple, Deanna Durbin, "declared that her true fans were not children but adults who wanted to fantasize about their vanished childhood."[6] All Greene did was to specify the fantasy, and for that he was chased to Mexico; though that didn't stop him from commenting on Ms. Durbin too: "Innocence is a tricky subject: its appeal is not always quite so clean as a whistle."[7]

Current films work obsessively with a single plot: a child, most often a boy, possessed either of no father or a bad one,[8] is isolated, sexualized, and imperiled, whereupon he or she runs into an adult, often a male, who is down on his or her luck, outcast, misunderstood, sensitive, on the lam, romantically irresistible—usually all of these, and always the last. The child falls in love, initiates the love, and it blossoms, fed eagerly by the child and resisted by the reluctant adult, who is, however, finally overcome as the love takes over, bigger than both of them. The plot creates a special space, harbors the pair for a few moments from an unfeeling world that soon, however, crashes in and kills or exiles the adult. Sometimes this plot is submerged or only hinted at, but it is so strong and so often repeated, so central to our erotic mythology, that we can complete the story ourselves from a few scraps. We have it by heart.

Not incidentally, this is the plot basic to most "Uranian" and child-loving, even pedo-pornographic, storytelling. It is the fantasy that animates Humbert Humbert as well as Holden Caulfield, the narrative that gives power to *Silas Marner, Oliver Twist, Little Girl Lust, My Frolics with Timmy, Shane,* and *The Client.* (The middle titles are invented; do not alert the authorities.) It is the plot that draws millions to movie theaters and helped to sink Oscar Wilde, when prosecutors noticed that some of his work had been published in a magazine next to a story (not by Wilde) called "The Priest and the Acolyte." That moony story tells of love between a boy and a priest that lifts them to ecstasy and to a mutual soft suicide when they are discovered. Her Majesty's prosecutors were incensed. We do not react mildly when our devious stories are set before us so bluntly, whether by Wilde or by Graham Greene, and still we keep paying to see Shirley Temple variants enact that story. Mainline television and movies give us androgynous Shirleys by the dozens, making possible an eroticism both covert and open. Matthew Stadler, reporting (hilariously) on a weekend of North American Man-Boy Love Association meetings, found that their secret eroticism was simply network television, the Disney channel, and mainline films: "I had found NAMBLA's 'porn,' and it was Hollywood."[9]

LUPICA'S '93 PREDICTIONS

The American Man, Age 10

Welcome to the world of preadolescent blade runners, where every little boy is warrior a lover, and a philosopher. A sneak preview of the twenty-first-century man. BY SUSAN ORLEAN

The conjunction of this image with *Esquire*'s motto—"The Magazine for Men"—is probably accidental.

Take one modern "totsy," Macaulay Culkin, who in his "prime" had cheeks like roses and lips like Monroe's, with better gloss. So many people went to look at him in 1990 that the viewing site, *Home Alone,* bagged more than $500 million. The same movie reappeared in 1992 as *Home Alone 2* and drained us of $375 million more. Even if one separates these twins, the older brother still ranks in the top five grossers of all time.[10]

Why? Because of Culkin and the way he is displayed, I think. This is the boy who, a few years ago, graced the cover of *Esquire* as "The American Male, Age 10," and that same year did bathtub jokes on *Saturday Night Live,* drawing naked butts and pretending to display his own. *Home Alone* prepared the way for a nationally admired centerfold. Though we do not receive the full pedophile plot in that film, we are titillated by an oblique sneak-up on the erotic narrative. Here, as in the standard plot, parents are rendered superfluous: self-absorbed and out of the way. The child is alone, in need not of protection but of love. As the fantasy develops and the child is actually attacked, we are allowed to relax in the face of his omnipotence. No intruders, burglars, molesters, or killers can touch him; he can rig bricks to brain them or wire doorknobs to electrocute them. The boy negates nervous parental (or audience) fears, assuring us, in this odd empowerment, that in a physical sense, he is quite OK alone. Don't call the cops; provide affection.

The bumbling intruders, both insanely aggressive and harmless in their obsession with the child, act as covers for us, perfect Three Stooges masks: we will never be forced to recognize ourselves in these clowns. They guarantee that this is a world without consequences, a cartoon world where there is no future: no one is hurt and pretty kids do not grow up. They are always home alone, waiting. Kevin (Culkin) begins the movie by announcing that it's not a *new* family he's after— "I don't want any family; families suck!"—and later entertains the idea that he has made his family disappear by the magic of his repugnance to them. Once isolated, he can exhibit himself to us, discreetly but fully, screened by a rich self-sufficiency and a periodic mock bow to family values—"I just want my family back"—that we welcome because it is so insincere and so nicely formulated to allow us to ignore what we are doing in this theater. We are so used to the alliance of sex and violence that here the overload of violence smuggles the sex along: Culkin's dialogue is sprinkled with pederastic winks: "horse's ass," "pain in the butt."

The sequel, which is somewhat coarser in its appeal and may have lost a few hundred million dollars thereby, runs on a joke about seeing people naked in a shower (guess who?), uses more pointed toilet humor, yucks it up about Culkin's underwear—"You can't be too careful when it involves underwear"—likes to talk about "naked rear ends," shoves the boy into a pool wearing a swimming suit many sizes too large, and you know the rest. It's really just a standard butt movie, I suppose, but that's all it takes.

What is missing from the standard plot is the misfit, the child's lover. No one is there to move in and adore the alone boy. The plot function is merely shadowed by the bogeyman neighbor in 1 and the pigeon lady in 2, both of whom educate and are educated by Culkin in standard Greek-love fashion. Each figure is, however, carefully kept dim and marginal, and neither is allowed to get close to Kevin.

That's the space kept vacant for us, and we have spent about a billion dollars jumping into it.

Culkin's career followed the predictable path of the adorable approaching fourteen.[11] Hollywood being what it is, no-longer-adorable children are inevitably induced to give it one more go with the pedophile plot, and it's like watching your great-grandmother frolic in a brief smock and ruffled panties. *Pagemaster,* which attempts to deal with the fact that we no longer want to see Culkin by no longer showing him to us, was a flop; and *Richie Rich* was a Whatever-Happened-to-Baby-Jane grotesquerie: the *Los Angeles Times* reviewer, reaching back into memory, called Culkin "irresistible" in the film,[12] but most of America reacted to this attempt to pass off an adolescent as a child as they would to the peddling of Rep. Sonny Bono as a bona fide cutie. The movie tries its best, providing the usual quota of butt jokes and flashing a cover of *People* proclaiming Culkin "Sexiest Man Alive," but it's wishful thinking. "Always watch your rear!" Culkin shouts in the film, perhaps realizing he can no longer count on others to watch it for him. Culkin's earlier-in-1994 *Getting Even with Dad* shows him cuddling up to a criminal, blackmailing the guy (Ted Danson) into loving him. It's the straight plot, but the film knows it doesn't have a child to put on display and feeds us our cherished tale in such a perfunctory way that we didn't bite, even with the bluntest cue jokes: "Lady, can I borrow your kid?" "Daddy, he's watching me pee." "Next time you see his face it'll be on a milk carton." Danson, perhaps desperately, said in an interview that the film was "a love story . . . the opposite of cute and glib."[13] Glib we don't mind, cute goes without saying; but love after thirteen doesn't work in this culture.[14]

Pure Adoration

The isolated-kid-finds-love plot counts for nothing if there is not at the center an adorable child, since the whole point is to make that child ripely available for our viewing. At its best and in its heart, the adorable child for us is always Shirley T,[15] a child so good at being adorable that she both defines it and looks like a caricature, in the same way Hemingway, Cheez Whiz, and Indianapolis are caricatures: they are perfectly what they are and, distressingly, nothing

Here Shirley
abandons, for once,
provocative-cute
for flopped-out
exhaustion.

else. Shirley Temple, America's sweetheart and top box-office draw,
also crystallized this form of American eroticism and shaped all sub-
sequent embodiments of it, from Margaret O'Brien to Brooke Shields
to Ricky Schroder and Culkin. American cute, one of our most successful exports, rolled off the thirties movie assembly line in a vast
succession of Temple films, of which I have seen five—and taken
notes on them too (what a scholar!).

The adorably cute here was a complex package of mugging and
giggles, pouting and bouncy recovery, sweet sayings and funny
phrases, dancing and reciting (both remarkably well), and an ability
to smile without letting the muscles around the eye contract as they
naturally do. She must have practiced that wide-eyed smile in the
crib, since she had it right from her debut in 1932 at the age of four.
Shirley Temple also had two even more vital skills: the ability to con-

ON THE GOOD SHIP LOLLIPOP

SIDNEY CLARE AND
RICHARD A WHITING

AS SUNG BY
SHIRLEY TEMPLE
IN THE FOX PICTURE
BRIGHT EYES
MOVIETONE

Here is a face so blank that the eyes, nostrils, and mouth threaten to disappear into the puffy flesh.

duct flirtations and the uncanny knack of imitating adults so well she seemed to be us (and us, her). Beyond this, she was blessed by nature not with beauty but with a total emptiness, a fat, round face with nothing in it and a body to match—like Ms. Potato Head. Into that vacancy audiences could project what they wanted, and what they wanted included voyeuristic pleasure. They wanted just as badly to avoid acknowledging that fact, as Graham Greene discovered. And Shirley Temple's comic strip-like being demanded so little for itself that it was easy to read into it the negations we wanted, innocence and purity. Had this Miss Piggy been beautiful, she would never have done so well, beauty always asking for distance and posing some threat. Shirley Temple was close, unthreatening, and void.

I don't mean to suggest that the actress was without talent or that all her fame just somehow happened. On the contrary, I was struck in watching the films (five, as I say) with how doggedly she worked at being cute. In *Poor Little Rich Girl* (1936), for instance, a clumsy adult lifting her hikes the child's skirt halfway up her back as he holds her, causing a shadow of oh-for-God's-sake annoyance to cross her face. But she frees one arm, tugs down her skirt, and goes right on with the demanding job of being darling. What a trouper. She must have been nearly worn out rearranging her skirts, what with all the strenuous piggy-back and ride-a-horsey going on in every single film I saw.

These movies also find the perfect plot for exhibiting her adorableness and making it into a comestible. Some of the films (*The Little Colonel* [1935] and *Wee Willie Winkie* [1937]) are satisfied with showing how everybody, and especially grandfathers (Lionel Barrymore and Victor McLaglen, respectively), can't get enough of her. Others employ the pedophile plot more openly. In *Curly Top* (1935), a handsome adult ("Edward") rescues seven-year-old Shirley from an orphanage, sets her down (after lots of manhandling) in opulence, lets her dance the hula, calls her a "designing woman," and gets in return a declaration: she longs to marry "Uncle Edward." The same orphanage-to-bliss plot is used in *The Little Princess* (1939) and elaborated in *Poor Little Rich Girl* to show how it's not really riches that count but Daddy.[16] In both, the motherless child plays out the erotic fantasy of separation and reunion (the father is initially presumed dead in one; in the other he's absorbed in his career), a reunion that consummates the myth of the adorable: it exists only for us and is entirely at our disposal. Daddy holds the little rich girl on his lap and croons (so nasally he must be sincere) about "that certain magic" she possesses: "Please let me make this confession, / You are my magnificent obsession," to which Shirley sings back (with a great increase in volume), "I love to hug and kiss you. / Marry me and let me be your wife."

Since then, a few hundred descendants have come from this line, many of them remarkably successful, even honored: Temple received an Oscar at five, Tatum O'Neal at ten, Anna Paquin at eleven, and Patty Duke at an aging sixteen; Brandon de Wilde was nominated at eleven and Jodie Foster at thirteen. Some films have been content to stand in wonder before this adorable child, offering one enticing scene after another in an attempt to achieve the groaning dessert table effect of a family album. *Richie Rich* tries for this tableau effect and fails, but *The Piano* (1993), *My Girl* (1991—with Culkin and Anna Chlumsky), and *Dennis the Menace* (1993) work better, the last in particular sacrificing plot to portraiture, giving us Mason Gamble in his coveralls (that didn't) and twice in the tub, with enough child molester jokes so we won't miss the point.

We have a history of celebratory films that invest superior wisdom, virtue, or prowess in the child. Stanley Kramer's *Bless the Beasts and Children* (1971) is perhaps most devout in its nostalgic child worship and its willingness to equate the child's purity with its incapacity. The blessed child is also helpless, isolated in irresistible virtue, and in need of love. In this film, as in the Culkin films, our spot is left vacant. A half dozen boys, each with parental monsters who range from hateful to dead, and all stuck in a summer camp that loathes them (it is Vince Lombardi macho; they are Shirley Temple sensitive), declare themselves "misfits" and band together. Wearing nothing but Jockey shorts through most of the movie, these oddly handsome pariahs make one attempt to come up to camp standards, fail miserably (but cutely), and are tortured for it: fresh urine is thrown in their faces and they are then lined up, bent over a fence, and spanked one by one. This radicalizes them for good, and they set off to free some buffaloes from hunters, recognizing that the trapped animals are "dings just like us." I won't tell you how it comes out (it's sad). The point is that this awful movie, with dialogue even worse, could have been made and released, much less praised, only in a climate of blind idealism, one that would be able not to flinch at the song ladled over the credits:

> For in this world they have no voice—they have no choice
> So—ooooo give them shelter from the storm!
> Keep them safe!
> Keep them warm (warrrrr-ummmmmm).

The same pedophilic nostalgia informs Rob Reiner's *Stand by Me* (1986), in which four outcasts with horror-show fathers get in trouble and stand by one another in homosocial devotion. But it's an image frozen in time: the film believes as passionately as J. M. Barrie that life ends at twelve,[17] the adult narrator at the end reflecting, "I never had any friends later on like the ones I had when I was twelve. Jesus, does anybody?" These charming kids (actually three adorables —Wil Wheaton, River Phoenix, Corey Feldman—and one clown, Jerry O'Connell, for balance) do the usual in bawdy talk and obligingly strip to their underpants in a central scene in which the lead cutie (Wil Wheaton) has to put his hand down into his shorts to extract a leech from his testicles,[18] camera following close up and breathless. Just as the Culkin movies are butt movies, this one is a balls movie: a junkyard dog is activated by the cry, "Sic balls." The eroticism here is really a sniffly kind, telling us we can never return to that golden boyhood, except maybe in movies. Even the twelve-year-olds seem perpetually on the verge of sobs at the prospect of losing one another when the dread thirteen comes.

Usually these static portraits of the adorable do not sink into the dismals. The uplifting *Free Willys* (1993, 1995, 1997) and the various *Black Beauty* films are more common, or the classic *Paper Moon* (1974), in which a nine-year-old Tatum O'Neal presents a powerful variation on Shirley Temple cute: a hard-surfaced, androgynous, rough-talking — "I need to go to the shithouse"—precociousness that imitates adult sleaze: smoking cigarettes, talking about sex, swindling. Of course, she's soft underneath, devoted entirely to the man who may or may not be her father (played by her real-life father, Ryan) and willing to fight for him. Exactly at the film's center the child enters into competition for the male with the adult woman (a hilarious Madeline Kahn) and wins by tricking her rival into having sex with a hotel desk clerk and arranging for them to get caught.

Before the triumph, though, the terms of the contest are explicitly laid out for us in a stunning scene. The child is furious that the man she loves has picked up a carnival floozie, Trixie Delight (Kahn), and allowed her to usurp the front seat. When they stop to pee, the child climbs a hill, sits pouting, and refuses to get back in the car. Kahn clambers, high-heeled and swearing, up the hill and pleads with the little girl as one woman-of-the-world to another: "You gonna ruin it, ain't ya? Look, I don't wanta wipe you out, and I don't want you wipin' me out, so I'm going to level with you, OK?" She argues that since all her attachments are short-lived—"I don't know why, but I just don't manage to hold on real long"—the child should wait it out: "Just for a little while. Let old Trixie sit up front with her big tits." She knows she doesn't have a chance, big tits and all, against the adorable child— not with the driver, and not with us.

A safer version of the sexually precocious adorable is familiar to us from movies in which the child gets adults back together, gets a single parent married, or senses better than the adults who should be bedding whom. *Milk Money* (1995) and *Sleepless in Seattle* (1993) slickly play on this, as do *Forever Young* (1992) and *Paradise* (1991), both starring Elijah Wood. In the first, Wood falls in love with Mel Gibson (displacing the love neatly onto a neighbor girl), tries unsuccessfully to get him to marry his mom, then reunites Gibson with his first wife. In *Paradise* the overt plot concerns the boy's ability to heal a sexually wounded marriage, the shadow plot showing him winning the love of Don Johnson—"I know you like me," he says to an aloof Johnson, and he's right. Boys know these things. Again, there is a displaced cover story of Wood and a girl his age, but apart from getting the kids into their underwear, it's a purely perfunctory sidelight. Adorable kids are not meant for other adorable kids.

Sexualizing the Child

The adorable child often talks dirty and may engage in imitation sexualized behavior, but the imitative quality, the make-believe, is often stressed so as to disguise the appeal, allow the audience its safety screen. Planting sexuality unequivocally onto the child requires a willingness on the part of the filmmaker to invent quite extraordinary sleights of hand, to be satisfied with a marginal movie, or to bear up under a storm of outrage. Let's take the outrage first. *Baby Doll* (1956), starring Carroll Baker as the thumb-sucking nymphet, was so drooling in its scenes of voyeurism and pursuit, of panting and squirming, that the absence of nudity or coitus did not keep the League of Decency from banning it and Cardinal Spellman from denouncing it. Baker candidly admitted trying to act like "an over-imaginative overheated pubescent," working herself up before shooting "into a combustible, near-volcanic state of desire," trying hard to suppress moans in the makeup chair, struggling to deal with the "fear of climaxing" if anyone inadvertently touched her.[19] Perhaps Cardinal Spellman knew what he was responding to.

I wonder what he thought of *Lolita* (1962) and the Brooke Shields films of the next decade. Stanley Kubrick's *Lolita* is perhaps the only mainline film to tackle the pedophile subject head-on, but of course it does everything it can to avoid that head-on collision. Kubrick complained that he "wasn't able to give any weight at all to the erotic aspect of Humbert's relationship with Lolita," [20] but his feathery touch was certainly enough to rock audiences. Perhaps Kubrick did much more than he thought, made even the standard cover stories into accusations of his audience, and the usual disguises into revelations. Although Lolita (Sue Lyon) is always clothed, and erotic play between the child and Humbert (James Mason) is indicated only indirectly (by such things as toenail painting), Kubrick made this film as offensive as perhaps any has ever been by ripping away many disguises built into the standard pedophile plot, so many that I'll just list them:

1. The kid is not cute but vulgar, not innocent but merely indecent; she is vastly informed (much better than the adult pedophile) on what she presumably knows nothing about, the mechanics of sexual performance.

2. The parent (Shelley Winters) forfeits any claim on the child (or us) by hating her so venomously—"the little beast!"—and by being so delightfully pretentious that she seems to have waived her very reality.

3. The pedophile is driven not by lust but by rapture, capturing the most subversive feature of Nabokov's original work: here is the great, the only, American novel about dizzying, transforming love.

4. When it is not elegiac, the tone of the movie is absurdist and comic, never shocked and certainly never pious. In fact, at several points piety is mocked: the preposterous mother is most earnestly sincere, which means most hilariously fake, when talking about God: "If I ever found out you didn't believe in God, I think I would commit suicide."

Lolita, then, plays out boldly every part of the pedophile plot except the central scenes, which can safely be left to the audience. Predictably, though, the boldness got it in trouble.[21]

Pretty Baby (1978) is just as explicit and just as troubling for those reasons. Brooke Shields, who at the age of eleven months was the Ivory Snow baby, nearly 100 percent pure, looks dazzlingly pure here too in Louis Malle's bathed-in-white vision of decadence. It's not just that the eleven-year-old Shields appears in her underwear usually and altogether nude several times, is whipped, talks about nookie, displays herself as a virgin "delicacy" (on a tray), and is auctioned off to a client of the whorehouse where she lives. The problem is that she likes what she does. Her mother (Susan Sarandon) is indifferent to her (until the contrived ending), but nothing is made of that, since the whorehouse atmosphere and the camaraderie among the whores, young (very) and old, is so agreeable. The audience finds a surrogate in a photographer (Keith Carradine) who has free run of the place and prefers taking "studies" to body contact—until the child seduces him, thus fulfilling our culture's central pedophile fantasy: the bewitching eleven-year-old launches herself at us. It's what Lewis Carroll dreamed of, and not just Lewis Carroll.

Compared with this, Shield's later film *The Blue Lagoon* (1980) is tame stuff, though it has even more nudity (using a body double for Shields) and more explicit sex talk: "I've seen you playing with it, Richard—I've seen what happens after you've been playing with it a long time." The children are scoured free of eroticism, both by the insistent artiness of the photography and by their quick move into unadorable adolescence.

Other films use more elaborate screens. Gavin Millar's *Dreamchild* (1985) allows a consummation-in-memory of pedophile love, as the eighty-year-old Alice finally admits at the end of her life what had happened at the beginning, the overwhelming love-gift of *Alice in Wonderland:* "At the time, I was too young to see the gift whole, to see it for what it was, to acknowledge the love that had given it birth. But I see it now, at long, long last. Thank you, Mr. Dodgson. Thank you." *Bugsy Malone* (1976) is a dress-up game in which Jodie Foster can vamp it up with impunity as a moll singing about giving sexual comfort—"Lonely? You don't have to be lonely—come and see Tallulah; she can take your troubles away!" So, unsurprisingly, is *The Little Rascals* (1994), in which children act out sexual passion, sexual jealousy, and sexual allure. *Little Indian, Big City* (1996) treats its near-naked little star (Ludwig Briand) as a precocious Don Juan who lures new adult "bedtime friends" to his hammock every night. *Interview with a Vampire* (1993) has a twelve-year-old moaning "I want some more!"— more blood, ostensibly, but also something more from her adult "protectors," Lestat and Louis. The cover here is that she isn't really twelve, but something like one hundred.

Movies that bluntly show kids or very young adolescents having at it arouse anxiety or leave too little room for audience participation to make much money. They exist, but without getting much official notice: Mark Lester in *Redneck* (1974), River Phoenix in *A Night in the Life of Jimmy Reardon* (1988), Eric Brown in *Private Lessons* (1980), and Jay North (Dennis the Menace) in *The Teacher* (1974), in which the teacher gets to possess the body all the neighborhood women want, his own mother included: "I find him very attractive—even if he is my own son."

Imperiled Adorables

Perhaps the most durable feature of the central plot we play repeatedly is the isolation and endangering of the adorable: parents or other potential helpers are fashioned as monstrous, indifferent, or dead, and then the child is put in such jeopardy that the call for help is unmistakable. Now and then, as in *The Little Girl Who Lives Down the Lane* (1976), it is an actual child molester who menaces the child (Jodie Foster, who the same year did a trashier version of the Brooke Shields child-whore for *Taxi Driver*). This film, something of a plea for children's rights, has the thirteen-year-old Foster hiding the body of her dead father (and the fact of his death) to avoid being smothered by adult protectors. She sleeps with a boy, which excuses a nude scene, but mostly she demonstrates that her apparent vulnerability is only apparent, that she needs no protectors at all. When the monster gets too close, she deftly poisons him, playing out for us in a different key the logic used so often in these films: love, not protection, is what the child needs. Jodie can do perfectly well home alone—just like Culkin.

Radio Flyer (1992) offers an even more disturbing (and therefore commercially disastrous) twist on this plot by making the home itself and the sadistic stepfather controlling it truly menacing. The melodrama here is so strong that it leaves no room for the audience to write the usual pedophilic romance. The isolation of the boy leads casts them not as available pinups but as victims of a fantasy that appears suicidal (for young Joseph Mazzello). The movie makes a pass at a *Stand by Me* pederastic nostalgia—"Before anybody ever grows up, there are magical things, impossible for adults, that can still happen . . . lost in the quick second between your twelfth and thirteenth birthday." But these secrets do not, as they do for Barrie or Stephen King, offer much of a refuge, and no drop-by adults offer the small boys (Mazzello and Elijah Wood) a chance for warm bonding. The script contains cute things for the kids to do, and the child actors are uncommonly gifted; but in the end there is no hope, for them or for us. The littlest boy goes sailing off the hill in a wagon, while Wood, who has been flashing his underpants through the movie as if he were in a different erotic world, is left behind.

Even more disastrous is *The Cure* (1995), a movie about a young boy's losing battle with AIDS and the passionate efforts of his loving best friend to find help. Though the film brings together Hollywood's two prettiest and most talented age-appropriate (eleven or twelve) boys (Mazzello again and Brad Renfro), the image of a dying child, later a beautiful corpse, seems dated now, even repulsive. Attempts are made to distract us from the sacrifice of Mazzello, but the down-the-Mississippi trip is merely terrifying, and even the erotics don't work well when played out in a hospital over the body of a dying boy:

> *Renfro:* "He [Mazzello] laughed his ass off!"
> *Doctor:* [lifting the sheets and looking at Mazzello's ass] "Is that where it went? I thought you were on a diet."

Mazzello giggles at this, invites our interest in his body; but his playfulness in the face of death is heroic to the point of being excruciating, hardly enticing. The Victorians who photographed kids in coffins and wept over dying Little Nell and Little Paul Dombey may have been able to take their necrophilic eroticism straight, but we need disguises when we freeze cute kids; and, to be fair to us, villains less appalling than AIDS.

More commonly these imperiling films (*The Great Santini* [1980] or *This Boy's Life* [1993]) are content to portray demonic fathers or stepfathers in order to open the door for superior replacements (guess who?). Some (*Maya* [1965], *Redneck* [1974]) seem to put children in danger only to undress them. The brilliant Charles Laughton–James

Agee film, *The Night of the Hunter* (1955), is a nightmare fantasy that uses all its energy to throw the children onto us (our surrogate is a child collector played by Lillian Gish). Pursued by Robert Mitchum in his best alligator man frenzy, two little kids run wildly through a dreamscape, are rescued, undressed, and spanked—the last two activities added for audience pleasure. Interestingly, the girl is made as bluntly unadorable as a movie child ever has been—Mitchum calls her a "poor silly disgusting little wretch"—in order to further isolate the luminous boy (Billy Chapin).

When an entire movie is devoted to wretches, it shows how easily child imperiling can turn to voyeuristic sadism, child adoring to child despising. In the 1996 *Kids,* which shameless critics pretended to admire, a conservative horror plot is played out with children as the central demonic spectacle. These kids, apparently ranging in age between ten and eighteen, not only insult family values but think pretty much exclusively about finding pleasure, mostly in drugs and sex. There's a surprise for you. The movie manages to titillate as it lectures, to make the kids into erotic spectacles at the same time it is presenting them as heartless louts.[22] The camera in the film lingers on a world of freaks, caresses them, making points so blatant and unpleasant that only the eros carries it off. When a character named Caper rapes a drugged girl named Jenny, the camera shoots the action around, more like *through,* a sleeping boy, maybe eleven, being bounced on the couch by the humping assault. We are allowed to envision—not given much choice but to envision—sex not only behind but astride the little boy, as well as with his two slightly older friends; and we are screened by the superficial outrage handed to us by the gloating camera. This is a movie that imperils kids only to tell us we needn't care about them. We are encouraged to find them repellant and alluring, the first reaction covering and heightening the second.

But these movies give us only bits and pieces of the full, unrolled dream tale. It's time now to consider films that play out the cultural fantasy without blinking: the lovely and lonely child bonds with the misfit adult. This plot runs so deep and smooth that it seems to be powered by its own juices, though it does have some trouble completing itself: having the bum and the kid live together happily ever after would provide a closure both dangerously explicit and dull; we go to movies to have our fantasies exercised, not fulfilled. Fulfillment, after all, is an end to enticement, and it's enticement we've been after all along, and the reason we invented children and this adorable movie plot in the first place. So these films end, usually, by suspending the fantasy, not completing it: bumping off or banning the misfit, sending the kid back to the parents. Such perfunctory endings often advertise their obligatory nature, signaling us not to take them seriously and thus guaranteeing that the fantasy is still alive, ready to be revisited.

One of the most sophisticated of these films, Clint Eastwood's *A Perfect World* (1993), offers a cunningly oblique twist on Culkin cute: an eight-year-old played by T. J. Lowther in a role that is given some substance, thus reducing its potential for exciting automatic or conventional responses. All the same, the movie acts out explicitly a variety of our most titillating narratives about child sexuality, in scenes that either reproduce or parody (depending on one's position) the child as object of sexual attention. Lowther's eyes never twinkle, seem to express some deep pain, and he twists his mouth so crazily and expressively that he often looks like a diminutive Dennis Hopper. He spends the first half of the movie in his briefs and the last half in a Halloween costume that gets torn so as, again, to exhibit his underpants.

Exposed and defenseless, the boy nonetheless finds liberation and love with the convict Haynes (Kevin Costner), who kidnaps him, actually rescuing him from a mother who, for religious reasons, prohibits everything the movie defines as good for kids: freedom, candy, parties, Halloweening, and (we assume) sex. Philip (he becomes "Buzz" while he's on the lam with Haynes) has a father, but he doesn't toss a ball around with the boy or "play grab-ass in the yard"; he isn't even at home—is, in fact, just like Haynes's father, "not worth a damn." With this between them, being alone and longing for carnivals and cotton candy, they forge an immediate, intense bond.

It's a bond cemented through an act of violence that helps define, for the film and for us, just what the relationship between Haynes and the boy is *not*. There was, you see, initially another escaped convict with them, one who had tried to rape Buzz's mother (Haynes stopped him) and who tries to assault the boy. Haynes has gone into a store for supplies, handing the boy a gun to control a man so vicious he looks like a deranged pit bull. This bad con in the backseat loses no time in taunting the boy for knowing nothing of guns, living with "split tails," aiming to "grow up queer." He leans forward for a "real man-to-man," asking the boy if he actually is a man. He then leers at the child's crotch, drools about his "cute little underwears," and reaches over to examine their contents: "Let's see what you got down there." Cackling like the redneck sodomists in *Deliverance,* he conducts a rough examination, and says, "Kinda puny, ain't it?"

Haynes delivers Buzz from this horror by killing the bad guy, thus cleverly delivering us too: the differentiation (good con/bad con, pure love/criminal love) allows us to enter fully into Haynes's wooing of the boy. The film shrewdly duplicates the scapegoating action we employ on a large scale with our repetitive criminal trials and other spectacles of our virtue. Having demonstrated our righteousness by taking such an active part in expelling monstrous evil, we can proceed with an easy heart.

Later, when Haynes jokes with the boy about sex, we know it's all good-buddy talk and educational besides. This is all so well done that the movie is able to pull off a quite extraordinary scene. As the boy's underpants get more and more grubby (and less cute), Haynes becomes distracted by them and decides Buzz needs new skivvies, which he buys and tells the boy to put on. Sensing that Buzz is shy about getting undressed, he asks directly, "You embarrassed cause I might see your pecker?" "It's—puny," says Buzz, twisting his face into a wretchedness that might afflict King Lear on the heath. "Let me see," Haynes says. "Go on. I'll shoot you straight." He bends over and looks: "Hell no, Philip. Good size for a boy your age." The smile that greets this reassurance would light up the carnival Buzz has never attended, but now, with Haynes's blessing, can run forever.

Costner says the penis is OK, and we are assured that it's OK and we are OK and it's OK to look. The movie, having gone so deeply into the fantasy, has to exert some mighty force to wrench itself free, since it cannot send the two riding off into the sunset, admiring one another's penis. So it contrives a climax so preposterous—Buzz shooting his love—it knows we won't believe it. The good con dead, the boy rejoins his mother and we are ready for the next artful kidnapping.

A Perfect World is echoed in recent kid-con films such as *The Pro-*

fessional (1994) and *The River Wild* (1994), and it reaches back to a multitude of earlier child-adult odd-couple movies, *Tiger Bay* (1959), for instance, in which twelve-year-old Hayley Mills is so drawn to a murderer that she risks everything to protect him. *Martin's Day* (1984) parallels that so closely as to be embarrassing to any group other than the film industry, which operates like Shakespeare in seizing on whatever plot lies nearest to hand. Here, young Martin (Justin Henry, about eleven years old) is kidnapped by disturbed escaped con Martin (Richard Harris) and taken on a series of adventures, all designed to minister to the kid's desires: for candy, an automobile and then a locomotive to drive, and acceptance so complete it leads to— surprise—a scene in which they pledge unto one another, "I love ya, kid!" "Oh, I love *you!*" The two Martins are not related, relatives not faring well in this movie: the boy's father ignores him, doesn't like him; and his mother's indifference is packed into the perky answering machine message the kid gets when he calls to tell her he has been kidnapped. Again, the child and the adult are sealed off in a perfect moment, shimmering in its nostalgic eros. The adult is so bluntly recapturing his own childhood that, at the end and in the lake at last, he sees in the boy his own sunlit self, naked and irresistible, as only our inner child can be.

Sling Blade (1996) is much more watchable but even more conventional, the loving outsider (Billy Bob Thornton) this time appearing under the guise of a released mental patient who years earlier killed his mother and her lover, and now is ready to kill again (this time not the mother, just the lover) to help the boy he loves. Because the mentally-retarded-as-well-as-diseased adult has such thick disguises (and because his twist is homicidal rather than pederastic, and thus less dangerous), he can express his love for the boy much more openly. The boy loves him back so ardently that the final murder functions as a redemptive sacrifice, a Sidney Carton or Opera Phantom renunciative love: greater love hath no man than to go back to the asylum for his beloved. In this film, adults, both the abusers and the lovers, have all the power. The child (Lucas Black) is simply there to look at and to receive benefits or blows as they come. The movie thinks it loves children but treats them as cute puppies.

For greater complexity try the exquisite *Savannah Smiles* (1982), in which Savannah (Bridgette Anderson) runs away from a pair of self-absorbed parents to find affection and peace with two on-the-run bumbling crooks. She manages to reach into their hearts and repair not so much their present—they are arrested in the end—as their pasts. In an astounding commentary on the power of the love of children and on the way memory is constructed, the tough con Alvie garners finally such a gift of grace as to heal the wounds he suffered as a kid. Alvie tells Savannah that the cousins he lived with as a child drove off with the family and abandoned him every Saturday, leaving him crying in the dust as they jeered: "I wasn't growed up then and didn't know men weren't supposed to cry." As a child, he got one present (firecrackers), played one trick, and, for that one moment of childhood, "Uncle Ludie, he took me out to the woodshed and he whupped me so hard I could hardly stand up." Alvie says he ran away then, so they wouldn't run away from him again ever: "But that's a long time ago, and I don't think about that never no more." Savannah knows better and teaches the crook not that crime doesn't pay but that love does. He doesn't forget the past; he gains a new past: the family stopped for him, pulled him to its breast after all.

There's a central scene toward the end in which Savannah, waking from a bad dream, stumbles over to Alvie, who gathers her up and dances with her to a heartbreaking country tune that captures the enormous power of adorable children to revive our sense of delight and vanishings. Here, with cops surrounding the place and the idyll of convict and child about to be blasted apart, they share, like Carroll and Alice on the "happy summer day," a spot of love, the terrible lyrics of loss washing over them: "If we could only hold on to this moment in time, / I'd be so much better off in your pretty world than I'll ever be in mine."

Here is the heart of the experience of this eroticism: Alvie hugs the child so tightly because he desperately needs what he can never again attain—what he never had until she came along and offered it. He squeezes her out of gratitude and a need that far exceeds the lust his hug may well contain. This fantasy of the perfect moment, a moment that is being lost as it is being held, is the thrilling bass support of nostalgic eroticism. It gives us the aching joy that informs "The Priest and the Acolyte" and ruined Oscar Wilde, not because he gave his culture what it didn't want, but because he gave more than it could stand. What was once a criminal plot is now standard fare, feeding on the sudden pain we feel when we look at that photograph, when we look at the laughing, happy child with us, our child—me, at the beach or at the park—and recognize with an intensity we can neither control nor tolerate that this great happiness we are experiencing now, right now, is already gone.

That is the intensity informing the wrenching *Man, Woman and Child* (1982), which tears the beautiful little boy from his adult lover, and *The Champ* (1979), which tears the adult lover from the heart-broken little boy. Slightly less agonizing are the bondings and partings in *The Client* (1994) between Susan Sarandon and small, needy Brad Renfro and in *The Man without a Face* (1993), between Mel Gibson and his tutee/lover. All these films do allow some happiness before these throbbing breaks, but it's a happiness skidding always downhill, loaded with ominous signs of the tragedy ahead.

This is getting depressing, so it's a relief to find a few lighter treatments of the theme, in the bizarre *Willie Wonka and the Chocolate Factory* (1971), *Meatballs* (1979), and *Indian in the Cupboard* (1996). *Willie Wonka* elaborates two central fantasies: the child who satisfies all his desires (endless chocolate and love), and the adult (Gene Wilder) who gets to choose from among contestants the child *he* wants. Little Charlie (Peter Ostrum) passes the test—the other kids failing because they are greedy, vulgar, untidy, German, and American (it's a film full of British bigotries). Charlie is given the factory, the everlasting gobstopper (an inexhaustible suckable candy), and Wonka's gobstopper hugs: "Don't forget, Charlie, what happened to the man who suddenly got everything he always wanted," Wonka says at the close. "He lived happily ever after." The *man* who got everything he wanted, note, not the *boy*.

Meatballs allows summer-camp counselor Tripper (Bill Murray) gliding room to swing his affectionate ironies around, particularly in the direction of one lonely, abandoned boy, Rudy (Chris Makepeace). Murray treats the fragile child as a tough street kid—"You gotta watch out for this guy; he's done time for car theft"—and vows to make him into "an animal." He poses and jokes and prods the boy into winning the big race, letting his guard down only once, when Rudy looks so tearful and solitary that even Tripper is driven out of his irony: "Look, you make one good friend a summer and you're doing pretty well." He makes that friend—they both do.[23]

Indian in the Cupboard (1995) has a nine-year-old boy (Hal Scardino) drawing from his complex inner life two simple-minded but dear-hearted grown-ups, "his inner adults," *Newsweek* nicely termed them.[24] These tiny adults are both toys and lessons for the boy, but the didactic plot is played down and there is a sense that this child, independent and capable, needs few lessons. What he needs is love, a need that is played out pretty directly between the boy and his Indian mentor/lover.

Recently, young girls have been cast in these androgynous roles without at all affecting the basic plot. A highly sexualized Natalie Portman in *The Professional* (1995) snuggles up to a con-on-the-run in a ghost version of *A Perfect World*. In 1996, Anna Paquin bonded with Daddy as they were able to work out their love by way of an airplane and a flock of geese, not so much triangulating as rectangling their passion. *Fly away Home* is slickly made, but its plot differs from the well-worn standard article only in being more directly incestuous, the hero-heroine of such plots generally flying away from, not to, home in order to find love. One genuinely radical movie, and one more determined to fix gender and avoid the androgynous-blended center, is *Matilda* (1996), which uses a comic fairy-tale mode to work out a moving child-adult bonding outside the family, a bonding that is unmistakably between girl and woman, woman and woman. Mother and father dissolve into unreality as the mode of the movie shifts from absurdist to homosexual romance.

Perhaps shadowing all these films is *Shane* (1952), in which the enigmatic and startlingly handsome Shane (Alan Ladd) inspires and gives so much love to Joey (Brandon de Wilde) that we often forget there's a father present (as does his wife). The mother warns Joey "don't get to liking Shane too much—he'll be moving on one day"; but Joey can't help himself—"Mother, I just *love* Shane!"—and neither can Shane, who teaches the boy to shoot and then has to do some shooting himself. The shooting locks them together, Shane reclaiming his own youth in the boy at the same time he pulls the boy into himself and his violence. The famous closing scene—"But we want you,

Shane"—reverberates because Shane also wants, exactly to the same pitch, the crying little boy.

The racking ending of *Shane* is revised happily (I keep slipping into the lugubrious) in *Second Best* (1994), in which two damaged people, adult (William Hurt) and boy (Chris Cleary Miles), stop pegging at one another and admit their love. At the heart of the movie, the forlorn boy deliberately bashes his head, goes to the timorous Hurt, and asks, in a thin, dreamlike voice, if he won't please kiss it, sobbing when Hurt gives it a peck, "Oh, harder or it won't work." Hurt kisses harder, which allows the boy, in the same pained voice that contains all his hopes, to plead, "Do you love me, then?" "Very much—probably more than is good for me," says Hurt. This movie completes the fable, joins boy and adult, and tells us, softly but insistently, that there's no loving too much, no love that's not good for all of us.

Leaving the Kids Alone

There are a few films that do not seem to absorb children or use them for purposes nostalgic or erotic, films with a wry vision so lucid as to see that the affection children can grow on is always wary and distant. These films pay their respects to children, see that even adorable children have a strange integrity that is so tough to fathom that it may be best just to record it and honor its variety and tenacity. *Searching for Bobby Fisher* (1992) does this, and Steven Spielberg manages it consistently, even in the oddly flat *Jurassic Park* (1993), in which the scientist learns that the brave and supercompetent kids are worth being around (and producing on his own) without ever trying to get close to them, save them, or bond with them. They are satisfied to like one another and part with a tip of the hat. *E.T.* (1982) also avoids making demons of adults, treating them instead as necessary encumbrances. There is an absent father again, but none of the kids seems to mind terribly; and the mother is hopelessly self-absorbed but benign enough and well intentioned. It's just that adult intentions don't matter much. The distance from the children is so marked, in fact, that the main child, Henry Thomas, again spending much of the movie in his underwear, is made an object for voyeuristic delight only. No one could get closer to him than Spielberg is—but the director is on the other side of the camera, in the bushes, only peeping.

Even more distant is *The Bad News Bears*, which offers nonadorable kids and an array of dim adults, the best of whom (Walter Matthau) learns to respect them and keep away: "Just go out there and do the best you can," he tells them. This is a movie that tries to allow kids not only the final say but all the says. Most adults are around only to be meddlesome and cruel. The most memorable things in the film are the many close-ups of kids' faces: they are stunned, shocked into disbelief and pain by adult viciousness. It's as if the kids cannot absorb the power of the narrow meanness driving the adults. The movie doesn't suggest that adults can ever cross the gap, only that they should get off the field so the kids can play.

5. Resenting Children

Into my heart an air that kills
From yon far country blows:
What are those blue remembered
    hills,
What spires, what farms are those?

That is the land of lost content
I see it shining plain,
The happy highways where I went
And cannot come again
—A. E. Housman

Deep as first love, and wild with all
    regret,
O, Death in Life, the days that are no
    more!
—Tennyson

The most adorable child is always, face it, the one in a self-portrait. Even the cutest of the children before us, Shirley Temple herself, is seen through an old photo and gradually finds herself melting into our attraction to the childhood we knew or imagine we knew. If that were the whole story, we would doubtless be an insufferably sentimental people with shockingly pampered, confused children; but we would be serene. But it's not that simple. When we spring the locks on the past, we are flooded not only by sunshine but by "an air that kills," bringing from the child within not restoration but "death in life." The poets always know. Our lolling nostalgia, child worship, and soft eroticism comingle with fear and repulsion. The child that brings life also threatens to end it; and we are always hugging the child with one eye on its jugular. Our adoration is violent and unsettled; our nostalgia the bitterest sweet.

What accounts for the agony that accompanies nostalgia, the pain we feel when we recall past happiness or look at beautiful children? Why do we resent that which we most desire, turn and rend what we have called into being? Why do we punish the child we prize most precisely for being that prize? It is as if somebody has to reimburse us for all we expend in mooning over adorable children, as if we could cover the guilt such longings bring to us by blaming the adorable child itself.

We manage this hocus-pocus by switching the costume we put on the child: idealized angels are made possible by matching devils. And it's simple economy to use the same body for both parts: the dream child becomes the demon. The dark side of our desire is projected outward onto the demon child, who occupies a variety of figures ranging from naughty to satanic, all of them alien to us, resistant, disobedient. This child is always running away from us, forcing us into a chase at least as alluring as the stasis offered by the perfectly adorable child.

But they are the same child. The monster is the logical continuation of the cherub, as our chief adorable, Macaulay Culkin, demonstrates in *The Good Son*. Culkin didn't extend his range, as some obtuse critics claimed, he just kept playing within it as we directed. Here, he gives us something to resent, the domestic angel turned so sour he kills people helter-skelter and even says the F-word. The movie spins out a strong fable of resentment, justifying not simply the milder forms of child hating—spanking, humiliation—but eradication: his mother deliberately drops him several thousand feet onto the rocks below. It's a scene that fits our needs so perfectly that audiences across America cheered.

The pleasure we take in rejecting children often forms a strong current even in the most cuddly of our cultural fictions, like Carroll's Alice books, which alternately fawn over the child, sobbing at her unresponsiveness, and snarl at her with barely disguised aggression. American comic strips have a long tradition of Sunday-after-Sunday punishments for naughty children (Buster Brown, Perry Winkle, Little Iodine, and the Katzenjammer Kids); and we love this plot in movies. In our desperate purification, we move what we think of as "children" into an unreal land where only mythic figures can live for us. It is a fairy tale that is always about to curdle: the child is always bad; the child always deserts us in the end, growing up and growing away. But why do we think of children in this way? Why do we construct for ourselves a child we find both alluring and tiresome, an embodiment of ourselves and a stranger, a dream come true and, when it gets too close, an enemy to escape or destroy? "So when," Barbara Ehrenreich asks, "did we start yearning for childhood and simultaneously hating so many of the little people to whom it rightly belongs?"[1]

To this set of questions I have a set (or miscellany) of answers, five and a bonus:

1. Deep within us is not just resentment but rage, infanticidal rage, all coming from a psychic core deeper than the desire to possess the mother or father. Such Oedipus/Electra complexes may, in fact, simply be a secondary drive to placate the parents and ward off their murderous impulses, since the desire to kill one's offspring felt by both

fathers and mothers (the Laius and Jocasta complexes, respectively) precedes it. According to Martin Bergmann's *In the Shadow of Moloch: The Sacrifice of Children,*[2] this parental drive sometimes to use children sexually and always to kill them is recorded in a history of child sacrifices that reached a turning point when Abraham's ready willingness to slay Isaac was blocked, the aggression thereafter being internalized and played out in a series of ritual substitutions: Bergmann mentions circumcision, and should have included spanking, assigning chores, and telling them they aren't working up to their potential. We participate heartily in a teen-bashing and child-hating discourse, applauding every new study that tells us about young superpredators, increased drug use, and declining SAT scores.

2. They outshine us. The modern "parent," a spin-off from the invention of the modern "child," has always had its character and duties defined retroactively: parents have to hustle to mold themselves anew in order to fit with the latest conceptions of the child. It may be only human to take offense at such treatment, but parents can find few outlets for expressing their anger, the child having seized control of the media. *Child* tells us that a tantrum is "a good sign," that a shrieking "I hate you!" is "a compliment, not an insult," showing plainly "that your child is secure"; we should treasure such moments. We see articles like "Full-Esteem Ahead,"[3] about a positive self-image, but not for parents, who have no image and must take orders: "don't take misbehavior personally"; "nurture, nurture, nurture"; "love unconditionally"; "don't presume that you own your kids"; "encourage independence"; "promote autonomy." If your child is making your life one long affliction, "try to figure out what needs she is trying to fulfill by misbehaving and then find ways to fulfill those needs as positive reinforcement." If you do these things, "your little engine [will be] thinking he can do anything." In case your child doesn't yet feel omnipotent, you'll be happy to learn that "it's never too soon—or too late—to start" power-boosting that little engine.

Those engines so drive public mythology that the rare keening protests that do get heard, that kids are, by and large, guilty of "parent abuse,"[4] for instance, seem almost obscene. Mostly we whine, worried that our self-sufficient kids may be part of us only if they go wrong, and not always then. Take Jeffrey Dahmer. Lionel Dahmer's *A Father's*

Story is a deep dive into himself to find the tie to his son, to locate an autobiography that will assure him that he had some role in this nightmare.[5] His sense of being seems to depend on it: he is driven to trace Jeffrey back to himself. If the child floats free of "the parent," maybe the parent was a fiction to start with.

Lionel Dahmer wants to understand not so much why his son did what he did, but where he fits in: Where did *I* go wrong? What about *me*? This is an account so intelligent and so bent on self-blame and on skewing the record that it broadcasts its own despair at finding a spot for the parent. Lionel often tries simply to announce that he's on to Jeffrey's perversions, having located "their distant origins within myself," that "the only difference . . . was that I had awakened out of a nightmare, and my son had awakened into one." But what was Lionel's nightmare, and in what way was he like Jeffrey? He worried a lot about details, could have spent more time with the boy (though he seems to have been more than usually attentive), lacked sparkling social skills, had trouble expressing feelings. Lionel ends wistfully, "I have come to believe that some of the compulsions that overwhelmed my son may have had their origins in me," a sentence that flaps so feebly in the breeze ("I have come to believe . . . some . . . may have"?) that it testifies only to the senior Dahmer's willingness to try hard.[6] "Fatherhood remains," he says, "a grave enigma," so grave (and enigmatic) that he warns every father after him, "Take care, take care, take care!" Of what? Take care that you not disappear entirely, find no place at all in your child's story, not even the villain's role?

3. Children demand everything, give nothing; they are ungrateful. This, the oldest charge in the book, echoes throughout classical literature, the Bible, and all parents' hearts: "How sharper than a serpent's tooth it is to have a thankless child!" moans King Lear—and my parents and yours, me and you. Samuel Butler (the elder) ascribed to Nature herself this cold indifference in children: "Nature hath order'd it so, that Parents have a great Inclination to the Love of their Children, because they cannot subsist without it: But takes no course that children should Love their Parents, because they have no such neede of it."[7]

4. Children desert us. Just as we are cementing the bond, they vanish: the adolescent, with a sexuality claimed for itself, bears no re-

lation whatever to the child who was there only a moment before, its sexuality denied, implanted. Peter Pan, coldhearted though he is, is a monument to eternal enticement, unlike his models, the Davies boys, who were so deeply loved by Peter Pan's creator. Those boys were there for Barrie only for a moment: "They had a long summer day, and I turned round twice and now they are off to school" (dedication to *Peter Pan*), over the cliff into the darkness. As Lewis Carroll knew, it's "all in a golden afternoon," a blip of time, that children exist; then they're off to find the night.

5. They do what they are told; they are good. I believe the chief cause of resentment against children is that they provide us with so few reasons for resentment. So many children want to please, try to do as they are told, imagine that what we are telling them we want is what we want. Wise children figure out that what we are after is the enticing naughtiness that comes from disobedience, their flight leaving open the child's spot so that we can occupy it.

Bonus. We resent children because resentment is in itself an erotic activity and provides excuses for even more erotic activities. The naughty child allows us to keep desire alive by keeping on the move and never falling into goodness. Desire desires desire, not fulfillment; and the naughty child is, at least in our imagination, the image that can always find ways to keep fulfillment and endings at bay. It is also true that the naughty child allows us (as goodness and obedience never do) to slip unconsciously into an imaginative sexuality that is almost obligatory in our culture: we make the bad kid into the Other (much as men do women) in order to idealize, beat, and generally mold as we like, all in the name of duty. We prescribe pretty clearly what we want, which is not Sid Sawyer but Tom—not the goody-good, the MENSA wretch, but the real kid, the child of our imagination. That child we can resent and honor with our desire. Smart kids know this.

That knowledge does them little good: no child can ever live up to our imaginative and nostalgic demands. The child can never fulfill our desire for it, a desire based on a void within us so vast as to be measureless: "desire implies a lack that no object can appease."[8] Children offer not appeasement but fuel, ways to keep our double-edged dreaming going.

American comic strips have traditionally offered up
child spankings for our enjoyment.

Spanking

The most resounding twist of resentment into desire is our tolerance
for spanking children, our culture being as reluctant to abandon this
custom as it is to acknowledge its pleasures. Even the Supreme Court
is anxious to insist "that children do not have a constitutional right
not to be subjected to harsh physical punishments."[9] The connections between sexual excitement and child beating have never been
hidden: they are mentioned in the *Satyricon,* by Festus, by Lucian, in
a 1669 "Children's Petition" to Parliament (directed against lecherous
schoolmasters and their "unquenchable appetites"); Rousseau traced
the formation of his sexual tastes to childhood spankings; Victorian
doctors worried about it, and Freud said the sexual arousals (and attendant problems) caused thereby were "well known."[10] I think it is
well known and just as well hidden; so we keep at it.

The American Humane Association claims to have evidence that 90
percent of parents of three- and four-year-olds have actually hit their

children. A large fraction of these will even admit that they do so: the National Committee to Prevent Child Abuse found that 49 percent of Americans said they spanked their children in 1993. The *Boston Globe* in 1995 reported that 90 percent of parents spank toddlers at least three times a week, two-thirds once a day; 52 percent of thirteen- and fourteen-year-olds get spanked, 20 percent of high-school seniors.[11] Some experts cited in the *Globe* article say those numbers are unrealistically low, probably because the sampling was drawn from the Northeast, where spanking is not so popular. But *Family Relations* gives similar statistics: 61 percent of mothers spanked their preschoolers in the past week; 26 percent three or more times; 5 percent during the interview on spanking practices. The number of spankings the average preschooler receives in a year: 150.[12] Even more ominous is a figure from a *USA Today* poll conducted in April 1994: 67 percent of those interviewed agreed that "a good hard spanking" is "sometimes necessary."[13] A "hard" spanking is always characterized as "good" or "sound," as something demanded by the child and delivered for its own sake.

About half the states still authorize corporal punishment in the schools and even the experts keep quiet about it: one 1994 content analysis "of 120 books on child abuse found that only 12 percent included an unambiguous recommendation that corporal punishment should not be used."[14] These books and the even-more-lenient child-rearing manuals often begin with a strong statement against spanking and then qualify themselves all the way into the other corner, admitting that it might be OK to spank in this or that situation and that other situations might even demand it. Some, like Doctor Spock, seem most concerned with assuaging the guilt the spanking parents might feel. *Time* reassures us that a recent study linking childhood spanking to adult violence is deeply flawed, needn't worry us.[15]

It is no wonder that even protective agencies such as Canada's Children's Aid Society differentiate appropriate from inappropriate physical force used on children, the former, which it calls "minor" ("may be perceived as necessary"), being nothing more than, say, "a gentle spanking," such an altogether nice thing that the society "would have no concerns" with it.[16] In this country, guides on what should be reported are more detailed: "*Reasonable corporal punishment should not be reported.* . . . To put it bluntly, parents are allowed to spank their children's bottom with their hands. In most jurisdictions, a hairbrush and even a belt (not the end with the buckle) can be used as long as no serious welts or cuts result." [17] In California, where I live, citizens are pledged not to "interfere with appropriate parental discipline," or to tell parents how to hold their belts during these appropriate beatings. My guess is that buckle beating would be regarded as "reasonable and age appropriate" so long as "serious physical injury" did not result;[18] and what's the chance of that? We're talking *serious* here: broken bones, hospitalization.

When we aren't doing it, we're talking about it. Mommy Dearest Joan Crawford lives for us only as a child beater—foaming, coat hanger descending; and Bing Crosby, who was about to fade from our minds altogether (too much manufactured cool), got new life when son Gary told us about looking back over his shoulder at his father during the beatings and seeing in his eyes "nothing—just boredom and dissatisfaction":

> My brothers got a beating once a week. I got two a week, sometimes three. Dad used to give it to us with a Western leather belt that had little silver points sticking out. He'd take our pants down and then methodically, very calmly, he would whip us till we bled. After he stopped, we'd go into the bathroom and look at our asses in the mirror. When we got older he used a chain or a cane with a big knob at the end. He'd hold it with two hands like a baseball bat, bend us over and then step into us fourteen or fifteen times.[19]

Going my way?

None of this quite compares with the furor surrounding the caning of an American teenager by the Singapore government in May 1994 on charges of spray-painting vandalism. Americans seemed to relish this event at least as much as publicity on penises being chopped off, and for exactly the same reason: it allowed us the chance to speak openly of a subject that, for once, really caught our interest. In a *Time* "Essay," [20] James Welch said Americans were "fascinated" by the caning because it "concentrated the mind wondrously" on a lively debate over "a due balance between individual and majority rights." My own feeling is that the national mind found itself wondrously concentrated not on rights but on buttocks, either generic or Michael Fay's particular set. Publicist David Schmidt said, "I can guarantee the exclusive pictures of his buttocks are worth at least one-half million — maybe more. People want to see his buttocks."[21] That seems reasonable. But no amount of money proved adequate, so we were forced to fall back on our usual substitute for actual buttocks before us: talk about buttocks. The flood of news and opinion articles, letters to the editor, call-ins, cartoons, jokes, and songs all had one thing in common: Michael was being whipped. Many times, before and after the event, we were dished the details: stripped, kidneys padded, butt exposed, bent over, strapped into a machine (usually illustrated, with cartoon cheeks), and thus ready for the official with the soaked rattan cane, which he administered after a short run, like a cricket bowler.

The tabloids did what tabloids do, which is also, more or less, what the respectable news magazines did. *Time* was relatively restrained, printing a good many letters on the subject but only three brief notices during this period and the essay referred to above, an admirable record marred only by a grotesque diagram bearing the title "Raw Data," which not only gave us (again) details on "How a Prisoner Is Caned," but allowed us to see, first in a smaller picture and then blown up, those very bare buttocks sticking out at us, just in case we'd like to take a swipe at them ourselves.[22] But this is nothing compared with *Newsweek*, which ran six stories (twice full-page ones), with titles straight from *Weekly World News*: "After the Caning, 'Mike's in Pain'" and "I Tried to Ignore the Pain."[23] The last, a follow-up interview, asked the boy such probers as: "What was the caning like?" "Who did the caning?" "How painful was it?" They got him to give us details Sade would have loved—and not only Sade, apparently: "I felt a deep burning sensation throughout my body, real pain. The flesh was ripped open. Now on one side there are brown blotches, about 2 inches in diameter, where the flesh was torn. On the other side are four straight lines." *Newsweek* neglected to give pictures, even to ask which side had the blotches, which the lines. Inquiring minds want to know. Anticipating its readership getting a little restless with just the one butt to contemplate, *Newsweek* ran a huge (for it) special on "Crime and Punishment," putting it with a straight face under "National Affairs," although it was the caning debate all over again. The article went on for six pages, with multiple illustrations and a virtuous essay by William J. Bennett, who said that our "pro-caning sentiment" was "justifiable outrage at what is happening to American society."[24]

The *Los Angeles Times,* being able to speak daily, told us what was going on or offered opinions on the caning twenty-one separate times, which must be some kind of record for an event that lasted, according to Fay, less than a minute. The headlines here were what you would expect: "US Youth Is Caned; Doctor Says He's OK" and "Fay Describes Caning, Seeing Resulting Scars." I want to know how he saw his own scars—did he crane around and peek, did the prison authorities give him a mirror, or did he take someone else's word for it?

Letters to the editor of the same paper during this happy time drooled more sloppily, even some of those protesting the sentence. But most expressed approval:

> Michael Fay deserves the "woodshed" treatment. . . . Were it not for the likes of bleeding-hearts ACLU, this kind of old-fashioned punishment might be just what we need in this country.

> I was caned twice while attending a British school. . . . I did not suffer any ill effects due to the caning and, in fact, throughout my life I've thought twice before breaking the rules.

> Michael Fay got what he deserved.

> It is time for him to take responsibility for his actions, quit whining, and accept his punishment like a man.

> The caning I have in mind doesn't have to be the Singapore type, brutally administered to the point of physical shock. It could be a more severe version of the belt-lashing my father used to give me. But I believe that would be salutary. And I am not alone in my view.

The last is not really from a letter but from an op-ed piece written by ex–New York mayor and spankee Ed Koch, entitled, liltingly, "We Used to 'Cane' in America; Let's Do It Again."

It came as no surprise when several politicians tried to climb on the bare-bottom bandwagon and gain popularity by keeping the discourse going, offering bills of various sorts that would attract attention and allow us to talk on about spanking, even after the sounds of the last interview with Michael Fay had echoed down the corridors of time— "Which buttocks was hurt most?" "Did you clench, did you flinch?" In California, State Assemblyman Mickey Conroy (R-Orange) proposed that young taggers (graffiti artists) be given up to ten blows with a wooden paddle by their parents in the courthouse, with the stipulation that if Mom and Dad didn't strike hard enough (what's hard enough?), the bailiff would take over. Conroy (and the rest of us) got the desired results: butt babble and punning headlines like "Paddling Bill Puts Conroy in Hot Seat." The bill was seriously debated and actually passed easily through one committee before barely being stalled in another by an eleven-to-eleven vote. Finally forced out of committee and given the strong support of the state attorney general (who said the activity would be wholly constitutional), the bill was finally, if narrowly, defeated. Conroy, blaming the defeat on freshmen congressmen "raised in the 60s who never knew the benefits of corporal punishment," vowed to find other avenues for peddling those benefits.[25] The 1996 film *Return to Paradise* capitalizes on this spanking mood, its opening sequence depicting an eleven-year-old boy being collared, depantsed, and repeatedly spanked by a buxom maid.

One of the things marking this sadomasochistic discourse, apart from its heat, is its tone of unremitting solemnity, which makes remarkable the few attempts to cut through the steamy monoeroticism. The *New Yorker* ran a lighthearted spoof by Bill Franzen that ended with tips for spray-painters traveling to Singapore: silence the mixing balls in the can; change labels so it looks like you're carrying silly string; watch the exercise video *Buns of Steel*.[26] And Don Martin offered in *Mouth2Mouth* a cartoon (mocking the explicitness of the Fay cartoons) that illustrated new and engaging penalties "that reflect the verve and diversity of today's crime." Complaining that Fay's caning was not only "primitive—it was dull," Martin proposed (and diagrammed) eye-snaps, pulling the eyeballs out about two feet and letting them fire back with a "Splabadap!"[27]

Like Fay's body, then, the naughty child becomes for us a national punching bag: the activity is aggressive, lustful, and righteous—a combination spelling bad news for the naughty child. We ask this naughty child to balance precariously between alluring otherness and threatening rebellion. The alluring child needs to be on the run, generally uncatchable (just) but making itself available now and then for correction. If he seems truly out of reach, then the child is a danger to us and we may begin to hate him, to regard him as a beast we maybe should just shoot down.

Demon Seed

It is an easy slide down to child hating. We seem now to be feeding on images of evil children to an alarming extent, frenetically publicizing juvenile crime and urging our politicians to compete for the toughest-on-children crown. In March 1994, thirteen separate bills were circulating in the California statehouse to try more kids as adults and lengthen their prison terms once we got them locked up. The legislative activity has remained steady ever since. The emphasis on punishment is so single-minded that, as a *Time* survey of the national mood puts it, "preventive solutions remain a hard sell."[28] It's as if all the ugly things we hoped to contain in "the adolescent" were leaking out and flooding backward onto the children, who are thereby made lethal, enemies of the people.

"Can You Spot the Drug Pusher?" blares the headline over a picture of eight cute elementary school kids, the cocky text below telling us, "the frightening thing is, that a kid is more likely to be pushed into drugs by some innocent-looking classmate" than by a puff-adder adult. Donahue runs a show on "Six-Year-Olds Sexually Harassing" (January 5, 1994), and Oprah's *Scared Silent* tells us that 60–80 percent of all sex offenders started their careers as teenagers, often young teenagers.

But even Oprah didn't see what was just around the corner: kindergarten harassers, toddler molesters. This peer-to-peer molestation produces experts like Bernice Sandler, who roams campuses and PTA meetings saying that kids molesting kids "is the most explosive and emerging type of harassment around today: first graders' crotches are being grabbed by fourth graders."[29] This move to spot the pedophile among yesterday's victims of pedophile predators has sometimes exploded in comic excess, as in the case of Jonathan Prevette, suspended from school for kissing a classmate on the cheek. The six-year-old,

It was difficult even for us to
see in Prevette the face of a
sexual predator.

originally charged with sexual harassment, turned out to be an engaging media presence, with bizarre self-possession, huge glasses, and the bearing and looks of *Our Gang*'s "Froggy." He drew a media storm, protests from all over, especially the right, Rush Limbaugh deploring leftist political correctness, Camille Paglia blaming the feminists, and Kathie Lee Gifford saying hey now, we've gone too far.[30] Over the protests of teachers, who called it "a slap in the face," Jonathan was chosen grand marshal of his town's Christmas parade.[31]

But this hilarious episode did nothing to deter the growing strength of the movement to spot and treat youthful (very) offenders. Just how strong is made chillingly clear in Judith Levine's brilliant *Mother Jones* analysis of the booming therapy industry treating and "rescuing" children who molest children.[32] Levine charts how these therapists, supported only by their own circular, self-confirming theories, have made huge inroads not only in "treating" tiny offenders but in separating them from their parents. With the help of "teachers and social workers, undereducated in psychology and overtrained (often by law enforcers) in sexual abuse,"[33] and thus apt to see sexual pathology in almost any act, children are removed from their homes and put through treatments that seem to have been drawn from William Burroughs's fantasies. All of this, Levine points out, rests on a belief that juvenile sexual acts of any sort are always far more meaningful than we suppose. She also sees that the removal of children from parents can proceed only by resurrecting the old nostrum of the cycle of abuse and the firm dogma that children would not be doing these things (masturbating, playing doctor, diddling themselves or others, fondling, attempting intercourse) if they were not themselves being abused. Where else would they get the idea? It seems to me also that this confusion of villain and victim, illogical as it is (aren't children supposed to be sexless?), suggests a terrifying extension of our story, as we reach for the monster role even into the ranks of the innocent. Our stockpile must be running low.

But it's also true that this demonizing of the young reflects our underlying unease and resentment, a malice toward the child that is clearest in the relish with which we greet and invent kiddy crime. *USA Today* runs a special cover story, "Teen Crime Surge Sparks Crackdown," and Richard Rodriguez writes an op-ed piece, "One day they are innocent; the next, they may try to blow your head off."[34] *Newsweek*'s deep plunge into the prophetic-fatuous, a set of visions called "The Millennium," is most confident about the future of crime: "Watch out!" its headline screams. "Aging Thugs Will Be Replaced by Younger, More Violent Criminals."[35] We can't get enough of this; it's worse than Michael Fay. Here are some random headlines, not invented:

2 Boys Charged in Gang Execution of 11-Year-Old
Youth, 14, Sentenced in Slaying of 9-Year-Old
Life of Violence Catches Up to Suspected Murderer, 11
Boy, 11, Who Cut Throat of Woman, 83, Gets Probation
Boy, 10, Accused of Murder in 1-Year-Old's Beating Death
Sylmar Boy, 14, Confesses He Shot Student for Backpack
Sister Held for Attempted Murder of Grandfather
Child Gives Another AIDS, NBC Reports
Boy, 12, Charged with Murder in Watts Slaying
Student Sentenced to Camp in Poisoning of Teacher
15-Year-Old Pleads Guilty in Pizza Deliverer's Slaying
Girl, 12, Sentenced to 20 Years in Fatal Beating of Child
Pupils Add Rat Poison to Teacher's GatorAde
Autistic Boy, 12, Arrested in Fatal Beating of Toddler
Boy, 6, Charged with Trying to Murder Baby
12-Year-Old Boy Held in Rape of Cousin, 4

What does this indicate—that children are going berserk or that we need to relocate our idea of evil? "Are [these things] harbingers of more preteen predators, children whom society should fear?" asks the

Los Angeles Times.[36] Professor John DiIulio believes there is a wave of superpredators coming, that the system "is not punitive *enough,*" that we have a "demographic time bomb" ticking away in the cellar.[37] *Newsweek* warns of "The Lull before the Storm," and *Time,* stealing DiIulio's metaphor, says, "Now for the Bad News: A Teenage Time Bomb."[38] Sentencing laws get tougher and more ingenious as children are tried and punished as adults—and worse. Colorado institutes a boot camp for young offenders, and California's attorney general says we should give up on rehabilitation ("it hasn't worked very well") and get down to the business of "reintroducing shame," publishing the names of any juveniles arrested for felonies, for urban violence, and for writing graffiti.[39] Perhaps we need to hear all this, need to stick monstrosity onto the child so we can pretend that, after all, it's the child himself who is the source of the pain that is visited on him. It's spanking with the stakes raised: it's what they've been asking for and deserve, a sound prison sentence, an old-fashioned trip to the electric chair. "No, Danny can't come out and play. Danny's on death row," a mother says in a terrific Mankoff *New Yorker* cartoon published August 4, 1997.

One especially gruesome case, the 1993 murder of a toddler in Liverpool, England, by two ten-year-old boys, gave us and the British a chance to talk about "inexplicable acts of evil." Such sonorous horror-show pronouncements rule out any other explanations for the crime.[40] With two demons on their hands, the British turned into a mob, screaming, "Kill the bastards" at their arraignment and conducting a spectacle-trial that made O. J. Simpson's theater look sedate. The murdered child's family joined in, the uncle calling a talk show to say he would kill the suspects, and the father adding, "One day they will be out of jail, and I'll be waiting for them."

Of course, the point is not that the grieving family would lose control but that the general public would do so, would unleash such hatred onto its children. Why do we need to do this? As Jesse Jackson says, "If you see a lot of children in the streets of Brazil shot down or shooting each other down, we say something is wrong with society. If that happens in Washington, New York, or urban America, we say something's wrong with the children."[41]

What are the facts here? What lies behind the common perception that juveniles are out of control, that their violence has reached new heights, that courts are soft on them, that we need more prisons, longer sentences, some get-tough all around? We get so tough we rush to execute junior-high students. "No other nation," Michael A. Males says, "puts juveniles to death"; but we have executed 300, 125 of them sixteen or younger, almost all of them black. Now, it's true that until a few years ago Pakistan, Rwanda, Bangladesh, and Barbados executed youths also, although never at our rate. But they have stopped, leaving us alone on the field.[42]

According to 1994 studies conducted by the National Council on Crime and Delinquency (NCCD), contrary to our "gut instincts," "juvenile crime, including violence, has not only not risen substantially, but also, by some indicators, has actually declined." By the end of 1995, all indicators, all official statistics, showed an even more precipitous drop in juvenile crime (even in juvenile arrests). Arrest rates for juvenile murderers, for instance, dropped 15.2 percent between 1994 and 1995, and 22.8 percent between 1993 and 1995.[43] The demographic projections of a future filled with child demons and superpredator toddlers has been shown to be "phony," "absolute hogwash" based on "faulty arithmetic and conceptual sloppiness."[44] But do we notice—or care?

As for courts being soft on delinquents, the NCCD's research shows that conviction rates in juvenile courts are often higher than in adult criminal courts, with punishments no more lenient and in some instances harsher. Arrest statistics "considerably overstate the true level of violent criminal behavior attributable to juveniles," since juveniles who do commit crimes tend to do so in groups. Much more significant, though, is what the council terms our "gut instincts" and how little these are troubled by facts. The report adds that though there simply is no crisis in juvenile violence directed toward adults, there certainly is a crisis the other way around: "America's youth are being killed in record numbers"—and not by gangs but, overwhelmingly, by parents and guardians.[45] The suicide rate among ten- to fourteen-year-old children rose 120 percent between 1980 and 1993.[46] Even the author of the sensational Kids Who Kill admits that the homicidal "kids" of his title are almost all in their late teens and that more than twice as many juveniles "kill themselves than kill others."[47]

The perception that we are about to be overwhelmed by young superpredators remains; ask anyone. Even white-collar kid criminals (as computer hackers) are projected: IBM runs a frightening ad that screams "Will a 14-year-old SOCIOPATH bring my company to its knees?"[48] Who is conjuring forth these demons? We seem always to need enemies, and we are in danger, as Robert Goodwin says, of making our children "the ultimate enemy." Pointing to "a tremendous increase in images of violent children" starting about spring 1993, Goodwin speculates that this barrage reflects "a basic assumption that most of the violence and illicit sexuality in society may be located in children."[49] The idea appears unthinkable when put in this form, but we don't put it in this form; and so we can think it and act on it.[50]

Tales of Resentment

Demon children did not, of course, suddenly appear in 1993; we have been concocting them for a long time and for a variety of purposes. I do think, though, that earlier demons may have functioned primarily to give an edge to erotic naughtiness, a fake sense of risk and danger. The current stories seem to have lost the campy sophistication that marks *The Exorcist* and *The Omen,* going now for images of the truly murderous. But this tradition of demonizing is never benign; it is not one that, in any form, bodes well for our children, and I do not wish to overstress recent deviations from it. From the start, it has played to our sense that kids have more than one foot in the nether world and may pull us into it if we give them the chance. Ads for John Carpenter's successful movie *Halloween* show, in front of the masked face of the adult Michael Myers, the beautiful child in the clown costume, the real killer. In this shot the child (the model is a girl) fades into the sharp, gleaming knife wielded by Myers, the point of dazzling light on the knife falling, surely not by accident, on the child's crotch. The bogeyman "Michael Myers Lives!" says the banner, lives as the demonic child within.

There is often a touch of the demonic even in adorable kids: Alice tries unsentimentally to decode Wonderland in terms of who eats whom, and Peter Pan is not only completely without conscience but "heartless," absolutely self-absorbed. And there is also a strain of anti-Romantic baby hating in our literary tradition: W. C. Fields picked up the classic assault on baby worship from Trollope, George Eliot,

The demon child is also beautiful.

and Samuel Butler. But all this amounts to a few light jabs compared with the knockout bolo punches aimed at the child by *A High Wind in Jamaica* and *The Lord of the Flies*. In *Jamaica,* the children are said to be reptilian in their emotional sensitivities, which means they feel nothing at all: the death of a "much-loved" adult excites in them only cold curiosity. Ruthless pirates are no match for creatures whose innocence exists only as a sentimental costume draped on them by adults, like lace on a cobra. And Golding's Wordsworth-upside-down is familiar to all: these boys do not trail clouds of glory but a smog of sulphur. Once released from adult control, they have nothing left but their nature, which is a black pit. At the end, the hero weeps "for the end of innocence, the darkness of man's heart," but there was no innocence to begin with, only the restraints applied by grown-ups. The darkness is not inside the men but in the boys.

Aggression against children gets even fuller play in films, where children are often cast as beasts to be slaughtered. Neil Sinyard speculates that the popularity of the *Nightmare on Elm Street* films stems from the fact that "at last, somebody is killing off those appalling American screen brats that audiences have had to put up with for so long."[51] Of course, we assembled and put those appalling brats there

McCormack's eyes match the insane purposiveness of Charles Manson's.

in the first place, precisely so we could prepare the way for Freddie Krueger's exemplary progress: from child molester to child killer. In any case, Sinyard captures (and perhaps shares) the glee with which we greet the massacre of the innocents, made a little less innocent so that we *can* massacre them.

An excellent example of this progression is the way Warner Brothers (in 1956) altered the ending of Maxwell Anderson's *The Bad Seed* to give audiences the child snuffing they wanted. In the shocker ending played on Broadway, vicious little Rhoda (Patty McCormack) foils her mother's plan to extinguish both of them (and thereby the defective seed), survives while her mother dies, and fiendishly winks at the audience afterward, making them complicit with her killings. Warner Brothers, knowing audiences would rather squash the child than join it, has Rhoda struck down from Above: a bolt of lightning sizzles her for good (I'm not making this up). And in a brilliant fillip, the filmmakers call the cast back for bows at the end and give us a domestic version of God's vengeance: the actress Nancy Kelly (playing the mother) yanks McCormack over her knee and gives her a spanking, a good spanking. Righteous murder, righteous sex, righteous voyeurism: the earthworm-level camera shoots straight up the child's dress.[52]

Rhoda's homicidal demonism is explained by some creaky idea of inherited madness, a version of the old Gothic "tainted blood" infecting the House of Usher and many another aristocratic lineage. These explanations are often a cover, usually a very thin cover, to allow us to go straight for the child without hesitating. As R. S. Prawer says of *The Omen,* "The gusto with which films like [this] wish for the child's destruction has something deeply suspect about it." He wonders further if there isn't a tie between the way we are being manipulated here and "the disturbing use made of child actors in pornographic films?"[53] There is something slippery in the way Prawer sidles from one scapegoat to another and resists blaming the audience. But he does draw up the crucial equation: the wish for the child's death is directly connected to our wish to possess the child. Watching these films can provide excuses to rip at the child. Children are said to be possessed (*The Innocents* [1961], *The Exorcist* [1973]), Satan himself (*Rosemary's Baby* [1968], *The Omen* [1976]), inexplicably taken over (*Village of the Damned* [1960, 1995], *The Shining* [1980], *Carrie* [1975]), sucked on by vampires (*The Lost Boys* [1987]), buried in sour ground (*Pet Sematary* [1989]), or liable to turn into panthers (*Cat People* [1982]).

More hostile still are movies that remove the disguise, wasting no time explaining why these kids are rotten. They just are. *The Innocents* flirts with this bluntness in a particularly spooky way, but many films don't bother flirting. *The Children's Hour* (1961) is an example of amoral, vicious youth who like being vicious and amoral, as are many motorcycle gang and juvenile delinquent movies of the fifties—*Blackboard Jungle* (1955), for instance, giving Vic Morrow a delightful opportunity to play to two primal feelings at once, justifying by his sullen, untamable rage our homicidal Laius/Jocasta complexes and also working out for kids an active fantasy of teacher murder.

Recent films of bad kids have generally been more simpleminded. *The Bad Seed* was remade with Blair Brown, and the 1992 *Mikey* uses as its killer a male version of sweet innocence, Brian Bonsall, fresh from being cute on *Family Ties*. *The Good Son* (1994) kills off the bad seed, and so does *Poison Ivy* (1992), in which the seducing, murdering, bourgeois family-wrecking Drew Barrymore gets hers. The *Halloween* films not only pulverize the horrid kid but find a way to do it again and again. The killer child here is made into the bogeyman, a litotes that marks a parable for our time. Finally, I might mention films that use direct substitutes, fetish or voodoo dolls for us to smash: the *Child's Play* series, in which "Chucky" the doll is both a child's toy and a child himself.[54]

Who Cares?

Playing off against (and supporting) this operatic spectacle of high Cs and murder is a blank indifference to the fate of children. When we want to indict the child we accuse it of being unfeeling; but I wonder if those charges are not projections. We may be so busy with our fantasies of adorable and demonic children, with exercising and denying our erotic nostalgia, that real-life children strike us as tiresome, hardly even there.

We value children very little. That's a crude statement, but why should the Dow Jones average soar and the situation of children become worse and worse? Between 1985 and 1995 the number of children living below the poverty line grew by 26 percent, now numbering one child in four; the population of poor kids under age six boomed—up 43 percent.[55] The most popular way of dealing with poor kids seems to be to put them in prison. We fix our eyes on sexual abuse, a comparatively minor problem, because it pleases us to talk about it. Meanwhile, about 2,000 children a year die in America from physical abuse and neglect, and 160,000 are seriously injured.[56] "Father Accused of Shocking Two Sons," using an electrified dog collar on them for refusing to exercise, says the article.[57] Emotional abuse is so widespread that we hardly bother to study it; and neglect, which accounts for the largest number by far of child abuse cases, is also almost certainly the most underreported.[58]

Across the world, some progress has been made in education and in fighting disease; but the condition of children is so needlessly catastrophic that you would think our concerns might stretch to include it. UNICEF says 10 million children will be orphaned by AIDS by the year 2000. Thirteen million children died in 1992, most of them from easily preventable diseases; diarrhea, curable with a cheap packet of oral rehydration salts, kills 1.5 million a year. Perhaps 1 billion children face malnutrition or starvation, disease and death, "mainly because we can't mobilize what we need to help them," says Dr. Charles McCormack, president of Save the Children. One and a half million children died in wars in the last decade; 4 million others were disabled, maimed, or brain-damaged. Child labor scandals are commonplace.[59] Apart from Norway and Sweden, no society in the world has taken any steps to recognize formally the rights of children.[60] Perhaps we feel they have none. Perhaps it seldom occurs to us to wonder.

When we do formally consider children's rights, it seems clear to us that even fundamental guarantees (the Constitution, say) are meant for "free adults," that is, for people, not children. The Supreme Court recently (June 26, 1995) declared breezily that the Fourth Amendment (on illegal search and seizure) does not apply to kids and that it is not necessary to have any kind of "individualized suspicion" to justify having any number of schoolchildren strip and pee. As long as we can tell ourselves we are hereby protecting innocence, we have no particular reason to suppose we may be imperiling it. Thus, following Justice Antonin Scalia's reasoning (for the majority), "communal undress" is not a violation of privacy; it's "for their own good," like spankings and religion. Scalia stressed that it wasn't just a matter of drug testing but of children's rights generally, that children possess only limited constitutional rights, having ceded them to parents and "to the temporary custody of the state as schoolmaster."[61] Children cannot be expected to know the world, their place in it, or what's good for them, the Court and country feel, so the issue of rights is moot. We'll take care of all that.

In this country, as many as two million children are homeless—runaways or throwaways. Throwaways. Speaking of kids and sex, the Office of Human Development Services estimated in 1989 that there were about 900,000 juvenile prostitutes in the United States. That was nearly ten years ago, and it's unlikely that there has been a decrease in the number of homeless kids or in the high percentage of those using their bodies to survive since then.[62]

Here are some of their voices:

I quit doing it and haven't done it in a year. I did it from thirteen to just before my seventeenth birthday. And I quit doing it. I don't see the sense in doing it again. I became more mature in my ways and stopped acting like a child. (Henry, seventeen years old)

There's a thirteen-year-old out there, he's been doing it for six months. I saw him in girl's clothes last night. I can see a seventeen-year-old, but thirteen!!! (Greg, seventeen years old)

I am glad I don't have to do it no more. It's dangerous. We traveled around in two's and we divided the money up evenly. Kids need love and understanding and a place to stay and some food to eat. (Nikki, nineteen years old)

I am experiencing the older side of life before I get there. I definitely know what it's like to be older before I'm older. I think kids need someone to love them. (Willie, sixteen years old)

If the kids are out there too long, their attitudes change. They lose everything they own, sometimes they lose their lives or their sanity or their virginity or whatever. (Bob, seventeen years old)

I don't feel safe all the time. It's scary. It's scarier at night. (Paul, fourteen years old)

If I ever grow up and get money, I'd give money to the shelters because I think they do a good job. They feed you and you sleep every night and you don't have to worry about where to go to sleep and there's people to talk to. You don't have to worry about not having friends. (Keith, fifteen years old)

Loving Them to Death

A spectacular 1994 murder in South Carolina, where a mother drove two little boys into a lake and then tried to blame it on an invented African American abductor in a stocking cap, sent the country into a short-term tizzy. These were white kids, and cute; and the old joke, quoted by *Time,* was that "God made them cute so we wouldn't kill them."[63] But cute is, first of all, in the eye of the cute maker; and, second, God doesn't do any child a favor by conferring cuteness, since the amount of homicidal rage directed at the child seems to be directly proportionate to its allure.

The question is why should we make such a fuss about this case when about thirteen hundred other children are murdered each year by parents or caretakers?[64] For the same reason, I suppose, that we focus on stranger kidnappings: it makes the actual problem seem to disappear. When we can be shocked at a single incident, it as much as assures us that such a thing is an anomaly. But the size of the problem indicates otherwise, as do suspicions that as many as fifteen hundred of the eight thousand SIDS deaths each year may actually be parental homicides.[65] Enough tiny children are shaken to death by their parents to justify the creation of a syndrome, "shaken baby syndrome," which can cause blindness, paralysis, severe brain damage, uncontrollable seizures, and, about two hundred times a year, death.[66]

Why do mothers and fathers kill their babies and young children? According to experts interviewed on NPR's *All Things Considered* (April 19, 1994), the reason is stress, linked to "being a single mom," "having no phone," "poor natal care," and "marital problems": "It could happen to anyone; anyone that has enough stress in their life may just lash out at their child and really want to do it." Since "enough stress in their life" is the same thing as having a life, this is not so much a diagnosis as an admission that we have constructed children as objects of an attraction so great and so inadmissible that homicide is one of the few solutions available to us.

If not homicide, then torture, which doesn't solve the problem but perhaps relieves the "stress." A man in Los Angeles who beat three children throughout an entire night until one of them died was said by the police to have "been putting these kids through some pretty significant torture,"[67] which I guess distinguishes it from routine torture. "You guys are so unfair!" screamed Donna Jo Artis when a Pennsylvania court sentenced her to two to ten years for beating her three-year-old son until he was lame, blind, and deaf.[68] A woman who seared her ten-year-old nephew's tongue with a hot knife and sodomized him with a baseball bat, Uncle Edward all the while in the next room watching television, was said by her attorney to be "lacking in parenting skills." After all, he said, "you walk over to Juvenile Hall and you'll see a hundred of these cases."[69]

The *Los Angeles Times* published the following letter on May 29, 1995, under the heading "Parent Responsibility":

> As a responsible parent I promise that if my kids start hanging around with a gang, or tagger crew or dance crew or whatever the disgusting little perverts call themselves, I will personally kick their butts. If I find that my children have participated in a group beating, I will take them outside and demonstrate the concept of pain. And if I ever find that my children have been involved in a killing, I will shoot them dead like the wild dogs they would be.

So, what's the point? First, we seem to be repelled by what attracts us, as are classic obsessive-compulsives who are so drawn to dirt that they cannot keep from washing. Martha Grace Duncan has applied this model brilliantly to analyze our complex love affair with the criminals we abhor,[70] a fitting parallel, no doubt, with children in our culture. But behind the obsessive-compulsive drive is a muddled confusion about our own lost childhoods, our fantasies and wishes, our cultural fables, all those pretty images, all those erotic dreams—and the real thing, which gets in the way, the child before us. We may be so caught up with children-in-the-head, to borrow from D. H. Lawrence, that children-in-bone-and-blood enrage us or fail altogether to come into view. Look, Ma, no hands! Who cares?

6. Myths, Legends, Folktales, and Lies

Whoever fights monsters should see
to it that in the process he does not
become a monster. —Nietzsche

Men never do evil so completely and
cheerfully as when they do it from
religious conviction. —Pascal

Fear of serious injury cannot alone
justify suppression of free speech and
assembly. Men feared witches and
burned women. It is the function of
speech to free men from the bond-
age of irrational fears. —Justice Louis
Brandeis

All the wild witches, those most noble
     ladies,
For all their broomsticks and their
     tears,
Their angry tears, are gone.
—W. B. Yeats

This is a chapter about alien abductions, the kiddie porn industry, satanic sacrifices, kidnapping rings, and monsters in the media. In another age it would have been about demonic possession, the influence of planetary motion, lands where dragons roam, and ether waves. Of course, it's not at all surprising that we have gentle legends, both urban and rural, and all manner of deranged stories and explanations hanging on to a weak existence simply because we are used to them and can't bring ourselves to disown them. Like my belief that killer bees (common in my neighborhood, despite official denials) will not attack me if I walk softly and carry no stick, mild stories live because we have some affable need of them and because we give them just enough oxygen. We generally let them out only at night, when we're alone. We protect ourselves from their full seductive force by employing our skepticism, our sense of the probable, our trust in moderate rationality, our tendency to think pretty much the same thing as our neighbor, our knowledge that nothing causes as much widespread distress as credulity.

But when it comes to child sexuality, we seem to have plunged into a 1990s credulity bath, where we're content to remain. Common sense isn't a great thing, but it's something; and skepticism is better; but exercising the two now makes one liable to prosecution.[1] Where is the tale about child sexuality and its enemies preposterous enough to be disbelieved? When Roman Polanski made *Rosemary's Baby*, he probably didn't conceive of it as a documentary; but it now looks like a slice of real life. Actually, Rosemary's satanic enemies are polite Gray Panthers who want fresh breeding stock, nothing to compare with today's hell-on-earth types who torture, murder, and eat their victims. These infernals from below join in attack with aliens from above, swooping in from other galaxies to plunge needles into us and do experiments that absolutely always seem to involve sex. Intergalactians and Satan's legions are both, no surprise, after children.

These folktales take such extraordinary forms, I believe, because our wild panic on the subject of children and sex effectively rules out moderation and reason. Both we and our children find ourselves in impossible situations: we make the child serve as the image both of what we desire and of what is altogether outside desire. But that is not our only dilemma. The erotic attraction to innocence is both forbidden (and thus, to some degree, forcibly repressed or at least denied) and so idealized as to be largely a fantasy attraction, cerebral lechery. And that, though it may sound like a protection, actually causes us additional problems: (a) since desire is so largely compounded of fantasy and so longs for its own perpetuation, the fantastic nature of our adorable child feeds the desire and makes it grow; (b) the fantasy can become so powerful it forgets it's fantasy; and (c) the fantasy creates images and expectations so unreal they make our children easier to hate than to prize.

I think this escalating ambivalence toward children, along with the unresolved and unacknowledged sexual tension we have loaded onto them, makes our stories about them increasingly outlandish. We become shrill, reaching back to myths of fiends in order to buy, through storytelling, some sanctity for ourselves. These are tales, always, about the tellers and their purity, a swelling purity that is able to (and must) confront Satan and alien galactic terrors. As the tension mounts for us, we haul to the surface daydreams and fears we once employed only for private entertainment. Nightmares are put into service as reality.

This chapter is about our flight from skepticism and urbanity, our rush for self-protection. Our wildest stories gain currency when tests of rational probability are suspended in favor of anecdote and testimony, supported by the demand that we accept narratives as valid if we cannot positively prove they are not. In our current version of the unanswerable, we are asked to accept testimonials as the final word: solid, not obviously demented people say aliens or satanists came and got them, and who are we to say it didn't happen? You had to have been there. If you withhold your enthusiasm you are suspect, may be in cahoots with the enemy. It takes one to doubt one.

How did we ever get ourselves into such a fix? Not, I suggest, by loving children but by being so perplexed by our heritage and the way it has constructed our feelings that we have mixed up love and power, have made a monster out of innocence, and have become so terrified by our children that we give them roles in the most dangerous stories of all, fairy tales. These are all twisted romances in which the villains love the children while the virtuous spurn them.

Legends are made to shield the legend makers, not the subjects of the stories. In particular, those stories known to folklorists as "subversion myths" arise from great social tension and a perceived threat to individual security; when such anxieties are collective and accompanied by a general will to believe, then anxiety-fed legends appear. Interestingly, such legends, by focusing anxieties on a specific threat and providing thereby a very simple explanation, do not so much ease the fear as give it fuel: "fear-provoking rumors both satisfy the need to reduce uncertainty and provoke even more anxiety."[2] The idea is not to erase the anxiety but to excite it, since it's the anxiety itself that is doing so much for us.

The Multi-Billion-Dollar Kiddie Porn Industry

We imagine that we have cause to believe, that reasons exist somewhere, that evidence shows, that the FBI confirms, that only criminals would deny—that kiddie porn is an international industry of gigantic proportions. According to Carl Raschke's *Painted Black,* "it has been estimated that there are at present about 300,000 children shackled to the taskmasters of 'kiddie porn,'" taskmasters who belong to "syndicates" who offer children to be passed around like "after-dinner mints" before they are "snuffed." Ellen Bass and Laura Davis don't mention the mints or snuff films, but they put the number of children involved in prostitution and pornography at between 500,000 and 1,000,000. Senator Strom Thurmond reports "a growing market" for kiddie porn, produced by drugging the children or buying them from unscrupulous parents.[3] The California Department of Justice, perhaps unsettled by such estimating, admits it is "impossible to make an exact assessment of the number of children in California who have been the victims of pornographic exploitation." And having said that, flies off into the murk too: "It is clear that by even the most conservative estimate, the number is alarmingly high."[4] Who would dare offer an estimate that was anything but alarming?

Doubters, and they do exist, are often accused of being molesters themselves, among those who profit, says Mike Lew, "from the sexual exploitation of children and who have created a multimillion dollar pornography and child sex industry and a powerful 'pro-incest lobby.'"[5] When we start entertaining seriously the notion that a pro-incest lobby exists, it is easy to start seeing horned hellhounds. But even the government bobs along, perhaps cynically, on this watery nonsense: President Clinton says he thinks there is a "scourge of child pornography" justifying "the broadest possible protections," and Attorney General Janet Reno says pornography includes not only the baby-on-the-bearskin-rug but clothed children too, if the images are "lascivious," lasciviousness being a quality the attorney general knows is perfectly clear to the average citizen.[6]

We could extend this carnival of myth-making forever, and that seems to be our plan, as we enter the thrilling world of cyberporn, a world without limits, and maybe unpoliceable. That doesn't stop us from policing it, of course, or at least talking about doing so, which is as good. In May 1995, Los Angeles filed its first criminal complaint alleging the downloading of kiddie porn from the net to a personal computer. The city attorney issued a statement saying that child porn and the children's access to sex on the net "is becoming an increasing problem," a problem met head-on in my town when police detective William Dworin, "posing as a pedophile," got into a net conversation with a man, made sure one thing led to another, produced when the time was right a search warrant, and then uncovered thirty-six downloaded instances of "child pornography" and forty-five of "child erotica."[7] In May 1995 the Senate banned smut from all on-line networks, imposing stiff penalties and never you mind how this can be enforced, adding to the bill at the last minute a demand that all servers restrict children's access, require age verification, and generally watch their step.[8]

By June, everyone was talking about the "two troubled teenagers" who, "lured from their homes by computer pen pals, simply "vanish[ed] into cyberspace," as *Newsweek* put it.[9] There was a lot more ink flowing about pedophiles on the net, how wily they are, and how we should pass some laws before things get worse.

It turns out there's no real evidence that pedophiles are using the net in this way, that they are having any success if they are, or that the talk is anything more than the usual alarmist titillation. The two troubled teenagers were lured in one case by another teenager ("it turns out, not a pedophile," *Newsweek* reluctantly admitted), and in the other by a boyfriend. Still, the principle's the same, and the talk does a lot for us.

Sensing this, both *Time* and *Newsweek* expanded this nonissue the next month into a huge spread. On July 3 *Time* ran a stunning cover of a wild-eyed blond child at a keyboard, cheeks flushed and mouth open (the better to pant with), staring in alarm (or fascination) straight out at us. The cover yells "CYBERPORN" and asks, "Can we protect our kids—and free speech?" The inside story, as usual, is so much calmer as to be contradictory. It cites a Carnegie-Mellon study showing that pornography is popular, makes money, is ubiquitous, is "a guy thing," and has a very wide range of subjects beyond naked women. Surprise! Researchers also found nothing on the internet that is not also in adult bookstores, and discovered that children are unlikely to gain access to such on-line material without trying very hard and using considerable skill: "If you don't want them you won't get them," says one sixteen-year-old who wants them. The article goes on to point out that there is no evidence that pedophiles are a danger to internet users or that they can be controlled if they become so. The overall tone is fairly moderate—but the cover does its job.[10] By the next week, *Time* was publishing letters from readers saying things like, "If we lose our kids to Cyberporn, free speech won't matter." [11] *Newsweek* missed out on the cover, but (same date) gave us a full six pages with a dullish come-on ("NO PLACE FOR KIDS? A Parent's Guide to Sex on the Net") and a terrific graphic, a blond boy gazing (longingly?) out at us through an imaginative list of alt.sex.titles (lingerie, spanking, masturbation, redhead). The article itself musters no alarming anecdotes and little indignation; but this species of pornobabble will mature, we know. Decency-on-the-net censoring legislation may have some temporary problems in the courts, but we are just getting started.

alt.sex.erotica.pornstar
alt.sex.erotica.redhead
alt.sex.fetish.orientals
alt.sex.fetish.shoes
alt.sex.girlfriends
alt.sex.homosexual
alt.sex.lingerie
alt.sex.magazines
alt.sex.masturbation
alt.sex.pictures.female
alt.sex.pictures.male
alt.sex.spanking
alt.sex.strip-clubs
alt.sex.telephone
alt.sex.voyeurism

The choice of shudder-inducing sites is not without wit: "magazines" is especially impressive.

At some point (right now) we need to inquire about the basis for these legends. If we look for studies of the actual material, the kiddie porn itself, we find nothing, since it is against the law to look at what may exist, much less own it. The distinguished sex researcher Vern L. Bullough reports somewhat wryly on how it is that we are kept from knowing anything at all about what we know so much about, and recounts the sad stories of a few professors who tried to do research in the subject and found themselves arrested for their pains.[12] Even in terms of the effects of such activities on the children involved, "there is no concrete empirical evidence" relating to the subject and nothing more than an "experts tend to believe" basis for the oft-repeated idea that pornography is a permanent record,[13] therefore permanently damaging, and that the abuse is repeated every time someone looks at such an image. This last notion, though widespread, also seems a little pathological, a confusion of image and subject usually found only in fixated voyeurs. But we hold it as if it were both healthy and true.

Myths, Legends, Folktales, and Lies   171

Even more widespread is the idea that such pornography is used by pedophiles to heighten their desire, that it leads to molestation, when "such evidence as exists, in fact, tends to deny the possibility of a connection between child pornography and abusive behavior." Many pedophiles may have viewed it, but "most researchers now believe that an interest in child pornography follows, rather than precedes, a sexual interest in children."[14]

The issue is not why scientific studies, or the absence of them, have not penetrated the public consciousness, but why we want to believe unlikely things in order to justify telling stories of denial, projection, and misplaced eroticism. We manage, for instance, prolonged government hearings which produce so much indignation that evidence is superfluous. In 1984, when there may still have been some commercially produced erotica of children, Senate hearings on "Child Pornography and Pedophilia," chaired by William V. Roth Jr., gave us customs officials and postal inspectors who, along with President Reagan, believed we were fighting not so much for children as for "the Nation's moral health." These witnesses, cheered along by Roth—"You are doing an enormous service in an area that is unbelievable"—told us what was plain already but can never be said too often: "As you know, Amsterdam is sort of the 1984 version of Sodom and Gomorrah." The commissioner of customs spoke with assurance of "a shocking cause and effect relationship between child molesting and child pornography," and a chief postal inspector, battling the idea that maybe there wasn't really all that much kiddie porn, said, "Its pervasiveness is evident in the number of investigations we have undertaken."[15] Such moonshine drifts up to us from a decade ago and still excites neither laughter nor outrage.

It hardly matters that there is no commercial kiddie porn being produced now in the United States. Let's say that: none, no kiddie porn at all. I'll let the exaggeration sit there a minute for health reasons before qualifying it. There is doubtless a cottage industry of sorts, a wary trading of photos and old magazines back and forth among a small number of people.[16] And there is the government, happily producing publications for sting operations,[17] sharing them, for all I know, with law enforcement people in your town and mine. A police seminar I attended at the University of Southern California in 1990 gave details of these publications and announced with pride that they were the only ones left in the field: only the government was producing and distributing child pornography.[18] The North American Man-Boy Love Association warns its members, "Save Your Life—Don't Try to Buy Child Porn," pointing out that all ads for such material are entrapment devices and that only police agents are working the field these days.[19] The police alone have access to this material; and, judging by my local paper, they are the ones acquiring a taste for it and being arrested for stashing it away.[20]

The survival of kiddie porn stories does not depend on the existence of kiddie porn, of cartels and rings and industries; the tales are independent of them. My own view is that our need to talk about these things so far outruns any cause to believe in them as to blot out reason entirely. We don't need kiddie porn to exist in order to get mad about it, investigate it, ban it, arrest people for having it, and wonder what on earth other people see in such filth.

Alien Abductions

If the existence of commercial child pornography and snuff films are urban legends that won't go away,[21] stories of visitations from molesting space aliens lay claim to even greater respectability. Dr. John E. Mack, Pulitzer Prize–winning author, prominent Harvard psychiatrist, and founder of the prestigious psychiatry department at Cambridge Hospital, says reports of such abductions by space creatures are accurate, that aliens are indeed intervening in our business, particularly our reproductive business, and that we should stop denying it. Dr. Mack's *Abduction: Human Encounters with Aliens* is a book so intelligent and calm, albeit resting entirely on testimonials, that it raises storytelling from the pages of cheap tabloids to the high plane of scientific meetings and academic journals.[22]

Mack points not only to the physical evidence of abductions (which he admits is a little frail) but also to the large number of such reports (mostly produced under hypnosis) from "experiencers" of sound mind, and to their consistency: all give the same report, tell the same story. This story is a story of sex, overwhelmingly, and of children: the aliens beam people up to undress them and set them on tables, so as

Aliens look a little like pin-up children in a carnival mirror: note the eyes and chin.

to penetrate them with things, conduct experiments, remove sperm samples, fertilize eggs, and raise, Mack says, "hybrid babies," along with "older hybrid children, adolescents, and adults, which they are told by the aliens or know intuitively are their own." These are stories about taking over our children, and though Mack regards these encounters as fundamentally benign and merciful, he admits many of the experiencers see them as "rapelike." Children themselves are often lifted up and tampered with, so often that experts before Mack identified such episodes with child molesting, satanic or secular.[23] Mack, however, partly because he is committed to the aliens' environmental program (which matches, point for point, his own), believes the children are not being molested but healed of the effects of molestation.

Not everyone is convinced that any part of Dr. Mack's argument is anything more than hokum. Hypnosis, some point out, can be used to convert fantasy into belief. No one has seen any hybrids, implants, photos, or really convincing souvenirs. The descriptions of aliens and their crafts change to match the novels and movies that are currently circulating. The news provided to us by what Dr. Mack insists are advanced and beneficent aliens is depressingly banal, entirely void of helpful tips, a new morality, or scientific wonder. And why, if they're so anxious to help, are they such sneaks, working with wires in the brains and impregnations rather than through prime-time television and radio talk shows?[24] But Mack's book does offer, as its *Atlantic Monthly* reviewer shrewdly points out, "the enticing possibility of debate unencumbered by fact."[25]

Mack's most sophisticated argument is that the phenomena under discussion cannot be investigated within the limits of our language, that our crude binary system is not simply inadequate but makes invisible (or absurd) what could be transforming. He says thinking of things as " 'true' or 'false' may restrict what we can learn" from these experiences.[26] That seems to me a winning point, though it's a point his detractors have ignored. I think it's not a question of whether these encounters take place but of how and why we speak of them and why they generate such heat. It's not truth or falsehood, in this sense, that is at issue but the stories we form and the investments we make in these stories. I don't really suppose we need visitors from the back of beyond to convince us that we are locked into binaries or that the stories we tell serve something beyond simple truth. Still, if they can help, I welcome them, though I draw the line at being probed or asked to father hybrids, even if I did know (as I would—intuition) which were mine.

Satanic Abuse

The will to believe is here the strongest, and may come easier to us, Satan having more credibility than space aliens—so much credibility, in fact, that the number of his believers rose from 37 percent in 1964 to nearly 60 percent in 1990,[27] and to 66 percent in 1995, moving Satan ahead of the Loch Ness monster and a live Elvis on the charts. Sixty-one percent of evangelical Protestants say they know the Devil exists because they have been tempted directly by him. That sampling may seem selective, but 37 percent of the general population reports similar archfiend encounters.[28] I propose that Satan's spectacular showing can be traced to the transfer of his story to children and child sexuality. So long as he was after the souls of businessmen and politicians, he struggled to maintain the grudging loyalty of barely a third of the population, and that third, you can bet, the most redneck-poor and downmarket—lousy demographics. Now, however, he has the young professionals, suburban Republicans, health-care workers, and

Christian moderates by the throat. He managed this turnaround by boldly redrawing his whole act, ditching the Faustian stage effects and emerging as the pattern child molester, which is where belief is at.

Recent satanic cult worries started to grow with the murderous activities of the Manson family in the 1960s and early 1970s, fed by rumors of cattle mutilations and other animal sacrifices. But it was the 1980 publication of *Michelle Remembers* that gave us our current quick spin. The same year saw accusations aimed at the Proctor and Gamble logo, expanding to encompass games (Dungeons and Dragons), books (*The Wizard of Oz*, school texts), and, especially, day-care centers. Jeffrey Victor's *Satanic Panic* summarizes sixty-two important North American rumor panics between 1982 and 1992 and gives details of twenty criminal cases between 1983 and 1987, all involving charges of satanic child abuse and all but one resulting in nothing whatever, the one exception being a plea bargain Victor says was likely a mistake. Despite comprehensive searches, there is no evidence that a ritual featuring satanic child abuse has ever occurred in this country.[29]

No evidence at all, and yet there is "an epidemic," fed by and demanding more criminal charges, excited talk, and books—like Carl Raschke's *Painted Black,* Margaret Smith's *Ritual Abuse,* and a few dozen others.[30] Raschke is the source of the epidemic talk, but Smith and the others would not disagree. Smith cannot understand how anyone would be skeptical, since the stories, garnered from hypnotized survivors, show a remarkable consistency in terms of details of the abuse. She itemizes those for us: friends murdered in front of me, buried alive with freshly killed bodies and body parts, put in a hole with snakes, baby kittens put inside my rectum and vagina, used as a prize in a poker game, married to Satan. To demonstrate how common these events are, Smith gives a frequency-of-occurrence tabulation: only 4 percent of the victims were rented out to other cults, and only 10 percent were hung upside down; but 36 percent were induced to breed children who were later sacrificed; 75 percent were forced to torture others; 88 percent were sodomized or required to sodomize others, and the same percentage had to participate in human sacrifices; 96 percent had to join in group sex; and 100 percent experienced "molestation or intercourse."[31] Through such activities these groups are said to be absorbing the potency of children—possessing their bodies and sometimes (most often) killing and eating them. The latter accounts for the fact that no corpses ever turn up, despite there being, says the Cult Crime Impact Network, fifty thousand human sacrifices every year by satanic cults.[32]

That this may seem improbable is, insiders say, hard proof of its existence: ritual abuse hides itself precisely by being farfetched, thus enticing our worst enemy, denial. The California Social Services Committee on Child Abuse Prevention identified the pervasive "denial of the problem of ritualistic abuse" in our society as its number one problem.[33] Added to denial is trickery. Renee Fredrickson, writing about repressed memories, says, "If you have memories that could not possibly have happened, first consider trickery designed to instill doubt. Ritual abusers combine sadism with intelligence."[34]

This unbeatable logic is often presented even more aggressively. Margaret Smith opens her book with an attempt to disarm skeptics: "If there is even a small chance that one ritual abuse claim is true, we owe it to all potential victims to explore the problem of ritual abuse in greater depth."[35] Here's sweet reason and moderation for you, only the plea is neither reasonable nor moderate, since science and society cannot throw their limited resources and attention after remote possibilities. Of course there's "a small chance" that one of the thousands of claims contains some truth; there's also a small chance that I'll start at right guard next year for the Detroit Lions. Exploring problems in depth means granting the basis of the problems strong probability, erecting hypotheses that seem reasonable and likely to be productive; it means, in short, believing in them for a time, *belief* being just what the sly Smith wants to wring from us. The satanists have no corner on the trickery market.

And, sadly, neither do the fanatics. The ritual abuse myth often becomes twisted into a gender issue, which brings into the fray feminists of great talent with better things to do: In 1993, *Ms.* published "Surviving the Unbelievable, A First-Person Account of Cult Ritual Abuse," all about infant sacrifices (the decapitation of the author's sister among them) and so forth.[36] The author repeatedly says that the way to stamp out ritual abuse is to "believe that it exists": "If we want to stop ritual abuse, the first step is to believe these brutal crimes occur." Belief is made into a moral principle, as it so often is in these cases, disbelief being identified with depravity or with the abuse itself: "I began to see where the well-orchestrated flood of 'witch-hunt' accusations was originating: from the molesters themselves."[37]

Not all believers are fanatics, of course, which in my view makes things worse. My own home town, Los Angeles, for instance, facing flood, fire, earthquake, financial ruin, and general unpopularity, decided to invest its money in investigating ritual abuse, charging the Los Angeles County Commission for Women to create a special task force and issue a report. The result (September 1994) is an easy-to-read, patient, question-answering pamphlet of thirty-seven pages. The pamphlet will provide future generations with a digest of what passes for wisdom on this subject, all of it offered with a severe air of assurance, as if anything beside our need to believe stood behind the paragraphs on dissociation, Multiple Personality Disorder (MPD), post-traumatic stress disorder, children's disclosures (and how to get them), along with the usual lurid details on sexual molestation, cannibalism, and ritual gougings.

The opening paragraphs of the report are worth quoting for their reporting of legend as established fact, their ability to make officious bullying stand for reason:

> Ritual abuse is a serious and growing problem in our community and in our nation. Ritual abuse is not a new problem, but society is only just beginning to recognize the gravity and scope of this problem. We are all in need of education on this issue. Parents need to be educated about the hallmarks of this abuse occurring in preschools and day care centers. . . . The concept of ritual abuse, that groups of adults would terrorize and torture children in order to control them, is frightening and controversial, raising for all of us problems of denial and fear of the consequences of such information.
>
> Despite detailed evidence of ritual abuse coming from child victims and their families, from adult victims, and from the professionals working with them, and despite the remarkable consistency of these reports both nationally and internationally, society at large resists believing that ritual abuse really occurs.

There remains the mistaken belief that satanic and other cult activity is isolated and rare.[38]

Well, *I* do not believe organized satanic cult abuse is isolated and rare; I believe it doesn't exist at all. But again, its existence is not so much the issue here as is the expenditure of so much energy, time, and money on talk that is highly charged but just as highly redundant, that repeats with high-tribunal certainty what nobody knows and advances the dubious, even the preposterous, as if it were a set of truisms our duty as citizens compelled us to embrace.

There are, of course, books that point out that "there is no evidence whatsoever for the existence of groups of so-called Satanists which sexually abuse children," no evidence that satanic cults of any sort ever existed outside of medieval legend.[39] Other books point out that these stories depend on nothing more than testimony, that they resemble novels and television specials very closely (and actual historic rites not at all), and that there is no physical evidence to support any of the macabre claims.[40] A large-scale study of twelve thousand accusations conducted at the University of California, Davis, turned up "absolutely no evidence about large-scale satanic cults—nothing," though the researchers did note that most alleged ritual abuse survivors were being treated by 2 percent of the therapists (which might constitute a cult of another sort).[41] Even the FBI experts throw up their hands at the failure of repeated investigations to uncover anything and say it's in the hands of mental health people "to explain why victims are alleging things that don't seem to be true."[42]

That's one point of view: that we need to stay where we are, keep on "explaining" things. Turning things over to the mental health people will certainly ensure that the talking goes on. But such talk is not cheap. We sustain it at a dear cost to our children. It's possible that this discourse on aliens and Satan will by its very absurdity alert us to what we're doing, but only if we are inclined to feel the absurdity, bring it home to ourselves, and stop the scapegoating. The National Center on Child Sexual Abuse issued a careful survey of the satanic abuse issue in 1990, "Ritual Child Abuse: Understanding the Controversies." It concludes that "since we lack consensus" not only on the phenomenon but on the terms we are using to debate it, "it is likely that the controversies will continue." The report urges us all to "exercise our critical judgment in evaluating what we see and hear from those who deny the existence of ritual child abuse and those who claim it is widespread." This amounts to encouraging more conversation on the subject; and that is more bad news for the children. Why should we be asked to attend to this unseemly nonsense at all? Why draw our attention to rumors that offer satisfactions so unworthy that we should be ashamed to accept them, rumors that draw our attention away from those who do need our help? Children need saving, but not from the cannibals, the decapitators, or the long-fanged worshippers of Beelzebub.

Kidnappings and Abductions

Why do we devote so much energy, concern, and money, so much organizational skill, so many competing centers and foundations, so much legislative know-how, so much fear and repetitive talk to the most insignificant problem facing our children: the risk of being kidnapped by a stranger? Let's review the annual figures again: about 575,000 runaways (more than 20 percent of these are throwaways); 354,000 children abducted by family members;[43] about 1 million children suffering physical abuse, and 1.5 million neglect; 140,000 serious injuries; 2,000 murders; and 200–300 stereotypical kidnappings. So what explains our focus on the last category? We need to stop claiming that it is "natural" to concentrate there and entertain the possibility that by doing so we magnify that event and make it central, much as *Jaws* made huge sharks the central feature of swimming, even in inland lakes and ponds. By magnifying kidnappings and dwelling on them, we are able to exploit them much as we do our other legends: we create monsters to deflect our attention from our own desires; we avoid confronting the problems that actually do press on us; we are able to produce and circulate the details of child molesting not only with impunity but with righteous fervor.

In order to examine this particular legend a little more fully, I return to the case of Polly Klaas, the most difficult case of all, since it's horror seems so fully to justify any response we might want to parade before it. Twelve-year-old Polly Klaas was kidnapped from a slumber party at her mother's house in Petaluma, California, and murdered shortly thereafter, though her body was not found for more than two months. I am trying to make a distinction here between the kidnapping and murder of the young girl, and the stories we have told about that event, a distinction we seldom make, because it is in our best interests, we feel, to make it appear that our stories follow naturally on the catastrophe.

Thus Noelle Oxenhandler's *New Yorker* essay, "Polly's Face,"[44] deals almost not at all with Polly or her face and concentrates skillfully on those who like to make the stories and draw the face: the article has more first-person pronouns than most Protestant hymns. Oxenhandler brilliantly generalizes this luscious egoism, makes it seem mythic and necessary: "It is impossible to remain rational about such a crime." Freed from rationality, we can offer our libidos a rich feast, primarily by allowing ourselves to be massaged by the idea of "horror," the keynote in Oxenhandler's mesmerizing chant. In a short two columns, she sings about "a unique horror," "the ultimate horror," "a primal horror," "the cosmic horror." This is a horror beyond all horrors and yet beneath and behind all horrors, particular and yet general, located in Petaluma and in the cosmos. This horror is made both unreal and oddly friendly, coming on us like an adventure and making us not only important but part of the ultimate, unique, primal cosmos. We are not drawn here to Polly's horror but to that felt by the neighbors and the universe. It is we who matter here, not Polly; and articles like Oxenhandler's artfully orchestrate and justify our egoistic self-indulgence.

Once we get into the soothing horror bath, we can tell other stories too. Donahue's "Child Abduction" show, run less than two weeks after the discovery of Polly's body,[45] set some of these in motion. Phil starts things off with some cosmic pumping, just to locate us in the land where it's "impossible" to be rational: he speaks of "the heart-stopping memorial" for Polly Klaas, "at which Linda Ronstadt sang, Joan Baez—both United States Senators from California, the Governor of California." (Only Ronstadt and Baez sang, I expect.) Donahue goes on to describe the search for the girl's killer as "the largest manhunt in the history of the universe. This is literally true." The puffery

Myths, Legends, Folktales, and Lies   181

makes the stories roll. Phil asks, "Is the incidence of this increasing?" Marc Klaas (Polly's father) says, "What we have to do is, we have to make sure that these kind of monsters, these evil men lurking in the night that are stealing our children out of parking lots, off of streets and out of homes are put away and never returned to society." That point is extended by a caller, who says he's eleven years old: "We're wasting space with these monsters. We should just kill them. Just kill them." A karate expert illustrates "a little drill" for children:

> Fingers, go! Fingers! Fingers! Fingers into the eyes! Push! Push! Switch! Switch! Fingers! Fingers! Fingers! Fingers! Palm! Palm! Palm! Palm! Palm! Palm! Palm! Hammer! Hammer! Hammer! Hammer! Hammer! Elbows! Elbows! Elbows! Elbows! Elbows! Grab the man now! Knee! Knee him up! Knee! Knee! Knee! Knee! Now thigh! Thigh! Thigh! Thigh! Kick the thighs! Thighs! Thighs! Shins! Pull him down! Pull him down! Okay, stomp! Stomp! Stomp! Finish him off!

Here are some other spin-offs from the tragedy, all of which, you'll notice, focus on us, and none on poor Polly Klaas. I'll provide only the lead-in; any of us can complete the story:

1. "In small towns and big cities alike, the innocent-looking 12-year-old's fate drove home the disturbing message that youngsters are not safe even in their own bedrooms."
2. "For some adults, the case has awakened buried memories of sexual abuse."
3. "Pictured above, Winona Ryder places a stuffed teddy bear in front of the Polly Klaas Search Center, reflecting the nation's bruised psyche."
4. "Governor Wilson said he almost lost it when Linda Ronstadt sang. . . . [He] then gave a tough speech pledging to fight for laws 'ensuring that career criminals become career inmates. . . . I mean, [he said], when I think of that son of a bitch [the man accused of Polly's murder], you cannot help but be angered. Did you see the picture of him smirking? Jesus, boy. I wanted to just belt him right across the mouth.'"
5. "Klaas Suspect Has Twisted Legal System since '70s."

Davis is caught looking aslant, a brilliant way to convey menace: who is he looking at?

6. "Polly is a tragic thing, but the real tragedy, if you ask me, is that America ignores all the rest of them."

7. "Members of other child find groups say media attention has created arrogance among some Klaas Foundation organizers: 'They're walking around like a bunch of movie stars.'"[46]

The case refused to go away, so useful was it to us. During the fall 1996 campaign at least three GOP congressional candidates linked their opponents to confessed killer Richard Allen Davis: "When Richard Allen Davis got the death penalty he rightly deserved for murdering Polly Klaas, two people were disappointed: Richard Allen Davis and [my opponent]."[47]

Then, at the sentencing on September 26, 1996, just as we were running low on fuel, Davis said it wasn't he who had molested Polly, but her father. "Just don't do me like my Daddy did": those were, according to Davis, Polly Klaas's last words. As Davis was explaining that any wish he might have had to molest the child was erased by the sickening spectacle of incest, Marc Klaas rose and shouted, "Burn in hell, Davis!" Having injected into the murder and abduction trial the possibility of even more child molesting, Davis set off even more talk, all of it predictable. Citizens sprang to their computers to get those letters off to the editor: "As a punishment for Davis, death is far too kind" "Is there any way to put his appeal on a fast track?"

"In a heartbeat, I would drop the pellet or inject the needle and send this scum on his way." The judge himself was in on this demonizing: "Mr. Davis," he intoned in pronouncing the sentence of death, "this is always a traumatic and emotional decision for a judge. You've made it very easy today by your conduct."

Before that, the prosecutor had forced on us images even we would not have asked for at such a time. "In my mind's eye," he said, "and I think on the mind's eye of the jurors and other people, there are images that will never go away." "I don't think I'll ever get these ideas or images out of my mind, and I suppose it won't be easy for others either." While these images included the usual monstrous hyperbole —Polly's grandfather said the atrocities of the Nazi death camps "pale in comparison to this atrocity committed by the defendant against society"—the prosecutor pulled us into the macabre sadistic sexuality in ways almost too direct, ways impossible without the screen of extreme outrage: he talked of Davis's fingers around her throat, "feeling her die," the image of her body, legs splayed, nightgown above her waist, her top untied.

After the sentencing, Marc Klaas gave a press conference. Klaas, "a visible, vocal advocate in the movement to protect children from predators,"[48] opened by saying, "We have been pursuing the death of Richard Allen Davis for three years. I am his worst nightmare. He went after the wrong family this time, and we are not going to rest until we get some kind of satisfaction." What kind? "The last thing Davis will see is my eyes, I hope." When asked about Davis's outburst, Klaas replied, "He's the one going down; I'm not." Leaving aside the rhetoric of the Old West here and the sense of a macho contest (and certainly allowing for Klaas's grief), this sort of talk so individualizes and psychologizes the issues that they become spectacular and really quite irrelevant to genuine social concerns. Klaas's actions and his advocacy movement ride the very top of the Gothic melodrama and thus remove the issue safely from the rest of us.

After all this, Raymond Brown, for Court TV, reminded viewers that they were seeing what should be an exercise in justice, not a tale told by Shirley Jackson. "Rage," he said, "is not a basis on which to make a fair and just decision, because rage makes you take it out on somebody, and that rage is going to be directed toward those who are most vulnerable and ugly. It's easy to feel sympathy for victims; it's very hard to say someone as ugly as Richard Allen Davis should get a fair trial." In the end, "It's how you treat the ugliest in society that matters." So shines a just man in a weary world—but nobody's looking.

Teenage Fornication

NBC News reported just this morning (November 18, 1996), during my granola, that a district attorney in a small Idaho town has found a law against fornication among the unmarried and has decided to bring it to bear against the youngest of these, as they seem to him a growing and undesirable group of criminals. He prosecutes both the kids and their mothers and fathers, reporting happily that early indications are his program is "working." Neither he nor the interviewer specified the desired end of his labor, but I guess it is to put an end to fornication out of wedlock, at least among teenagers.

In California, we are also fighting teen sex, "putting the jail in jail-bait," as *Time* puts it, by saying to males over eighteen who have sex with women under eighteen (and vice versa?), "We'll give you a year to think about [what you've done] in the county jail."[49] That's our governor speaking, a leader when it comes to devising ways to put people behind bars. Other states are moving in this direction, in some cases forcing the fornicating teens who get themselves pregnant to marry. In addition to resurrecting the language (and action) of shot-gun weddings and jailbait, the state's director of social services, Eloise Anderson, "advocates sentencing the men to jail, placing the girls in foster care, and putting their babies up for adoption"—period.[50]

Why are we singing this song? A 1995 Carnegie-Mellon/University of Chicago study found that teenage mothers "are just as likely to obtain a high school diploma and to have the same earnings potential as other teenage girls. Nor are they more likely to participate in government-sponsored welfare programs."[51] If they had their children later in life, the taxpayers would save nothing. But is there an epidemic of teenage childbearing to begin with? Is there really a problem? Here are the clearest facts: "Roughly 12 percent of children born in the United States in any given year have teenage mothers, both married and unmarried; the vast majority of those mothers are either

18 or 19 years old, and thus teen-agers only in the most technical of senses. In point of fact, the data indicate that teen-agers have been producing children at about the same rate for most of the century."[52]

The simplest conclusion is that we have this problem because it suits us to have it.

Monsters of the Media

Here's a comment that would in another age have seemed mad, but now seems insipid, a sure sign that a legend has hold of us: "Poisoning by media is even more harmful than poisoning by cigarettes or saturated fats, because it destroys not just individuals, but culture."[53]

One of our most telling legends allows us to attack the messenger, not the message, always a good game and one with a long history. According to a recent poll, 67 percent of Americans blame the "problem of low morals and personal character in this country" on "television and other popular entertainment." While those answering the poll were allowed to pinpoint more than one cause for moral degeneration, and while more people (77 percent) landed on "breakdown of the family," it is notable that the media did worse than the schools, the churches, economic conditions, and even politicians.[54] We hear constantly these days that television violence begets real violence, hear it so often that, according to yet another poll, 79 percent of us firmly believe it, even in the absence of evidence to support such a causal relationship. Our present First Lady, also undeterred by rationality, says she knows full well that "news violence harms the young."[55] Oliver Stone agrees: "Every night on the news it's back-to-back murder and body bags."[56] Hillary Clinton, Stone, and just about everybody else are convinced that the problem lies in the media, that the victims are the children, and that it's up to us to put a stop to it. An idealized "child" becomes the paradigmatic viewer of news programs, which are then challenged to find a different reality to tell us about.

All this leaves television stations, moviemakers, and print journalists a little baffled. Television in particular is bashed by columnists and by basher-in-chief Janet Reno, who threatens to come down hard on them unless they get rid of mayhem. She tells the Senate Commerce Committee that "the regulation of [television] violence is constitutionally permissible."[57] As usual, Reno speaks for the surface hysteria of our country's silliest people. Still, some producers in places like Seattle, Albuquerque, and Oklahoma City scurry to put on what they call "family sensitive" news,[58] believing surveys that tell them viewers are fed up with violence, crime, lurid details, sex, nudity, and grossness generally; that they want to see kittens rescued from trees, good works, school talent shows. The reason these producers find themselves in places like Seattle and Oklahoma City is that they are no wiser than Reno.

In fact, another poll asking Americans what sources of information they really trust revealed that we have found a home with the media, and that television is the most credible source of all: 49 percent said they believed our nation's leaders; 60 percent believed the church; 68 percent believed newspapers; and 73 percent believed television news.[59] These are likely the same 73 percent who said that this news is altogether too violent and sexy and that they are shocked, shocked by it every night. What does this mean? It could mean that we trust the accuracy of the news but wish it weren't so vile; or it could mean that we trust it, like it the way it is (which is largely why it is the way it is), and feel the need to say we don't.

Our legends give us a way to send directions to the media on what we want, get it (except in Seattle and Oklahoma City), and then blame them for giving it to us. The media function as an important node in the broad cultural circulation of desire, a circulation of desire that always flows in and through children—but in a strange way. We want to have a means of gabbling about the media that positions us as the protectors of children; we want a discourse about children's innocence and susceptibility that is also a discourse about our probity and concern. The media are nothing if not sensitive recorders of public desire.[60]

This works so well that alert presidential candidates can base campaigns on the moral ascendancy granted by attacking Hollywood. Bob Dole's spring fling at the movies, "nightmares of depravity," met with fervent assent, 71 percent of Americans agreeing with him generally, according to a *Los Angeles Times* poll, and an even higher number expressing assurance in a *Time* poll that media violence numbs people to violence, inspires young people to be violent, and tells us violence

Myths, Legends, Folktales, and Lies   187

is fun and acceptable.[61] According to the same *Time* poll, more people blame American consumers for the problem than hit on the entertainment industry, and favor "tighter parental supervision" as the best means for dealing with the issue (overwhelmingly opposing government restriction or censorship). Such injections of good sense do not, however, diminish the pleasure we take in hating the media, just as we enjoy heartily conjuring up a ringleading Satan and space invaders.

The media is a reflector of a complex excuse that manages also to be a triumphant claim: that we will do everything in our power to protect our children from a world and a set of impulses that we had no part in creating and no part in distributing. We pretend that we don't know how these things got there, that we think it's high time things were changed. Such trumpery talk leaves our children right where they've always been. I do not believe our needs are cosmic or infernal, though, and I do think we can find better things to do with them than pour them out, guilt-free, onto children.

Sleepers

In late 1996, a movie emerged that played on our pulses well enough to make it the top box-office draw for several weeks. In another age, *Sleepers,* written and directed by Barry Levinson, would seem a film for thugs, but now it is a popular entertainment, playing the hysteria that lies all too near our cultural heart. The story is about four pretty boys from New York's Hell's Kitchen, little rascals with sweet faces and no more than mischief on their minds. They don't swear, not really, and as for sex, the most experienced among these eleven- to fourteen-year-olds has kissed a girl twice—tee hee. These boys spend a lot of time in their underpants, as boys will, and they are attended by their faithful priest, Father Bobby (Robert DeNiro), who, in the line of Don Murray, Pat O'Brien, and Bing himself, knows how to adapt Jesus to real life and play basketball too. The film is set up, in other words, in the pederastic mode of *Stand by Me:* the opening line is "This is a story about friendship that runs deeper than blood."

These sterilized Brady Bunch boys decide to steal some hotdogs from a vendor and, one thing leading to another, kill a bystander, by the freakiest accident, not their fault. But they are sentenced to reform school, where Kevin Bacon and other white guards (the black guards are nice) watch them undress (so do we) while drooling and then beat, sodomize, and otherwise torment them. The sadism is more emphasized than the sex—the boys give Bacon a blow job, not the other way around—partly to ward off charges of homophobia and partly to screen us from acknowledging the eroticism we are being given.

The myth takes hold here: first, this event determines absolutely who these boys *are:* identity is formed in sexual trauma. Second, the problem is one of monsters, evil without institutional or cultural resonance. The voice-over tells us that "most if not all the others belonged there" (at the dungeon/reform school). That is, we needn't concern ourselves with anything outside the immediate psychodrama: the institution is just fine, the system is fine, and so are we. Third, child molesting is not only worse than murder but fully justifies revenge killing and vigilante justice.

When the film hops forward to show us the revenge, two of the four boys are obsessive killers, murdering, apparently, about once a week; another is a beginning journalist, not doing well; and Brad Pitt is an assistant district attorney assigned to prosecute his two old friends, now charged with shooting Kevin Bacon—over spaghetti, a few dozen times, starting in the crotch. So, the plot shrieks forward: the journalist covers Brad Pitt going after the other two. But he's not really going after them, for they have "remained caring friends," cemented together by what they went through and able to empathize with things like murder. So, they deliberately hire (for reasons unclear to me) the worst defense attorney they can get, Dustin Hoffman, and feed him lines; and Brad Pitt deliberately blows the case, with the help of some old friend drug dealers and Mafia bosses, who murder witnesses and the like. Father Bobby agonizes off-screen (thank God) over whether he should give them an alibi under oath—that is, whether he should commit both perjury and blasphemy—and decides to do so. (I hope I've spoiled the ending for you.) Nothing, you see, is as important as child abuse—not drug dealing, not organized crime, not murder, not the church, not the truth, and certainly not God.

The ending is true to the premises of our cultural panic. The two boys get off and gather for a party with the two who helped them, remembering old times together, but with so much pain. Brad Pitt

Myths, Legends, Folktales, and Lies   189

leaves his girl and never marries, ever, because—well, you know. The journalist, in time, is granted a modest promotion, as a hedge against utter bleakness. The two wild ones are shot down shortly afterward in gunfights. That's because you can't escape what you are, the film reminds us, and they are children of molestation. Wally and the Beaver would have turned out this way had Kevin Bacon got hold of them.

We can make up better stories than this.

7. The Trials: Believing the Children

The prologues are over. It is a ques-
   tion, now
Of final belief. So, say the final belief
Must be in a fiction. It is time to
   choose.
— Wallace Stevens, "Asides on the
Oboe"

Your belief will help create the fact.
— William James

It is convenient that there be gods,
and, as it is convenient, let us believe
there are. — Ovid

Nothing is easier than self-deceit. For
what each man wishes, that he also
believes to be true. — Demosthenes

Trial by jury, instead of being a security to persons who are accused, will
be a delusion, a mockery, and a snare.
— Thomas, Lord Denham

Criminal trials are what we turn to when talk shows fail us. These trials imitate art, copying the formal features and fervor brought to their highest development in *Oprah, Hard Copy,* and movies of the week. The extended trials now showing on a continuing basis across the country thrive as the material base for all our dramas of display and disavowal. By way of these trials we can denounce the monsters while enjoying monstrous pleasures, cover our eyes while peeking through our fingers.

Such trials present us with the illusion that we have a painful duty to perform, allow us to confront what we pretend we are reluctant to contemplate: the enormity of pedophilia. We operate under the pretense that we need to hear the details, repeatedly, because we cannot imagine such things for ourselves: "He did what? Say that again—I didn't catch it." We can affect difficulty in bringing our minds to focus on such activities, and thus justify the parade of images and stories. We have it arranged so that even the flood of sex talk proves how little it means to us.

What does matter to us, we say, are the children, the victims we are pledged to believe (so long as they are saying what we want to hear) and protect. Every trial speaks to our certainty that the children are made happier and safer, given more of what we know childhood should be, by the public examination of their enemies. Let's start here, with the children and what we are doing for them.

Ellie Nesler's Son

Ellie Nesler's son is named Willy, Willy Nesler. He is now about fourteen-years old, living, I think, in Jamestown, California, where in 1993, in April, he was in a courtroom waiting to testify in the preliminary hearing of one Daniel Driver, accused of seven counts of child molesting. The papers say Willy Nesler was one of the alleged victims; they also say that, according to his mother, he was vomiting wildly the morning he was scheduled to tell his story in court. Before he got the chance to speak, his mother took control, silencing her boy and the accused forever. When Daniel Driver looked at her with what she took to be a smirk, Ellie Nesler, goaded beyond her limits, bolted from the courtroom, filched a .22 semiautomatic from her sister's purse, charged back in, and plugged the guarded, manacled Driver in the head and neck five times at close range, proclaiming, "Maybe I'm not God, but I'll tell you what: I'm the closest damn thing to it." [1]

I mention Willy Nesler because at this point he becomes silent, a vacancy at the center of the story—filled up and written on by his mother, the press, and the nation's outrage, our own included. He never speaks again, so far as I know, so completely is he now a character in a drama controlled by our fantasies. Willy Nesler becomes our main but stereotypical character, the empty and violated child whose story we know so well there is no need for Willy now to tell it: we hear it from within ourselves, spoken by our needs. Once the accused is out of the way and the child is rendered merely a figure in the play of our desire, we can proceed to our usual business.

In this case, Willy Nesler's mother thrust herself between us and the speaking child, blocking his words just in time. In the scores of accounts I read of the trial, Willy appears only as "Ellie's boy," "Nesler's son." [2] Often he isn't even mentioned. Ellie Nesler steps forward, gun blazing, and becomes the projection we can use for a while to contemplate with impunity her thoroughly sexualized boy; and then we can disown and discard her. For a moment, Ellie grabbed the headlines, became a vigilante June Cleaver, protecting her chick in a way dear to the hearts of nostalgic thugs: "Danny Driver smirked once too often," Patrick Buchanan smirked. [3] Defense funds sprang up, fueled by spaghetti suppers; schoolchildren were forced to write thank-you

Ellie Nesler pictured in a pose
that combines pathos and
heroic determination.

notes; T-shirts and bumper stickers sniggered "Nice Shootin' Ellie";
Hard Copy and Charles Kuralt descended on Jamestown. All this so
we could do as we liked with our image of Willy Nesler. We could
sentimentalize him erotically, as a townsperson did by saying, "His
little soul died the day he was molested,"[4] or we could indulge in the
full-scale fantasies scripted by Ellie's attorney, who asked the jury to
"pick a child you know and look at their innocence and sweetness"
and then imagine that child being violated.[5]

This didn't last very long. For a while Ellie gave us a story so compelling in its combination of Gothic simplicity and family values that
it was irresistible. But Ellie's story never sold. The crowds of media
talent drawn into Jamestown from Los Angeles and New York, like
vultures to roadkill, fled even more quickly. Ellie was abandoned—
left to fend for herself in the trial and reduced to claiming that she
was "acting for God" in firing away, that she was insane at the time
of the killing, and, in a last-ditch, double-barreled bid for sympathy,
that she had been molested herself as a child and was now suffering
from a fatal disease. But the attempt to put it off on God and the in-
sanity defense both failed,[6] and nobody cared by then whether or not
Ellie had cancer or even whether those she named, her father's poker
buddies and a state senator,[7] had sexually abused her.

What happened was that Ellie turned out to be complicated, not
the simple heroine we needed for a Gothic tale but a woman with a

past, a past we didn't want. Her life had been a hard one, not pictur-esque hard but gritty, grinding hard. She had a minor criminal record; she had taken drugs, perhaps on the morning of the shooting; she had threatened to kill Daniel Driver months earlier. We no longer had the blunt melodrama that placed the screen of outrage between us and our object of interest, which had never been Ellie or Driver but always Willy Nesler, the breached, silent child. Without the screen story, we were left to face the music ourselves or search for other stories. Since the stories are not hard to find, we hesitated not a second in getting out of Jamestown and leaving Ellie to her sentencing—ten years.

By the way, I heard in October 1994 on a news radio station, just before the traffic report, that Willy Nesler had run away from wher-ever he was staying, from whomever was tending him. I didn't catch the details. However, both the Pasadena and the San Bernardino Free-ways—I can use either—were a mess.

McMartin

The McMartin trial, which dealt with allegations of child molestation and ritual satanic abuse at a Southern California preschool run by the McMartin family, began with charges (354 counts, 41 witnesses, 369 alleged victims) in the summer of 1983 and didn't end until the summer of 1990, the trial itself running, with one short break, from April 1987 until July 1990. This longest criminal trial in U.S. history trailed off into acquittals, deadlocks, and declarations of mistrials, all signaling that we had other spectacles to attend to and could finally let this one go. But along the way we provided ourselves with seven rich years of narratives about animal sacrifice and demonic posses-sion, about games of "tickle" and "naked movie star," about Raymond Buckey's underwear and his collection of *Playboy* magazines, about children and sex.

This trial ripened into a brazen cultural showing off, as if some-one had double-dared us: could we really sustain an enticing story that long? Operating like a chain letter or any number of games that end only in exhaustion, the McMartin trial set the record, established the outer limits of double-dealing, erotic-hypocritic ingenuity. At one point, Pam Ferrero, one of the prosecutors, referred the court to "official transcript, page 55,000." I was there, you see, and was alert to the fact that page 55,000 had been written some time ago and that we were now well into six figures and roaring on. You may wonder why I was there rather than preparing to teach *Julius Caesar,* and the reason is that it was my duty to go and record the story and be part of it. That was the least I could do.

It all started on August 12, 1983, when Judy Johnson called the Manhattan Beach Police Department and was connected to Juvenile Officer Jane Hoag. It was an electric splicing from the beginning, Hoag not only believing every word Ms. Johnson fed to her but acting on it. And what Judy Johnson said was that her son had been sodomized by "Mr. Ray" (Raymond Buckey). Johnson later went on to claim that Buckey habitually wore masks and capes, stuck the boy's head in a toilet, and forced an air tube in his rectum. Within a short time she had also accused a member of the Los Angeles School Board, an AWOL Marine (she couldn't place his name), three "models" from a local health club, and her ex-husband of sodomizing the boy. When prosecutors entered the case, she told them what she hadn't trusted Ms. Hoag with: that Mr. Ray could fly and that he had stapled her son's ears and run scissors into his eyes. Within two years Ms. Johnson was diagnosed as suffering from acute paranoid schizophrenia; in 1987 she died from alcohol-induced liver failure.[8]

So what? Roland Summit, the UCLA psychiatrist who served as an adviser to the McMartin parents (and still believes something dark and obscene was going on at the school), rightly points out that Judy Johnson's sad eccentricity, even madness, cannot reasonably be used to discredit the case: even if the origins are questionable, we would still need to explain what "could mobilize police and the entire group of more conventional, trustful parents."[9] That surely is the issue. Why did Officer Hoag and others after her swallow the whole story— knees, knuckles, and head? After a month's hard work failed to turn up either evidence or corroboration, Hoag turned the matter over to her boss, the chief, who got things rolling (and certainly started the evidence flooding in) by sending a letter to all the parents.

The letter asked parents for "assistance" in case "288 P.C.," a case of "child molestation," including "oral sex, fondling of the genitals, buttocks or chest area, and sodomy, possibly committed under the pretense of 'taking the child's temperature.'" The letter also asked for information on photos "without clothing" and on the activities of Ray Buckey: did he leave with a child during nap time, did he tie children up? "Please," parents were asked, "question your child," find out if he or she is a "witness" or a "victim," fill out the enclosed information form, and return it within a week, thank you very much.

That did it. The children were turned over to an interviewing group called Children's Institute International (cii), who managed to find 369 victims among the 400 children questioned. In 1984, Ray Buckey, his mother, sister, grandmother, and three other teachers were arrested and charged with various combinations of the three hundred plus counts of child molesting. Over the years (and years) charges were dropped and refiled, and the number of defendants shrank. The original show, with seven defendants and as many lawyers, was like an Edna Ferber epic, loosely formed and dramatically slack. Eventually we had only Raymond Buckey and his mother, and finally, in a move to achieve maximum dramatic intensity, Raymond by himself.

The prosecution did its part by keeping up a show of having more evidence than it was quite ready to release, evidence of a kind that would, once aired, utterly transform things. Prosecutors held press conferences full of high-potency hints, seldom making the mistake of producing anything material. When they did—as with the cape they said Ray Buckey used—the public was disappointed: the cape was very flimsy and clearly a child's toy, not nearly big enough to fit Mr. Ray or strong enough to sustain him aloft. And it was a mistake having children pick the molesters from photographs, since they tended to choose shots of people like actor Chuck Norris and even the Los Angeles city attorney.

So, for evidence, the prosecution had only the direct testimony of the children and the tapes of the cii interviews. The first, I thought, was usually very powerful, if sometimes contradictory: the children spoke with an assurance that was unmistakable. Even Ray Buckey said it was obvious they were not lying, were telling what they took to be the truth. But the cii interviews raised questions about just where the kids might have found the "truth" they were telling. These interviews were often so bullying and so loaded, so intent on getting "disclosures," that kids who were not forthcoming or who denied outright what the interviewers wanted to find were often attacked—"You must be dumb!" "Are you stupid?" "What good are you?" The encouragement to tell all was often put in terms that would make me accuse my own sister, if I had one:

"You have some yucky secrets, don't you? Wouldn't you like to put them in the box and get rid of them?"
"Are you really sure you don't have yucky secrets?"
"C'mon! A lot of your friends have told us their yucky secrets."
"Mommy and Daddy would be very happy if you got rid of those yucky secrets."

Even the prosecution now admits that these Gestapo-like grillings made the case tough to win,[10] particularly, I think, since the prosecution had nothing much to offer except the fruits of these interrogations.

But that didn't keep us from attending closely to—hardly believing and yet hardly daring not to believe—the charges that were detailed. Here is a summary, by category:

The expected: fondling and the like, of which little was made, it being so entirely predictable in this plot
Improper games: the naked movie star game, the cowboy game, the alligator game, the doctor game, horsey, and tickle
Sadism: rape, sodomy, penetration with pencils and silverware, being urinated and defecated on
Terrorism: threats, killing of animals (horses, rabbits) by means of baseball bat clubbings
Satanism: visiting cemeteries to exhume and cut up corpses; abuse by black-robed people carrying black candles in an Episcopal church; teachers flying; naked nuns and priests in tunnels under the school; blood-drinking
Unclassified: airplane trips to places like Hawaii

There were also prolonged discussions of things like Raymond Buckey's *Playboy* collection—"Did you buy them for the interviews, Mr. Buckey?"—and his underwear:

"I ask you to look at this photograph, Mr. Buckey. Are you wearing underwear here?"

"I don't know; I seem to be fully clothed—you know, for playing volleyball."

"I didn't ask you that, now did I? I thought I asked you whether you were wearing underwear. Perhaps you could stop evading the question?"

"Could be."

"Could be what?"

"Could be I was wearing underwear."

"That's the best you can do?"

"Sometimes I did and sometimes I didn't."

"I didn't ask you about other times, did I now, or about your general practice? Correct me if I'm wrong. Perhaps I can persuade you to bring your mind back to the picture you seem so anxious to avoid."

["Objection!" "Sustained." pointless yammer]

"Let's try again. You see the picture, Mr. Buckey?"

"Yes."

"That's a start, don't you think?"

"I agree."

"OK, now I have a very simple question. You ready?"

"Yes I am."

"Are you wearing underwear in the picture, at the time it was taken, not the previous Tuesday or the Monday following, but as you were standing there? Hmmmm?"

"Well, the only way I can answer that is to say that I think sometime around this time I stopped wearing underwear when I was playing beach volleyball—I played volleyball a lot—because it got wet if I went swimming and was uncomfortable—and . . ."

"Mr. Buckey [Misssturrrr Buck-keeeeeee]. May I take it that you refuse to tell me?"

[Objection—and etc.] [11]

I cite this not because I suspect you of having any more interest in the issue at hand than I—and my interest is under control—but because it illustrates how well the prosecution, and the defense too, played its part, keeping before us images of naked children, naked perpetrators. The spotlight is here on Raymond's underwear, not because it matters two pins but because it evokes its own absence: Raymond's not wearing underwear!

Finally, though, we abandoned McMartin and went on to other things, leaving a huge mess behind. This case, and copycat cases that came in its wake, left a permanent mark on day-care operations— "You really need [now] to be careful not to set a child on your lap too long, not to hug them too hard," says a preschool owner[12]—and on those who need their services: how much more guilt do working women need shoveled on them? Often it is worse than guilt, a judge in Michigan actually removing a three-year-old girl from her mother because the mother was using day care thirty-five hours a week while taking classes in Ann Arbor.[13] We notice, too, that McMartin did not teach us caution or restraint, much less sophistication: "the not-guilty verdict spawned even more vigorous—some would say reckless— accusations against alleged abusers."[14]

The McMartin case also set out for us what seems to me the most dangerous feature of our talk and storytelling about child molesting: its unvarying attraction to a single narrative mode, a pinched mode in which all problems are reduced to playing "find the villain," actually "find and kill." The 1990 film *Unspeakable Acts* replays the McMartin trial, reversing the ending and thus bringing it more into accord with the most hysterical version of our main story: the accused are always guilty. The prosecutors in the film cite McMartin, saying, "We are going to learn from their mistakes," and here, as so often in Hollywood, history is rewritten to come out better: "something so evil, so dark," is identified with perfect clarity and punished.

One notices that even when there is a backlash on the McMartin case, when writers, as they now often do, decide it was all a witch hunt, the story stays the same. Only the roles are switched, the defendants becoming the victims and the monster role being taken by the media, the district attorney's office, poor Judy Johnson, the parents generally, or the cii interviewers. The 1995 hbo movie made by Abby and Myra Mann, with Oliver Stone, retains the plot and tone of original McMartin lore and simply flip-flops the roles, as if the Three Little Pigs were now breaking in on the Wolf. The Manns, playing the same old game, see it as a case of the molestation of innocence: "In their opinion, the McMartin students were abused by the legal system, not by the Buckeys," and Stone agrees that we have in the past simply placed "the victim hat on the wrong head."[15]

In the end, it just doesn't matter.[16] What infects us here and does so much damage to our children is the plain simplemindedness of this story: it is so crude and blunt, so ill-adapted to helping anybody do anything—except keep the story going. As one of the attorneys said of the case and its cultural moment, "They created this monster, and it developed a life of its own. There was no one in control."[17] The police came to believe that interlocking satanic rings were woven throughout the Manhattan Beach area, involving, they estimated, twelve hundred child victims; and they proceeded frantically to close nine more schools and blacken yet more lives and reputations.[18] One McMartin spin-off resulted in a $7.3 million award to four adults in Pico Rivera wrongly accused of child molesting. But the award came eleven years after the fact, making it, the *Los Angeles Times* says, "a victory of sorts" for people whose lives had already been ruined.[19]

The popularity of this brutally superficial story guarantees that it will continue to grind up not just the accused and the accusers, but anyone caught in its gears: the parents, the children, all those involved in copycat prosecutions, nervous day-care operators and the children they refuse to touch, the teachers who lost their jobs and careers, the Buckeys, especially Raymond. Denied bail and thus sentenced to five years in prison for nothing, Raymond Buckey deserves the last word here. Now attending college under his own name—"I've thought of changing my name or dyeing my hair. But I'll deal with it, because I respect my name"—he is remarkably thoughtful, even courteous about the wave that engulfed him: "I'm not stupid enough to say poor, poor me." Though he admits to being "tired of those sideward glances," he can muster still some light irony: "I always wonder how I'll write my résumé—there'll be this seven-year gap. What am I going to say I did during those years—courtroom observer?"

Buckey says he learned to respect those he met in jail, many of whom faced "horrendous fear and uncertainty" with "dignity." He speaks of McMartin now as not a personal but a cultural disaster: "The sad thing is that no one has really learned anything from McMartin.

Things have gotten worse." Everywhere there are new wild cases: "defendants are getting ruined. The kids are getting ruined. Everyone is getting ruined." [20]

Menendez

Menendez is *McMartin II,* an artful variation on the usual staged drama of child molesting masking as an exercise in justice. *Menendez* shows how far we have come in our ability to write and produce these spectacles, making once-flashy McMartin now look crude and bumbling, much as *Hamlet* exposes the rawness of its sources. *Menendez* is postmodernist porn, the defendants in this classy Beverly Hills murder trial re-creating for us the Sadian theatre they said had been their childhood (he tore off my hairpiece! she yelled at me! he fucked me!), while others talked about what was talked about and what others suggested was being talked about right over there in the other room.

More people know the details of the Menendez brothers' trials than are confident about who won the Napoleonic Wars, so I'll just mention that they have a lot to do with children, sex, and the weight we give to their coming together. The trials offered a test of how much we want to hear the stories of child molesting and to what extent we take seriously the notion that the violation of innocence counts for much more than, and justifies the taking of, life. If, as we often say, molestation is worse than murder, if innocence is truly more valuable than life, then surely we were no more than consistent in allowing the Menendez boys their argument.

Judging by the public response and the deadlocked jury in the first trial, it's an argument so strong it can override for a time what looked like a stacked deck: Two rich and arrogant young men, no longer children by any stretch of the word and to all appearances free to leave home if they didn't like it, planned and executed a grisly murder of parents who posed no imminent threat whatever, who were eating berries and ice cream and filling out a college application form for one of their sons. Not only did these sons shoot the parents repeatedly, they retired to reload and then finished off a bleeding, crawling mother. They then covered their tracks: made a sobbing, well-rehearsed call to 911, hired a computer expert to erase a dangerous hard disk, and concocted a remarkably phony memorial service. Mostly, though, they spent money, and fast: $15,000 on three Rolex watches, $70,000 on a Porsche, $300,000 on a down payment for a chicken-wing restaurant, $50,000 for a tennis coach, and an unspecified amount (at least I can't find it) for another car. They got their stories crossed on where they bought the guns and were caught in the lie; they confessed to their shrink but never mentioned to him their alleged history of sexual abuse. Still, they spoke so well and so to the point of our interest that many found—and find—them worthy and handsome victims.

Lyle Menendez, who has been compared with Judy Garland and Montgomery Clift as a "great neurotic actor,"[21] testified that his father, whispering that, like Greek warriors, they were using sex to get tough, started toughening him when he was six, taking nude photos as well. The next year, Lyle said, oral sex began; and at age eight, "object sessions," using shaving or toothbrushes. Lyle cried, with a tough-guy sob, "He raped me." Not only that, he testified the next day that he had, as an eight-year-old, molested his fellow defendant, Erik, then six, with a toothbrush. "I'm sorry," Lyle said to his brother, right there in the courtroom, not omitting the sob.

According to most spectators, Erik is not so gifted, despite his acting ambitions, and poured out too many details without his brother's mastery of narrative pace and flow. Erik talked all in a rush about the taste of his father's semen, sweetened with cinnamon; he spoke of his mother squeezing blisters on his penis and otherwise "checking him out"; he mentioned categories of incestuous activities and the names each had—Knees, Nice, Rough, and Sex; respectively, oral, hand, needles and tacks, and anal. He was too eager to add flourishes: his father lighting candles and slowly placing them about the room before saying to the boy, like an X-rated Vincent Price, "One last fuck before I kill you." Still, even Erik managed to do the job.

We collected fat benefits from this trial, no matter what our stand on the brothers' innocence or guilt. In fact, as with McMartin, that position hardly mattered so long as we adopted a high and severe moral tone. Many (Alan Dershowitz and Susan Estrich at least weekly) used the occasion to op-ed huff about vigilante justice, the rampant evasion of responsibility in America today, or the failure of "the system." We had Menendez books and television movies—hawked with

The sweaters do it all.

trailers telling us, "the story you know so well is a story you don't know at all."[22] There were documentary specials (a good one on Fox hosted by ron Reagan), a bustling Prodigy "Menendez Bulletin Board," and the growth of Court TV around this delectable spectacle. As if answering to all this clamor, the defense finally tacked up in court, for all to see, some of the naked pictures, taken years before, when the boys really were children.

One alternate juror confessed to Donahue, "Phil . . . it was sickening. . . . I could *visualize* this pedophile father—he's down the hall in the bedroom, he is sodomizing his six-year-old child."[23] What is being visualized sharply is a child, a figure in this drama so important that it seems to replace the actual bodies of the grown-up and athletically bulky Lyle and Erik. Both were referred to, not only by their attorneys but by many of our deputies in the press, as children, kids, boys, sometimes prefixed by "little." It is this image of the child that we were paying for in the trial, and we used the besweatered young men as transparent agencies, peering back through them to the child within, down the hall in the bedroom.

In the end, at the end of the second trial to be exact, we seemed ready for new theater and so disposed of Lyle and Erik as we had Ellie before them. They were found guilty, the jury saying it "had sympathy but no doubts" in sentencing them to life imprisonment,[24] the sympathy possibly warding off the death penalty, though jurors by now seemed weary of the same old child abuse stories, which read this time like twice-told porn, not arousing. The crowds were tiny, in part because the Menendez brothers, now older, worn, and without the high-school sweaters, were no longer disguised as "boys."

And That's Not All

Just to indicate what we all know but perhaps aren't writing home about: it's not just the big trials we have going for us, the litigational Super Bowls; there are lots of local contests too, small excitements to sustain us between major celebrations. Here are some examples drawn mostly from my hometown, a staid place.

1. "Man Accused of Molesting Girl on Plane": a story about a twelve-year-old girl who "said she was groped by another passenger during a flight from Los Angeles to Las Vegas."[25] The girl said she cried loudly and repeatedly, "Stop touching me! I don't like it!" but nobody helped her, a flight attendant snubbing her, and the "lady behind her" telling her to "be quiet!" How exactly was she "groped"? "He touched my breasts . . . and the inside of my leg." The alleged toucher was arrested and the airline expressed regret. Three days later a small piece appeared, in section B, page 2, saying a guy across the aisle "was keeping an eye on her" during the flight and saw no groping, heard no cries for help. Six weeks later an even smaller piece appeared saying the charges had been reduced from "open and gross lewdness" to "annoying a minor," since, according to the district attorney, "there was no touching that was specifically sexual."[26] If there were further notices I missed them; but since I would not have missed them, there were no further notices. We'll never know if it all just went away, vanished when we got tired of hearing and talking about it.

2. "Psychologist Convicted of Molesting 2 of His Students."[27] I mention this one because it shows what happens when the *Menendez* defense is overdone. Here the accused claimed that the two students,

one of whom was his foster son, had "repeatedly raped and beaten" him and threatened to lie and turn him in if he complained, which he was too embarrassed to do, since he was, after all, an adult, being, he said, molested by boys, albeit boys of fourteen and fifteen who were "troubled" (the article says) and in a special school. Anyhow, his story was met only with giggles (I'll wager), and (this much is clear) he got ten years for "oral copulation and lewd conduct."

3. "Staff Misconduct Alleged at S. Pasadena Private School."[28] I almost passed over this one, thinking "misconduct" might have to do with embezzlement, dress code violations, arson, or something just as trifling. But then I saw "Sheriff's Department Juvenile Investigation Bureau," "a multi-victim, multi-suspect, multi-allegation investigation," which, "based on the allegations made, [offered] a potential of serious misconduct." However, this was no McMartin; the parents supported the school and angrily ridiculed the Keystone Cops sex investigators. Five weeks later, a humiliated police chief had to admit "no major revelations," nothing at all in the way of "significant developments": "No one thing has led us to something else." When no one thing can be found that leads to some other thing, what is one to do?

4. From Boulder, Colorado,[29] comes a richly detailed item about a man accused of confronting a high-school student at the local recreation center. Now, I'm not clear about all this, since there are rather more details than I can sort out, but I think the boy claimed the man got an erection looking at him while they were both in the communal shower and then approached him at a urinal and asked, according to one account, if the boy would "like to get together" or, according to another account, let him "suck on my penis." The man then suggested they go "for privacy" to the English department at the University of Colorado (certainly nobody working late there!), at which point the boy said he made an artful excuse and fled. The prosecution claimed that the defendant, a popular children's rights advocate in town, was Jekyll and Hyde: "As a heterosexual, he is an overachiever, a wonderful father and husband"; however, "he's got a homosexual side, a hidden side that nobody knows about." "This defendant," said Deputy District Attorney Mary Keegan, "is a closet homosexual. It is that part of James Keane that committed this crime." The jury, at least some of whom were brighter and less bigoted than Ms. Keegan, deadlocked.

5. "Criminals in the Classroom" is a whole series that ran in front-page hotness in the *Charlotte (N.C.) Observer* for three days (March 20–22, 1994). Each day featured a thoughtful lead-in: "She was 5 years old, and she refused to wear a dress to school. When she wore a dress, she told her parents, she sometimes found the hands of Rock Hill elementary school principal Billy Campbell beneath it"; or "For criminals with teaching ambitions, North Carolina is a land of opportunity."

6. In East Wenatchee, Washington, a SWAT team stormed a church and arrested Pastor Robert Roberson, who was handing out groceries from his food bank at the time. His wife was nabbed at a local community college, where she was attending class. They were charged with, among other things, leading ritual orgies in the church, forming the congregation into a mass of child molesters and rapists. As the charges expanded from the mouth of the foster daughter of Robert Perez, the town's lone sex crimes investigator, the tales of sacrifices, of shouts of "Hallelujah" as "the wild thing" was done, and of dozens of leading citizens doing dozens of abominable things swelled. After nearly five months in jail, the Robersons were brought to trial and acquitted on all counts. Even after the verdict, prosecutors remained firm in their contention that there was (even as they spoke) "an epidemic of sexual abuse in East Wenatchee and its twin city, Wenatchee."[30]

7. Finally, from East Liverpool, Ohio, where a recent Notre Dame football coach and I grew up, I fulfilling the promise that was evident even back then, he failing to do so. This item is from the wire service, however, East Liverpool no longer having anyone living in it under seventy and thus not much troubled with pedophiles: "HOUSTON. A judge wanted to punish a piano teacher for molesting two girls ["fondling 9 and 10-year-olds"] . . . so he ordered him to stay away from the keyboard for 20 years." The judge said he wanted to "take away the most important thing in his life," in other words do something dog-dirty mean, no matter how illogical and irrelevant: "I don't know anything about pianos—I don't like pianos!" said the judge, slurping back drool as he spoke.[31] I expect people in East Liverpool liked that story. I know I did. The Notre Dame coach wouldn't get it.

Since we started by losing track of Willy Nesler, perhaps it's time to see if we can get the child back. The question is this: What do we take the child, particularly "the molested child," to be? I've been arguing that neither figure is natural, both being manufactured according to specifications that fit adults' needs, not theirs. The endangered child, the molested child, the child of innocence: all are formulated by us, one way or another, as the child without means, the incapable child. The child needs us badly enough to justify our rushing in only because the child is "pure": without the ability to understand, size things up, act. We insist so much on the child's inability, seem to feel such desire to find this weakness in the child, that perhaps we are stuffing it in there ourselves.

Take the issue of children's testimony. When we really need to hear from children, we seem to feel that's just the time we should be giving them the words we know they should be saying. Who would trust a child to tell us what a child knows, feels, or has experienced? According to *Women's Day*, 20,000 children testify every year in sex abuse trials, and another 100,000 are investigated.[32] What do we hear them saying, and when do we believe them? It seems to me that we believe children are being entirely truthful when they tell us what we know beforehand to be the truth.

That sometimes means filtering out things we don't want to hear or things that don't seem within even the stretchable bounds of the truthful: "Mr. Benny killed a giraffe at school" we don't even hear; "Mr. Benny took off his clothes, killed the rabbit, and made me drink the blood" is truth. As Ellen Bass and Laura Davis put it, "Children don't often say, 'My brother molested me six times,' but in their own way, all children 'tell' that they've been abused." You just have to know how to hear their language. The examples given by Bass and Davis are these: "Don't make me go to Poppa's house" ("a very clear message"); "I don't want to go to Boy Scouts anymore"; "I don't like Mrs. Johnson."[33]

I suppose Bass and Davis would say we should also be detecting "telling" when kids say, "I like Fred" or "I'm indifferent to Fred" or "Who's Fred?" or "Fred's a fool." We sometimes have to hear in circles, according to the "child sex abuse accommodation syndrome," which was originally offered as an explanation of why some children who make accusations may be frightened into withdrawing them, but is sometimes twisted to justify leading questions or even to offer proof: if the child retracts an accusation you can be sure she or he was molested. But if a child is likely to be frightened by the charged cultural climate into retracting, isn't a child also likely to be incited by a charged climate into accusing? Where's the syndrome to explain that? Some people believe children always tell the truth about sexual abuse; some feel just as strongly that they do not.

Why would we suppose that children are *unable* to lie? When people say, as if it were an argument, "Do you suppose the children are just making those horrible things up?" the best answer is, "Why not?" It's not in the best interests of the child to presume that she simply hasn't the capacity to make things up, hasn't the imagination to project and entertain possibilities, hasn't the wit to lie. We should respect children at least enough to acknowledge what is plain: they have independent powers of thinking and assessing; they have considerable will; they can be deft and witty; they can be complex; they can be imaginative. They can be generous and fine; they can be narrow and nasty. Why would we want to devise impossibly simple standards: they always lie, they always tell truth? Even dogs are more intricate. These abstract rules would make sense only if we were dealing with an abstract essence-of-child.

I have a feeling that this is all important and that I've let it slide by too quickly, so I'm going to return to the McMartin trial to hammer at this one last time, to try and fix the point that this "child" we are defending isn't a "child" any child would want to be. To do this, I'll repeat a bit taken from my book *Child-Loving* as a finale.[34]

> "I believe," Buckey's attorney says, "the children believe what they are saying." What the three children called in the last trial say is that Raymond Buckey molested them—engaged them in games involving nudity and improper contact, fondled them, forced them into genital and oral sex, sodomized them, urinated on them—and then insured with threats their silence. Asked what he thinks of the children's stories, Raymond Buckey says on the stand that he thinks children are more honest than adults.

In fact, he says, "all children are honest as to what they believe." Buckey allows that statement to stand for a dramatic moment before quietly adding: "but that doesn't make what they believe right." To a very large extent, what is at stake in the McMartin trial is just that: whether what the children believe to be "right" is "right." . . .

Oddly, absolutely everyone in the courtroom agrees that the children are now and always have been telling a perfectly straight story (the narrators are reliable), but it is possible, perhaps probable or certain, that these narrators are limited, that they (a) are telling a story that never happened, (b) are telling a story that has been fed to them or severely distorted by others, (c) are telling a story that has shifted over time, (d) are telling a story where the events are right but the actors are not, (e) are telling a story where the actors are right but not the events, (f) many of the above. The argument between defense and prosecution comes down to an argument about narrators, genre, and tone, finally about interpretation. It is a literary argument about texts, a quarrel between authors and critics.

The prosecution claims that the children's evidence should be read in a "straightforward" and "common-sense" way. If they say something happened, it happened; their words are to be interpreted by means of the no-nonsense equipment we bring to bear on any text in daily life. The prosecution claims the texts offered by the children are not, as we used to say, "literature" and need no special attention beyond regarding them as "true." The prosecution further claims, in the manner of authoritative medieval exegesis of scripture, that where discrepancies are unavoidable we take whatever furthers the prosecution's case as true and disregard the rest. Though the children have told many different narratives, denied the truth of narratives told previously and recanted them, switched the modes or settings or even actors in the stories; the prosecution still sticks by its rules of interpretation: the child is always telling the truth when it says molestation occurred (and is never telling the truth when it says it didn't); if the latest version of a child's narrative confirms the prosecution's case, then that story is to be believed (if it doesn't, it isn't); the child's language needs no "interpretation" but is transparent and directly mimetic, says the prosecution (allowing for some few exceptional cases which the prosecution will clarify for us). The prosecution does not really disagree with Mr. Buckey, then: "all children are honest as to what they believe, but that doesn't make what they believe right." The prosecution imposes its own view of how to fix on what truly is "right"; it certainly doesn't trust the children to do that for them. That children are honest as to what they believe, then, simply renders the search for truth more open; it does not give any authority to the child but rather transfers all power to the adult storytellers. The child becomes an empty signifier, or, rather, an infinitely plural one. The child's testimony becomes a spilling out of game counters and an invitation to all adults not simply to play but to make up the rules of the game. The child can never author its own story. The prosecution seizes hold and tells the story it must have.

The position of the defense as regards the children is very little different. The child's complete and uncomplicated veracity is accorded a respect almost absurd to anyone who has ever spent more than a few seconds with an actual child. But it serves the purposes of the defense as well as the prosecution to erect this myth of a spotlessly honest child, since it also empties out the child and makes it incapable of any independent action or thought. That the child is completely honest means that the child is incapable of not being honest; its veracity is unwilled and hence merely automatic. The child's relation to the matter under consideration is thus innocent and powerless. The child will report with entire sincerity whatever enters its head and takes up lodging there.

Such a child, our child, is judged unable to interpret, even to interpret its own story; all it can do is lay out the story in some impossibly unmediated language so that the real interpreters can have a go at it. The prosecution's child cannot author; the defense's child cannot interpret. The honest child cannot write, cannot read; the child of molestation is functionally and conveniently illiterate, not because the pedophile wants it that way but because we do.

In this, though, we aren't much different: both of us really yearn for this empty, incompetent "child," and if we don't find it, we know well enough how to manufacture it.

8. Accusing the Stars:
Perversion among the Prominent

Love and scandal are the best sweet-
eners of tea. —Henry Fielding

The trials themselves are so spectacularly obtrusive they get in the way of the talk about them, in the same way an English football match gets in the way of the exciting mayhem before and after, going on a vacation gets in the way of anticipating or remembering it, sexual activity gets in the way of erotic fantasy. The trials are there to feed the discourse, but there's often too much there there. We do better with shadowy events or fabrications we can make central because they are so murkily indecisive, never pressed before a jury, and thus open to endless speculation. Here's how we do it: take a prominent person (or a person in a prominent position) and splotch his or her image with stories about children and sex, acknowledging that these are only rumors, of course, maybe only rumors, though we're never sure of that from day to day, as new rumors come out. It's not necessary to go so far as actually to believe anything; no one needs to commit herself. Just keep the talk coming: the Supreme Court justice with the Senate page; the child psychologist with up to four hundred patient-victims; Calvin Coolidge with Baby LeRoy. Even the Dionne quintuplets, not in the news since the reign of George VI, get in on the show by accusing their father.[1] Prate and babble and gabble and gab and dither and whinge and gurgle and coo.

You'll find in this chapter a selection of child sex talk-fests that have latched onto a position or person in our culture prominent enough to elicit a gasp of happy disbelief. We have college presidents, teachers, Boy Scout leaders, and priests; and (turning to personalities) Woody Allen and Michael Jackson. That list of the prominent isn't as rangy as you might expect: we are missing, for instance, politicians, literary

How many files were combed, I wonder, to locate this particularly suggestive pose?

theorists, and sports figures. But there are reasons for their absence, as we shall shortly see.

What we need for scandal are prominent people who also carry with them the erotic, in one of two packages: the presumption of extreme innocence or obvious self-contained sexiness. Thus, priests or Boy Scout leaders, Michael Jackson or Woody Allen.[2] Politicians and athletes do not fit well because, for one, we no longer pretend that politicians are innocent, and as for sexy: Jesse Helms? Clarence Thomas? Alfonse D'Amato? Ted Kennedy? Sports figures seem to us not so much innocent as imbecile and far too elephantine to be sexy. Still, I predict that this last is an area ripe for storytelling. Forget those football tub-o-guts and contemplate the future of basketball cuties or tennis hunks. Why literary critics and theorists are overlooked is a mystery. I can explain most things, but not that.

The Distinguished College President

In 1993, Richard Berendzen, ex-president of American University, capped off a series of talk-show appearances by publishing *Come Here: A Man Overcomes the Tragic Aftermath of Childhood Sexual Abuse.*

Berendzen had received some attention in 1990, when he was bumped from the presidency into a Johns Hopkins treatment center, into court, and onto *Nightline* (with Ted Koppel), all for placing a series of phone calls to people advertising in newspapers as child-care providers. In these calls, made from his office at American University, Berendzen would try to induce the other party to talk about children and sexuality, sometimes by saying everyone bathed or slept together at his house or practiced nudity or did a lot of punishing—"how about you?" If he got a response (which he did once too often), he would discuss incest, domination, and "many forms of child sexual abuse." At this point, Berendzen stops giving us specifics and turns to irritating metaphors: "The conversations . . . plummeted into Hades."[3]

If this had been all there was to it, American University would have buried the matter (and Berendzen) fast and we would have hurried off to the next event. But Berendzen and his coauthor, Laura Palmer, managed to tack this shabby anecdote onto our main molestation story and thus gave it considerable time in the spotlight. The book's subtitle presents the pitch—"the tragic aftermath of childhood sexual abuse"—making the main story not sexual harassment but sexual victimization. Berendzen's wife is used throughout the book as a kind of shill for this product: "At last it all made sense to her: 'you were a victim as a child, and now you are a victim again—all this because of the original abuse.'"[4] The obliging wife puts with all the subtlety of a hammerhead shark the belief that sustains the author and us: sex with children stems from previous sex with children and will lead to more sex with children, thus extending this story along the timeline of the past, present, and future; as history, journalism, and sci-fi.

Even so, the book is so self-congratulatory throughout, so smug in its mock-humble self-aggrandizements that we may find the fun hardly worth a slog through the fatuous life of a small-time college president: "A university, after all, is defined by more than libraries and laboratories, bleachers and books; it is defined by people." But the details promised in the "come here" part of the title are undeniably delivered: "Come here" was the ominous yet commonplace phrase that the author's mother used to summon him into the world of her strange lusts. The molestation is presented as a memory all the more vivid (and useful as an explanatory tool) for having been so long buried. Berendzen says he "lived two childhoods, the one I remembered and the one I repressed," the one he repressed coming back only much later when he again heard the words "Come here."[5]

His mother arises out of this recovered memory like one of Thurber's wives, just in proportion as his father recedes in a kind of cartoon symmetry: "My father was as passive as my mother was dominant"; and she was so dominant and ferocious, both in her beatings of the boy and her sexual wallowings, that she becomes the mother of all monster mothers. Releasing "a lava flow of hot madness," this mother was "a Texas rattlesnake," a "great horned owl" that searches out its prey "in the blackest night" and locks the boy in her talons, "a hurricane" whose eye is "charged with a ferocious hunger." This was a set of parents unlike any other: "I didn't have most men for my father. Or most women for my mother."[6]

Struggling sincerely (as I have no doubt he is) to understand and reclaim himself, Berendzen finds ready to hand a narrative offering him a medical/psychological status that releases him from the ordinary logic of individual responsibility. We stop asking why he made those calls, stop looking for immediate clues, because, as his wife and the master story tell us, *all this because of the original abuse.* On the one hand, then, this cycle-of-abuse story elevates as it explains Berendzen, makes him a special case; on the other, the story is intelligible and available for use in this case only because it has such broad circulation and, in its way, applies to everyone in our culture. The story works because the condition it describes is so common and confers uniqueness because it is one of a kind. In order to understand Berendzen, we need to hear all the unparalleled details; but we then process his recitation by referring it all to a story we've heard a million times before.

Despite the unruly metaphors and the tendency of his book to maintain one pitch (the atrocity scream) throughout, Berendzen does now and then break through the automatic prose to reveal something of his dogged valor and candor. He speaks openly of the confusing pleasures he felt in having sex with his mother and resists submitting those pleasures to pat explanations. His honesty about the self-serving trustees and administrators, fairweather friends, who slunk away from him at the first hint of trouble, is bleak and never self-pitying; and his corresponding gratitude for the loyalty of students very moving. He does tell Ted Koppel that "my childhood abuse did not absolve my adult behavior."[7]

Such things are rare, though, the author generally finding it convenient to reproduce the deals we have made with one another about child abuse talk: K-Mart-quality commonplaces about sex-as-power, "control," "denial." In the last chapter he reprints a speech he made that someone must have told him he should look on with pride: "Let me state it more bluntly: Child abuse is the most prevalent and yet least recognized evil in America today. It gnaws at the soul of our nation. America, wake up!" As his wife had said to him earlier, "Somebody better start talking frankly about child abuse. . . . Somebody's got to break the wall of silence, the denial."[8]

Teacher Sex Scandals

As we turn to teachers and away from administrators, we notice a quantum leap in public interest, partly because teachers are in closer touch with children and partly because they represent something more palpable and absorbing than mere billboards of officialdom like college presidents. Teachers have become lightning rods for these stories, popular teachers being especially vulnerable because of their popularity: Mary Baxter (see chapter 1) was Teacher of the Year, and therefore just the one to haul into court.

It may seem odd that our culture could conceive of an ordinary classroom as a bordello, a place charged with exotic passion (rather than with the smell of wet wool, peed pants, and old uneaten lunches). But most of us take care to know next to nothing about what actually goes on in classrooms (the daily demands for inventive labor), and erotic suspicion finds its best food in ignorance. Thus we both glamorize (as we ridicule) and resent (as we depend on) the teacher who seems to be "reaching" the child, teaching her and actually gaining her attention. We might imagine that there's only one way this could be happening, and that way is sinister. We tend not to inquire too deeply into why we think that way: it suits so very many of our purposes.

So we arrange, in addition to the criminal trials involving teachers, a flow of concern, breaking forth in talk. We are concerned, let's pretend, about teaching being a haven for pedophiles. Thus we have a right to our worry, a worry we pay others, like Connie Chung, to fan. Chung did an *Eye to Eye* coyly entitled "Back to School" (February 3, 1994) that gives us the lowdown on how "convicted child molesters" have "hid their past to gain access to elementary school children." "It sounds outrageous and it is," Chung says. "If you want a job as a UPS delivery driver or cleaning up our national parks, you have to undergo a criminal background check. But there's a job that convicted sex offenders seem to have no trouble getting." The reporter feeding this to Chung (Roberta Baskin) assures her that the rotation of child molesters through our nation's schools is "not as unusual as you think," due to "a system" that "allows child molesters to move from school to school and find new victims." Even if s/he's caught and convicted, an offender "doesn't go to jail; he gets another job as a teacher." What a system!

As an expert in all the system's workings, Mr. Ken Lanning is brought on by Baskin and Chung to raise the level of anecdote (of which we've been given plenty) to sophisticated generalization. Mr. Lanning, who, Baskin says, "investigates pedophiles for the FBI," reports that "a true pedophile will find a method of access to children, and as a schoolteacher, not only can you find children, but you can specialize in whatever grade you want to gain access to." Baskin asks him to elaborate: "Now if your child gets molested by a dirty old man in a wrinkled raincoat or something like that, that's easier to deal with," he says. "But when you find some, what I call, pillar-of-the-community pedophile or molester in your midst, the general reaction is to get him out of your midst." Out of my midst, pillar-of-the-community pedophile!

Be Prepared

Scout leaders are natural figures in the stories we tell, because they have at their disposal a setting even better than the classroom: the forests and campgrounds of America. In 1996, a Cub Scout leader (Dana Point, Orange County, Troop 713) "crossed the line into lewd conduct" on a camping trip to the beach. In addition, he was convicted of earlier molesting two other "boys he befriended through scouting." He "showed no reaction to the verdict," the reporter noted, and that's the worst sign of all.[9] In a much more notorious case on the West Coast, a young Boy Scout chaplain-counselor (I think; the *L.A. Times*, with its mind on other things, never did make his position entirely clear) admitted to "having sexual contact with more than 50 Boy Scouts." He chose a setting, officials said, that "gave him discreet contact with the boys," perfect "isolation": Santa Catalina Island. Richard Walker, identified as a national Boy Scouts spokesman, said the admitted pedophile had been in contact, discreet or otherwise, with more than five hundred boys, the names of each being provided to the police, our main story generator.

A local Boy Scout executive, anticipating some criticism for entrusting boys to this chaplain-counselor, said, "The Boy Scouts does the best it can to ensure that campers are safe."[10] Since that "best" appears to some none too good in the face of what may have happened on the island, the Boy Scouts are tightening their net, fighting against atheists and homosexuals, and, at least in California, losing the first fight but holding their own in the second. Two boys who definitely did not believe in God and wanted to say so but just as definitely wanted to be Boy Scouts (why?) won the right to be so, and in Orange County too. But thirteen-year-old Timothy Curran, who identifies himself as gay and wants to be an assistant scoutmaster, was told by the Scouts and then by a judge that he couldn't. The judge said the Boy Scouts had the right to determine "its own standards of morality" and that doing so was "neither offensive or [sic] improper."[11]

Of course, I can't say the Boy Scouts are so stupid as to identify pedophilia with atheistic homosexuality,[12] and there is some danger that these restrictions may not only shut off the stories but shut off the supply of new volunteers altogether. There's such a thing as being too careful, as the executive director of Big Brothers/Big Sisters of Northwest Ohio pointed out in a letter to the *Toledo Blade* responding to an editorial. The original editorial (which I confess I did not see, my friend there sending me only the response to it) apparently called for sorting out anyone with an interest in children. The executive director, with some alarm, observed that the screening already going on was fine-toothed, and that "given the sacrifice of time and money our fine volunteers make each week for the Littles they serve, eliminating anyone with a strong interest in children would ensure a radical reduction in the number of matches that could be made."[13] Point well taken; but if they heed my advice, the Big Brothers/Big Sisters of Northwest Ohio will stop calling the children "the Littles," as if they were delicate miniatures living amongst the ferns.

Children and the Clergy

A local radio station broadcast the following: "Concerning the San Diego scandal involving priests and young boys, an unnamed source, speaking for the board of inquiry, said, 'without going into graphic detail now' . . ." Not go into graphic detail now? All across Southern California, dials turned as disappointed listeners sought out a less squeamish station. Not me, since I'm a scholar with no interest in vivid details and a lot in the cloudy big picture. Besides, the same station, quickly ridding itself of savorless official sources, told us what was going on: "charges of fondling, oral sex, anal intercourse, and other practices."

Clerics molesting children: that's the best occupational story we have. Priests especially are devised as the only nonsexual beings in our culture except for children and are thus nearly as vacant and erotic.[14] It is natural that they should figure prominently in these stories, just as they have in Gothic novels and in pornography—from medieval smut to Lewis's *The Monk* to a host of Victorian and modern tales of broken celibacy vows. One recent example, the three-hour Canadian film *The Boys of St. Vincent,* shown in the United States in 1995, rests squarely in this silly tradition, offering not a single surprise or deviation, not a single new idea, nothing you would call an "idea" at all. It has, not surprisingly, been widely praised.

CNN ran a seven-part series, *Fall from Grace,* beginning on November 14, 1993, with a follow-up program, *Child Molestation and the Church,* on December 7. The program begins with a meta-meditation by an unnamed woman on what it means to think of the subject at all: "It's such a threat to just even believe that a priest, a holy man, could molest children." Father Andrew Greeley follows, saying, "When a priest abuses a child, he's abusing Jesus." Confronting both the threat and the blasphemy, the show goes on to contemplate the idea of incest (the priest as "father"), secret vices and perversions ("an attractive hiding place for men struggling with deviant sexual urges"), the peculiarity of celibacy, and the tie (which doesn't exist) between homosexuality (assumed to be rampant among priests) and pedophilia. And this is CNN.

The same program also allows us to gauge the size of the problem: about five hundred priests and Catholic brothers turned in since 1982; an estimated two to four thousand child sex abusers (out of fifty thousand Roman Catholic clergy);[15] and an enormous drain on the church's coffers for settling or fighting these cases, about $40 million a year now, with estimates that "the American Catholic church will pay out more than $1 billion to victims by the end of this century." Insurance companies are starting to take a hard line on covering clerical abuse cases, and some archdioceses are budgeting big dollars in anticipation of settlements. The fact that Pope John Paul II reportedly regards all this merely as a social problem peculiar to America and Canada seems to guarantee that we will not run out of stories soon. CNN quotes the pope: "While every human means for responding to this evil must be implemented, we cannot forget that the first and most important means is prayer." The pope, like the rest of us, finds the solution in a coalition of alarm and talk.

What are people saying about this set of stories? Perhaps you already know, or can guess, so I'll just offer a sample:

> We made some mistakes, but "the church and the rest of society didn't have the understanding (of) pedophilia" then as it has now.

> In the same courtroom where, a century earlier, Lizzie Borden was acquitted of murdering her parents, the 58-year-old former priest sat impassively through the unusually long parade of victims' impact statements.

> And my suggestion, if you'll let me finish, was that we're probably talking about a form of homosexual attraction here. The entrance of homosexuals in the Roman Catholic clergy is only 10 or 15 years old. Prior to then, they wouldn't have been allowed in. I know some priests who are disciplined homosexuals, and they're very good priests. But I think it relates to that problem, but of course, the gay community doesn't like to hear that sort

of thing. Then, of course, we're dealing, apparently, with people who are abused in their own childhood. I think that's the interesting issue which is: Do they seek out the comfort of the priesthood with its laws of celibacy so they don't have to deal with their own sexuality. Again, the experts seem to talk about this.[16]

Experts do seem to talk about this—and not just the experts.

Such talk is fed by charges and possibilities, farfetched or not. The late Cardinal Joseph Bernadin of Chicago, for instance, was accused by one Steven J. Cook of having molested him in the mid-1970s when Cook was a teenage seminary student, the charges having been delayed because the memory hadn't been recovered until recently. But by November 12, 1993, helped along by hypnosis therapy, Cook said he was sure, had taken two polygraph tests, and knew it was Bernadin to whom he had been delivered by another priest (also a molester, Cook said) for purposes of fondling and sodomy. Now, Cardinal Bernadin had been a leader in urging the church to meet the issue of pedophilic priests head-on and had instituted a set of tough policies for dealing with the problem. The ironies were irresistible.

A few months later, on February 28, 1994, Mr. Cook dropped all charges, saying that "if he knew in November what he now understood about the limitations of recovered memory, he would never have sued Bernadin."[17] Bernadin said he harbored no ill feelings against Cook, though he didn't officially excuse CNN, which not only had broadcast the accusation by Cook—"It shatters your soul, it shatters your life. [Bernadin] has to pay a price."—but had delayed it a few days to coincide with the opening of a national Catholic bishops' conference in Washington. Just as we directed.

More recently and unthinkably, the Los Angeles Times was delighted to bring us a case involving two rabbis. Federal authorities alleged "that the ultra-orthodox rabbi, Israel Grunwald, fondled the minor and that his assistant, Rabbi Yehudah Friedlander, sexually molested the girl." The girl in question was a fifteen-year-old on a flight from Australia, traveling alone. She said Grunwald leaned over an empty seat, admired her jewelry, and fondled her breast. He then, she said, relinquished his seat to Friedlander, who "fondled and molested her while she was covered with a blanket, trying to sleep." The story was apparently confirmed by "a passenger from Michigan," who said a rabbi groped the girl under a blanket for five to eight minutes.[18] The passenger later talked to the flight crew, who contacted authorities, who arrested the two rabbis at the airport on May 31, charging Friedlander with sexual abuse of a minor and Grunwald with abusive sexual contact. On June 14, Friedlander was indicted by a federal grand jury, and in November he "admitted that during the flight he reached underneath the teen-ager's underwear and touched her genitals without her consent."[19] At the sentencing, the girl's father said she had been transformed by the incident from "a gregarious, outspoken, friendly girl" at the top of her class to a depressed insomniac with plummeting grades. "He violated me in the very deepest way possible," she said.[20] There were, by my count, eight articles, long and detailed ones, about the fondling. Why?

Woody Allen

The talk that swirls around individual stars is even more satisfying than that generated by professions. People such as Woody Allen and Michael Jackson outshine their occupations and magnetize our attention so fully that it is no wonder this tale of erotic children would somehow, sooner or later, come to ensnare them. It's true that they are connected to the story only by talk: nothing was proven, no charges were filed; but talk is what we want, all we want.

Take Woody Allen. "If Woody Allen is a child molester, I will publicly kiss Pat Buchanan," said Dick Cavett,[21] testifying, I think, to his belief in Allen's innocence and not his longing for the honey of Mr. Buchanan's lips. Still, the connections are telling. I understand the witty Cavett to be mocking not only right-wing frenzies over child molesting but the general eroticizing of the discourse.

Allen built his career on the absurd metaphysical and sexual pretensions emanating from his wizened dried apple of a body. Ridiculing his own lust for truth, immortality, and younger women, Allen has played relentlessly on the clichés of pop psychology, pop philosophy, and pop horniness. He has been successful because he can tickle our desires and fears, actually work his way inside them, and still give us considerable distance, allowing us always the protections of his own

Allen here seems so
absurdly self-absorbed
he fails to notice he is
missing a trunk.

inventive comedy, impossible body, sweet pathos. More plainly, he
allows us to be perverse and lecherous by parodying lust and lechery,
gives us some exercise for our dark side by making it seem, for a moment, acutely funny: "I'm doing a sociological study of perversion;
I'm up to child molesting" (*Bananas*).

But Allen woke one day to find the delicate balance of this comedy
shattered. It was as if bad elves had come in the night and taken him
from sophisticated Manhattan to a land where only soap opera stories
had currency and where minds were so granular that jokes about sex
were understood as confessions. Woody always thought Los Angeles
was hell; but that was before he found himself in Omaha.

For those of you who have forgotten the founding facts (as if they
mattered) of this case, here they are, at least as I remember them.
After seven years of marriage to Mia Farrow and soon after the birth of
their son, Satchel, in 1987, things began to cool in the marriage, if you
know what I mean. Soon they stopped having sex together, Woody
says; and Mia says, through her lawyer, Alan Dershowitz, that Woody
started having sex with Soon-Yi Previn in December 1991. Soon-Yi

Previn is Mia's daughter by way of her former husband, Andre Previn. Soon-Yi says she was twenty-one when all this broke (August 1992), though others say she was nineteen. She and Allen apparently took no notice of one another until in 1991 he asked her to go to a Knicks game, then another, then another—and, well, you know how Knicks games are. Allen, keep in mind, is not her biological (or any other kind of) father, was not married to her mother, and did not live with Soon-Yi, who was unarguably a consenting adult (at twenty-one or even the rumored nineteen).

In January 1992, Ms. Farrow discovered—was "shattered to discover," as *Newsweek* put it—nude photos of Ms. Previn at Woody's apartment. Around this time, though not necessarily as a result of this discovery, the couple started wrangling about a joint custody arrangement for Satchel and two other children, Moses (fourteen) and Dylan (seven), whom Woody had adopted with Farrow. Meanwhile, Farrow had adopted two more children by herself in 1992, continuing a practice (she's adopted seven over the years) her friends regard as saintly and Woody regards as a pathological form of collecting, dangerous to the children and to him. Anyhow, negotiations were going badly and got worse. In August 1992, Mia, in effect, turned Allen in to the police for molesting Dylan (having first recorded a conversation with Dylan, which supporters say delivered the goods and skeptics say was the result of rehearsal and cruel coercion). Allen responded by suing for custody of all three children, suggesting Mia was an unfit mother. He gave interviews to magazines he surely detests, *Time* and *Newsweek,* and held bizarre press conferences, one to confirm his love for Soon-Yi (the same day, August 17, the Connecticut police confirmed they were investigating charges of sexual abuse against him). Mia wasn't saying a lot, allowing her martyrdom and her view of Allen to come out by way of friends and her spokesperson-children, the Dylan tape being released and Moses being sent before news cameras to denounce his father: "That person is capable of doing it to anybody; people like that should be locked up."

By this time we had all the fuel we needed and pretty much all we'll ever get. It was plenty to ignite the talk. Some of it is comical: Rosie O'Donnell shrieks on an HBO comedy special (April 29, 1995) that Woody has "a great idea: adopt a kid and when she gets to be 16, you fuck 'er. It's called INCEST, Woody, PEDOPHILIA—get a dictionary!" Some of it is political: Newt Gingrich twitters, "Woody Allen is currently having nonincest with a nondaughter for whom he is a nonfather . . . because they have no concept of families."[22] Who's "they"? They is the monster, the child molester, the little guy with the red hair, the—well, the cop in *Bananas* says it perfectly: "He's a bad apple, a commie, a New York Jewish intellectual Communist crackpot. I don't want to cast no aspersions." Allen is so perfect for this part that we won't let him out of it no matter how much he protests. The protests are beside the point, make him sound like his own favorite character, Fielding Melish: "This trial is a travesty of a mockery of a sham of a mockery of a travesty of two mockeries of a sham. I call for a mistrial."

Only a pest, a Fielding Melish, someone who doesn't get it, would say Woody Allen is innocent—or guilty. It doesn't matter which. The parts have already been cast, and Allen is firmly set in the role of child molester. Not that his is the lead part, or that, in truth, we take him all that seriously. In this drama, we pay to see the child, and we run things backward, set the film in reverse, so that the twenty-one-year-old Ms. Previn somehow gets younger and younger, folds into the body of the seven-year-old Dylan. Our fantasies are caught in the merging of the young woman Allen says he is having sex with and the small child he says he certainly is not having sex with. Soon-Yi is reported to be younger than she says, and rumors (obviously false) abound that she is "mentally handicapped" (that would make her "just like a child," wouldn't it?). *Time* runs a column, "What Is Incest,"[23] which allows experts to answer the question we were all afraid to ask and to see that though what is going on between Woody and Ms. Previn can hardly be called "innocent" (why not?) and is "surely an abuse of power" (why?), it obviously is not incest.

So why deal with it under that category? Why not ask if it flies in the face of the Council of Trent or Robert's Rules of Order? Because *Time* is circulating public desire, and public desire is working on the assumption that somehow Soon-Yi and Dylan are the same, that those nude photos show more than we've been told, that more children are involved, and that we now have license to contemplate it all. Adult women are often collapsed into little girls in our sanctioned public pornography, in fashion and film particularly; but this case makes the process both material and fantastic, palpable and perfectly safe.

This may explain why both the prosecuting attorney who dropped the criminal case and the judge deciding custody behaved as if Allen were both guilty and an annoyance. The prosecutor, explaining why he wasn't filing charges, insisted he had a strong case but didn't want to put Dylan through the courtroom ordeal—never mentioning that both state investigators and the Yale–New Haven hospital said the charges were unfounded, that Dylan had imagined it or been coached. Kate Stith, a Yale law professor, may say she has "never heard of another case where the prosecutor spoke so directly and so inappropriately about a case he wasn't going to prosecute," and Nat Hentoff may label the prosecutor's conduct "one of the most egregious disfigurings of justice I have ever come across"; but he did what we pay him to do.[24]

The judge did his part by raging against Allen for taking up with Soon-Yi, for possessing "no parenting skills," and for acting toward Dylan in a way that was "grossly inappropriate."[25] He then gave sole custody of all the children to Farrow, making it practically impossible for Allen ever to see any of them. That ensured further appeals and gossip incitement: Farrow gabbled later about the difference between "inappropriate" and "sexual" behavior, saying what Woody did to Dylan in play time was too "intense" and adding that, yes, she had "thought he had a homosexual relationship" with someone,[26] as if that were germane.

And it went on: more appeals, Mia changed Dylan's name to Eliza and Satchel's to Seamus, Woody threatened to make a documentary of the whole business, and still more appeals, not to mention a March 1995 Fox television miniseries, *Love and Betrayal: The Mia Farrow Story*. The *New Yorker* ran a long, slack piece on Woody as a "peerless stylist" victimized by humorless Puritans,[27] and more interviews bloomed. To Liz Smith, Woody exclaimed, "It's been fun! It's been fun being the bad guy in the press. And I can afford it."[28] And on *NBC Dateline* (November 29, 1994) he said the whole nightmare has been very valuable to him: "Apart from pain to the children, I wouldn't trade the last two years' experience." He said he has come to believe in "the power of distraction": "It is possible in this vale of tears to avoid coming face to face with the position you're in." "I've managed," he said, "to achieve being shallow *and* unhappy."

Allen then slipped through the cracks, apart from some random sniping: the *New York Times* ran an op-ed piece calling him "irretrievably creepy," and *Time* listed him among the week's "LOSERS" when one of his custody appeals was "laughed out of court."[29] But his new movies were doing well and nobody much minded any more. He had done his job.

Michael Jackson

Michael Jackson is not, as you thought I was going to say, another matter. It's the same thing: talk that may be reckless but is also unmalicious, which we prove by buying his records, going to his concerts, and declaring our "belief" in him. We concoct friendly little jokes: he has been making improper advances on his inner child; the problem with the marriage was that Lisa Marie wanted children right away and Michael preferred to buy them dinner first; you can tell when Michael's having a party by all the Big Wheels parked in the driveway; he told Lisa Marie he wanted children — but he meant for his birthday.

Along with the jokes, of course, there were the charges being leaked regularly by lawyers or sold to *Hard Copy* by Jackson's ex-employees: "He did not seem to mind when [Blanca] Francia [ex-maid] saw him in the water with a 9- or 10-year old guest, their underpants clearly visible atop a heap of towels alongside the Jacuzzi. She assumed that beneath the swirling water they were nude."[30] Francia's surmising mind sinks beneath the bubbles and takes us with it. Francia said she later saw Jackson with her own son "in a room," and though "unable to make out what they were doing, she admitted to being 'nervous.'" I'm getting nervous myself. A Jackson driver — ex-driver, of course — said he saw Jackson with his hands down a boy's underpants; another ex-maid said she saw him "giving the famous Michael Jackson crotch grab to this little boy — over and over again"; and an ex-cook claimed he saw Jackson "groping Macaulay Culkin . . . as the boy was engrossed in a video game."[31] I expect the crotched-grabbed boy and

Michael gleams forth
like a crazed mime.

the singularly engrossed Culkin were in their underpants, since the entire army of ex-Jackson employees seem to be in the grips of an unremitting underpants fetish.

Of course, as with Allen, there was a case of sorts that sparked things and opened all these images up for us, a case that never went anywhere and probably never had anywhere to go, though it dragged its slow length across months and months like a weary python. Once again, I'll tell you what I remember of the actual facts here, some of which I have checked. In August 1993 (why do these things always bloom in August?) allegations of sexual abuse of a thirteen-year-old boy surfaced. Things became confused. Private investigators moved in, a whole sea of attorneys, including some big shots like Johnny Cochran and, for a couple of days, Gloria Allred. Countercharges were fired back, claiming the boy's father, a "dentist to the stars" and aspiring screenwriter, was simply trying to get money from Jackson, urging the boy to lie in order to feather his own nest. The well-connected dentist was, in any case, involved in trying to get custody and seeking some kind of victory, bragging on tape, "If I go through with this [the lawsuit, presumably], I win big time; there's no way I lose." Meanwhile, the police raided Jackson's Neverland ranch and took away fifty boxes (of what?), and a grand jury was called.

Many boys were interviewed by police and more by television reporters. Jackson's special friends had included the famous—Emmanuel Lewis (from *Webster*), Corey Feldman, and Culkin—as well as a good many others who came forward to talk about their relationships with him. All this testimony was top-notch, despite Culkin's vexing silence. Each of the friends earnestly told of their belief in Michael and detailed how innocent their own relationship with him was. Some, perhaps not helping Michael to the extent they hoped, eagerly told of spending the night in the same bed with the singer—but it was a big bed, nothing happened, the cuddling was only friendly. One ex-boy, Terry George, told anyone who would listen that Michael did call him and talk dirty, telling the then twelve-year-old George that he was masturbating as they spoke; George hastily added that, though it sounded like "phone sex," it wasn't at all "a dirty old man thing," but just "a way of expressing affection."[32]

Meanwhile, the unnamed (but easily traceable—I mean, how many fathers are dentists to the stars?) boy who had sued supplied salacious details to the police about his dealings with the man he said nicknamed him "Rubba." Jackson, he said, kissed him often, progressing to putting his tongue in the boy's mouth, which the boy did not like but learned to tolerate, and then to the grabbing of buttocks, and then to various stratagems for getting one or both of them naked, then to lying atop one another and creating mutual erections, then to "masturbating me with his mouth," then to mutual masturbation.

Meanwhile, Jackson, who was on tour in places like Singapore and Hong Kong, collapsed, canceled the tour (Pepsi deserted him; Sony re-signed him), went to drug rehab, welcomed to his side Elizabeth Taylor (who believed in him), sparked a lot of controversy about why he wasn't returning to the United States, returned to the United States, sued *Hard Copy,* had the NAACP protest the handling of the case, was strip-searched (to see if his genitals matched the description given by the boy), went public (December 22, 1993) with protests against "being forced to submit to a dehumanizing and humiliating examination . . . [of] my penis, my buttocks, my lower torso, my thighs, and any other area that they wanted to," settled the civil suit, saw the criminal charges melt away for lack of evidence, married Lisa Marie Presley (sparking another round of jokes and a *Time* poll [August 22, 1994] that revealed only 4 percent of Americans thought the marriage would last "forever," presumably meaning until death parted them), started planning a new tour, and, to the chagrin of the 4 percent, was divorced.[33]

Like Allen, Jackson was forced into the monster role in this melodrama, and he doubtless suffered. Yet there was surprisingly little direct attack. His own sister La Toya was the major exception, issuing periodic statements about her brother's "crimes against young people," claiming she simply could not stand by and "be a silent collaborator," though (dear La Toya) she didn't blame him really because he was (she claimed) molested by a relative as a child and thus couldn't help himself. "He is a pedophile," said La Toya, but "I don't blame him; he's sick."[34]

Beyond that, things were either sweet or no worse than mildly acrid, even from the standard founts of bitterness. The *National Enquirer,* perhaps because Jackson has used it for his own purposes in the past, satisfied itself with things like an interview (December 14, 1993) with ex-cook Johnny Ciao about Jackson and boys "naked except for underwear" (what an odd way to put it). Even this article qualifies its attention to Jackson by giving us a picture of Ciao looking like a demented garbageman, dressed in a chef's costume he must have been wearing night and day since 1977, doing something disgusting with his dirty, pendulous hands to meat (I think), and drooling over this project as if it excited him almost as much as underpants—thus making it tough to trust him entirely. And even Roseanne, who can be counted on to express colorfully the least admirable positions available to weak understandings, was satisfied with testifying that Jackson "is the perfect picture of a child molester," saving her more considered analyses for the parents of Jackson's child friends: "stupid fucking assholes."[35]

This tendency on the part of those certain of his guilt to attack the

SPEAKING OUT for the first time, Jac
son's former chef, Johnny Ciao, says i
caught Michael emerging from the pla
room in only his underwear.

At least Mr. Ciao is
not himself pictured
in his underwear.

parents, to slip right by Jackson, was marked and curious, as if we
were both asserting our own righteousness and protecting the star. It's
not Jackson who's at fault, we seem to be saying, but those who naively
assume that relations with him (or any adult) can be nonsexual. Let
me reprint a letter to the editor of the *Los Angeles Times* that catches
our will to utter passionate denunciations that are oddly off-center,
as if we needed to be superior to someone but needed also to protect
the sexually enticing images surrounding adult-child relations:

Jackson may or may not be guilty of molesting the young boys he befriended. But without question, the parents of those boys are guilty of contributing to the delinquency of a minor and they should be held accountable and thus prosecuted.

Parents who are willing and knowingly allow such a relationship between a 35-year-old man and their young son are largely responsible for the consequences of the relationship.

When are we going to place responsibility where or on whom it belongs? [36]

If it doesn't matter whether Jackson is guilty or not, what kind of "delinquency" are the parents contributing to? The writer wants to lay on the parents a guilt she is also anxious to withdraw from Jackson, thus preserving the eroticism of adult-child contacts and attacking those who might deny it.

Most were not anxious to blame anybody, content to enjoy themselves (ourselves). Kids kept buying his records and scoffing at the charges; a poll taken by *Entertainment Weekly* just after the story broke showed only 12 percent put any stock in the charges, and Jackson later won the Children's Choice Award, as 75 percent of the 100,000 schoolchildren polled chose Michael Jackson as the world's top "ideal role model." Even the locksmith employed by the police to burglarize his place said he liked Jackson, respected "the good he has done in the world," and hoped the police didn't find what they were looking for.[37]

By summer 1995 Michael was pretty much back in business. In June of that year he issued the blockbuster album *HIStory*. Though it did not quite set records for initial sales, his single "Scream" entered the Billboard Hot 100 in June 1995 as number 5, the highest debut ever. But these successes were nothing compared with his spectacular marriage and the use we could make of it. In a June 14 interview (Michael and Lisa Marie) on ABC's *Prime Time Live*, Diane Sawyer raised the issues we all knew needed airing:

"Did you ever sexually engage, fondle, have sexual contact with this child or any other?"

"Never, ever; it's not in my head and I'm not even interested in that!"

"Why did you settle?"

"I talked to my lawyers and I said, 'Can you guarantee me that justice will prevail?' and they said . . ."

"What is a thirty-six-year-old man doing sleeping with a twelve-year-old boy?"

"I have never invited anyone into my bed — ever. Children love me. I love them. They follow me. They want to be with me. Anybody can come into my bed."

[Lisa Marie]: "They jump into bed with him!"

"Is it over, the sleep-overs where people have to wonder?"

"No — because it's all moral. It's all on the level of purity and love and just innocence. If you're talking about sex, then that's a nut — that's not me. Go to the guy down the street, cause it's not Michael Jackson."

Sawyer then announced what of course we all knew, that she is an important intellectual: "I didn't spend my life as a serious journalist to ask these kinds of questions." That being the case, she ran clips of others asking these kinds of questions: were Michael and Lisa Marie having sex and truly enjoying it. "Yes, yes, yes!" said Lisa Marie impatiently, adding that those doubting it "can eat it."

The marriage ended, but it provided plenty of tired jokes and innuendoes while it lasted: "Scared Moms Drag Their Kids Indoors as Michael Jackson Cruises Streets," said the *National Enquirer;* and, in the same tone, *Newsweek* said Lisa Marie "reportedly complained" (yeah, sure), "How come he can find time for other people's children but not mine?" *Esquire* (using the headline, "Dub Me! Rub Me!") reported that Jackson requested a British knighthood "for his work with little children."[38] Jackson stays in the news, of course, given his lavish plans for new industries, the flaps over his recordings (racist lyrics?), his marriage late in 1996 to Debbie Rowe, and the birth of his baby.

Jackson's importance to us, however, seems to outrun the current news or scandal, even to be somehow detached from it. For one thing, he has always been figured as puzzling, a sexual dilemma, in that he blurs so exotically the boundaries of age, gender, and race. From the time a thirteen-year-old Tatum O'Neal was dating him, he has been figured inside the discourse of sexuality more than the discourse of music or entertainment. Jackson is the one who shuns sex or battens on it, collects girls or men or boys. Is he gay? Is he bisexual, transsexual, transvestite, androgynous, in love with the Elephant Man's remains? The speculations—he took hormones, he had a sex-change operation, he had got Brooke Shields pregnant, he was going to marry Clifton Davis—became so frenzied that Jackson issued (on September 5, 1984) what must be the most exasperated public statement ever, insisting that he didn't take hormones, hadn't had eye surgery, and that he planned one day to marry and have children, whom he, by the way, loved.

But more fully than others playing the role in this drama of child loving, even more fully than Allen, Jackson is seen as himself a child, thus doubling the *frisson*. He is ordinarily explained in reference to his childhood: the unnatural life of a child star and the emotional and physical abuse he suffered at the hands of his father: "sometimes with a belt; sometimes with a switch. I'd try to fight back, just swinging my fists. That's why I got it more than all my brothers combined. I would fight back and my father would kill me, just tear me up."[39] An expert interviewed on *Good Morning America* (November 26, 1993), one Brenda Wade, Ph.D., explains it this way: His tragedy "is quite understandable, given his background. Here's someone who was an abused child, by his own report. We know that his siblings also say there was abuse. And he had no childhood. He didn't have the opportunities to be with other children, to play, to have normal relationships with people. And this doesn't make for a very healthy human being in the long run."

The terms of this form of understanding are, of course, so loaded as to be useful only if one starts by assuming that Jackson needs to be explained in terms of a deficiency. There are other possibilities. His own view, repeated many times, is that he likes children, finding them more honest and less self-serving than adults. They also provide him with a source of energy: if he's tired, "I'll dash off on my bike and ride to the schoolyard, just to be around them. When I come back to the studio, I'm ready to move mountains." He also, perhaps revealingly, finds children safe: "They can't hurt you."[40] They can, as he now knows; but one sees what he means.

I see no reason not to locate Michael Jackson in the tradition of

Romantic idealism that often attaches artists to youth, as it did Lewis Carroll, Mark Twain, John Ruskin, J. M. Barrie, and many other minor artists among the moderns. It shouldn't surprise us that some might find ways to take seriously, to literalize the pastoral and Romantic exaltation of the child. Many of Jackson's friends, Elizabeth Taylor especially, seem to find this view of him wholly satisfactory. Many others, however, reach for darker models, or at least more complex ones, often those in literature, Peter Pan coming to hand with embarrassing readiness. The parallel can be illuminating: Peter with his lost boys trying gamely to turn the world into a vast playground and resisting with all the energy in their near-naked bodies the efforts of adults to contain them. Jackson's subtle abilities to woo his audience coexist with a defiance so blunt that young people everywhere respond immediately: Jackson looks the way *he* wants to look, dresses outrageously, adorns himself, and doesn't obey gravity, much less parental strictures: if you feel like it, he says, then grab your crotch and wave it right in Dad's face.

But I think this American hero is also a part of a more nostalgic and dangerous tradition, one represented most clearly by Holden Caulfield's desire to catch and hold the innocence he knows he really cannot contain. Holden says, in lines that refuse to go away, no matter how often we call them corny:

> I keep picturing all these little kids playing some game in this big field of rye and all. Thousands of little kids, and nobody's around—nobody big, I mean—except me. And I'm standing on the edge of some crazy cliff. What I have to do, I have to catch everybody if they start to fall over the cliff—I mean if they're running and they don't look where they're going I have to come out from somewhere and *catch* them. That's all I'd do all day. I'd just be the catcher in the rye and all. I know it's crazy, but that's the one thing I'd really like to be. I know it's crazy.[41]

Michael Jackson, away with his boys at Neverland, with nobody around—nobody big, I mean—does all he can to keep them from falling. They are all running, not looking where they're going. He'll catch them—or we will. And then what? What does our nostalgia buy for us, or for those caught in our net?

9. Recovered Memory

It isn't so astonishing, the number of things I can remember, as the number of things I can remember that aren't so. —Mark Twain

Memory belongs to the imagination. Human memory is not like a computer which records things; it is part of the imaginative process, on the same terms as invention. —Alain Robbe-Grillet[1]

Elizabeth Loftus was molested when she was six and shrugs it off. "It's not that big a deal." —*Psychology Today*

When we picture our own childhood, what do we see? Reaching back into memory, we locate a figure all but irresistible. We were the child other people yearned for, not that such allure made us so special. Irresistible is what a child *is* in our culture. We could not find an un-alluring child within if we tried, and why should we try? Why should we not locate the origins of our being in a child that is both innocent and erotic, pure and violated? The rewards for conducting the search in this way are considerable; and it's the best kind of search: we never come up empty. What we find when we ask whence we sprang and why we are the way we are is the child fashioned by our culture, a culture that seems to understand itself and formulate its fables of being in reference to child molesting.

That looks more like an unearned conclusion than an engaging introduction, I know; but recovered memory is such a tumultuous subject that it's best to clear off some ground on which to stand. I am not, I should say, interested in contesting the claims of either the recovered- or the false-memory groups, but rather in trying to understand why this issue exists at all and why we find the claims and counterclaims so arresting. Why do we frame the issue of memory and erotic childhood as we do, and why do we develop a thirst for quarrels that take place within that frame?

Recovering memories of childhood sexual abuse would not be a practice or a topic of such absorbing interest to us if it did not satisfy so many needs. I do not mean by this simply that abuse provides an "excuse" for bad lives and bad acts. It may, but such an analysis is so trivial and self-righteous that it stops inquiry just where it should begin.

Citing the "abuse excuse" as a sufficient explanation is like saying Marilyn Monroe was popular because she was female. If we explore why people so often read their pasts in reference to an overwhelming image of the overwhelmed child, raped and silenced, we won't be satisfied with blaming them, with saying they are trying to beat the rap. We read our pasts as dramas of child molesting, first of all, because that's the way pasts are constructed in our culture. Why we do that, why we find recovered memory so riveting, where this is leading, what it's costing: these will be the questions haunting this chapter.

Let me take out of hiding a couple of observations that will help us as we go. First, we have learned from Foucault that while repression is a good metaphor for explaining the mental and cultural operations that say no to us, this machinery does not often operate by prohibiting; it creates. So, we might hypothesize that memory, like all agencies of power, does not work primarily by crude proscription but by fabrication. Our culture does not spend its energies trying to outlaw what it doesn't like; it puts into operation what it does like. Memory may repress now and then, but its authority lies in its ability to build. Memories are made, not retrieved; they are made anew each time by artists, not hauled to us by forklift trucks.

Further, to say that memory is a construction (and hence not a slick retrieval of some prior event) implies that at one time there was an event that was not a construction, some pristine present with which we were fully at one. Where is this event that doesn't ask us to interpret and construct it, even as it is being played before and through us? It's not simply that I misremember Grandma yelling at me for stealing the pie when I was four (it wasn't Grandma but Aunt Sally; it wasn't pie but ice cream; I wasn't four but nine; it wasn't me but my brother); it's that I misread the event at the time, if there was an event. That is, no pure, whole, independent event is there for me; it exists as a form to be read and acted, then and now.

My reason for setting off such high-sounding platitudes is to draw attention not to pure reality and whether or not memory is acting up, but to the nature of our constructing apparatus. Why do we form our pasts and our lives as we do? Where do our memory plots come from? Why do they assume the shape they commonly have these days?

I suggest that our memories are structured as much by deep cultural needs as by raw experience, that we draw our plots largely from a cultural storehouse made available to all of us in pretty much the same form. I am not talking here about Jungian archetypes; I mean that our preoccupations and the stories that give them power are not necessarily individualized, and, more important, that the relentless individualizing we engage in draws our attention away from cultural analysis. A cultural analysis is not meant as an evasion of responsibility—shut up Alan Dershowitz—but as a means of getting closer to knowing the ways our heritage may be driving us into corners—simply by giving us so few stories to tell, by starving our inventive capacities.

The story of recovered memory locks together the fascinating tales of multiple personality, childhood sexual activities, criminality, people in therapy telling secrets, hidden pasts, sudden discoveries that explain all. The usual story gets rid of all complexity and ambiguity; everything that was hidden (totally) is now clear (totally). This cultural fantasia manifests a boozy democratic hospitality, a hearty American come-on-in quality. By expanding the story of child molesting into the past and into the recesses of all our memories, we make sure no one is left out.

Even if we think that we don't enter into this, that our childhood (therefore our present being) wasn't molded by molestation, we are, according to many experts on the subject, probably wrong:

> If you are unable to remember any specific instances . . . but still have a feeling that something abusive happened to you, it probably did. . . . Often the knowledge that you were abused starts with a tiny feeling, an intuition. It's important to trust that inner voice and work from there. Assume your feelings are valid. So far, no one we've talked to thought she might have been abused, and then later discovered that she hadn't been. The progression always goes the other way, from suspicion to confirmation. If you think you've been abused and your life shows the symptoms, then you were.

> If a memory fits your sense of the past, and, in the long run, you feel better for having dealt with it as real, then accept it

as true. . . . The more you know about what to look for with repressed memories, the more you find. . . . The existence of profound disbelief is an indication that the memories are real.

If you ever had reason to suspect that you may have been sexually abused, even if you have no explicit memory of it, the chances are very high that you were.

Incest is so common as to be epidemic. . . . Repression in some form is virtually universal among survivors.

When clients tell me they have no recollection of whole pieces of their childhood, I assume the likelihood of some sort of abuse.[2]

If we remain unconvinced, we are given lists of symptoms and urged to read backward from them, being sure that they mark childhood sexual abuse, even (especially) if we have no memory of such abuse. Trusting the symptoms will allow us to recover the memories and to recognize, meanwhile, that we were indeed molested. As you doubtless know, these lists commonly reach such length and breadth that no human alive could escape. Take me. From John Bradshaw's famous list of four, I am certainly caught by at least two: I have trouble knowing what I want, and I tend to follow suggestions other people give me. Bradshaw says even one *yes* means "you can count on some damage having been done to you in your early developmental stage." I try Renee Fredrickson. Big mistake: I seemed to know things about sex before they were explained to me; I am preoccupied with thoughts about sex; I often have nightmares (chased by bears); basements terrify me; I hate going to the dentist more than most people (more than anyone); certain foods nauseate me; I have odd sensations in my genitals; I do not take good care of my body; nothing seems very real sometimes; sometimes really violent or strange pictures flash through my mind; I startle easily; I daydream. That's a dozen, and there are another twenty I lied about (but who wants to admit "I pick at my body too much" or "There are certain things I seem to have a strange affection or attraction for" or "I began masturbating at an early age"?).[3]

It is not my purpose here to indict Mother, to ridicule the recovered memory movement, or to join in the backlash. That backlash, in fact, seems to me so much a part of the problem and so unlikely to dislodge the main story that I devote the next chapter to it. The point is that the story of recovered memory has, one way or another, kept the erotic scapegoating story of child sexuality tantalizingly before us for a long time now. So eager are we for that story that books parading their own naiveté sell millions of copies. For instance, the mammothly successful *Courage to Heal* offers a circus of appeal to anecdote, reasoning from "raw experience," a disdain for theory—"none of what is presented here is based on psychological theories"[4]—a serene disregard for complexity, an inability to imagine other explanations for the phenomena the authors observe, and a reckless imprecision stemming from an addiction to their own nostrums. But this book has had such consequences that "it would have to be considered one of the most significant publications of the century," Lawrence Wright ruefully admits.[5] Bass and Davis feel sure that the dinkiest inkling of suspicion means molestation, that, given enough work, you'll recover the memories; or if you don't it doesn't matter, since life's rufflings can have but one source.

Here's the standard line. Child molesting is an epidemic, and memory holds the secret. Because the trauma of sexual assault is unbearable, children deny the facts, repressing them and commonly expressing this damaging repression through neurotic behaviors, often being forced to create for themselves multiple personalities in order to lock away the trauma. Memory guards the vault. The fact that memory may not yield up the secrets readily licenses us to talk at greater length about hidden pasts, to read more subtly and discover more and more erotic hints, to refer more and more behavioral patterns to central images of children involved in sexual activity. States rush to extend the statute of limitations in these memory cases so that all of us will have more leisure to devote to recovering stories of childhood sexuality.[6]

Repression

In order to provide us with this cascade of new images, supporting notions are smuggled in. One of these is a dubious model for memory itself, a point that will occupy us later; others concern repression and the general way the mind handles shocking or unpleasant material.

By repression I mean simply the capacity of the mind to hide out of sight, disguise and block, make into lapses, what it cannot handle directly. Two questions about repression arise: Is there such a thing? Is it activated in cases of child molesting? The second question seems easier, but it isn't, since most of the literature simply reports what therapists and analysts have observed, and they have observed contradictory things: Michael Yapko says repression very seldom is evident in cases of trauma, that the victim "knows *and has always known* that the abuse occurred," but Lenore Terr says that repeated (more extreme?) trauma makes the operation of repression more likely.[7] Most reports seem to side with Yapko, but the talk goes on inconclusively.

It can do so largely because "repression" itself is such a loose baggy monster of an idea. A debate in the *Harvard Mental Health Newsletter* conducted July–October 1994 on whether or not there is such a thing as repression foundered on different ideas about what it might be. Dr. Adolf Grunbaum argued that there is no empirical evidence at all to support the idea of "repression proper," and Dr. David S. Holmes, admitting it is impossible to prove that repression does not exist, colorfully and with some heat said, "We are no more justified in using the concept to explain a patient's behavior than we are in expecting the patient to ride home on a unicorn." On the other hand, sidestepping the unicorn question, Dr. Mardi J. Horowitz said that "we need not define the term as Freud did a century ago," and that, redefined, it could be very useful, although never, he added, in the dramatic and blunt way certain movies and enthusiastic therapists tend to claim.

What's interesting in all this is how a way of understanding forgetting becomes hardened into a mechanism, not simply by those who wish to repudiate it but also by those who wish to claim it for their own ends. If repression is a machine or an on-off device, skeptical doctors can cite the failure of decades of research to detect it; and the recovered-memory people, ignoring the empiricists, can go on assuming it operates like a border guard or an alarm system. If, on the other hand, repression is (as Freud himself developed it) an explanatory metaphor, it can become part of a strategy to ward off knowingness. Freud told the story of repression to keep alive the possibility that answers can often hide behind other answers, that we should not rest just because a conclusion (or a diagnosis) is plausible, its very plausibility sometimes being a clue that it is "screening" deeper answers. Freud posited that there is psychic material that is always hidden, and he distrusted the impatient scurry to settle down fast with the first answer that came along. Freud developed a figure of speech, hoping to curb our fear that if we didn't find certainty right off we might never find it. Repression for him was a way of asserting the mind's depth and its capacity to elude the pedantic application of commonsense models.

Getting Rid of Freud, Getting Back to Basics

But it's precisely Freud's siding with complexity and ambiguity that makes him anathema to those who want to see repression as a tool for hammering into place the simple facts. Hence the assault on Freud. While the concept of repression is central to the defense of recovered memory stories and the strong erotic images arising from them, Freud's complex use of repression does not give us an open sesame into the scene of child molesting. In fact, he suggested that what is often being repressed is complicity, not rudimentary victimization.

Similarly, those who line up on the other side, viewing recovered memory therapy as mostly mumbo-jumbo encouragement to false memory retrieval, often extend their attacks to include all psychotherapy and Freud too. Frederick Crews, for instance, views Freud as "the true historical sponsor of the 'false memory syndrome,'" the one who authorized this amateurish delving into the "secrets" of the mind.[8] These critics often reject repression altogether, and while they're at it dump everything else its most famous proponent stood for. These two sides, imagining that they are eyeing one another murderously over a vast moral and intellectual chasm, in fact form a cozy oneness. Both want to retrieve a trust in brute fact, actual experience, and objective truth; and Freud's ironic sophistication dumbfounds them.

But it was the recovered-memory people who went after Freud first, urged on by Florence Rush's *The Best Kept Secret: Sexual Abuse of Children* (1980) and Jeffrey Moussaieff Masson's *The Assault on Truth: Freud's Suppression of the Seduction Theory* (1984). Rush and Masson argue that Freud abandoned the seduction theory because he was anxious about the hostile reaction of his Vienna medical peers to a paper he gave in 1896, "The Etiology of Hysteria." That paper discusses the hypothesis that the chain of associations that constitute memory will, in the case of hysterical symptoms, eventually lead us back from one apparent cause to yet another until the analyst reaches the traumatic sexual experience, child molesting, the root cause. To be more precise, it is not really the trauma itself that causes the hysteria or even the memories of that trauma but the *repression* of those memories. It is true that the paper was received coldly, and Masson and others have been satisfied that this rejection was the sole cause for Freud's cowardly revision of his views, his retreat from the clear truth he had uncovered.

What actually happened was that within less than two years Freud began to wonder whether such a simple solution could apply to such a varied set of problems as those presented by hysteria and whether the whole adult nation around him could be populated by child molesters, which is what the commonality of hysteria would require of his seduction theory. To make a fascinating story boring but brief, Freud came to see that child molesting (the seduction theory) "retained a certain share, though a humbler one, in the etiology of neurosis."[9] In other words, children indeed sometimes are seduced and traumatized, repress the memory, and are made neurotic by the terrible strain caused by repressing—*sometimes*. But repression, Freud came to think, does not always, not even often, operate in such simple and melodramatic ways. More often, repression works to mask something much more intricate than isolated victimhood, something more compounded of pain, guilt, desire, longing, and a host of other feelings that are, he felt, associated with a primal story in which humans live and form our being, one we can never glimpse fully and must repress.

In other words, Freud posited a repression that can keep erecting screen memories until the cows come home, camouflaging the terrible Oedipal story we must hide from. Moving behind the seduction theory, Freud hypothesized a more charged scene of mutual seduction and longing, involving not simply a threatening adult but a child filled with sexual desire and needs probably as voracious and dangerous as any adult's. Put another way, what Freud put in place of universal childhood seduction was the theory of the unconscious and the dark Greek tragedies that hover inside it, never fully realized and never giving us an easy, uncontaminated part to play. It's this unending complexity, this ambiguity that never untangles, that neither side of the debate can tolerate.

To imagine that Freud erected all this as a timorous apology for having posited the seduction theory, that he offered as a peace offering to the establishment such shocking (far more shocking) ideas as infantile sexuality and universal perversion, is, as Peter Gay rightly observes, "preposterous."[10] It is equally absurd to read Freud's revision, momentous as it was in the history of psychoanalysis, as a recantation. As Lloyd DeMause has shown, later in his life Freud repeatedly insisted that child sexual abuse is no mere fantasy: "There was," DeMause persuasively insists, "no 'great reversal,' no 'suppression of seduction,' no 'betrayal of the child,' no 'assault on truth.'"[11] All the same, Freud clearly relocated the origin of the story away from a material scene, straightforward and unmediated, and onto a memory of that scene; and then he further complicated the power of memory and the way we read the stories it tells. Rather than a mechanical means of recapturing stories, memory is organic; instead of being an innocent agency, it is highly charged and devious, entwined with fantasy and our least-acknowledged needs. The memory and the mind that produces it are part of a fallen world: infinitely complicated, corrupted, and never completely within our grasp.

We are maddened by this uncertainty, this suspension between images that never quite come into focus. Were we seduced or is that memory a screen for our own appalling desires? Or is it not a matter of *or;* is there a mixture, a hazy overlay of scripts and dark memories, wishes, and fantasies? Are we victims and perpetrators too, participants and observers? Why do these questions unsettle us to the point that we're willing almost to dismiss Freud with a few slogans and a mugwump anger? It's not that we are suddenly stupid or unwilling to live with complexity. It is, I think, that our need for lurid and yet protected stories about child sexuality was put in jeopardy by the inventor of child sexuality. Freud spun stories that catch us, grant us no immunity; nobody is safe and nobody is innocent: not the child and not us. When we reach back into memory in Freud's world, we come up with something that looks far less like our current porn and more like—well, like *Antigone* or *Oedipus*. And that, of course, is exactly what Freud said.

Anyhow, that's not what we want right now, so we license *Time* to run an issue that asks, expectantly, "Is Freud Dead?" In the accompanying article, *Time* gestures toward balance but lets us have what we want in bold centerpieces such as this one: "In the ultimate accounting, psychoanalysis and all its offshoots may turn out to be no more reliable than phrenology or mesmerism." Most of the article is an attack on Freud's life and character, an attempt to pin on him the excesses of recovered memory and satanic abuse therapists, an account of the success of drugs in treating mental disorders, and so forth, most of it entirely irrelevant to Freud's work and achievements.[12] The point seems to be that a rejection of Freud and every other smarty-pants idea in the psychological line puts us back in the drama of the real, assures us that it happened and that we not only can watch but have a duty to do so.

This reassuring piece is followed immediately in the same issue by a devastating article on the false-memory syndrome entitled "Lies of the Mind," which reviews the criticisms of recovered memory, includes some sarcasms on alien possession ("people are trying to please the hypnotist"), argues that MPD is implanted by aggressive therapists, and generally rips into the whole memory industry.[13] The conjunction is curious, as if *Time* were offering us the chance to oust both Freud and recovered memory, dismissing from our tales of child molesting both repression and memory. Maybe it's time, *Time* whispers to us, we returned to home base. Psychiatry professor George Ganaway says what we're all thinking (but says it better, being a professor): Because of false-memory scandals, "society may end up throwing the baby out with the bath water—and the hard-earned credibility of the child-abuse-survivor movement will go down the drain." Rather than lose that hard-earned credibility, we are prepared to wash away Freud and even memory. *Time* suggests that perhaps it was a mistake to turn to a complex agency like memory in the first place and proposes that we get back to those uncomplicated tales that, however redundant, suited our purposes: "No one questions that childhood sexual abuse is widespread and underreported. . . . Indeed, many, perhaps millions of Americans . . . ."[14] That's a tune we know how to dance to.

But actually, Freud is probably not in danger, nor is memory, even recovered. *Time* is just providing a reassuring backup, the reliever warming up in the bullpen in case our star hurler gets in trouble.

Should the fable of recovered memory fail us, no need to worry, we've still got a story. Actually, we have pretty much the same story and the same talk about it. Discussions of Freud, repression, false or true memory retrieval can all be managed so as to incite the images we require.

Benefits

Let's say the story of recovered memory and the skepticism about it are part of a larger drama of violated sexual purity given an intensely personal turn. It's this larger drama that concerns us here, that drama and the ease with which its preset plot accommodates the quarrel. When we enter into the controversy, what are we doing: what assumptions are we agreeing to grant, what beliefs to honor? When we discuss whether one can (and commonly does) repress childhood sexual trauma and later accurately recover it (usually in therapy), we confirm a cluster of fundamental beliefs, give our support to a range of connected cultural assumptions. These are the beliefs and assumptions I have been calling our "main story," the story of the erotic child that could never be told if we did not subscribe (however automatically) to a set of views that are no more than artificial forgings, some of them dubious and most of them superannuated.

So, what does this story of recovered memory offer?

1. An affirmation of our gut feelings and needs, an endorsement of what we "know" over what we might have to demonstrate or argue: intuitions, not proofs, are what matter, a vital foundational belief if hysterical rumor stories like this one are to flourish. If pushed, we say that we are, after all, telling a story of how we were hurt, which we certainly wouldn't do if it weren't true. This is astonishing logic, but it often glides by us. Here's an example, from Oprah's January 17, 1991, show, "Too Scared to Remember":

> *Oprah:* Well, how do you know those memories, as you call them, are not something that you have seen in a movie or read in a book or conjured up in your head? How do you know that's you?
> *Sherrie:* But, you know, why would you even want to conjure this up? This is so awful. When I remember it, I don't want to re-

member it. You know, I haven't seen any movies—I have physical memories. The body remembers, even though the mind forgets.

The mind is subject to the body, reason to impulse, evidence to assertion.

2. Far more important than excusing all, this story explains all—provides a reassuring causality and a linear, simple plot. In place of uncertainty and ambiguity, it tells a plain tale, the simplest of all stories—"something happened." What happened was the formation of our being; this is the story of who we are. Renee Fredrickson argues that learning to claim absolute self-knowledge is worth all the pain that comes from uncovering these buried demons: "When you retrieve your repressed memories, you get the tremendous reward of knowing your own history. Needing to know who you are and where you came from is a powerful drive in people."[15] Notice that according to this etiological model, where one came from is equated with what one *is*, and what one *is* is the child of molestation.

3. The child given to us is the Romantic child, allowing not only a continuous selfhood but also a child that is somehow still us. The boundaries of childhood expand: the child is made the source of past pain and of present suffering and rejuvenation. The explanations that matter come from our childhood, are answered by the child. When we really want to know, we ask the child within, the riddler who holds the secret to our psychic (and erotic) life. To test this, try to get sympathy for something that happened to you when you were twenty, then ten. In this sense, adults not only don't matter; they hardly exist. So dominated by the drive for these images are we that we have turned the whole world into a kiddie matinee. There's one stage and one figure on it.

Often, this "child" who is so exalted bears only a slim relation to the child whose material presence cannot ever match the beauty of the fantasy child or the child inside. What is exalted is a "child," but it's not the child we live with, the one we're as likely to resent as worship. Also, by pressing our origins into the realm of sorrow and pain—we always spring from abuse—we submit our erotic drives to the strange focus of sadomasochistic theater, and that's not good news for children.

4. The recovered child is so insistently and fundamentally erotic that the fact goes without saying. It's as if the depth of this erotic investment made it possible for us to ignore it. It's only when we wonder—which we never do—how it could be that half or more of the adults in this country are driven to unspeakable criminality, which we must believe if we swallow the statistics, that we come to the conclusion that they simply cannot resist the allure of the child. If the child is not beguiling, what sense does any of this make? What sense does it make for us to tell these stories of retrieving the lost child except to confirm what we cannot speak—that children are so erotically charged as to be magnetizing?

5. The recovered-memory story absolves us from responsibility for peeking at the child, justifies our enthusiastic voyeurism. Not only are we engaged in an important voyage of recovery, we are suffering as we go. We deserve sympathy, not censure.

6. We feel the need to examine these stories of recovered memory, of child-abuse-in-the-head, not because we are especially interested, but because it is our duty as responsible citizens to be informed. This is a vital issue of the day; it needs airing.

7. As I mentioned before, all these stories (and their angry refutations) personalize the issue unmistakably, make it always a medical and never a social or cultural issue. Whether we are talking about victims or survivors, monster fathers or unscrupulous therapists, we are talking about personal horror stories with more or less rootless villains, not those who grow out of cultural need and historical necessity. The memory that is feeding us traumas, true or false, is the memory of isolated occurrences. If there are many of these memories, this story tells us that it's simply because there are many survivors and pedophiles—not because a terrible social fable is playing itself out through them. We have become adept at resisting any generalizing that would endanger our Gothic theater of sin and punishment.

Some Narratives

Most arguments about recovered memory rely on anecdote for support, on one detailed horror story or another. I'll detail one or two of the most famous, one or two being plenty, since they are all the same. Their uniformity is used by one side as proof of their truth, by the other as proof that it's all mass hysteria. Uniformity seems to me consistent with the way our culture has organized its understanding of child sexuality as a pornographic tale, pornography also having a notoriously high redundancy quotient.

In 1990, Eileen Franklin-Lipsker became the first person in history to prosecute successfully on the basis of a recovered memory, this one coming to her suddenly when a small gesture made by her daughter triggered a flashback. All at once (under hypnosis, it later turned out), she found herself seeing back twenty years through that gesture to an eight-year-old friend raising her arm in a hopeless effort to avoid the deadly attack of a rapist: George Franklin, Eileen's father. A spectacular trial and conviction followed, along with two books (one by Eileen), a television movie, talk show galas, and general palaver.

Never mind that the evidence presented was trivial (apart from Eileen's unshakable memory, which directed her to recall two other murders by her father), so shaky that a little pressure on the facts six years later resulted in George Franklin's release.[16] Still, after this case, the flood. One of the better-publicized stories is that of Donna Smith, beautifully written up by John Taylor in *Esquire*.[17] In the fall of 1991, Donna Smith, then seventeen, was seeing her social worker–therapist, the latest in a line of a dozen. This one, Cathy Meyers, reported that in November Donna began to "split," and that the new personality (seven-year-old Jackie) was able to remember vividly that her father had raped Donna when she was twelve. Thereupon, the authorities put Donna in a foster home and arrested the father. At a Baltimore hospital, more personalities emerged. There were six at first (another Donna, Jackie, Sarah, Squashie, and Ashley), then scores more, some of whom detailed abuse of her brothers, which caused the sheriff's department to charge in and rescue them, dragging them screaming from the home.

The stories Donna told were lurid, but sometimes mixed up her father and a neighbor—or had them participating in the same activities and employing the same dialogue. The details of these are reproduced, of course; it would be irresponsible to omit them:

At first he kept licking my stomach, then kissing my legs. Then he moved down between my legs. . . . After a little while he would use his fingers at the same time. . . . I remember my father sitting on the bed next to me, and standing up to take his clothes off and sitting me up and telling me to suck his dick . . . and he said, "Daddy's milk will come and you will drink it."

The jury couldn't decide: deadlocked, mistrial.

These cases customarily remain suspended, uncertain and thus available to us to mold and use as we like. There is, of course, a terrible cost. Donna seems desperately unhappy now, with very little in her life to keep her going apart from her treatment and her illness. Her parents are not allowed to speak to her, even on the phone and even if Donna were to call them; they are $100,000 in debt to lawyers; the mother, despite the dropped charges (and against the father, after all), lost her license to operate her in-home day-care facility; the father had to take a second job and is exhausted. Donna is not yet ready to say that her parents are themselves multiples, "but I've thought about it."

Probably best known is the case of Paul Ingram and his two daughters in Olympia, Washington, the subject of Lawrence Wright's *Remembering Satan*. The twist here is that Ingram, when arrested, was not only willing but eager to fit himself into the standard script. Although he remembered nothing, and though the charges grew to include not just molestation but satanic abuse, Ingram figured that he may have repressed the memories and set about finding them. As a dutiful member of our culture, Ingram accepted the inevitable and, somewhat charmingly, sought for means to make the memories come to him efficiently. Though he was at first befuddled, unable to *see* himself (as he kept saying) doing these things, he soon hit on a method whereby memories matching his daughters' charges could be summoned forth: he would pray himself into a trance and then find himself able to write down minutely detailed accounts of what he and his friends had done.

Meanwhile, the daughters were expanding their field to include their mother, two older brothers, two male friends of their father, the sister of one of these friends, many members of the sheriff's department, and others. Richard Ofshe, a psychologist at Berkeley and well-known skeptic in this field, was called in and concluded that the case was mass idiocy. Ingram was almost certainly guilty of nothing more than being suggestible. Nevertheless, the prosecution went forward, despite the absence of any evidence other than the girls' ever-changing testimony: "At no time," Wright says, "did the detectives ever consider that the source of the memories was the investigation itself." But it was not just "the investigation itself" stoking these cases, not just ignorant and zealous provincial lawmen who had watched too much Oprah. "The investigation itself" was fueled and given its structure by a culture that demands satisfaction in the form of these dramas. The question is not why the Olympia people and Paul Ingram himself took their roles in this script to heart, but why we have written this particular script and granted it so much authority over our lives.

The standard sad coda: the charges against Ingram's friends were finally dropped, but not before the usual draining of finances and wrecking of reputations. The family has been slashed to pieces, left with nothing but horrific roles to play, whether or not these include being victims in satanic rituals. Paul Ingram came to doubt the validity of his recovered memories, decided, in fact, that they were bogus, and tried to withdraw his guilty plea. He had, however, already confessed, and according to state law, there was no way to stop the legal grinding, which here took the form of a twenty-year sentence, which he is currently serving.

Part of the fun we exact from these cases comes, as I've said, from their irresolution, the teasing quality of these lady-or-tiger endings. Is he guilty or not? That's one of the questions that keeps us going, precisely because it can so seldom be answered. I can easily imagine myself, even without praying and trances, finding ways to confirm other people's memories. I can conceive of a cultural story so large and insistent it could shove me into virtually any slot and make me fit. I believe any person in this culture could be made to adopt memories granted *by that culture.* We could all remember being molested or molesting.

Memory

All of which raises the question of what we know of memory, a question that is not going to be answered in very dispassionate terms by those hacking away at one another in the recovered-memory pit. Let's ask the novelists instead. Of course, memories often come to us armed with guarantees of their own accuracy, guarantees (as with Paul Ingram) in the form of their visual power—we can *see* them—and in terms of the feelings we get from them. Eileen Franklin described this verifying feeling to Larry King, a feeling that gave her the certainty to prosecute her father:

> *Ms. Franklin:* I just know what a memory feels like and these feel like memories.
> *King:* Explain. What do you mean?
> *Ms. Franklin:* When the memories come back they feel like memories. They don't feel like— [18]

We all know the feeling, and we are beginning to see that such feelings, strong as they are, tell us nothing about whether or not a memory is "accurate." As Elizabeth Loftus puts it, "The truly horrifying idea is that what we *believe* with all our *hearts* is not necessarily the *truth*." [19] People in the grips of a delusion pass lie detector tests easily, and we all find our memory narratives arriving through verifying channels and thus appearing as "memories," feeling like memories, vivid and unmistakable. Our memories become, in Steven Rose's words, "biologically real," even though they may have only a "narrative truth" and not "historical truth." Memories suggested by therapists, for instance, or by family legend or by the culture at large will be impossible for us to discriminate from memories of a punch in the nose that left a scar we can now examine. All are stored not in some computer memory, but mixed together in various parts of the brain, recalled in narrative form, and constructed anew each time we summon them. This invented story is "memory," always "fabricated" and not just recalled. [20] There is thus no structural difference between true and false memories, and no way to test any story fed to us by memory by referring it to the vividness of a "feeling." The human mind is constructed on a plan that "practically guarantees people will 'remember' things that never happened," partly because memories are scattered (like a teaspoon of milk stirred into a bowl of water, Loftus suggests) and need to be reconstituted when needed. [21]

Memory, then, is a powerful storytelling agency, but its constituent parts are either highly unreliable or highly inventive, depending on how you look at it. Memory, as *Time* colorfully puts it, is "nothing more than a few thousand brain cells firing."[22] We don't store videotapes; we pack away billions upon billions of fragments that we must, every time, shuffle into a satisfactory narrative. What counts as satisfactory changes according to the demands of the occasion.

Rose suggests further that the child's memory, eidetic (photographic) and unselective, is very different from that of adults. Along about puberty we learn to be selective, to notice some things and to ignore others. As part of an adaptive process and in the interests of efficiency, we learn to store what is likely to serve us and block the rest. We learn to forget, an art children (as we all know to our discomfort) have almost no grasp of. The result is, Rose says, "that our adult memories are strangely disarticulated from our childhood ones."[23] If so, reaching back into childhood "memory" is an attempt to activate a part of the mind (the child's memory) now lost. That doesn't stop us from recovering memories; but it may suggest how poignant, open, and dangerous those memories are. It may also suggest that their heavy charge of eroticism is laid on not by the past but by present needs.

The happy point is that what our memories do for us they do awfully well. I can remember my dear mother taking a whole day off to take me swimming, then out for halibut, then to *A Night at the Opera;* I can remember my father once telling me I had wonderful conversational skills; I can remember Sally Fox in high school letting me touch her breast, even though she was pretty and cool and hardly in the grips of lust for me—did it just out of sheer lovingkindness, as Thomas Hardy would say. The degrees of confabulation and fantasy and repression and egomaniacal wish fulfillment working in these memories are, I suppose, about the usual quota. But the memories warm me and do no harm, so far as I can see.

I think that is more than we can say for our obsession with a core memory fixed in childhood sexual experience. Such an obsession tells the story of the erotic power of the child and the inability of the adult to resist it. It makes that story the primal story, the origin of being. It persuades us that this tale, though everywhere the same, is an idiosyncratic one, thus discouraging us from examining our surroundings, our history. I think we need neither sanctify nor trash our memory, but rather ask what it is giving to us. Why do we keep getting back the same story when we ask for memories? Why do we need it? What is it doing for us? What is it doing to us? Why would we rather think of catastrophic trauma than of going with Mother to *A Night at the Opera,* or, even better, of cool Sally Fox's breast?

10. The Backlash, the Counter-backlash, the Reaction, the Resurgence, the Return, the Reform, the Restating the Whole Thing for Clarity

Certitude is not the test of certainty.
—Oliver Wendell Holmes Jr.

Who shall decide when doctors disagree?—Alexander Pope

An intellectual hatred is the worst.
—W. B. Yeats

A man cannot be too careful in the
    choice of his enemies.
—Oscar Wilde

It's not that we don't want to solve cultural (and personal) problems; it's just that we don't seem to care much for problems that present themselves to us as solvable. Most of the problems we find pouncing on us are not solvable anyhow, because we take care that they not be. I don't mean we bedevil ourselves by making up problems that are actually *unsolvable*, but that we find ways to fashion problems that provoke multiple and competing solutions, all clamoring for our allegiance and thus vexing us, tantalizing us, and assuring us they won't go away. It stands to reason that we concoct predicaments because we are attracted to them. So why would we bring them into being in a form that would be easy to dismiss, gag them just as they started singing? If we solved them, they would go away and take with them the anxieties and desires we wanted to tickle. We don't call up cultural problems from the vasty deep for cameo appearances.

The most certain way to keep a problem around and in view is to place it between contending camps and let them fire solutions at it. You might think this would take its toll on the problem, but it does just the opposite: problems wax fat on such bullets. Problems grow up in such close friendship with solutions that they exist in a kind of dance. In our case, the child-molesting problem flourishes in partnership with a general solution that tells us what we need is talk. I'm not saying the solution came first—that we invented child molesting in order to talk about child sex. But I think the reverse causality—that the existence of child molesting necessitated the talk about it—is just as suspect. The problem and the cure are happily married; it doesn't matter who proposed to whom, they came into being together, made for each other.

After a time there is so much agreement about the solution that it becomes tedious and begins to wither, shrinking the problem with it. Then it's time for a backlash, which can generate a counterbacklash, a counter counter—all entering into a symbiotic relationship with the problem to keep the party going. As the charges and countercharges change, they adapt to one another; and more important, the "problem" changes shape to accommodate the more complex dynamic relations. What looks like wild disharmony seems to me, then, sweet concord. The backlash always comes on the scene like Outraged Reason in the allegory: as a judicious check, a skeptical brake to runaway zeal. But it functions to pep up a waning conversation.

In our case, assured talk and assured prosecutions have been followed by indignant protests, which have spawned indignant restatements, which have spawned accusations, which have spawned careful assessments, which have spawned further loud disagreements. As the centrality of child sexuality came to dominate not just our courtrooms but our therapists' offices, as we located our dilemmas not just in the backrooms of day-care centers but also in the backrooms of our memory, satanist dens, and alien spacecraft, we found ourselves running out of room. We needed a shift in focus in order to locate new territory, and we found just that in a new contest, a backlash in which both sides of the argument join together to focus not only on the problem but on *approaches to* the problem. Recovered memory is a bountiful subject, but it has less to give than arguments *about* recovered memory.

The backlash, so goes the argument of this chapter, is playing the same game that was going on before it was called out to take its position on the field: it accepts the same ground rules, the same discourse, the same controlling metaphors. It does not propose to curtail the discussion but to extend it, and to extend it with only such modifications as will artfully reexcite without fundamentally redirecting our interests. It does so by quarreling—but quarreling, as Touchstone says in the last act of *As You Like It*, "by the book," which means quarreling in such a way as to entice more quarreling. Touchstone is a master of this vital social practice and outlines for us the stages through which a quarrel progresses according to form: the Retort Courteous, the Quip Modest, the Reply Churlish, the Reproof Valiant, the Countercheck Quarrelsome, the Lie Circumstantial, the Lie Direct.

I would say we are having our fun now mostly in the territory around disputes churlish and counterchecks vicious, having lost patience with courtesy and modesty. The tone with which each side refers to the other is seldom moderate; for example: "The authors of *The Politics of Child Abuse,* one of the most biased (and superficial) books on this or any subject, argue . . . ."[1] The mutual loathing is so marked that Louise Armstrong's witty description is not at all hyperbolic: "And—with flak flying about who is mendacious and who misremembering; who is possessed of true wisdom and who merely possessed; who is venal and who is in fact multiple who's—[incest] has become the subject of one of the great screaming matches of all time."[2] True, though it's not just incest but any child sex; and it's not just any old screaming but screaming on key.

Each side accuses the other of being parochial, of listening only to itself, of being less devoted to disinterested investigation than in confirming its own superstitions: "Only information affirming that abuse is the root of psychological or physical disorders is allowed within the echo chamber that passes for professional discourse [in recovered-memory therapy]." The point is amplified by Dr. John F. Kihlstrom: "False memory syndrome is especially destructive because the person assiduously avoids confrontation with any evidence that might challenge the memory. Thus it takes on a life of its own, encapsulated and resistant to correction."[3] Encapsulated stories banging against one another. I hope to show that all camps find such echo chambers useful: the conservatives, backlashers, counterbacklashers, and those imaging they are above the fray.[4]

There is so much so-alike indignation bouncing about here that the enthusiasm we feel in wading into the (let's say) twenty-seven backlash books and thirty-one counterbacklash books soon turns to rue as we swim into deep déjà vu. The same authorities are cited, the same arguments are used, the same sneers and telling mots, the same absolutely irrefutable clinical studies.

This is not a battle designed to go anywhere, largely because it is so formally constricted: certain positions are always unexamined; certain questions are never asked. There are, in fact, so many agreements between the two sides that it's almost like Harvard v. Yale—the game could never be played were not both sides and their supporters pretty much interchangeable. We cannot escape this discursive trap by an act of balancing, a judicious toting up of the virtues and vices held by each side. It's not, I'm going to argue, a matter of being moderate, avoiding name-calling, trying to find common ground. We often hear calls for "a more sober, genuinely truth-finding forum . . . a non-adversarial . . . sanctuary for academic-quality clinical research."[5] But that's like looking for a way to assess calmly the claims of religion in a revival meeting being stormed by club-wielding members of Atheists United. The terms for neutrality do not present themselves when the whole landscape is contaminated by the assumptions of war.

The backlash, the counterbacklash, traditional talk about child molesting, and the plea for scientific objectivity join hands with the images and desires circulating around child sexuality. They maintain their cooperative hostilities by agreeing to three basic points: (1) never to acknowledge that such cooperation exists; (2) never to ask why the subject at the center, child sexuality, is of such magnetizing interest; and (3) never to let the talk escape the anecdotal, thus avoiding historical, sociological, and literary paradigms that might disrupt the talk.

The Backlash

In 1991, Dale Akiki, a San Diego church day-care volunteer, was arrested and charged with thirty-five counts of sexually abusing, torturing, and kidnapping nine (sometimes reported as ten or eleven) children. Held without bail for two and a half years and then the focus of the longest trial in San Diego history (seven months), Akiki was acquitted of all charges by a jury that deliberated only seven hours and came out full of wrath at "lawyers," "overzealous prosecutors," "the parents," "the child sexual abuse syndrome" (whereby things like fear of water or doctor's offices are made into telltale symptoms), and "therapists on a witch-hunt." The anger of the jury led to more anger, expressed in such places as *People,* the *New York Times,* and *Inside Edition* (December 15; transcripts available). All these accounts emphasized Mr. Akiki's disabilities—"mentally retarded and physically deformed," blurted out the *New York Times*[6]—his sweetness of temper and heart, the absurdity of the charges (blood drinking; murdering giraffes, elephants, and a human baby; hanging the children from a chandelier), the complete absence of physical evidence, the tendency of society to pick on "odd-looking" people, the view that this sort of thing had gone on too often, that we were losing our heads, and that we should have no more nonsense.

It was the backlash, the all-right-now-that-does-it-you-went-too-far-and-got-me-good-and-mad reaction to what an observer from Britain (a country always prepared to generalize about American excesses) called our "national neurosis," our tendency to find criminal child molesting where it doesn't exist as a result of our "self-righteous child-welfare police" and their ability ("corrupt and incompetent" as they are) to induce, through "Gestapo-style" methods, accusations of child abuse, two-thirds of which are likely spurious.[7] We might resent these sneers from England (probably not; we Americans are so generously good-natured in a brutish sort of way), but does the view that we have a national neurosis brought on by a genetic tendency to stupidity and hysteria share something with our own media's reports of the Akiki trial? Both carefully refrain from asking why this particular subject should so fascinate us (and the British too) at this time; and both isolate cases and personalize them, just as they isolate and personalize the general issue, making it a matter of individual health and secluded demons. It's the same melodrama.

It is understandable that official backlash organizations, formed in the center of the battle and often from its victims, should be preoccupied with tactics and local aims. VOCAL (Victims of Child Abuse Laws), founded in 1984, and the more recent False Memory Syndrome Foundation (1992) do what they can with their rage; but what they can (or want to) do does not seem to include studying why our culture should be so fixated on sex with children and how we might deal with that fixation. Of course group members set their eyes only on the enemy, but why are the rest of us playing find-the-fiend?

For now, let's try to get a grip on things by listing the faces of the enemy as seen by the backlash:

1. *Self-help-for-abuse-victims books.* Carol Tavris's rocket-launcher

essay, "The Incest-Survivor Machine,"[8] argues that such books, trading back and forth like baseball cards their "misinformation, faulty statistics and unvalidated assertions," not only offer simple answers for intricate questions but, much worse, try hard "to *create* victims." Blaring forth their "scientific illiteracy" with fervent conviction, these books damage lives and draw women away from thinking of social change by offering them mere "psychological solace."

2. *Survivors and victims themselves.* Few backlash works directly create monsters out of accusers, but many come close. It is a position that affords us considerable moral superiority and is thus never unpopular, as the success of the 1996 film *Primal Fear,* about a lying altar-boy "victim," attests. Writers in the backlash commonly take a snide position in relation to the people duped by these people and the charges they issue. It's but a step from here to saying that everything would be fine if dumb people only got better guidance—like, say, from people in the backlash. Even Tavris, whose article I admire, leaves the impression that these moronic books can succeed only by getting the full allegiance of millions of moronic women—I mean, how else could there be a problem for the backlash to take up? Who is it that's reading these idiotic books?

3. *The evasion of responsibility.* Alan Dershowitz's *Abuse Excuse* doesn't so much blame victims as a mushy swoon afflicting the whole culture—every one of us and don't you deny it: we snivel, we pass the buck, we are unmanly, we can't stand the heat but want to be in the kitchen, we blame others for things that are our own damn fault.

4. *Feminist fanatics.* Frederick Crews suggests that the audience for the self-help books has been created in part by feminists such as Andrea Dworkin and Susan Brownmiller, with their vision of rape as a commonplace pedagogical tool of American fathers.[9] He points out that such "incitement to militant victimhood" is not in "the best interests of women," all of whom will be happy to have Crews clarifying for them their best interests and chiding them for their little excesses.

5. *The media.* It will come as a big surprise to you that one of the chief enemies of the original movement serves just as well for the backlash. The media—gotta love 'em! Virtually everyone in the backlash abuses the media. Our ability to mount a ferocious witch hunt is strong, Crews says, "thanks to the power of our sensation-seeking

media to spread the illness."[10] During the 1996 presidential campaign, Robert Dole (with almost no resistance from President Clinton) went even William Bennett (our virtue czar) one better in worrying television, rap music, and Hollywood. "It's filth!" Bennett cried. "You have sold your souls," said Dole to Time-Warner; and, as for Hollywood, it was "marketing evil," "nightmares of depravity."[11] The public said, at least to pollsters, that they couldn't agree more with Dole and his rhetoric drawn from Jonathan Edwards's famous Puritan sermon, "Sinners in the Hands of an Angry God": 71 percent said so, and 61 percent thought things were getting worse and worse.[12] People fumed for a while, talking about sex and writing letters to newspapers. Of course, their tastes and buying habits changed not one iota, and they didn't vote for Dole.

6. *Parents.* Parents are said to stuff these stories into children with such force that they become a sickness within the child, poisoning it and many innocent people besides. Parents do this because they are mean, suggestible, neurotic, unable to imagine their children *not* being violated, so conscientious as to think it is their duty to have an abused child, or involved in a custody dispute and willing to load up the child with a fabricated horror story and then fire it. The last villainy is the one most publicized; for example, Jeanne Bishop, "a public defender in the overcrowded courts of Cook County, Illinois," almost daily sees "parents using their children as weapons."[13]

7. *Lawyers.* If you were surprised the backlash picked on "the media," you'll be flabbergasted to learn it also names as enemies our attorneys. Ann Landers, speaking out against false memories and falser accusations and for "common decency," fingers "lawyers who see an opportunity to make a killing by nailing a well-known (or well-heeled) person."[14]

8. *Therapists.* Here's where most of the fusillade is going, straight at therapists, many of whom have read or written books (*The Courage to Heal, Secret Survivors*) and are now, as *Time* puts it, "harming patients, devastating families and intensifying a backlash against mental-health practitioners," a backlash *Time* is enthusiastically promoting. Even the popular Dr. Frank, who regularly invites readers to "Ask Dr. Frank" in *Psychology Today,* says to "Heartbroken Sister," "I share your outrage at the irresponsibility of therapists," at "this strange therapeutic witch

hunt."[15] Therapists are accused of eagerly implanting false memories in patients,[16] often using hypnotism or various memory "aids" that amount, critics say, to nothing more than construction tools, as these therapists would themselves realize were they not so tied to outdated notions of what memory is and how it works. Lawsuits against therapists have become common, and not a few are successful, ever since a Napa Valley (California) father won $500,000 in damages from a therapist for implanting through "quackery," the jury said, memories of sexual abuse in his daughter. A defense lawyer interviewed in the case said therapists really are not detectives: "They are trained to see the world as the patient sees it and work within that framework."[17] Whatever one thinks of this as a defense of therapists, it seems to me a provocative comment on the way the backlash, the counterbacklash, and all of us tend to see the world through the story of the sexuality of the innocent child and the assault on that innocence. I think the backlash, and our culture generally, has been content to "work within that framework."

The Backlash in Detail

I wish I could get by with the assertions above, but I realize I have made the backlash sound so narrowly focused and homogeneous that you will hardly believe me unless I take some pains (and give you more) in examining some of the principal works in this movement. Many of these are brilliantly conceived, courageous, witty, and possessed of many other virtues, none of which will figure in this account, our purpose being to analyze the deeply conservative nature of this backlash, its fervent dedication to playing by the rules. Here are some instances:[18]

Wounded Innocents, by Richard Wexler, is a rich-in-detail, never-tiring attack on the child-saving system (foster care and protective services) in the name of the family. Wexler bases his attack on the assertion that more than half of all accusations are false and result in catastrophic family destruction: "There are more than a million such nightmares in America every year" (p. 12). The rhetoric of the book is pure (and entertaining) horror show: "The war against child abuse has become a war against children" (p. 14). This war has been launched by "child savers" who hoke up "panic-inducing numbers" (p. 94) and a hysterical argument that has had an alarming result: "Americans eagerly surrendered their most fundamental liberties to the child savers" (p. 15). These child savers (called "invaders") are, left and right, "destroying children in order to save them" (p. 28). *Destroying* children, you notice, just as child savers say they are *rescuing* them. Danger seems to be everywhere and to ask for the same response, no matter which side you're on. It's the same hair-raising story of apocalyptic terror. So immersed is he in this story that Wexler lets fall his best insights (and there are several) without having a way to pick them up. He sees, for instance, that the "medical model" on which child saving is based is itself never going to allow us out of a cycle of blame and treatment; but he has left himself no geography in which to explore that idea, much less build a new model.

True and False Accusations of Child Sex Abuse, by Richard Gardner, is a classic in the field, much loathed by traditionalists and other antibacklashers. It is, I think, both the most vigorous and the most timid of the backlash books, which is perhaps why it has attained such prominence. Gardner offers brilliant and often withering analyses of symptoms lists (how-to-know-you-were-abused-by-consulting-present-problems), of dangerous nostrums such as "children never lie," and of the intellectual limitations of those he names as chief enemies: the "validators" (therapists, police, social workers) of this "present sex abuse fiasco" (p. 263). These validators, Gardner says, are not evil conspirators or scientists with a mission but dumbos, ignorant victims of "the progressive deterioration of educational standards throughout the United States." "No one," he says, "can deny that there has been a deterioration in the public schools." We get the feeling we had better not deny it, or he will sic William Bennett and Rush Limbaugh on us. Even though the only evidence he offers comes down to SAT scores, we have to go along. Beyond these scores (which have been rising) he has only anecdotes: "I have had secretaries whom I have had to let go after a week or two" because of their "egregious errors in grammar, punctuation, and spelling," a weakness that infects not only those who seek employment with Gardner but, he says, the whole culture. Teachers are stupid and lazy, he says, school nothing more than a "winter camp"; and nobody flunks, nobody works, nobody knows anything, nobody cares (pp. 316–18). Things weren't like this when Gardner was a boy!

The extraordinary reactionary quality of this discourse recalls Allan Bloom and other golden age myth spinners, but it also signals an important quality of the backlash generally: its ability to generate a lot of noise without disturbing the main story, to look like a protest while drinking coffee with the bosses. Gardner's own assault on the therapy industry has been carefully positioned so as not to ruffle the costume: he said on CNN's *Crossfire* (March 1, 1994) that there certainly *is* a repressed memory syndrome and that "sexual abuse is widespread"; elsewhere he has granted that "the vast majority of sex allegations of children are likely to be justified (perhaps 95% of them)."[19] Having granted so much, one wonders what he has left to write about. He tells us: "What I am saying is that there are two tracks," widespread sexual abuse, just as everyone is saying, and "a parallel witch hunt" (CNN *Crossfire*).

This may seem simply befuddled: why not mount a witch hunt if there are witches? But Gardner actually seems to me clearer than most of the backlash true believers. He sees that his work is custodial, that the backlash is programmed to sweep up messy areas like repressed memory so we can enjoy the main story in surroundings more befitting their bourgeois suburban ethos. It's an artful gentrification of our pornographic narratives.

Suggestions of Abuse, by Michael Yapko, is another well-informed and very smart book going after ignorant therapists and the harm their smug, know-nothing self-righteousness does. Yapko's is a calmer and much more precisely reasoned book than most, but it plays strictly by the rules of the backlash and observes the role doled out to the backlash discourse in the master plan. He begins with the usual disclaimer: "I want to state emphatically at the outset of this book that while it is clear to me that abuse is a widespread phenomenon, the exact role of repression . . . ." He sums it up thus: "*Abuse happens, but so do false memories*" (p. 21). The "but so do" has the same function as Gardner's "second track," separating the critique from the main body of belief and securing that belief from disruption.

Yapko then presents the results of a survey he conducted among 865 "qualified professionals with advanced degrees," results that really do seem as horrifying to me as the news that most butchers feel there is no real difference between rat and cow, that germs are a myth, and that meat improves with age indefinitely. More than half of Yapko's respondents thought hypnosis can recover memories as far back as birth; a little more than half believed hypnotically retrieved memories are more accurate than ordinary remembering; almost two-thirds made no effort to distinguish between true and false memories; and 41 percent said that memories from the first year of life are accurately stored and ready for retrieval. These blunders are, he moderately says, "sometimes outright dangerous to their clients' well-being" (p. 60). But, like Gardner, he aims even this carefully protected story at a safe target: "the culture of blame," our tendency to blame our parents for everything (p. 145). That's as far as his generalizing goes, questions about the history, satisfactions, and source of this phenomenon being folded into a blanket of silence. The backlash starts to look more conventional than the traditional story.

The Abuse Excuse, by Alan Dershowitz, need not detain anyone long, as it refers all manner of current ills (all current ills) to not taking responsibility. Dershowitz is a master of bunkum rhetoric, of the grandiose vacuity that announces his own authority: the abuse excuse "is dangerous to the very tenets of democracy" (p. 4); it "threatens the very fabric of our democracy" (p. 5); "what is at stake is . . . the very nature of our experiment with democracy" (p. 319). One can hear the Gilbert and Sullivan chorus: "Yes, he's a very, very, very, very, very, very, very lofty man." Dershowitz sounds like the comic prig in the Victorian operetta telling us all to do our duty, an idea the Victorians themselves found both sweet and silly. Dershowitz cruelly portrays daytime television as "a bevy of sobbing women and men justifying their failed lives by reference to some past abuse, real or imagined" (p. 5). Failed lives? Anyhow, this book, like the others, hovers noisily over the subject—our respect for the overwhelming power of childhood sexual abuse and our willingness to see it everywhere—without lighting. The noise is calculated to pacify us, signaling us to be calm: it's just a matter of getting tougher, growing back our stern fiber, recalling a day when men would rather die than mewl.

Hidden Memories, by Robert Baker, is a very readable, because acrimonious, romp with the "rumor mongers and petty paranoiacs"

(p. 40) who have somehow capitalized on our collective density, susceptibility to the appeal of urban legends, and dread, to make a startling number "of ordinary, seemingly sane individuals believe" ridiculous things, as if we shared "a world view closer to the demon-haunted world of the superstitious medieval peasant than that of a skeptical, scientifically-oriented American living in the 1990s" (p. 9). He has in mind satanic cults, aliens, and past lives, mostly, though he is full of colorful talk about the whole shebang. "What on earth," he asks, "would motivate people, even momentarily, to take such things seriously?" (p. 10). A question, certainly, to be asked; but after asking it Baker drops it in favor of ranting. He does suggest, feebly, that science education be improved, since the average "skeptical, scientifically-oriented American" seems to him neither skeptical nor at all up on science. Beyond that, however, he too directs his fury and his considerable vituperative talents to conservative ends. Why, indeed, would people be *motivated* to take such things seriously? That is the question, the very question, Dershowitz would say. The backlash raises it, and then, with considerable skill, shields it from exploration.

The Myth of Repressed Memory, by Elizabeth Loftus and Katherine Ketcham, is an important book because it comes from a major figure in the backlash community and represents a fascinating attempt of someone inside the battle to find a position outside the firing lines. Loftus calls herself a moderate, an enemy of simpleminded polarizings, and directs the momentum of her book toward a meeting with Ellen Bass, coauthor of *The Courage to Heal* and traditionalist guru, as if it were an oldtime East-West summit. What happens at that meeting is, however, what happens in the book as a whole: promises of new vistas collapse into the same familiar landscape. A potentially momentous meeting of minds becomes an absurdist impasse—babbling at cross-purposes, petty misunderstandings. Instead of finding new territory to explore together, Bass and Loftus drop back into the old trenches, failing to challenge in any way the status quo.

Loftus, the best known of those disputing the accuracy of memory generally and recovered memory specifically, is herself a psychologist who has done experiments demonstrating how memory can be corrupted and has used the fruits of her experience as an expert witness in many celebrated trials across the land. But despite the fact that she has indeed been vilified (and once, in a plane, beaten over the head with a magazine by a woman in the next seat), it is hard to see how she could be more accommodating, more anxious to remove the sting from her analyses and confine their application to a limited service area. She tells Bass at the end, "I am only interested in this isolated subject of memories that are labeled 'repressed'" (p. 214), abandoning the rest of the world to the incorrigibly amateurish Bass.

The book opens in the same deodorizing way, assuring us that Loftus means in no way "to attack therapy" (p. xi) or to debate "the horror or the reality of sexual abuse" (p. xi). Scattered through the rest of the book are careful delimitings of the subject: "We are only questioning the memories commonly referred to as 'repressed'" (p. 141). Since she cannot forever bottle her terrific intelligence and subversive experience, her impatience with the standard line and her disgust with the excesses of survivor therapy do show through. She is not as colorful as Bradshaw or Gardner, but she gets off some good lines on symptom lists, naive beliefs in the accuracy of memory, and "McTherapy."

But finally she returns home, delighted that she and Bass have met and confirmed, pleasant women that they are, the stark binaries that define the unproductive, spirit-sapping backlash. "We looked at each other, trying to gauge the depth of the chasm sculpted by our separate realities" (p. 210), an image she finds so altogether satisfactory (sculpted chasms?) that she indulges herself in repetition: "we looked at each other across that great ideological chasm that divided and separated us" (p. 219). Tweedledee and Tweedledum settle into "overstuffed chairs" in "the fourth floor . . . large suite with a commanding view of the snow-covered Olympic Mountains"—never mind that this is only the Seattle Hyatt—and, with that good-natured resignation characteristic of large minds, sigh, and accept the fact that history itself has declared that they be isolated; bad luck for history.

Making Monsters, by Richard Ofshe and Ethan Watters, is often reviewed with Loftus and Ketcham, as if they were one, which they pretty much are. Ofshe is the other half of the best-known pair of popularizers and high-paid expert witnesses speaking on the wobbly inaccuracies and constructedness of memory. This book is much angrier than Loftus's, and thus more fun, waiving all the twaddle about finding a moderate stance. It is also more careful in outlining the various flaws and lies in traditionalists' claims. Still, the satiric energy of the book is directed to preserving the nature of this standard narrative, in which there are, as always, monsters and pure guys, the pure guys always being the ones writing the book before us. In fact, Ofshe and Watters seem to recognize that the melodrama they are in allows them no alternative but to take up the position assigned to them. They don't put it that way, of course, since they imagine themselves rebels; what they say is, "Finding the middle ground in this debate is like finding it between those who proclaimed the world flat and those who believed it to be round" (p. 182).

These backlash books not only sanctify the main story, the story of the traditionalists, but also mimic it. Through the use of disclaimers and other isolating strategies, they remove inconvenient debris, act as the scavengers for our culture's most dubious narrative organisms. Beyond this, they employ the same rhetoric, characters, and plot as the melodramatic, Gothic mode that guarantees the survival of the main story. So long as we are inside a horror story, monsters need never fear. They'll start worrying when realism comes along, or comedy—when Abbott and Costello meet Frankenstein. And, finally, the backlash extends and prolongs the child sex coo, elaborates it, and allows us to keep talking the same talk while giving us the illusion we are rejecting it.

You Scratch My Backlash and I'll Scratch Yours—The Counter

The backlash never expected to be allowed to have its own way. The idea was never to overrun the traditionalists but to settle into a long and loud tiff with them. That the traditionalists would counterattack was certain, since the backlash could not but promote it. That counterattack would surely generate new topics, backlashers assumed, or, if it didn't (and it didn't), would at least keep the voltage up, reinject the personal element, and bring onstage a whole new cast of enemies. The backlash made it possible to attack not just pedophiles (who, doubtless to their delight, disappeared from the discourse for a short time) but also the traditionalists. There were, even the traditionalists would admit, more of them than pedophiles; and that made for a noisier war, especially when the traditionalists, perhaps a little tired of pedophiles, could attack the backlashers.

One reason it was so easy to attack the backlashers was that they were so familiar. It was just a matter of returning serve, keeping the rally going, like old-friend tennis players making minor adjustments to meet very minor changes in their rivals' strategy. Here we find books whose titles show that it's just a matter of learning a new trick or two, not a whole new game: *Shifting the Burden of Truth: Suing Child Sex Abusers: A Legal Guide for Survivors and Their Supporters,* for instance.[20]

But an odd and wondrously hopeful thing happened, at least now and then: in launching their attack on the backlashers, a few traditionalists recognized the kinship and began to wonder about it. As they were attacking the backlashers for switching categories, relying on anecdotal evidence, appealing to unreason, creating demons, painting only in black and white, and depending entirely on sensational formulations, a few noticed that they were repeating attacks made on themselves, lobbing back the same shells. I haven't found many who have chosen to pursue the possibility that both the traditionalist and the backlash scripts are located within a master script and are functioning to serve a slightly hidden agenda. Nevertheless, this is a major new development.

I should acknowledge that most of the counterbacklash parade sticks to the established route. There are a (very) few making small and sensible practical points about the dangers of the backlash. Therapist Richard Rose points out that the lawsuits against therapists will not be good news for those who need help, frosting the relationship and making the therapist keep one eye on the client and one on a series of other parties who might be involved in some future litigation; and Dershowitz argues persuasively that overusing the abuse excuse in court will stretch things "to the point where a swing of the pendulum is inevitable" and legitimate defenses will be difficult to sustain.[21]

More common, alas, is a blunt reassertion at a higher pitch of the old traditionalist points, an arguing technique that is as irritating as it is common. Renee Fredrickson says that although "blaming the therapist is really popular right now" (she's a therapist herself), the real problem still involves "people being abused, hurt, tortured, and being told that it didn't happen, encouraged to forget."[22] Fredrickson is speaking for adults recovering memory; the authors of *Child Sexual Abuse* make the same point as regards children:

> The danger of such groups [the backlash] is that they perpetuate the myth that children's stories are often not credible. However, the converse is true: children rarely produce accounts of abuse which have not occurred. The large majority of victims are never able to reveal the abuse: they have been trained, coerced, or cajoled by the abuser into deceiving the world.[23]

More generally, we hear that "the danger is that books like 'Making Monsters' and 'The Myth of Repressed Memory' will once again silence women and men from speaking—and being believed—about very real abuse, and will create a new breed of experts who will once again presume to know the truth."[24]

Notice that the "very real" here is assumed to be experience itself and not some explanation of it, thus the sneers at "a new breed of experts." This traditionalist view holds that experience somehow holds its own truth and that any question posed to it is hostile. Abuse, our understanding of it, its place within our culture, and its remedies are assumed to be self-evident. Such arguments are not effective parts of the counteroffensives; they represent failures to recognize that the war, while still on the same battleground, has begun to use slightly different weapons. Lumbering old muskets will no longer do.

The more wily counteroffensive begins by identifying the enemy and abusing him: "It is suddenly trendy to belittle," "A chic literati denounces all late remembered abuse as false," says Roland Summit, inventor of the accommodation syndrome and a man with expansive ideas about chic.[25] Others reach for stronger language. Sandra L. Bloom, pointing out that the backlashers are quick to use shoddy science to attack what they term the traditionalists' "pseudoscience," compares them with deniers of the Holocaust. Robert B. Rockwell, touching all the bases, says, "The 'False Memory Syndrome' is a sham invented by pedophiles and sexual abusers for the media"; "I can only speculate," he adds in another essay, "that the pedophiles and child pornographers have the money to mount massive public relations efforts." E. Sue Blume says Carol Tavris's essay "places her directly on

the side of the molesters, rapists, pedophiles, and other misogynists."
And, writing from a Dutch perspective (easily translatable), Dr. Fred
Jonker sees that "the purpose of the backlash is to enforce silence
about the reality of child abuse."[26]

This naming and characterizing of the enemy soon spills over (as
in many of the examples above) to impugning his motives. Mike Lew
lists seven motives for the backlash, ranging from mental illness to
stupidity to vested interest. Backlashers include those in the grips of
our old friend denial, those imagining that the sex abuse fuss is "this
year's fad"; those who haven't gotten the word; apologists for child
sex; "romanticists"; and people who have reason for seeing the "multimillion dollar pornography and child sex industry thrive."[27]

But there is more wit than that among the counterattackers, as
there will be in those who counter the counterers. Many will spot the
circularity of this discourse, its energetic circling of a center that is
never spoken. A few have already commented on the way this warfare
is oddly defensive and enormously redundant, the way the two sides
seem so cooperative that they almost look like one. Louise Armstrong
best characterizes this commentary, and is consistently observant and
witty too. In both *Kiss Daddy Goodnight: Ten Years Later* and *Rocking
the Cradle of Sexual Politics: What Happened When Women Said Incest*,
she takes an unsentimental, alternately wry and angry look at the history of talk (which is all it has been, she says) on incest in the last
decade or so. Her books represent one of the few instances of this sort
of analysis we have, and it is a fine one, though in my view it turns
too quickly from the implications of its explorings.[28]

Armstrong analyzes how a political argument on rape was reduced
by our culture to a personal issue, medicalized, and turned into discourse. Arguing that "the powers-that-be . . . use *noise* to achieve the
same end that was once served by repression," she turns a weary eye
on her earlier belief that enough talk would lead to action: "We really
thought the conversation about incest would be self-liquidating."[29]
She notes that the curtain she raised by discussing incest led not
to action but to discussion groups, and she calls the medical therapy establishment "our society's sanitation engineers," charged with
transforming anger and pain and insight into a language of "personal
pathology and recovery." It manages this, she says, by isolating for

concern the *individual* and making all problems internal and unproductive: the culture thus takes political women and puts them "'in recovery,' as though that were a geographic location."[30] Further, by creating monstrous bogeyman distractions like MPD, satanism, and self-help recovery books, this protective discourse makes the problem at once everywhere (all are victims) and nowhere: it is so sensationalized it is unreal, so pathologized as never to be available for action. Here is Armstrong on the overall effects of this discourse:

> But it was not our intention to start a long conversation. Nor did we intend simply to offer up one more topic for talk shows, or one more plot option for ongoing dramatic series. We hoped to raise hell. We hoped to raise change. What we raised, it would seem, was discourse. And a sizable problem-management industry. . . . It was not in our minds . . . ten years ago, that incest would become a career option.[31]

Armstrong will not thank me for ignoring her main thesis—that there is but one enemy and one basis for the backlash: our culture's granting "permission for male sexual abuse of the children in their care and trust."[32] This is, she says, a part of everyday living, simply assumed as a male prerogative that will not be given up easily—thus the backlash and what she refers to constantly as "the war." For me, all this is a distraction from the stunning analysis she keeps beginning and often carries on for some time before she remembers her thesis about patriarchal rape. It's like watching a great dancer attached to heavy weights.

And just to show that it's not simply Armstrong who harbors the hope that is to be found in the counterreaction, consider what Lenore Terr has to say. Terr is often a witness for the traditionalists, but she is also a fair-minded person who realizes that it's not always a question of who's right but of what question is being asked and whether we have to pose it always in the same form. She notes that false memories do occur and that they are troubling indeed. But she goes on to suggest that not all false memories are "deliberately planted," that "well-meaning people can inadvertently receive well-meant suggestions from their therapists, their friends, their families, or the police, or pick up notions from the books they read and the movies and television shows they watch, and come to believe they have experienced something that never happened."[33]

Terr is onto something: a new way to tell the story and to receive into ourselves the possibilities we have feared for so long. These are "well-meaning" people she is talking about, well-meaning people and "well-meant suggestions." Instead of a war, Terr imagines a large amount of innocent bumbling; instead of a national plot she imagines a national story; instead of a group of demons stalking every playground, school, and family, every therapist's office and couch, she locates the "well meaning." It's no longer a paranoid but a comic world, a world and a tale we can live within more easily, don't you think?

The children too. We've pretty much lost track of children the last few chapters, so maybe it's time we brought them back in and asked what they'd make of a new script, not perfect or anything—like it *would* be, duh!—but well meaning.

So glance back at the meeting of Elizabeth Loftus and Ellen Bass that I rendered in such a sarcastic and mean-spirited way earlier. Actually, I am moved that they like one another and moved too that they both regret the gap that divides them. No need to ridicule that gap or the regret. But there's also no need to regard the breach as permanent. What if we tried to see these two experienced and well-meaning women in a well-meaning way, tried to conceive a plot in which they could stop depending entirely on strained goodwill and would not have to "respect their differences." Maybe we can send them back to their overstuffed Hyatt lounge chairs and let them find a tale to tell that doesn't require leaping chasms, asks only that they rubberize themselves. This is a story I'll have a go at in the next chapter. I need help—from those like Ellen Bass and Elizabeth Loftus and all the well-meaning people who know we haven't yet got it right, haven't hit on that once-upon-a-time that will show us how to live and how to be, will give us that story that will allow us to love children without exploiting them.

11. *Other Stories, Other Kids* —————

I, the Muse's priest, sing for girls and
boys songs not heard before.
—Horace, *Odes*

Surely it was time someone invented
a new plot. — Virginia Woolf, *Between
the Acts*

What would it be like to have available different stories about the child, to try our hand at a new story-telling, and then to open ourselves up to these new tales, teach ourselves to be receptive to strange and novel stories? Rather than confronting current scripts, doing battle with them, what if we move to a theater around the corner: more light and air, replace the curtains, freshen the scenery. And a new plot, maybe a comedy or even a musical. I like a Gershwin tune — how about you? It might be healing, or at least a break for the children. Psychoanalyst Adam Phillips says that "the art of psychoanalysis is to produce interesting redescriptions: redescriptions that the patient is free — can bear — to be interested in."[1] Maybe we can cure ourselves of our addiction to these ruinous Gothic stories of child sexuality by reviewing the situation and then redescribing it in a way we can bear to be interested in.

And what if we don't need a cure, what if all the pain we are causing and feeling is unnecessary, a result of our not getting the story right? Maybe we don't need surgery but recess. Phillips describes psychoanalysts as artful spin doctors: "The aim of psychoanalysis is not to cure people but to show them that there is nothing wrong with them." Nothing wrong with them that a better tale won't put right. It's a question not of a diseased culture but of a blundering one, stubbornly loyal to the lousiest route available: a stupid cow lurching through brambles only a few feet from a smooth country lane, chewing on nettles instead of sweet grass, protecting its calves by trampling them.

Like psychoanalysis of the sort Phillips discusses (a sort perhaps not so easy to find in the Yellow Pages), our new maps and new stories

need not be all that different from the old ones. It's not transformation we need but jiggling. The old story we've been abusing for the
entire book, the story of innocent (erotic) children and fabulous (but
ubiquitous) monsters, has its heart in the right place. It sees that the
problem lies somehow in the investment our culture has made in the
sexual appeal of children; it tries to center that problem in order to
save the children it loves. The difficulty comes in all the fudgings that
have crept in, the failures in nerve, the veerings and skewings. The
eroticizing of children is blamed on somebody else, as if it were an
accidental and freakish thing we could wipe out by being sufficiently
sanctimonious. Yet, this old story has many features worth washing
off and saving. Down deep, it wants to do right by the child.

The Happy Child

For some time we have aligned childhood and happiness so closely
that they have become one. Whatever grim realities actual children
face, and they face plenty, we cannot entirely lose the sense that an
unhappy child is an indictment of us all, that pain and starvation,
abuse and hopelessness are monstrous when visited on children, not
to be borne. The most moving and enspiriting thing I know is a laughing child, the total absorption of the child in the full altogether of its
pleasure. This is the child of Blake and Wordsworth, the child that
defines so much of our culture's ideology and so much of what we all
are. Its negation, the suffering child, is still, for all our callous protections, the image we cannot stand before without acting. This child of
Dostoevsky and Dickens—beaten and starving, asking for more and
told to move on—strikes deeper into our capacity for compassion and
our willingness to act than any other image in this world or beyond.
I say that despite the thousands of little people who suffer and die all
around us. It is still true, and the story we now have, for all its faults,
knows it is true and tries its best to build on that fact.

This Romantic heritage of the child, the happy child or the child
as happiness, is not one we are likely to lose or, in my view, would
be well served by losing. It hits a nerve, and it is still a potent call
to action. We construct our beings and our culture on the assumption that happiness is the birthright of every child. Our current story

seems to give both us and our children so little access to that happiness, though, that we are obsessed with its denial, with the outrageous withholding of happiness. We want to make somebody pay. We've gotten ourselves into the middle of a twisted, ironic narrative that uses this belief in happiness as the basis for seeing and causing unhappiness all around us.

But we don't want to lose the core of our heritage: a belief in the right to happiness and a way of constructing the child in reference to that right. Even when we are being most caustic and subversive, we want to grip hard the story that says we have the capacity to grant to this loved child a full, entirely unearned seed-time of joy. It may seldom so be, but we are not wrong to insist that it always should be so. Even Freud, no sentimentalist when it came to children or anything else, found himself so unable to keep from smiling in their presence and so moved by their apparently unalloyed bliss that he could not but make that happiness—its haunting loss, its allure—central to his explanation of adult struggle. In a touching passage that concludes *Jokes and Their Relation to the Unconscious,* for instance, Freud says that we seek in jokes, in all humor, for a "euphoria" that once came to us easily, "the mood of our childhood, when we were ignorant of the comic, when we were incapable of jokes and when we had no need of humour to make us feel happy in our life." [2]

No need to collapse into a nostalgia that will soon have us so wrapped in our own past that we are offended by present-day children. We need to treat this image of the happy child with poise if it is to work for us and for the children and allow us to escape the desperate stories of protection we have devised. Perhaps we can reimagine the boisterously happy child as a countermodel to the child whose happiness is always under siege. We are so worried about children that we project our worry into what they *are;* and we scurry then, with the best of intentions, to bury them within corpulent and suffocating narratives of danger.

We have been so busy reinventing the child as a being at risk sexually that we have allowed the happy child to wander out of our range. We have made the child we are protecting from sexual horrors into a being defined exclusively by sexual images and terms: the child is defined as the sexual lure, the one in danger, the one capable of at-tracing nothing but sexual thoughts. The laughing child has been replaced in our cultural iconography by the anxious, fretting child—really, a grotesquely sexy little adult. Not a kid, not a companion, not an ally; just an unhappy undersized thing, tormented by being cast in terms that allow it no room to move: the child is the sexual being whose essence is that it has no sexuality at all. What a part to play! Defined in terms of negation and denial, the child shouldn't surprise us by devoting itself to vengeance. The wonder is that so many are forgiving, loving—even happy.

Getting Started on New Stories

It isn't easy to start new stories, or even to think of them. It's not like we were ever asked which stories about children we would prefer, not like we ever started fresh with no story at all and were asked to choose. We were born in the middle of a story already in progress, and we were told this was the way things were. How can we, even if we want to, see things differently and find a different story? I have heard that people of other cultures don't hear the sound cats make as "meow" but as something else ("whoo-pee," maybe, or "ain't we got fun!"); but I can't stop hearing it as "meow" just by an effort of will. I yam what I yam, as Popeye says, and so are you; and what we are is within a story that has passed itself off as truth for a long time. It's who we are and how we see ourselves. How do we get outside it?

Tough but doable. In Michael Moore's *Roger and Me,* Pat Boone, who knows a lot about General Motors, having sung for them for so long, says Board Chairman Roger Smith strikes him as "a can-do kind of guy." So are we all, fatuous Pat included, and we can find ways into new stories if we want to. But a part of all of us isn't so eager to give up stories that would never have developed as they have were they not providing a fair pay-off: erotic titillation, a stamp of virtue, guarantees of immunity. But we're well-meaning people as well as energetic ones, and I think we see what we're doing to ourselves and our children.

We aren't monsters, and we can do without monster stories. Abandon the Gothic: that's the first step. That doesn't mean we should turn around and create a backlash, a point I take without you reminding me that I made it earlier. We don't want to create enemies, not real enemies—fools, maybe, and bumpkins, those who dislike parties, and old people who don't want young people having fun or sex, the traditional feathery and unthreatening enemies of comedy. I suggest we try out visions of the world and stories cut out of those visions that are easier on us, more relaxed and tolerant, more in tune with a culture that is certainly not safe but is also unwilling to spend all its energy and joy seeking safety.

We need a new mode for our stories and a new set of possibilities that will allow us to see what might happen if we trusted ourselves more. We can tell tales about childhood, adventure, and risk that are not so paralytically predictable; we can invent stories about the present, love, and even sex. We will find, perhaps, that it's less a matter of finding a new cultural tradition than looking further at our old one, reimagining our Romantic roots and the Romantic investment in the child. Even in our father, Wordsworth, we will find in familiar lines momentum not for grief but for sustenance:

> Though nothing can bring back the hour
> Of splendour in the grass, of glory in the flower;
> We will grieve not, rather find
> Strength in what remains behind

Wordsworth's child, we may find, is not a stultifying being-at-risk or an invitation to a nostalgic wallow; he is a tonic and a good beginning for a story, a strong comic tale. It's not that we've been trapped by Romantic images of the child. We haven't been nearly Romantic enough.

Bad Habits We Need to Lose

If we are to find our way to happier stories with more open possibilities, we need first to eliminate a variety of habits we've picked up in repeating our Gothic scapegoating tales. I'll list some of these tricks-o'-the-trade we learned for telling the old story and now need to lose, fast. I've used lists to give up alcohol, tobacco, meat, and sloth. It works, and I'm now a walking hieroglyph of successful self-improvement brought about by good lists.

1. Stop looking for monsters and their victims. If we look, we'll find them. If we don't, we won't. Such activity seems to promise so much, but it (and the tales-of-terror mode directing it) really is a fraud, making all of us pay heavily for nothing.

2. Stop listening to simpleminded stories. Most Gothic tales demand that we cease thinking as we listen and think even less as we repeat them.

3. Stop welcoming appeals to blind hatred. We don't need to exercise this faculty, and it seldom gives us stories we can use for anything other than more hating.

4. Stop employing our wit to find sinister motives, dark causes for all effects. Not every hug is a fondle, nor every squeeze molestation; all erotic feelings are not bad, nor are we in need of rules about what constitutes erotic trespass. Ann Landers ought to use the intelligence she is blessed with to do better things than tell "Concerned Cousin in Springfield, Mass." that she should tickle into motion her worries about an uncle's attentions to his daughters. Concerned Cousin admits that the girls "seem to love their father," but the oldest weighs more than four-hundred pounds and is "bright, but unmotivated." Cousin, further, has been wondering about all the hugging in public: "For years, I've wondered whether my uncle was sexually abusing his daughters." Rather than tell her to get a hobby, Ann urges her to act: "You cannot stand by and remain silent and do nothing. A young girl who weighs 400 pounds did not get that size for no reason."[3] People wear extra clothes, put on weight, or become anxious for many reasons, some of them good.

5. Stop treating all family life as if it originated in the House of Atreus. Gary Gilmore's brother Mikal wrote a book (*Shot in the Heart*) that *Time* says shows how the "Gilmore parents, haunted by their past, took their frustrations out on their children, dooming them to lives of anger and abuse as well."[4] Let's stop imagining that parents "doom" children to anything and that life is nothing more than a plod through a predestined bog.

6. Stop tracing everything backward, looking always to the past for sources, explanations, and excuses. Find stories that are future oriented or at least optimistic about dealing with present problems. For instance, for all my bragging about self-improvement, I am a little be-

hind in aerobic exercising. But tomorrow is another day, and if not tomorrow then next week, which promises to be less busy.

7. Stop passing laws. We have sufficient prohibitions and safeguards; and if we don't, we can count on lawmakers to cover any suddenly perceived gap in an hour or two with a few score edicts and no-nonsense penalties. These laws, almost always punitive in the area of our concern, give us the illusion that we are doing something. As sociologist Barry Krisberg, president of the National Council on Crime and Delinquency, says of parental-responsibility laws (laws punishing parents for the crimes of their children): "They don't appear to cost much because they don't do anything." These "dangerously naive" laws, he says, ignore real social problems and propose that people will suddenly become perfect parents if threatened with large enough penalties.[5]

New Stories

Once all those bad habits are out of the way, the old story itself seems new, transformed from a bellowing nightmare into an everyday realism that is almost banal. The problem of child eroticism immediately seems less grand than it was, so much less grand that we may wonder why we ever manufactured such elaborate and costly evasions. Children are billed as erotic by our cultural heritage, and we are caught square in the center of the sweep of that heritage: So what! How would it be if it turned out that we didn't have to wait around until our perceptions changed or our heritage moved (glacially, glacially) into new channels, that we could, right now, handle the problem?

Our first set of new stories, then, would construct themselves as quotidian realism's response to demonic horror: if there's a terrifying noise in the cellar, it's probably mice, or Cousin Laura entertaining her boyfriend. If it's a stranger come in through the window, invite him to dinner. Switch the mode. As Dickens says, "The play is, really, not *all* Wolf and Red Riding-Hood, but has other parts in it."[6] Let's find them, not forgetting the openhearted gulls, the naive, the generous; and the stories issuing from the unguarded—from Mr. Pickwick, Forrest Gump, Chaucer's Franklin, Cordelia, and Edward Lear. It's a comic story with great appeal, and it often does the job. In our case, it would tell about child sexuality and our response to it as if the issue were of some importance and considerable interest but not terribly special, certainly not a cause for panic. That children are sexualized or eroticized, and that we all, in some measure, respond to it would then seem unremarkable, not at all worth the reckless frenzy of denial and scapegoating with which we now meet those facts.

The new story, the simplest of all, would not begin by assuming there is a problem, much less a monumental one. We would simply admit that "children's sexuality *does* exist and anyone who tries to deny it is wilfully ignoring the evidence," that "sexual activity is commonly observed in children, and steadily increases during the school years and adolescence."[7] Further, we would not regard as remarkable statements like "Those being honest will also admit to finding immense pleasure in both their child's sensuousness, and the sensuous contact they themselves have with the child."[8] Such assumptions would rid themselves of their protective defensiveness and become commonplace, common knowledge. Indeed, such things are common knowledge now, although we hardly have room for them in the current story. The candid authors of *The Courage to Heal*, however, do make brief mention of the common desire of children to "test limits, sexually as well as in other areas," and of the fact that "parents often have sensual feelings toward their children."[9]

This simple tale, then, says in a simple way that children are devised by our culture as erotic and that we are bound to find them so. Such a story taps into the easy good sense of *The Courage to Heal* on this point, into our ability to recognize that the erotic is, after all, a large territory in which we move all the time; that our being there seldom surprises us or makes us likely to assault the nearest thing in sight; that there is nothing horrifying about the conditions of erotic pleasure, either in arousing or responding to it; that a participation in the erotic is neither criminal nor harmful. Criminal and harmful things are criminal and harmful, and that can be true of money dealings, entering a building, driving a car, or loving another.

Behind this simple story is both a more complex view of sexuality and sexual responsiveness and a more complex view of what constitutes an "adult" and a "child." But not all that complex, since the notion of a *range* of erotic feelings and responses is a notion most of us hold and all of us live by and in. It simply is not true that we perceive every image, being, and stimulus in our world as either erotic or not. It's always a matter of degree. I find virtually everything in my world erotic to some degree, the exceptions being trivial (and not ones I can call to mind); and I am certainly representative. For me (and you too) it is no hardship to live with a scale of erotic responses and to find pleasurable even the sort of low-grade, background erotic hum we experience at a cafeteria or on a bus. Feeling erotically buzzed or even highly charged does not mean entering automatically into a different order of being. Human beings do not have a rutting season, do not spray or howl at the moon or start humping the legs of guests at parties.

The erotic feelings we have toward children are not, in themselves, a problem—or at least not a problem we can't handle. Becoming part of that problem *is* the solution. Denial does nobody any good and drives the desire into the lying, scapegoating babble, where it thrives and does terrible harm. Erotic feelings are not rape.

I am, I know, trying here to empower a more rationalist story, one that admits the irrational, certainly, but one that also relies on the ability of adults to be grown-ups, to exercise some control, some wit and decency. We can see for ourselves, without hauling out demons and holding witch trials, that raping, molesting, and assaulting little beings is wrong and cruel. To have our erotic lives wholly under the spell of children is, as even pedophile fiction always acknowledges, both sad and comically puerile. We can see these things, and we can deal with them. We'll be better off armed with good sense (a sense of decorum, a sense of humor) and native kindness than with all the police and horror tales and harum-scarum tactics in the world. So will the children.

I think this rationalist approach will also, no doubt very slowly, act to moderate our aesthetics of desire. Trusting to our good sense will, in time, make the focus of our erotic preferences a bit more sensible. Erotic preferences, after all, are largely a formal matter: like learning to appreciate new architectural forms or new fashions. But even if this argument is not my strongest (it is hard for me to imagine a weaker one), I think we can depend on our sense of the ridiculous, our sense of what is fair, and our sense, finally, that we can be ingenious when we put our minds to it.

Admit all this openly and we at the same time issue an invitation, easy and relaxed, to our best storytellers to find tales of healing and happiness. I am fully aware that I need help here; we all do. The solutions will come not as a set of prescriptions but as a casting call for the best creative talent to devise and make stick a cultural story about children and sexuality that is out in the open and does not bolt at the first sign of complexity. We always do well with what is in the open. It's when we play hide-and-seek with inconvenient facts that we become ungainly and start hurting the very ones we fear for.

In the meantime, we should keep hugging kids, playing horsey, bathing them, and taking pictures of them naked on rugs (not bear rugs), just as we did before we had the wits scared out of us. If you find yourself getting too excited, going too far, wanting to incite or not to stop—then stop. If you are hard-pressed, then indulge in voyeurism, which is child abuse only by elastic standards and seems to many children at least as funny as it is invasive.

Try to emulate Coach Buttermaker in *The Bad News Bears:* get the hell off the field and let the kids go at it by themselves. Recognize that your interest in kids, even your own kids, is pitched much higher than theirs in you. Get out of the way. Say, like Walter Matthau to his team, "Go out there and do the best you can," and then watch. Even Holden Caulfield realizes he can't spend his life with cute kids, much less catch them before they get so very uncute. All he can do is "watch" them. Make the best of it. Take the model of Joe Gargery in Dickens's *Great Expectations.* Joe's love for Pip is so powerful that he knows when he must leave. Not only does he separate himself from the snobbish boy in London, he tears himself away even from the now-restored sweet friend he had been nursing:

> Not wishful to intrude I have departured fur you are well again dear Pip and will do better without
>
> Jo
>
> P.S. Ever the best of friends [10]

Not wishful to intrude, we should all departure while the kids are well, maintaining our friendship as distance, even if an erotic distance. I think this stoic story is also available to us, once we wash away the hysteria.

Of course, saying such things and asserting we can manage perfectly well without Gothic monster stories will seem to some a feeble answer to the dangers that lurk out there. I think the dangers are themselves largely a function of the stories told about them, but I am aware that the rational and the stoic stories I've told depend on mechanisms of reason, control, and clear vision that we have come to distrust. Distrust these things, however, and we have little left but the police.

We need new stories because they will create a way of imagining new actions and new beings. Inside a different set of narratives, we will see and plot differently. I think the conditions for rethinking laws, families, orphanages, welfare, discipline, and sexuality can be made available to us only through what I have been calling stories. With these stories will come the opportunity to conceive the child and its welfare, its body and its feelings, in ways that will be unusual and can hardly fail to be more productive and happy than those we have managed with our current melodramas. I am *not* arguing that we should wait until the hearts of men and women are transformed before doing anything; but unless the hearts of men and women are changed, softened, we will lack the capacity and resources to see the problems, much less imagine the solutions.

So I see no need to apologize for promoting stories that, along with the sensible, the romantic, and the stoic, strive to make us care. Dickens, for instance, sometimes caricatured as a writer of melodramas, regarded himself, with some justice, as a stern realist, a realist with a faith in the ability of his art and the real facts he was describing to open the hearts of his readers and make them eager for change, for pure compassion's sake. For Dickens, it was not the child's innocence that was in danger but its life; he did not think people loved children in a sick or perverted way but that they did not love them at all, simply did not care. I think his analysis is powerful still, that our frantic babble over outrages to the sexual being of children is a mask for our lack of concern, our willingness to overlook the battered and the starving, the impoverished and ill educated, those without comfort and without hope.

Let's take just two familiar Dickens fables. Oliver Twist lives amidst the tender mercies of the workhouse and the orphanage, symbols not of institutional mismanagement or corruption but of social hard-heartedness. It's not that we need better workhouses or more laws; we need love. Further, Oliver lives among thieves and prostitutes of all ages, but he is endangered not by sexual predation or abuse caused by the criminals but by ravenous hunger caused by the virtuous. When he asks for *more* he is asking not for protection or safeguards but for plenitude. Dickens is protesting against a world that is niggardly and wizened, cold and unkind; in it one fears not invasion but being shut out, left to die. We seem to have forgotten that primal fear—and the central fact of the lives of our homeless and cast-off children.

Similarly, Dickens's crossing sweeper Jo, in *Bleak House,* is murdered by a society that doesn't care if he sells his body, doesn't care at all about anything to do with the boy. He is told always to "move along," resting nowhere, given no home and no peace. "Dead!" Dickens thunders over the corpse of the poor, wasted child, "and dying thus around us every day!" Dying thus around *us* every day while we spend our energies chasing phantom abductors and trying cases of daddies photographing children in the tub.

Now That We've Got the Stories, What?

With a collection of these realist, romantic, comic, stoic, and human-ist stories circulating, we will make current the plots that will allow us to devise the laws and regulations, the institutions, the popular nonfiction books, the new perceptions of children and their lives that will, I believe, make things happier. They cannot easily be worse; but I do not wish to make the argument tilt to the negative. I think, instead, that we can make good stories, that there is ample reason to trust our own well-meaningness. Again, let's get Ellen Bass and Elizabeth Loftus back together, and arrange a million other meetings like it and tell the participants to regard themselves as storytellers charged with creating tales about the happiness of children, stories Blake would like and Lewis Carroll and Dostoevsky and Gandhi and Groucho Marx. That'd do it, I do think.

Political and legal action should begin to consider all the dilemmas that touch the lives of children, not just those transgressions (abduction, incest, sexual abuse generally) we enjoy talking about. The disproportionate energy, money, and concern we load on sexual abuse is ridiculous, draining what is needed for the much larger issues of physical and emotional abuse of children, neglect, poverty. The attention lavished on stranger abductions is criminal self-indulgence because it clearly serves not the children but the prurient interests of the general public. Under the new paradigm we will divert money away from useless hot lines and into support for education and relief for bone-mangling poverty.

No child should ever be thrown away, homeless, or alone. I think we will agree, probably do agree; new stories will lend new urgency to such mandates.

No child should ever be struck in the name of discipline, nor should we tolerate for one minute the practices of other cultures in this regard. We should be, in this case, closed-minded and provincial. If other cultures make hitting kids a commonplace or an honored tradition, then other cultures are wrong and had better stop it right now—at least when their members immigrate here. No kind of political correctness requires tolerating cruelty toward the helpless.

Again, I am not claiming that these material changes and others like them need wait on cultural transfigurations or the full acceptance of a new story. The generation of a new plot not only causes but is caused by the development of new programs and new political positions. It's a cooperative, symbiotic relationship between political action and storytelling.

Speaking of storytelling, the new plot would also generate a new breed of self-help books, books that would envision the world as a field of opportunities, not a recovery room, with plots directed toward action, not recuperation. There would be no allowance for rationalizing selfish brutality in the new paradigm—no tough love or tough luck either. The focus would be on the responsibilities of the present and on the grown-up. No more inner children! We are adults and need to tend to the children outside.

Within a more hopeful paradigm, we will be more inclined to hear children speak—to ask them to do so and listen to what they say. As it is, we seldom bother to inquire about how they're doing. Children are now and then polled as to their opinions, asked such loaded questions as whether television depicts "too much sex before marriage, too much disrespect for parents, too much dishonesty and aggressive behavior."[11] And they answer, overwhelmingly and mostly with straight faces, "Oh yes, yes indeed." Teenagers become very good at telling us what we want to hear, especially when it seems to them funny: "Did they give you that one about too much disrespect for parents and whether TV caused it, for Christ's sake? What morons!" Now and then, they are asked, by accident, something they care about and tell us something we don't want to hear: for instance, that they aren't given enough information on sex and reproduction.[12] Generally, however, we are careful to pose only the questions we know are safe, in the form guaranteed to confirm that problems are somebody else's fault, somebody else's responsibility, and that we ourselves are about as upright and fault free as human beings can ever be expected to be.

Being less terrified and less defensive, we will be more willing to regard children as humans equipped with voices.

An Unsafe World

There are signs of discontent, signs that our Gothic way of viewing the world is not giving us all we want—or anything we want. We have drawn in on ourselves so fiercely that we have narrowed the range of our explanatory stories to monster hunting, to parables of overwhelming danger, suspicion, the desperate search for safety. Willing to go after a vision of absolute protection, we have invested heavily in the dream of safety: jailing a record percentage of our population, distrusting everyone, finding no touch preferable to an ambiguous touch. Don't be touched, don't be spoken to, don't be looked at: what kind of goal is that?

Robert Samuelson writes in *Newsweek* that we simply "cannot afford absolute safety," especially when the huge price tag buys us benefits that are "trivial or nonexistent." *Newsweek* also, in a separate article, raises questions about what a terror-charged atmosphere does to children: what is "the psychic cost of raising [children] in a state of hypervigilance?"[13] Why, to put it in my terms, have we become locked into a story that gives us no choice in the matter? Are the benefits such that we cannot forgo them for the sake of the children?

Are we so tied to the sneaky thrills, the cheap and nasty hypocrisy, the fiddling little flutters that we get when we speak of these matters—outraged, solemn, and aroused?

Do we not care who gets hurt so long as we get our fix of porn-babble?

Of course we care, and deeply. We didn't invent our current fables; we woke to find ourselves already in their embrace. Our current myths of anxiety came up from deep roots and have gradually choked out the more open and delicate growths: the stories of possibility and adventure, of pleasurable contact with people, animals, things, and ideas. We have it in us to reimagine a set of stories not so tied to safety, not so cringing and cautious. There are stories of potential and risk, of excitement and possibility, stories that take pleasure in the present and look forward to the future. We need stories that aren't afraid to leave home.

When my daughter Anne was three and her sister Elizabeth midway between one and two, we went one night to a circus held in a barren field near a small village. After the circus, I was standing outside in the now-muddy meadow talking to a person I didn't like very much and paying no attention to Anne and Elizabeth, guessing, insofar as I guessed anything about it, that they were by my side. They weren't. I remember thinking that the reason I didn't much like the friendly person talking to me lay deep within me and wasn't pretty. I also had to pee and was wondering if this field, once freed of my vexatious talking companion and the few hundred others who were beating it out of there (the crowd was small but enthusiastic), would serve my purposes.

When I noticed the void next to me, I saw that Elizabeth had done her wobbling zigzag over to the edge of a ditch so deep it was like a ravine and that Anne had gone with her and was blocking her from plunging into it—and into certain injury or death. I ran over and did the expected and right thing, said they shouldn't do that and it was dangerous and watch out and be careful. I then thanked Anne for tending to her baby sister. Anne, unmoved, said, "She thought there was an elephant down there."

My incubus of a friend, not using this opportunity to leave, approached: "That's a deep ditch there. They should fill it up."

Anne stared at me, maybe expecting me to detach myself from such sentiments. I did nothing. Finally, she repeated, "She thought there was an elephant down there."

Friend: "Elephants don't live in ditches or in England."

This triple-dyed ass was beating me to the punch every time. I wish I could say that I found a way to counter his killjoying, or looked for one.

Anne knew when she was outnumbered. She also knew what she knew about her sister and the dark pit—I guess. But after all, I was there and it was a pit.

If I had it to do over again, I'd do better.

We have it to do over again.

Appendix —————

"The First National Conference on Young Performers," sponsored by the Screen Actors Guild, took place in fall 1995 in several ballrooms (East, West, and Grand) of the Universal Sheraton, Universal City, California. The Universal Sheraton, I found, is just down the hill from Universal Studios and its popular fun park. Tour buses smogged up the steep grade before and behind me, and I wondered if people parking at the hotel—I had a free pass for that—could stroll as they liked into the exhibit area and see the acclaimed "Jurassic Park" show, the "Psycho" house, and the real Jaws. No, they could not.

The conference invitation, which I had received for reasons I will reveal later, contained a letter from Barry Gordon, president of the Screen Actors Guild (sag) describing the concerns those of us gathered would be addressing. Pointing out that "the Entertainment Industry is practically unique in its need for and use of minors" ("as you are well aware"), Gordon said that these children often fared well "during their performing experiences," but that good treatment had "not always" been extended "to their lives outside performance." Consequently, it made sense to have a conference "addressing the position of the young performer as a professional, as a child and as a future adult."

As it turned out, nobody there, not even Gordon, thought the treatment of minors during their performing experience was anything to crow about. In the afterlife (beyond fourteen), it was neglect and treachery all around. In fact, the young performer as child and as future adult, and certainly the adult as ex–child performer, was ensconced deeply and, to me, convincingly in the role of victim. But this is getting ahead of things.

Walking into the ballroom was not exactly like walking back in time, although just about every face looked familiar. It was not a high-school reunion, where all but you have weathered alarmingly. It was just the opposite: time had ravaged only me. Not one of the grown-up child actors had let themselves go even a little since last appearing on-screen. All their features were bright: skin like peaches, breasts like plums, hair lush and carefully windblown. Nevertheless, it had been a long time since their days of full exposure; some, though not all, had grown a little taller, and most looked wiser, had about them a worldliness that was subtly different from the winning arrogance that had made them so arresting at age nine.

There was a "Timmy" or two from *Lassie;* "Wally" from *Leave It to Beaver;* "Kitten," "Betty," and "Bud" from *Father Knows Best;* "Rusty" from *Rin Tin Tin;* "Margaret" from *Dennis the Menace;* "Jeff" from *Donna Reed;* "Jody" and the oldest sister from *A Family Affair;* the little boy and his girlfriend from *The Wonder Years;* one of the Waltons; the kid from *Julia;* a very large number from films; and a host of others whose faces seemed strikingly memorable, though I did not remember them. I was not, I'm glad to say, struck as I sat there with any politically reprehensible thoughts, like imagining I had dropped into Munchkinland; but I did think of a *Twilight Zone* episode in which, bingo, all small children suddenly became forty-five.

I wondered if others assumed I was an ex-star, perhaps well known in my time, the time of *Intolerance* and *Wings.* I wondered too, while waiting for the opening ceremonies, who the genuinely unrecogniz-ables might be. The ones who were not recognizable were also, in every case, not pretty either, which is why I didn't notice them at first. But as I settled down some, I realized there were many there whom the program identified as deputy mayors (well, one deputy mayor), writers, producers, officials from the Directors Guild of America, agents, securities brokers, financial analysts, entertainment lawyers, studio teachers, accountants, coaches, stuntpeople, labor commis-sioners, personal managers, psychiatrists, and "academics." None of these people was much to look at. I was, by the way, one of the "academics," perhaps the only representative in my category, like the deputy mayor, and thus bearing, with him, a heavy charge.

The conference turned out to be notable for the passion and intelligence it sent forth onto some questions and the bland indifference it expressed toward others. Generally speaking, this was a get-right-down-to-business conference, concerned with "the profession" and the way it operated, ways already known to all the insiders but not to me. Legal issues were raised, but not as often as financial ones; horror stories, very good ones, were told about conditions on the set, about agents, and about parents. Many sensitive ideas were advanced to help children cope with their hothouse life while they were working and with the pain of finding themselves, overnight, not working at all, meeting puberty and total unemployment simultaneously.

But why does this happen? Why do we create these conditions? Why does the public yearn to see twelve-year-olds and avert its eyes from kids of fifteen? Why does attraction turn to repugnance? Why do we have child actors at all? What cultural needs do they serve? Why put children on display? Why do we want to see them? What is it we want to see? What should we be "protecting" child actors (or any children) from? Is the idea of protection somehow at odds with talk about the rights of the child as professional wage-earner? Who is the enemy? Is it the family? Why should children not have a right to their earnings, all of them? Why are child actors (unlike, say, child tennis players) imaged as weak, ignorant, enfeebled?

But I wasn't thinking of these things right off. I was thinking that my plan of taking notes on a pad with a pen was strikingly anachronistic for the Universal Sheraton. A nice pad and even better pen had indeed been provided, as decorations only, signals of bounty. Everyone else was wired—computers, phones, beepers, recorders. But the food was extremely good and plentiful, even the morning food, and I decided to stop worrying and start eating, since I'd never see pastries like these at an academic do.

The conference began with some startlingly good warm-ups, delivered by people who knew how to get on and off the stage fast and smoothly. This was true even of the deputy mayor, Cody Cluff, whose fill-in-the-blanks welcoming speech convinced me that Los Angeles was happy to have the film industry here, regarded this conference as a very good thing, and wished we would accomplish each and every thing we hoped to—accomplish. The other welcomers seemed anxious to strike a moderate tone: the acting president of SAG, Sumi

Haru—"We have come a long way since the days of the exploitation of kids like Coogan"—and Jeanne K. Russell, national chair of the SAG Young Person's Committee[1]—"Most ex–child actors occupy a middle ground between going on to win Oscars and posing for mug shots."

But Barry Gordon, former (by a few days) president of SAG and a candidate for Congress, more accurately caught what turned out to be the mood of the conference, which did not seem inclined to celebrate progress or the successful adjustments made by some ex–child stars. Gordon said the experience for kids was always rough and often disastrous, that changes were needed, and that this was to be an action-oriented, crisis-centered conference. A child actor himself, Gordon told us what Danny Thomas had told his mother: "If your son is in show business and has been there since the age of three [as Gordon had], get it out of your head that he's normal." Gordon left us with that, and we understood: we got it out of our heads that there was much here that was normal or could be understood with our normal perceptual tools. The lives of child performers, during and after, are not what we suppose or are easily able to suppose. We also do not much want to know about the real lives of these kids, perhaps because we like things just as they are, and perhaps because the suffering of these children is not disconnected from our needs, a point we are even less anxious to have thrust upon us.

In any case, the first speakers, writer William Blinn and producer Lloyd Schwartz (son of Sherwood), spoke of the emotional mistreatment of child actors and their need for protection. Bobby Porter, an adult whose size—he said he is four feet nine—and athletic ability make him a perfect stunt double for kids, then launched the series of horror stories that were to flood the conference. Detailing vividly the "tragedies" of kids mistreated on sets, subject to all sorts of bends and loops in labor laws and to tyrannical blackmail from the adults surrounding them, Porter suggested a world whose glamorous surface masks what sometimes edges toward drudgery, exploitation, or even child slavery.

Jon Provost, a long-running Timmy on *Lassie* and master of a fierce irony, read to us regulations concerning the treatment of animals and insects in performance, telling us to substitute "child" where "animal" or "insect" appeared in stipulations such as "No one on the set shall be allowed to play with, fondle, or pet the animal"; or "Nothing can be done to harm an insect, or permanently alter its appearance or behavior." He socked home his point with an anecdote of filming a stirring episode in which he and Lassie were on a raft, flying out of control down the Sonora River and into the rocks. Unable, apparently, to rehearse the scene (or to explore underwater conditions), the adults involved directed young Provost to get on the raft, hit the water when the raft broke up, and swim for it. He did all of that, but he cracked his head hard on a submerged rock and was floundering, the director and the film crew cheering on what they took to be his method acting. There was nobody whose job it was to help Provost, but Rudd Weatherwax, Lassie's trainer, had stationed several men to rescue the dog, and one of them finally recognized the little boy's plight and tugged him to shore.[2]

Another eloquent speaker, Eddie Hodges (*The Music Man* on Broadway and many films, including *Hole in the Head*), identified himself as "one of the walking wounded who practices psychotherapy." Hodges, like many after him, told how the industry isolates the child and plays not only to his sense of being special, uniquely talented, but tells him he is wanted, now and forever: "You got a great future in this business, boy!" Hodges said his childhood was a series of lessons in deceit, for him and for his family: "We all tried to make it look as if we were having a damned good time." And then came the inevitable rejection and pain: "Hollywood left me before I grew up." "For years," he said, "I felt guilty and ashamed—later bitter and burned." Hodges recognizes the excruciating banality of his patterned story of drugs, depression, and alcoholism; sees that his narrative is the narrative of so many of these kids who offend us by no longer being cute. He has made it out to the other side, clinging to some disturbing questions: "How did any adult miss the fact that I had these problems? Why such a sink-or-swim attitude?"

In fact, it's really a swim-and-then-sink reality, given that all but a tiny number of child performers are given the boot once and for all at puberty.[3] We want cute, and adolescents are not cute. When adolescent parts are called for, they are played by actors not uncommonly in their thirties, and always cute. It's children we seem to long for, and we relentlessly throw them away when we're finished with them.

Hodges, speaking for many, said, "We sacrificed our mental health for the Hollywood dream." In some cases, the sacrifice demanded has been even heavier.

And for what? One would imagine that these children, however messed up, pile up big bucks and provide themselves with a future more grotesquely attractive than military retirement at forty-five: the golden years can start at fourteen. However, a surprising number, including Jackie Coogan most prominently and even Shirley Temple, find themselves without much money when they reach their majority. John Whitaker, a kind of Macaulay Culkin of the late 1960s and early 1970s, said he came through pretty well, but even he fought with his parents over money. I got the feeling that such battles are nearly as inevitable as the outcome—kids lose, partly because Congress has exempted performing children from child labor laws, partly because the Civil Code grants to parents "the custody, services, and earnings of the unmarried minor," [4] and partly because kids are easy to blackmail.

Lauren Chapin, who had been under contract to Columbia as a child star and played "Kitten" in *Father Knows Best*, said she had to battle through the courts to have a bare 10 percent of the 25 percent of the gross she had earned turned over to her when she became sixteen and was legally emancipated. Got that? By law, parents can hold on to 75 percent of the child's earnings—on the grounds that they have unusual expenses and that children are parental property anyhow. That leaves the child with, at best, 25 percent of her earnings; and in Lauren's case it was tough going, even after emancipation, to get 10 percent of that quarter. When she got her 2.5 percent, her mother sued her to recover that. I didn't have the heart to ask for the results of that last wretched battle.

Ms. Chapin's story, I should have said, was reported during the afternoon "Work Session": four hours of concentrated discussion on three topics, take your choice. My choice was "Child Development, Impact of Celebrity, Transition to Adulthood," which I chose partly because I saw that Provost, Tony Dow, Gigi Perreau, Fred Savage,[5] and Lauren Chapin would be there, and partly because the other work sessions were devoted to "Current Working Conditions" (which sounded like a rehash of the morning's horror show) and "Legislative Changes, the Coogan Law, Financial Responsibilities" (which sounded important, addressing nuts-and-bolts areas I had neglected utterly, would never read about, and therefore ought not miss; so I did).

My session was wonderfully scatterbrained and anecdotal, just the thing for me. Chapin focused on the way children in "the business" get their money plucked from them, and others chimed in on that chord too. Sybil Jason told how her earnings had been siphoned off by an uncle. Jason must have had a fair amount of money too, as she was a successful child star of the 1930s who costarred with Al Jolson, appeared in *The Little Princess* with Shirley Temple, and was once billed *over* Bogart (so she said, and who am I to doubt it?). "How many examples do you need," she asked, "of child stars, when reaching twenty-one, finding the cupboard bare?"

Not too many, as it happened, since many of the participants were more concerned with forms of exploitation that were more insidious, went deeper. Gene Reynolds, a former child actor and now president of the Directors Guild, argued that "the child actor is in a master-slave relationship"; more accurately, a slave surrounded by a confusing array of masters, all supremely demanding and apparently irresistible. Parents, coaches, directors, agents, managers: each presents himself as the one who knows best, who can collect (without asking) the child's complete trust, take control, more or less as if the child were not there. It was this erasing procedure that seemed to stir the bitterest anger. Who ever asks the kid?

Though the child is, in one sense, loaded with "premature responsibility," Reynolds pointed out that there is no way the child can do anything in reference to that responsibility, what with its absolute dependence on adults. The responsibility, therefore, can give the child great anxiety and a false sense of importance, but no real maturity, no chance to mature. "Children," he said, "suffer for the narcissism of the parents, parents possessed by the child's career. I don't know how you're going to be able to deal with that."

All the best speakers offered similarly frightening and rather nihilistic analyses. Those who saw furthest seemed to discover more and more traps. Tony Dow (Beaver's older brother), an unassuming man who spoke thoughtfully and with a capacity for generalization unusual at the conference, didn't blame parents; in fact, did not cast the problem as a melodrama of victims and villains. Dow saw the damage to child actors as intrinsic to both the methods of production and the demands of the audience. The problem, he said, is not money, danger on the set, parents reliving their childhood, or evil producers and directors.

In fact, most parents are sensible and most people in the business are kind; many children get their money, have fine tutors, and are very well treated on the set. And they are still badly damaged because the very mechanisms of movie and television production demand that they be isolated, focused on work. In addition, Dow said, the child is made, willy-nilly, an object of voyeurism, a creature "in this really strange fishbowl, where everybody's looking at you." Such children, he said, learn one thing only: how to be objects of attention and desire, adept at pleasing people and being cute. "You never get to try things," he said. "You develop only one ability, to be a good little kid." That "good little kid" image is dangerously static, allowing no growth or variation and promising to the child inside it that nothing will ever change: "You lose all ambition, because everything seems to be there—everything."

Dow's comments came very close to shifting the focus away from "the business" as an isolated problem and toward the general culture in which this business is located. Dow seemed to be suggesting that the child actor is locked into a particular object position, the focus of a cultural gaze that seeks to freeze the cute child in a mesmeric trance, denying it not only growth but movement, really any sort of agency. In other words, Dow's expansive ideas tended to be genuinely subversive, bypassing questions of protection, compensation, and blame for a brief glimpse of cultural dynamics, especially sexual dynamics.

But his views were quickly assimilated into the preparation of a working paper that would be presented to the assembled conference the next day; and we went on as before, hearing stories of how children who were unable to muster adequate screams for horror movies were stuck with pins until they could, of more and more rapacious parents, of film companies that leave California and film just across the state line to avoid the weak-but-better-than-nothing child labor laws here.

The day's work was done, followed by free time, which I spent asking ex-stars what it was like to work with Brian Keith, Jodie Foster, Donna Reed, Lassie. I love those stories. Then there was a dinner at Wizardz on Universal City Walk, a hilariously neoned collection of eateries and shopperies right there on the same hill (but also not offering sneak-in access to the rides). During dinner, provided by SAG and terrific, I spoke with writers who had screenplays and television people who had ideas for new shows. I seem to have lost my notes on these talks, which were, anyhow, the usual L.A. dinner (or bus ride) conversations.

The next day we met to hear the group reports, and I did manage to learn a bit about the law, especially how the Coogan Law, which protects a percentage of the child's earnings, applies only to contract work, said to be only about 5 percent of child work in the business. I also heard some eloquent and stirring candor from Paul Petersen, the moving force behind the conference and the president of A Minor Consideration, a support and lobbying group for child actors, past and present. Petersen, a well-published and brilliant scholar as well as a worker in the field, said that the treatment of children in the industry exposes the hypocrisy of our professions about family values and our deep concern for the child: "You see what happens," he said, "when children *really* become valuable commodities." "These kids," he continued, "are mostly white upper-middle-class kids," whose parents are free to do as they like and practice the values they espouse: "and look what they do!" "Look on parents with a jaundiced eye!" he suggested. They are the ones who make the idea of a self-sufficient child or even a child with earnings of its own utterly "alien."

But is it the parents? The conference, with its emphasis on protection, seemed deeply confused on whether to appeal to parents' better instincts or to slaughter the lot of them, whether to regard the child as weak and in need of sheltering, or self-sufficient, in need of empowerment. I wondered, as I listened to Petersen's informed and passionate remarks, whether it was enough to talk tough about parents, conditions on the set, even the laws. On this last afternoon, the conference was flooded with new participants, current child actors and their parents, maybe five hundred of them.[6] They were all cute as buttons, of course, and seemed much more aware and self-possessed than the generally uncertain, frazzled parents they had in tow. These children, ranging in age from about five to maybe thirteen, were already grooved, perfectly adapted in body and spirit, or so it seemed.

Looking out on this assemblage of cunning winningness, John Whitaker promised, "We are not going to let this happen to you!" He was referring explicitly to the puberty cutoff, the cold dumping of children at the age of acne; but he was including all the other horrors we had been hearing about, the financial, emotional, and physical exploitation of children. All of this, the conference seemed to be saying, must and will end.

It seemed to me, though, that the audience itself had already been shaped by our culture in such a way as to belie that promise and that hope. These kids had been formed to fit an image and to satisfy a demand, not by their parents or even by "the industry" but by all of us. Why were they all pretty, vacant, acquiescent? Why were a good 75 percent of them blond? Why were 99 percent of them white? Why were they there at all? Why did we, the rest of us, want to look at them? Who was creating the demand for these small bodies—and why? Was the conference taking part in the usual hugger-mugger by so resolutely avoiding central questions about the culture?

Tony Dow's words came back to me, his suggestion that children are being posed before us on movie and television screens in answer to deep and terrible cultural needs that have everything to do with our desires and nothing to do with the welfare of the children. His tactful and oblique references to voyeurism, to the use of children to satisfy displaced sexual needs, brought up an issue not otherwise considered by the conference: Who looks at children and why?

As Graham Greene suggested in discussing Shirley Temple, these children are provided to us as totsies, not because the industry is corrupt or because parents are consumed with blind greed but because we demand it. The plight of child actors may not seem to demand much of our attention or sympathy. How much can we care about a few thousand show-biz kids who feel sore because they get swindled out of their earnings and robbed of a normal childhood? A normal childhood is not that great anyhow. But maybe these special, even privileged children, forced into fishbowls so we can look at their changeless bodies and eternal cuteness, can reveal something to us besides their devious erotic charm. Perhaps they might hold a key to the otherwise mysterious hypocrisy we exercise in proclaiming our child-centeredness as we bash and jettison our actual children, attend shoddily to their health, education, and welfare as we croon endearments over them.

How do we understand our constant sexualizing of children and our quick denials of that activity? How can we stop creating so many victims, both in Hollywood and outside? Perhaps Tony Dow, Lauren Chapin, Paul Petersen, and their friends can tell us.

Notes

Introduction

1   *60 Minutes* executive producer and creator Don Hewitt bristles at the idea that his show is slithering downward toward tabloid journalism: "We've never caved in to the Bobbitts, Dahmers and O. J. Simpsons. We do stories on Lloyd's of London" (*Newsweek,* November 28, 1994, p. 76).

2   A few months later (October 17, 1994) the same group did appear in daylight, on *Donahue*—"Roseanne's Family Speaks Out"—telling the identical story more fully, helped along by suggestions from the audience: "Hello. I wanted to ask the—ask you did you ever consider the fact that Roseanne is unhappy with herself, which is why she's pushing the family away?"

3   Declared in August 1990 by the Advisory Board on Child Abuse and Neglect of the U.S. Department of Health and Human Services.

4   Quoted in Douglas J. Besharov, with Jacob W. Dembrosky, "Child Abuse: Threat or Menace: How Common Is It Really?" posted on *Hey Wait,* Thursday, October 3, 1996; and in *NRCCSA News* 5, no. 2 (March–April 1996): 8. Secretary Shalala is, I should say, referring to a report that covers all forms of child abuse, but as I shall argue, we often code "child abuse" so strongly as "sexual molesting" as to make them synonymous.

5   For a parallel analysis of this maneuver in reference to a different sex crisis, see Philip Jenkins, *Pedophiles and Priests: Anatomy of a Contemporary Crisis* (New York: Oxford University Press, 1996).

6   See Ellen Bass and Laura Davis, *The Courage to Heal: A Guide for Women Survivors of Child Abuse* rev. ed. (New York: HarperCollins, 1992): "If you are unable to remember any specific instances . . . but still have a feeling that something abusive happened to you, it probably did" (p. 21); or Beverly Engel, *The Right to Innocence: Healing the Trauma of Childhood Sexual Abuse* (New York: Ivy Books, 1990): "If you have ever had reason to suspect that you may have been sexually abused, even if you have no explicit memory of it, the chances are very high that you were" (p. 2).

7   March 7, 1994, pp. 6, 8.

8   As for glee, I can cite the reaction of policemen attending a special all-day seminar conducted at the University of Southern California's Delinquency Control
Institute by an expert in child-molesting crimes, R. P. "Toby" Tyler, in October
1988. When the previous year's figures for convictions were announced, there
were murmurs of approval; but the figures for suicides brought forth hearty ap-
plause. As for anger, see Don W. Weber and Charles Bosworth Jr., *Secret Lessons*
(Harmondsworth: Penguin, 1994), concerning the trial of Richard Van Hook, an
Illinois teacher found guilty of molesting students. Though he maintained his
innocence steadily, after the conviction he shot himself, whereupon the director
of the local rape and sexual abuse center "erupted in anger": "He's raped those
girls again. He's stolen their right to see him punished" (p. 351).

9   I have a file of examples, a recent one citing a Florida prison where a steel bar
was used by one convict (not convicted of a crime against a child) to beat to
death another (who was) (*Los Angeles Times*, October 3, 1996, p. A16).

10 According to the National Institute of Justice's *Research in Brief*, "The vast majority of childhood sexual victims are not arrested for sex crimes or any other
crimes as adults" (March 1995, p. 2). Since arrests constitute about the only evidence here, these would seem to be suggestive data.

11 *Newsweek*, June 13, 1994, p. 31.

12 According to the massive study of state statistics released in April 1996, *Child
Maltreatment 1994: Reports from the States to the National Center on Child Abuse
and Neglect,* all forms of sexual abuse combined add up to 14 percent of the total
of officially maltreated children: 53 percent are neglected, 26 percent physically
abused, 5 percent emotionally abused, and 22 percent "other." See *NRCCSA
NEWS* 5, no. 2 (March–April, 1996): 8.

13 Vern L. Bullough, "History of Human Sexual Behavior in Western Societies,"
in *Pedophilia: Biosocial Dimensions,* ed. Jay R. Feierman (New York: Springer-
Verlag, 1990), p. 86.

14 This historical development is traced in my *Child-Loving: The Erotic Child and
Victorian Culture* (New York: Routledge, 1992), the last chapter of which contains the seeds of the present book.

15 Actually, the grandmother says this about Mary (Karen Balkin) in William
Wyler's film version of the play (1961).

16 Representative Mark Souder (R-Indiana) found himself in hot water when he
argued: "The only law that [the FBI] clearly established [David Koresh] broke
that I can see so far is he had sex with consenting minors. Do you send government troops into large sections of Kentucky and Tennessee and other places
where such things occur?" Souder made matters worse by saying he didn't know
Koresh was sleeping with ten-year-olds; he thought they were fourteen. (*Time,*
August 14, 1995, p. 18).

17 Oliver Goldsmith, "Song," from *The Vicar of Wakefield* (1776).

18 *Crier Report,* Fox News Channel, April 28, 1997.

19 *Newsweek,* June 3, 1996, pp. 64–65.

20 By the way, these cultural directives equating the enticing with eternal youth operate with special ferocity on women, but not only on women: think of Tom Cruise, Michael Jordan, John Kennedy Jr., Matthew Broderick, Dan Quayle, Prince Charles, David Letterman, Jimmy Connors, Tom Brokaw, Stanley Fish, Luciano Pavarotti, Mick Jagger, Jack Nicholson, Bob Hope—cute little boys forever.

21 Asked to rate for sexual allure photos from three age groups—child (age seven), adolescent (seventeen), and adult—all judges (male and female, all ages) chose the adolescent girl, with adolescent boys not far behind. Though children did not win here, they generally did much better than adults, and one might wonder if the researchers unconsciously protected themselves from more upsetting results by choosing as "a child" such a young image. What if the photos they used had been of twelve-year-olds? For the study and its results, see Howard E. Barbaree et al., eds., *The Juvenile Sex Offender* (New York: Guilford Press, 1993), p. 147.

22 There are, of course, less happy forms of scandal. Vern L. Bullough, emeritus professor of history and sociology at SUNY Buffalo and a distinguished historian and sex researcher, found himself with a nearly one-hundred-page FBI file, branded as a "security risk," and when he once traveled overseas on a Fulbright Fellowship, identified to foreign agencies as "a dangerous subversive"; see *Lingua Franca,* May–June 1994. Even garden-variety scandal can be disabling, as when it successfully identifies skeptics of the standard line as the enemy or as fellow-travelers with the child molesters. For an analysis of this phenomenon, see Jeffrey S. Victor, *Satanic Panic: The Creation of a Contemporary Legend* (Chicago: Open Court, 1993), pp. 252–53.

1. *Trapped in the Story*

1 Partly to protect the innocent people involved in this trial and partly to avoid inadvertently participating in the ongoing civil suit, I have changed the names of the plaintiff and his family, the defendant and her family, the students who testified, and the high school. I have not changed the name of the public officials involved or the newspaper and its reporter.

2 See *Glendale News-Press,* March 8, 1994, p. A1; March 17, 1994, p. A1.

3 *Glendale News-Press,* March 8, 1994, p. A1.

4 Interview, May 18, 1994.

5 She so stated when signing him into therapy.

6 Testified to in the trial: *The People of the State of California v. Mary T. Baxter.* Alan's exact age at the time of the alleged molestation is uncertain, but Mary recalls him saying he was one and a half years old. His speaking of this abuse to Mary Baxter led to the October exchange of therapeutic letters that was to loom so large in the trial.

7 Testimony in the trial, reported in the *Glendale News-Press,* March 10, 1994, p. A1.

8   His close friend Kim Hart told sheriff's detective Julia Pausch that Alan "told her that he thought he was 'in love' with his teacher." See Los Angeles County Sheriff's Department Supplementary Report of June 11, 1993, file 493-03374-0757-127, p. 2, filed by Julia Pausch, LASD Child Abuse Detail.

9   Interview, May 18, 1994.

10 *The Pickwick Papers*, chapter 34.

11 Characterizations offered by the prosecution, according to the *Glendale News-Press*, March 15, 1994, p. A12; and March 18, 1994, p. A1.

12 The characterization (rather restrained for this discourse) offered by the defense, according to the *Glendale News-Press*, March 15, 1994, p. A12.

13 From interview with Mrs. Baxter, May 18, 1994, details being confirmed also in testimony offered during the trial.

14 Alan's account is vague on this and all other dates.

15 File 493-03374-0757-127; Detective Julia Pausch's report "Oral Copulation with a Minor," 288A(B) (1) PC, pp. 9–11.

16 The first in the original (June 2) report to Detective R. Fornay; the second in the June 11 report filed by Detective Pausch.

17 Pausch report (June 11).

18 *Glendale News-Press*, March 9, 1994, p. A1.

19 March 16, 1994, p. A1. Mrs. Baxter told me the tattoo is actually on her right hip. "But who," she commented, "expects the media to be accurate? Besides, thigh is much more salacious, doncha think?"

20 *Glendale News-Press*, March 8, 1994, p. A1; March 16, 1994, p. A1; March 19, 1994, p. A14.

21 *Glendale News-Press*, March 11, 1994, pp. A1, A4.

22 *Glendale News-Press*, March 11, 1994, p. A4.

23 Interview, May 18, 1994.

24 See Detective Pausch's report of her interview with Mrs. Baxter of June 18, 1993.

25 Interview, May 18, 1994.

26 November 4, 1992, p. A1.

27 March 5, 1994, p. A12.

28 The prosecution had claimed it was "relative to the threshhold [sic] issues," a powerful metaphor that doesn't exclude much, since anything might be on the threshold (*Glendale News-Press*, November 4, 1992, p. A1).

29 *Glendale News-Press*, March 12, 1994, pp. A1, A4.

2. Inventing the Child — and Sexuality

1   Phillipe Ariès, *Centuries of Childhood: A Social History of Family Life*, trans. Robert Baldick (New York: Knopf, 1962). See also Lawrence Stone, *The Family, Sex, and Marriage in England, 1500–1800* (New York: Harper and Row, 1977); Richard Lewinsohn, *History of Sexual Customs*, trans. Alexander Mayce (New

York: Bell, 1958); and Peter Coveney, *The Image of Childhood. The Individual and Society: A Study of the Theme in English Literature,* rev. ed. (Baltimore: Penguin, 1967). It's also worth noting that in the colonies "men" included most of what we would now think of as "boys": Guy Butler, *When Boys Were Men* (Cape Town: Oxford University Press, 1969).

2   See Keith Thomas, "The Changing Family," *Times (London) Literary Supplement,* October 21, 1977, pp. 1226–27; and Linda Pollock, *A Lasting Relationship: Parents and Children over Three Centuries* (Hanover, N.H.: University Press of New England, 1987), pp. 11–13.

3   The quotation is from "My Heart Leaps Up." I acknowledge that Wordsworth often laments the great distance from childhood, the aching sense of what is lost—"nothing can bring back the hour / Of splendour in the grass, of glory in the flower" ("Ode: Intimations of Immortality"), but he always insists there is a residue, a powerful memory tie connecting us to the child.

4   Sigmund Freud, *Group Psychology and the Analysis of the Ego,* trans. James Strachey (New York: Norton, 1989), pp. 89–90.

5   Ibid., p. 90.

6   See Diane H. Schectky and Arthur H. Green, *Child Sexual Abuse: A Handbook for Health Care and Legal Professionals* (New York: Brunner/Mazel, 1998), which cites a host of studies indicating that most "latent" children are thinking about sex, masturbating, and engaging in sex play not at all infrequently.

7   *Child,* June–July 1996, p. 38.

8   Jean-Marc-Gaspard Itard, *The Wild Boy of Aveyron,* trans. George Humphrey and Muriel Humphrey (Englewood Cliffs, N.J.: Prentice Hall, 1962), p. 59.

9   Ibid., p. 11.

10 Ibid., p. 4.

11 Ibid., p. 11.

12 Ibid., pp. 17, 33, 18, 66.

13 Ibid., p. 35.

14 Ibid., p. 91.

15 Ibid., p. 59.

16 Ibid., p. 25.

17 Ibid., p. 52.

18 See Russ Rymer, *Genie: A Scientific Tragedy* (New York: HarperCollins, 1993).

19 In late 1994, a particularly appalling New Age movie version of this wild-child story, *Nell,* was released. It is a film so content with its own soft-mindedness that it defiles ideas of noble savagery: "so much transcendent ultraviolet" from "Nell's unpolluted spiritual radiance" "produces an intense case of soul-burn," *Newsweek* observed (December 19, 1994, p. 64). This Jodie Foster vehicle defines Nell's innocence as asexuality and then tries to cure her of her fear of men by giving her a view of a benign doctor's penis (bathed in moonlight), just to let her know how harmless it is. The film has trouble getting its own cynicism straight.

20 I'm indebted in this discussion to Michael Moon's brilliant "'The Gentle Boy

from the Dangerous Classes': Pederasty, Domesticity, and Capitalism in Horatio Alger," *Representations* 19 (1987): 87–110.

21 Horatio Alger Jr., *Ragged Dick* (1867; reprint, New York: Collier Books, 1962), p. 40.

22 Ibid., pp. 61, 43–44.

23 See Moon, "'The Gentle Boy from the Dangerous Classes.'"

24 *Mark, the Match Boy* (1869; reprint, New York: Collier Books, 1962), p. 382.

25 *Los Angeles Times*, August 15, 1994, p. A5. In the 1996 elections, a parental rights amendment was rejected in Colorado, but backers pressed ahead with plans to place similar initiatives on the ballot in twenty-six other states.

26 *Los Angeles Times*, May 15, 1994, p. A16.

27 Lionel Dahmer, *A Father's Story* (New York: Morrow, 1994).

28 From a review by Dr. Louise Bates Ames of Anthony E. Wolf, *It's Not Fair, Jeremy Spencer's Parents Let Him Stay Up ALL Night: A Guide to the Tougher Parts of Parenting* in the *New Haven Register*, April 23, 1995, p. D3.

29 *Child*, September 1994, p. 100.

30 Ava L. Siegler, "Battle of Wills: How to Handle Your Child's Defiance," *Child*, September 1994, p. 32.

31 This line is lifted from J. M. Barrie; see Andrew Birkin, *J. M. Barrie & The Lost Boys* (London: Constable, 1979), p. 8.

32 John Bradshaw, *Homecoming: Reclaiming and Championing Your Inner Child* (New York: Bantam Books, 1990).

33 Ibid., p. 253.

34 Beverly Engel, *The Right to Innocence: Healing the Trauma of Childhood Sexual Abuse* (New York: Ivy Books, 1990), pp. 63–64.

35 Ellen Bass and Laura Davis, *The Courage to Heal: A Guide for Women Survivors of Child Sexual Abuse*, rev. ed. (New York: HarperCollins, 1992), pp. 58–59.

36 Mike Lew, *Victims No Longer: Men Recovering from Incest and Other Sexual Child Abuse* (New York: HarperCollins, 1990), p. 177.

37 *National Enquirer* cover, April 30, 1996; *Time* cover, April 22, 1996.

3. Myths of Protection, Acts of Exposure

1 October 14, 1996, p. 28.

2 Examples are everywhere. *Child* magazine published a special issue on modesty, telling us that children need to feel they have control over who sees their bodies and running as a caption under a large picture, "It's natural for school-age kids to become shy about their bodies." The picture is of a school-age kid, shy about his body but exposed in only his underpants, arms crossed warily across his chest, looking angrily at all of us who do not "value his feelings" (June–July 1996, p. 40).

3 *Los Angeles Times*, December 28, 1993, p. A16.

4 See Ronald M. Holmes, *Sex Crimes* (Newbury Park: Sage, 1991), pp. 34–35.

5 Emily Driver, "Positive Action," in *Child Sexual Abuse: A Feminist Reader,* ed. Emily Driver and Audrey Droisen (Washington Square: New York University Press, 1989), pp. 194–95.

6 Liz Smith column in *Los Angeles Times,* January 4, 1994, p. F2.

7 I am aware that there is a backlash afoot, but I believe the backlashers are playing by the same rules as the friends of the standard line on this subject. See chapter 10.

8 *Time,* January 17, 1993, p. 47.

9 *Los Angeles Times,* March 20, 1994, p. E4.

10 February 2, 1995, p. B6.

11 Quoted in and commented on by Gary B. Melton in his foreword to *Preventing Child Sexual Abuse: Sharing the Responsibility,* by Sandy K. Wurtele and Cindy L. Miller-Perrin (Lincoln: University of Nebraska Press, 1992), p. vii. For a patient analysis of the social construction of this problem, see Martin L. Forst and Martha-Elin Blomquist, *Missing Children: Rhetoric and Reality* (New York: Lexington Books, 1991), pp. 55–113.

12 Danya Glaser and Stephen Frosh, *Child Sexual Abuse* (Toronto: University of Toronto Press, 1993), p. ix.

13 Roland Summit, foreword to *Sexual Abuse of Young Children: Evaluation and Treatment,* by Kee MacFarlane, Jill Waterman, et al. (New York: Guilford Press, 1986), p. xi.

14 The first from Beverly Engel, *The Right to Innocence: Healing the Trauma of Childhood Sexual Abuse* (New York: Ivy Books, 1990), p. 33; the second from Mic Hunter, *Abused Boys: The Neglected Victims of Sexual Abuse* (New York: Lexington Books, 1990), p. 25.

15 *Basic Facts about Child Sexual Abuse,* 3d ed. (Chicago: National Committee to Prevent Child Abuse, 1988), p. 13.

16 The first statement comes from *Basic Facts about Child Abuse,* 3d ed.; the pamphlet is now in its fourth edition, 1993. All this does indeed come from the NCPCA.

17 See Forst and Blomquist, *Missing Children,* pp. 63, 68.

18 Ibid., p. 31.

19 Reported in Brett Kahr, "The Sexual Molestation of Children: Historical Perspectives," *Journal of Psychohistory* 19 (1992): 193. To be fair, the Berlin findings are "preliminary" and the British ones come from a questionnaire. All the same, Kahr says, these "findings still clamor for outrage and action" (p. 194).

20 Dr. Frank Pittman, "Ask Dr. Frank," *Psychology Today,* May–June 1994, p. 95.

21 "The Universality of Incest," *Journal of Psychohistory* 19 (1992): 139.

22 Beverly Gomes-Schwartz et al., *Child Sexual Abuse: The Initial Effects* (Newbury Park: Sage, 1990), p. 14.

23 Kathleen Coulborn Faller, *Child Sexual Abuse: Intervention and Treatment Issues* (Washington, D.C.: Department of Health and Human Services, Administration for Children and Families, 1993), p. 16.

24 Jon R. Conte, *A Look at Sexual Child Abuse* (Chicago: National Council for the Prevention of Child Abuse, 1986), p. 3.

25 Glaser and Frosh, *Child Sexual Abuse,* p. 5. A Fort Collins (Colorado) eye doctor was reported by the *Denver Post* (March 26, 1995, pp. 1A, 15A) to have committed suicide in a Denver motel room after police discovered hidden camera-VCR set-ups he had placed in his home's bathrooms and bedrooms to tape, among others, his thirteen-year-old daughter's friends. Despite his death, the case goes on, entirely because "people want to know if they are victims." The police could, of course, destroy the tapes, but that would rob the citizenry (or much of it, apparently) of its claim to victimhood. What's the point of being a victim unless you know it?

26 *Los Angeles Times,* November 13, 1995, p. A28.

27 "Child Abuse: Threat or Menace," World-Wide Web posting, October 3, 1996.

28 In order, see Peggy Martinelli, ed., *Find the Children Directory 93-94,* vol. 8 (Salem, Ore: Jadent, 1993), p. 5; "Stranger Abduction Homicides of Children," *Office of Juvenile Justice and Delinquency Prevention, Juvenile Justice Bulletin,* January 1989, p. 3; Gerald T. Hotaling and David Finkelhor, *The Sexual Exploitation of Missing Children: A Research Review* (Washington, D.C.: U.S. Department of Justice, 1988), p. 2; Forst and Blomquist, *Missing Children,* p. 70.

29 Karen McCurdy and Deborah Daro, *Current Trends in Child Abuse Reporting and Fatalities: The Results of the 1993 Annual Fifty State Survey* (Washington, D.C.: National Center on Child Abuse Prevention Research, 1994).

30 According to a study by the nonprofit Population Reference Bureau, reported in the *Los Angeles Times,* February 2, 1995, p. A12.

31 Accompanying pamphlet, p. 5.

32 *Los Angeles Times,* December 20, 1993, p. E2.

33 See, e.g., Jane McCord and Lauren Shapiro Gonzalez, "Disclosure Patterns in Psychotherapy," in *Behind the Playground Walls: Sexual Abuse in Preschools,* ed. Jill Waterman et al. (New York: Guilford Press, 1993), p. 65.

34 John Crewdson, *By Silence Betrayed: Sexual Abuse of Children in America* (Boston: Little, Brown, 1988), p. 32.

35 *Los Angeles Times,* March 14, 1994, p. E2.

36 *Los Angeles Times,* October 24, 1993, "Calendar," p. 85.

37 So said Dr. Joyce Brothers in the *Los Angeles Times,* August 15, 1994, p. E9. See also Mic Hunter, *Abused Boys: The Neglected Victims of Sexual Abuse* (Lexington, Mass.: Heath, 1990).

38 Ronald M. Holmes, *Sex Crimes* (Newbury Park: Sage, 1991), p. 34; Mike Lew, *Victims No Longer: Men Recovering from Incest and Other Sexual Child Abuse* (New York: HarperCollins, 1990), p. xvii.

39 See, e.g., his *Sourcebook on Child Sexual Abuse* (Beverly Hills: Sage, 1986), pp. 62–63.

40 Wurtele and Miller-Perrin, *Preventing Child Sexual Abuse,* p. 17.

41 Hunter, *Abused Boys,* pp. 42–43. Note that much of the controversy over A. M.

Holmes's nervy 1996 novel, *The End of Alice*, dealt not so much with her pedophile male killer but with his correspondent, a college girl writing of her seduction of a twelve-year-old boy.

42 *Los Angeles Times*, February 13, 1994, p. B2.

43 *Los Angeles Times*, May 29, 1994, p. A25. Later that year, perhaps in a copycat case, a fifty-one-year-old fund-raiser for Burbank High School, Salle Dumm, was accused of seducing a seventeen-year-old high-school football player. The boy said she murmured to him, "Do this for your team. I can help out your team financially."

44 July 25, 1994, p. 54.

45 *Los Angeles Times*, July 12, 1994, pp. A1, A17.

46 *New York Times*, international edition, April 2, 1997, p. A4.

47 April 18, 1994, p. 40.

48 *Los Angeles Times*, August 3, 1994, pp. A1, A8 for Nepal, p. A4 for Brazil.

49 *Los Angeles Times*, July 13, 1994, pp. A1, A12.

50 "The Universality of Incest," *Journal of Psychohistory* 19 (1991): 142.

51 Ibid., pp. 147, 143, 149, 157.

52 On the assaults in Guatemala, see *Los Angeles Times*, April 1, 1994, p. A13; April 2, 1994, pp. A1, A22; May 16, 1994, p. A13; also *Time*, April 18, 1994, p. 48. On alleged misuse of children in other countries, see Victor Perera's op-ed essay, "Behind the Kidnapping of Children for Their Organs," *Los Angeles Times*, May 1, 1994, pp. M1, M6, which contains charges vigorously denied by the U.S. Information Agency: ibid., June 4, 1994, p. B7.

   Newsweek ran a skeptical piece (June 26, 1995, p. 33) on these charges-that-will-not-go-away and on two much-honored documentaries, *The Body Parts Business* (Canadian) and *Organ Thieves* (French). *Newsweek* notes the harm done—a decline in lifesaving organ contributions in these countries—and traces this myth to old stories of ogres and Jews stealing Christian babies. Of all anti-U.S. propaganda hits, this one is called "the greatest lie of all," a lie, *Newsweek* ruefully notes, that "lives on."

53 The sources cited in this discussion are *Los Angeles Times*, October 22, 1996, p. B6; *Newsweek*, September 2, 1996; (for Reuters) *Los Angeles Times*, August 19, 1996, p. A11; *Stern*, August 29, 1996; *Johannesburg Citizen*, August 31, 1996, p. 15; and *Time*, September 2, 1996.

54 *Time*, September 2, 1996, p. 25. The quotations are, in order, from Dr. Fred Berlin, founder of the Sexual Disorders Clinic at Johns Hopkins; A. Nicholas Groth, Florida clinical psychologist; unspecified ("what does seem clear"); and Dr. Chester Schmidt of Johns Hopkins.

55 *Remembering Satan* (New York: Knopf, 1994), p. 50.

56 See *Lingua Franca*, March–April 1994, pp. 8–11.

57 May 24, 1996, p. 1.

58 December 20, 1995, p. A16.

59 *Los Angeles Times*, April 10, 1994, p. E5.

60 *Pasadena Star News,* August 13, 1996, p. A3; *Los Angeles Times,* September 18, 1996, p. A10.

61 Sally Jessy Raphael, "Not in My Neighborhood," transcript 1560, August 30, 1994.

62 *Los Angeles Times,* September 9, 1994, p. A18.

63 *The Abuse Excuse and Other Cop-outs, Sob Stories, and Evasions of Responsibility* (Boston: Little, Brown, 1994), pp. 100–11.

64 *Los Angeles Times,* February 10, 1996, p. A17.

65 Ibid.

66 *Los Angeles Times,* June 24, 1997, pp. A1, A12.

67 California's first local Megan's Law target not only found his house picketed by neighbors, who had been alerted by police flyers, but was hounded by sign-toting, bullhorn blaring, 911-dialing people whenever he left the house. His employer heard the noise and immediately fired him, prompting his nearest neighbor to reflect that all the community had managed to do was secure his presence: they got him fired, and "this will make it harder for him to move" — to move or to live at all, one might say. See *Los Angeles Times,* January 15, 1997, pp. A3, A14.

   Community notification laws seem to work well in providing us with a focus for sanctimonious outrage and not at all to provide safety or to deter. Elizabeth Semel, board member of the National Association of Criminal Defense Lawyers, calls the whole thing "an orchestrated train wreck"; and Jerome G. Miller, clinical director of the Augustus Institute (who "has treated more than 500 pedophiles"), says these laws do not stop "truly compulsive" molesters, and rob "borderline pedophiles" of the support they need to stop. In other words, the laws create lots of noise, more molestation, and more talk. Nice job. Quotes are from *Los Angeles Times,* May 25, 1997, p. A25.

68 *Los Angeles Times,* June 23, 1996, p. A1. The Child Sex Offender Registration and Community Notification Act was passed as part of the omnibus crime bill in January 1996.

69 *Los Angeles Times,* October 14, 1996, p. A8; November 11, 1996, p. B5.

70 Frank E. Zimring, "The Truth about Sex Offenders," *Los Angeles Times,* May 5, 1997, p. B5. The quotes from Governor Wilson are also from this op-ed piece.

71 *Los Angeles Times,* September 26, 1996, p. A19.

72 July 3, 1995, pp. 47–50.

73 July 22, 1996, p. 33.

74 *Los Angeles Times,* February 15, 1994, pp. A1, A6.

75 Quoted in Barbara Dafoe Whitehead, "The Failure of Sex Education," *Atlantic Monthly,* October 1994, p. 64. In January 1995, this same magazine printed a variety of protesting letters and a strong response from Whitehead.

76 MacFarlane, Waterman, et al., *Sexual Abuse of Young Children,* p. 255.

77 Jill Duerr Berrick and Neil Gilbert, *With the Best of Intentions: The Child Sexual Abuse Prevention Movement* (New York: Guilford Press, 1991), p. 37.

78 *Child* authority Dr. Penelope Leach points out that most children who are snatched do cry and that it does no good, that others in the vicinity simply

assume it's the parents making the kids cry, since parents so often do that. Dr. Leach says the answer is increased vigilance; it might also be helpful if parents did not induce children to cry so regularly.

79 Berrick and Gilbert, *With the Best of Intentions*, p. 40.

80 Ibid., p. 41.

81 *Los Angeles Times*, January 12, 1994, p. E6.

82 *What Every Kid Should Know about Child Abuse* (South Deerfield, Mass.: Channing L.Bete Company, 1994).

83 Berrick and Gilbert, *With the Best of Intentions*, p. 90.

84 This private school is, I think, no longer in business, ruined, perhaps, by the competition (unfair) coming from Los Angeles County Parks and Recreation. According to a flyer my granddaughter (the same) brought home from kindergarten, these courses are run as a public benefit to foil sexual predators: "Weekly safety awareness information addresses the lures strangers use to attract and abduct children and teens!" (exclamation point in original).

85 See Diane H. Schetky and Arthur H. Green, *Child Sexual Abuse: A Handbook for Health Care and Legal Professionals* (New York: Brunner/Mazel, 1989), pp. 217–18.

86 February 1977, pp. 19–24.

87 *People*, December 20, 1993, pp. 84–90.

88 Richard D. Mohr, "The Pedophilia of Everyday Life," *Art Issues*, March–April 1996, a slightly different version also appearing on http://www.guidemag.com/features/pedophilia-mohr.html; *Newsweek*, June 24, 1996, pp. 64–65. See also the June 1997 issue of *Spy*, with its startling "Sexy Little Girls" cover entitled "Jailbait." The surprisingly acute and detailed (that part is not surprising) essay (pp. 42–49) talks a lot about "the new Lolitocracy" in film, modeling, and advertising; mentions girl gymnasts; and concludes, feebly, that if men were more manly they wouldn't be attracted to Natalie Portman, Anna Paquin, Alicia Silverstone, and Christina Ricci.

89 See *Los Angeles Times*, January 13, 1997, pp. E1, E6. The officials quoted are Mike Maki, president of EPIC International Associates, and Charles Dunn, publisher of *Pageantry* magazine.

90 We got even more of this in early 1997 when the murder of JonBenet Ramsey allowed us (by way of our obliging media villains) to wax indignant about beauty pageants—what kind of people would do that to a six-year-old child?—as we were watching endless videos of a little girl made up to look like a cross between Dolly Parton and Joan Rivers. She pranced once again for us on the screen and sang and did a mock striptease, and we blamed it all on vulgar parents, greed, or "the South." Of course, no one has been able even to invent a connection between the pageants and the grisly murder that gave rise to the publicity, but so what?

91 *Child*, February 1996, p. 16.

92 *Time*, September 26, 1994, p. 75.

93 *Newsweek*, January 19, 1995, p. 73.

94 *Newsweek*, August 28, 1995, p. 57.

95   June 17, 1996, p. 66.

96   As of this writing, thirteen states have laws requiring photo developers to scru-
tinize photographs of nude children, all of which are "suspect," and report what
seems *really* suspect. Perhaps not ironically, many magazines reporting this
problem run a picture of a nude child, just to make sure we know what one
looks like; see, e.g., *Child,* September 1996.

97   Richard B. Woodward, "The Disturbing Photography of Sally Mann," *New York
Times Magazine,* September 27, 1992, p. 52. For a brilliant and subtle examination of the issues involved here and also of the art, see Anne Higonnet, "Con-
clusions Based on Observation," *Yale Journal of Criticism* 9 (1996): 1–18.

98   David Pagel, "Mann Captures the Images of Childhood," *Los Angeles Times,* August 4, 1994, p. F3. Mann is not alone in creating controversy along these lines,
of course. Robert Mapplethorpe and Jock Sturges are two other well-known examples.

99   Mann's statement is quoted in Woodward, "Disturbing Photography," p. 52.
George Dimock, in a brilliant paper delivered at a 1994 conference at Kansas
State University on "the child," called Mann's statement "crippling," which seems
to me exactly right.

100 For further discussion of child stars, see the Appendix.

101 From a study done by the U.S. Advisory Board on Child Abuse and Neglect; reported in the *Los Angeles Times,* April 26, 1995, p. B1.

102 *Los Angeles Times,* January 9, 1994, p. M4.

103 *Los Angeles Times,* December 25, 1993, p. B3; "America's Children: How Are They
Doing?" American Humane Association, Fact Sheet 8 (Englewood, Colo., 1994).

104 Drawn from the following sources: *Time,* April 18, 1994, p. 68; "America's Children: How Are They Doing?" American Humane Association Fact Sheet 8; transcript of *All Things Considered* (NPR), November 13, 1993; *Los Angeles Times,*
July 18, 1994, p. A18; Sylvia Ann Hewlett, *When the Bough Breaks* (New York:
HarperCollins, 1992), p. 14; transcript of *All Things Considered* (NPR), February 6,
1994.

105 *Los Angeles Times,* March 12, 1994, p. E1.

106 *Morning Edition* (NPR), January 4, 1994.

107 Quoted in Marian Wright Edelman, *The Measure of Our Success: A Letter to My
Children and Yours* (Boston: Beacon Press, 1992), p. 96.

4. *Home Alone with the Adorable Child*

1   Mark Twain, *Adventures of Huckleberry Finn* (New York: The Library of America,
1982), p. 812.

2   J. D. Salinger, *The Catcher in the Rye* (Boston: Little, Brown, 1951), p. 224.

3   Preface to *Peter and Wendy* (entitled *Peter Pan* in this edition) (New York: Signet,
1987), p. 1; "Prefatory Poem," *Through the Looking-Glass* (Berkeley: University of
California Press, 1983).

4   See John Russell Taylor, ed., *Graham Greene on Film* (New York: Simon and Schuster, 1972), p. 92; an appendix (pp. 276–77) summarizes the Shirley Temple libel action. Greene's review was called "beastly" by Temple's attorneys and "a gross outrage" by the Lord Chief Justice, who found in Miss Temple's favor. Even the defense (which seems to our eyes groveling) admitted, "The fact that the film had already been licensed for universal exhibition refuted the charges which had been made in the article." If the licensers said it was decent, audiences could not react indecently? Possibly the beleaguered defense was being snide. I hope so.

5   See his review in *Night and Day*, October 28, 1937, pp. 184–85.

6   See Marianne Sinclair, *Hollywood Lolitas: The Nymphet Syndrome in the Movies* (New York: Holt, 1988), p. 44.

7   Quoted in ibid., p. 58.

8   The mother, if there is one, is seldom demonized and is often mildly sympathetic—she just is never very important one way or the other. In these films, mothers never (except at the very end, in routine plot conventions) rescue the child from isolation or serve as the main monster: they haven't the power or the erotic force for either role. If the central figure is a girl, the absence of the mother is even more common. The father is, if incest is in the air, the central figure; otherwise, he plays the shadowy role mothers play in boy movies.

9   *Stranger*, March 20, 1997, p. 15.

10 Or it did when *People* said it did: December 13, 1993, p. 46.

11 He has been replaced by an equally full-lipped look-alike, Jonathan Taylor Thomas, who has the advantage over Culkin of being able either to defer puberty or to undergo it without showing visible signs. The *Los Angeles Times* (December 21, 1995, p. F1) identified him in its headline as "Heartthrob and Hot Property," noting, trusting us to supply the causality, that at fourteen he can easily pass for ten.

12 December 21, 1994, p. F9.

13 *Entertainment Weekly*, May 27, 1994, p. 34.

14 Sadly and predictably, Culkin now flashes before us only in small bits of parenthetical sadism, exercises in cruelty so smug that they seem to arise out of the feeling that we have some grievance against the boy, that this figure we called into being and slobbered over is now an affront. *Time* printed an ugly picture of the boy (a very small picture—not like the old days) and a notice: "Hard times: first 14-year-old MACAULAY CULKIN hit 'that awkward age'; now his parents are splitting up" (June 3, 1995, p. 61). In a messy and very public custody battle, Culkin's mother accused the father "of trying to destroy the movie careers" of Mac and his little brother (*Los Angeles Times*, June 27, 1995, p. F1). By May 1996, *Time* was running nasty columns with pictures of a homely former home-aloner, telling us (May 6, p. 91) that his father had slapped him; in August (even uglier picture) Culkin was trying to get at his trust fund to pay his parents' rent (August 19, p. 95); in October, he was being passed over for *Home Alone III* (October 7, p. 101) in favor of what *USA Today* called "A new Macaulay" (November 21,

1996, p. 20). The following April (1997), *Time*, finding an even goofier picture of him, said the custody battle appeared to be over (April 14, 1997, p. 101) — but don't bet on it. What's more dispiriting, the two parents growling over a career that is no longer alive or the public getting high on the shredding of this young life? Culkin really was better off home alone, without parents — and without us.

15 I don't mean to suggest Shirley Temple inaugurated either the cult of the adorable or its representation in screen children (or screen adults-as-children). F. Scott Fitzgerald's pre-Shirley *Tender Is the Night* (1934) remarked on "the current youth worship, the moving pictures with their myriad faces of girl-children" (New York: Scribners, 1961), book 3, chap. 8. Shirley simply stands for us as a powerful embodiment of a tradition older and wider than she.

16 *The Little Princess* was remade in 1995, in a version too witty, perhaps, to make money.

17 Quoted in Andrew Birkin, *J. M. Barrie & The Lost Boys* (London: Constable, 1978), p. 8.

18 Underpants fetishists who are also pederasts must have a hard time keeping up with the American films that cater to them. Culkin seems to have resisted being so displayed, but the two major boy stars on either side of him chronologically seemed happy to oblige: Ricky Schroder in *The Last Flight of Noah's Ark* and Elijah Wood in *Paradise* and *The War*.

19 Quoted in Sinclair, *Hollywood Lolitas,* p. 101.

20 Quoted in Alfred Appel Jr., *Nabokov's Dark Cinema* (New York: Oxford University Press, 1974), p. 229.

21 A new version that "won't flinch from the story's perverse erotic center" (*Newsweek,* November 13, 1995, p. 90) was due out in late 1996, but it was delayed (*Newsweek,* December 16, 1996, p. 70): dilatory filmmaking or distributor worries about the touchy material and new child pornography laws? One thing is clear: many of the touchiest scenes are being cut, despite the fact that they were shot with a body double for fourteen-year-old star Dominique Swain. The director, Adrian Lyne, gamely says, "I think the film will work, if people can get past the subject matter" (*Esquire,* February, 1997, p. 55), which is a bit like saying, "Arsenic cereal will be a big seller, if people can get past dying from it."

22 "The cinematic point of the movie," says Richard D. Mohr ("The Pedophilia of Everyday Life," p. 30), "is to linger on naked boys. . . . Again, moralizing becomes both a vehicle to advance, and a buffer to acknowledge, prurient interest."

23 The lifeless 1996 *Flipper* tried for a similar summer vacation romance between Paul Hogan and Elijah Wood, but nobody's heart was in it, doubtless because Wood was by then lumpy, gangly, and undisguisably adolescent — not at all the requisite cute.

24 July 17, 1995, p. 60.

5. Resenting Children

1   *Time,* November 4, 1996, p. 100.

2   Martin S. Bergmann, *In the Shadow of Moloch: The Sacrifice of Children* (New York: Columbia University Press, 1993).

3   Kevin Leman, "Full-Esteem Ahead," *Child,* August 1994, pp. 82–85. The article does include some cautions against overcharging your child with power and autonomy. I read these qualifications as maddening complications that make the job of parents even more impossible, since every recommendation is accompanied by a caution, almost a contradiction.

4   "Little Big People," *New York Times Magazine,* October 10, 1993, pp. 28–34. Of course, these are Yuppie brats and Yuppie parental whimpers. The discussion will move to more significant and much larger portions of our child population before long.

5   *A Father's Story* (New York: Morrow, 1994).

6   Ibid., pp. 212, 215, 253. His mother seems to have felt this way too. She wanted Jeffrey's brain preserved, hoping scientists would study it "to determine whether biological factors were behind her son's behavior." She seems to have shared the father's wish to drive back to family origins, even of terror. The judge, however, ordered the brain destroyed (*Los Angeles Times,* December 13, 1995, p. A24).

7   Samuel Butler, *Prose Observations,* ed. Hugh De Quehen (Oxford: Clarendon, 1979), p. 95.

8   Adam Phillips, *On Kissing, Tickling, and Being Bored: Psychoanalytic Essays on the Unexamined Life* (Cambridge: Harvard University Press, 1993), p. 58.

9   Alan Dershowitz, *The Abuse Excuse and Other Cop-outs, Sob Stories, and Evasions of Responsibility* (Boston: Little, Brown, 1994), p. 102.

10 See my *Child-Loving: The Erotic Child and Victorian Culture* (New York: Routledge, 1992), pp. 255–63.

11 Barbara F. Metz, *Boston Globe,* April 27, 1995.

12 *Family Relations* 44, no. 2 (1996).

13 *Los Angeles Times,* August 10, 1994, p. E3; see also "The Use of Physical Discipline," American Humane Association Fact Sheet 12 (January 1994).

14 See Panel on Research on Child Abuse and Neglect, National Research Council, *Understanding Child Abuse and Neglect* (Washington, D.C.: National Academy Press, 1993), p. 189.

15 *Time* (August 25, 1997), p. 65. *Time* gives over its article to pro-spanking enthusiasts, to the notion that such punishment is definitely not child-abuse, and to a large picture of a mother angrily spanking a small girl draped over her knee. The caption to the picture pounds in *Time's* (our?) attitude: "BAD OLD DAYS? Not necessarily."

16 David A. Wolfe, *Preventing Physical and Emotional Abuse of Children* (New York: Guilford Press, 1991), p. 11.

17 Douglas J. Besharov, *Recognizing Child Abuse: A Guide for the Concerned* (New York: Macmillan, 1990), p. 67.

18 *The California Child Abuse and Neglect Reporting Law: Issues and Answers for Health Practitioners* (Sacramento: California Department of Social Services, Office of Child Abuse Prevention, 1991), pp. 3, 16.

19 In Suzanne Somers, *Wednesday's Children: Adult Survivors of Abuse Speak Out* (New York: Jove Books, 1992), p. 91.

20 *Time*, May 2, 1994, p. 80.

21 Quoted in *Newsweek*, December 26, 1994, January 2, 1995, p. 86.

22 *Time*, May 16, 1994, p. 38.

23 *Newsweek*, May 16, 1994, p. 41, July 4, 1994, p. 36.

24 *Newsweek*, April 18, 1994, pp. 18–23.

25 *Los Angeles Times*, January 30, 1996, p. A4; January 31, 1996, p. A3.

26 May 16, 1994, p. 110.

27 Reprinted in *Harper's*, November 1994, p. 28.

28 "Going Soft on Crime," *Time*, November 14, 1994, pp. 63–64.

29 Reported in the *Colorado Daily*, April 14–16, 1995.

30 See *Time*, October 7, 1996, p. 64.

31 *Los Angeles Times*, December 19, 1996, p. A43.

32 "A Question of Abuse," *Mother Jones*, July–August 1996, pp. 32–37, 67–70.

33 Ibid., p. 35.

34 *USA Today*, March 17, 1994; *Los Angeles Times*, December 19, 1993.

35 *Newsweek*, December 26, 1994, January 2, 1995, p. 122.

36 April 26, 1996, p. B8.

37 See James Traub, "The Criminals of Tomorrow," *New Yorker*, November 4, 1996, p. 50.

38 *Newsweek*, December 4, 1995, p. 40; *Time*, January 15, 1996, p. 52.

39 *Los Angeles Times*, January 17, 1995, p. A3.

40 With one exception: the boys were sexually abused as children. Though there is no real evidence to suggest that such things went on (or were important if they did), Blake Morrison, in a long piece in the *New Yorker* (February 14, 1994, pp. 48–60), not only advances the abuse excuse as about the only rational explanation but says that possibly the boys were themselves perverts. As perverts, their primary motive was to assault the toddler sexually, the murder being secondary, a punishment or silencing. Astounding.

41 "Why Do We Blame the Children," transcript 112 of *Both Sides with Jesse Jackson*, February 26, 1994, p. 1.

42 Michael A. Males, "Executioner's Myth," *Los Angeles Times*, May 4, 1997, p. M1.

43 *Los Angeles Times*, August 9, 1996, p. A9.

44 See Franklin E. Zimring, "Crying Wolf over Teen Demons," *Los Angeles Times*, August 19, 1996, p. B5.

45 The NCCD study is by Michael A. Jones and Barry Krisberg, *Images and Reality: Juvenile Crime, Youth Violence and Public Policy* (San Francisco: National Council

on Crime and Delinquency, 1994), pp. 1, 3–4. Michael Males says that "a youth under age 18 is three times more likely to be murdered by an adult than another youth" (Los Angeles Times, May 7, 1997, p. M1).

46 Time, July 22, 1996, p. 41.

47 Charles Patrick Ewing, Kids Who Kill (New York: Avon Books, 1990), p. 75.

48 Time, June 17, 1996.

49 Robert Goodwin, "On the Function of Enemies: The Articulation and Containment of the Unthought Self," Journal of Psychohistory 22 (1994): 93.

50 Sometimes, as in the case of teenage pregnancy, we do: we seem to want to believe that skyrocketing teenage pregnancy is "a powerful marker of a society gone astray," a causal agent in crime, unemployment, poverty, and moral decline. So felt the National Campaign to Prevent Teen Pregnancy, which in early 1997, with the help of Hillary Clinton and MTV, launched a huge campaign that included the commissioning of a study of the issue. Big mistake. The study, done by V. Joseph Hotz, a UCLA scholar, shows not only that teenage pregnancy is declining and has done so steadily since 1991, but that we were wrong to focus on teenage pregnancy in the first place because it is clearly a symptom and not a cause: it makes no difference if very poor women are teenagers when they have children; putting off getting pregnant makes no difference. In short, "teenagers do not have problems because they have babies; they have babies because they have problems." Instead of a titillating issue we can moralize on, Hotz shows, we have a structural problem that we cannot lay on the young, on sex, or on shocking immorality. See Los Angeles Times, May 24, 1997, pp. A1, A14–A15.

51 Neil Sinyard, Children in the Movies (New York: St. Martin's Press, 1992), p. 12.

52 And that's not all, as we are given a reprise of Shirley T, demented but still there: Rhoda, writhing her cute little body, plays a game with Daddy (and other adults she wants to wheedle): "What will you give me for a basket of hugs?" "I'll give you a basket of kisses." At the movie's start, she and Daddy tell one another how much they'll miss these baskets—"Oh, I'll miss your basket of hugs!"—and exchange pledges of what looks like passion: "Oh Daddy, I love you! You're so big and strong!" We can find little Rhoda adorable and also justify killing her because she is desecrating what she is also consecrating.

Patty McCormack returned in late 1995 on a video release of Mommy ("Never let her tuck you in"), apparently an homage to The Bad Seed (Los Angeles Times, December 25, 1995, p. F8).

53 Quoted in Sinyard, Children in the Movies, p. 71.

54 One lonely but glowing exception is the exuberant and subversive Gremlins (1984), which sides with the killer brats.

55 Reported in Jonathan Freedman, "A 'Dow' for How America Values Its Kids," Los Angeles Times, June 21, 1994, p. B7.

56 See Understanding Child Abuse and Neglect, p. 1. The 160,000 figure is for 1990.

57 Los Angeles Times, May 26, 1996, p. A28.

58 See Understanding Child Abuse and Neglect, pp. 93–94.

59 Action against worldwide exploitation of children is most potently focused now in Free the Children, an organization founded and headed by Craig Kielburger, a thirteen-year-old Canadian activist who has been very successful in persuading heads of state to alter child labor laws, and a little less successful in altering consumer practices. This children's campaign is aimed at ending the oppression of children and, Craig's father wrote to me (Craig himself was on a European political trip at the time), "the empowerment of children—the channeling of the creative energy of young people to positive social change."

60 For material on these issues, see *The State of the World's Children 1994*, issued by UNICEF (New York: Oxford University Press, 1994); Penelope Leach, *Children First: What Our Society Must Do—and Is Not Doing—for Our Children Today* (New York: Knopf, 1994); and a special report in the *Los Angeles Times* by Robin Wright, "The Littlest Victims of Global 'Progress,'" January 11, 1994, pp. H1, H4.

61 *Los Angeles Times*, June 27, 1995, pp. A1, A10.

62 *Confronting Sexual Exploitation of Homeless Youth: California's Juvenile Prostitution Intervention Projects* (Sacramento: California Office of Criminal Justice Planning, 1991), pp. 21–22. The quotes that follow are also from this document, pp. 160–82.

63 November 14, 1994, p. 43.

64 See "Why Parents Kill," *Newsweek*, November 14, 1994, p. 31; Martin L. Forst and Martha-Elin Blomquist, *Missing Children: Rhetoric and Reality* (New York: Macmillan, 1991), p. 53. The *Los Angeles Times* puts the figure of "child-abuse deaths" at two thousand but cites no sources (December 6, 1996, p. A33).

65 "When Is Crib Death a Cover for Murder?" *Time*, April 11, 1994, p. 63.

66 *Los Angeles Times*, December 6, 1996, p. A1.

67 *Los Angeles Times*, March 29, 1994, p. B3.

68 *Newsweek*, April 11, 1994, p. 23.

69 *Los Angeles Times*, September 17, 1994, p. A28.

70 "In Slime and Darkness: The Metaphor of Filth in Criminal Justice," *Tulane Law Review* 68 (1994): 727–57.

6. *Myths, Legends, Folktales, and Lies*

1 See Elaine Showalter, *Hystories: Hysterical Episodes in Modern Culture* (New York: Columbia University Press, 1997). Showalter analyzes some of the same phenomena dealt with in this chapter, locating still other causes.

2 See Jeffrey S. Victor, *Satanic Panic: The Creation of a Contemporary Legend* (Chicago: Open Court, 1993), p. 38, also pp. 37–73; and Robert A. Baker, *Hidden Memories: Voices and Visions from Within* (Buffalo: Prometheus Books, 1992), pp. 330–31.

3 Quoted in Lawrence A. Stanley, "The Child-Pornography Myth," *Playboy*, September 1988, p. 41.

4 Carl A. Raschke, *Painted Black* (New York: Harper and Row, 1990), p. 208; Ellen Bass and Laura Davis, *The Courage to Heal: A Guide for Women Survivors of Child*

Sexual Abuse (New York: Ivy Books, 1990), p. 21; *Child Abuse Prevention Handbook* (Sacramento: Office of the Attorney General, 1993), p. 16.

5 Mike Lew, *Victims No Longer: Men Recovering from Incest and Other Sexual Child Abuse* (New York: HarperCollins, 1990), p. xv.

6 See *Los Angeles Times*, November 13, 1993, p. A35, for Clinton statement; *Time*, November 21, 1994, p. 36, for Janet Reno's comments.

7 *Los Angeles Times*, May 18, 1995, pp. B1, B4.

8 *Los Angeles Times*, June 15, 1995, pp. A1, A23.

9 *Los Angeles Times*, June 16, 1996, p. B6; *Newsweek*, June 19, 1995, p. 42.

10 Even so, a red-faced *Time* had to admit that the study it was using was one whose ethics, methodology, and authorship were in doubt. Instead of 83.5 percent of Usenet images being pornographic, for instance, "pornographic files represent less than 0.5 percent of all messages posted on the Internet" (*Time*, July 24, 1995, p. 57).

11 *Time*, July 24, 1995, p. 8.

12 "History of Human Sexual Behavior in Western Societies," in *Pedophilia: Biosocial Dimensions*, ed. Jay R. Feierman (New York: Springer-Verlag, 1990), pp. 82–85.

13 See, e.g., Robert Lee Pierce, "Child Pornography: A Hidden Dimension of Child Abuse," *Child Abuse and Neglect* 8 (1984): 486.

14 John Crewdson, *By Silence Betrayed: Sexual Abuse of Children in America* (Boston: Little, Brown, 1988), pp. 246–47.

15 See my *Child-Loving: The Erotic Child and Victorian Culture* (New York: Routledge, 1992), pp. 378–81, for a discussion of these hearings and the issue of child pornography generally.

16 I hold by this despite such occasional roaring headlines as "International Child-Porn Ring Smashed." This particular smash, heralded as nabbing the leaders of "one of the largest child pornography rings" operating anywhere, occurred in San Diego in November 1995. When we look at the details, though, it turns out that the videos were obtained from Mexico, Asia, and Europe and then "mass produced" (copied) in the San Diego house. The volume of this ring allegedly amounted to upward of 500 videos a month worldwide, although only 387 videos were found in the raid. If this was one of the largest "rings" (though it seems to have been a solo operation, geometrically a point and not a ring), how many of these pennyante operations does it take to add up to the "multi-billion-dollar industry" we're hearing about? See *Los Angeles Times*, November 4, 1995, p. A22; January 19, 1996, p. A20.

17 See, e.g., Crewdson, *By Silence Betrayed*, p. 243: there is no city in the United States where it is sold; what is produced circulates among "a few thousand practicing pedophiles."

18 This was a special seminar conducted by child abuse expert R. P. "Toby" Tyler.

19 *NAMBLA Bulletin*, June 1993, p. 11.

20 See the *Los Angeles Times*, March 17, 1994 ("Ex–Probation Officer Pleads Guilty to Child Porn Charges," p. B2), and June 24, 1994 ("Officer Charged with Posses-

sion of Child Porno," pp. B1, B4). To be fair, the first case seems to have involved photos from Thailand; but the latter were filched from police files.

21 Cecil Adams did a brilliant analysis of the snuff film legend and found no evidence whatever of a single snuff film existing now or at any time in the past: *Los Angeles Reader,* July 9, 1993, p. 62. As this article may not be readily available, I'll be glad to send a copy to anyone interested.

22 John E. Mack, *Abduction: Human Encounters with Aliens* (New York: Scribner's, 1994); see also C. D. B. Bryan, *Alien Abductions, UFOs, and the Conference at M.I.T.* (New York: Knopf, 1995). The conference mentioned in the title was co-chaired by John Mack and dealt with his favorite topic. The evenhanded *New York Times* reviewer (Dean Koontz) of Bryan's book said, "Although clearly an intelligent and dynamic man, Dr. Mack sets standards of proof that are more suitable to theological debate than to a scientific inquiry" (June 11, 1995, p. 14).

23 Mack, *Abduction,* pp. 38, 39, 18–19.

24 These and other objections are reported in *Chronicle of Higher Education,* July 6, 1994, p. A10; and in a hilarious letter to the *Los Angeles Times Book Review* by David Brin, September 4, 1994, p. P11.

25 *Atlantic Monthly,* May 1994, p. 194.

26 Mack, *Abduction,* p. xi.

27 Gallup poll cited in David Lotto, "On Witches and Witch Hunts," *Journal of Psychohistory* 21 (1994): 388.

28 See *Newsweek*'s special "Do We Need Satan?" November 15, 1995, pp. 62–68.

29 In late 1995 the University of Toronto Press published *Satanic Ritual Abuse: Principles of Treatment,* by Colin A. Ross. According to the publisher's blurb, "there is increasing evidence that ritual abuse does take place." And it continues, "Although Dr. Ross has found no evidence of a widespread Satanic network he is open to the possibility that a certain percentage of his patients' memories may be entirely or partially historically accurate. In treatment he recommends that the therapist adopt an attitude hovering between disbelief and credulous entrapment." Notice the traps set in this bit of hokum: increasing evidence, which does not exist, paves the way for the skeptical Dr. Ross, who has (not yet?) uncovered the widespread satanic network, but meanwhile recommends that therapists hover gracefully. This is a university press speaking.

30 Raschke, *Painted Black;* Margaret Smith, *Ritual Abuse* (New York: HarperCollins, 1993).

31 Smith, *Ritual Abuse,* pp. 195–97, 77.

32 Cited in Lotto, "Witches and Witch Hunts," p. 374.

33 "Ritualistic Child Abuse in California" (Sacramento, April 1991), p. 1.

34 *Repressed Memories: A Journey to Recovery from Sexual Abuse* (New York: Simon and Schuster, 1992), p. 165.

35 Smith, *Ritual Abuse,* p. vii.

36 Elizabeth S. Rose (pseud.), "Surviving the Unbelievable," *Ms,* January–February 1993.

37 Lloyd DeMause, "Why Cults Terrorize and Kill Children," *Journal of Psychohistory* 21 (1994): 510.

38 "Ritual Abuse: Definitions, Glossary, the Use of Mind Control": Report of the Ritual Abuse Task Force, Los Angeles County Commission for Women," September 1, 1994.

39 Victor, *Satanic Panic*, pp. 299, 297.

40 Baker, *Hidden Memories*, p. 329.

41 *Los Angeles Times*, November 8, 1994, p. A22.

42 Quoted in Elizabeth Loftus and Katherine Ketcham, *The Myth of Repressed Memory* (New York: St. Martin's Press, 1994), p. 203.

43 This figure, which I haven't reported before, is from D. Finkelhor et al., "Children Abducted by Family Members: A National Household Survey of Incidence and Episode Characteristics," *Journal of Marriage and the Family* 53 (1991): 805–17. The other figures were reported above.

44 Noelle Oxenhandler, "Polly's Face," *New Yorker*, November 29, 1993.

45 December 14, 1993 transcript 3881.

46 All quotes are from the *Los Angeles Times*, in order: December 8, 1993, p. A1; ibid.; December 8, 1993, p. A2; December 13, 1993, p. A3; December 12, 1993, p. A1 (headline); December 10, 1993, p. A38; January 10, 1994, p. E2.

47 *Los Angeles Times*, October 11, 1996, p. A3.

48 *Los Angeles Times*, September 27, 1996, p. A18.

49 *Time*, January 29, 1996, p. 33.

50 *Los Angeles Times*, September 29, 1996, p. A30.

51 Ibid.

52 Kai Erickson, reviewing Kristin Luker, *Dubious Conceptions: The Politics of Teen Pregnancy*, in *New York Times Book Review*, September 1, 1996, p. 12.

53 Op-ed piece by Donella H. Meadows, "Junk Media," *Los Angeles Times*, September 22, 1994, p. B7.

54 *Newsweek*, July 13, 1994, p. 36.

55 For poll, see *Los Angeles Times*, December 18, 1993, p. A1; for Mrs. Clinton's comments, see headline in *Los Angeles Times*, March 5, 1994, p. A21.

56 *Time*, August 29, 1994, p. 66.

57 *Los Angeles Times*, March 6, 1994, p. M3.

58 *Time*, June 20, 1994, p. 55.

59 *Los Angeles Times*, March 16, 1994, pp. A1, A9.

60 This is not to deny that the media can sharpen the focus of or help to give desire certain shapes. What is at stake is the media's putative position as originator.

61 *Los Angeles Times*, June 14, 1995, pp. A1, A24–A25; *Time*, June 12, 1995, p. 26.

7. The Trials: Believing the Children

1 Quoted in *Los Angeles Times*, July 23, 1993, p. A26.

2 It wasn't until *Redbook* published Beverly Lowry's account of the imprisoned

Ellie Nesler's struggle with cancer, "Should Ellie Nesler Go Free?" (August 1994, pp. 82–85, 114–17), that Willy's name surfaced. It is possible, of course, that his name was withheld from the newspaper accounts out of consideration for his age (though this is by no means a universal practice); but such erasures still have the effect of eroticizing the emptiness. They also fold the child into the adult, as a possession or an extension: "Ellie's boy" is really a part of Ellie (Ellie's foot), a function of Ellie (Ellie's job), and an object (Ellie's afghan).

3   Quoted in Alan Dershowitz, *The Abuse Excuse and Other Cop-outs, Sob Stories, and Evasions of Responsibility* (Boston: Little, Brown, 1994), p. 51. Buchanan had company and lots of it, at least for a while. An op-ed piece I did for the *New York Times* (May 31, 1993) drew a couple of fierce personal letters, saying Ellie should be "lauded" for doing in "this degenerate [*sic*] Daniel Driver" and castigating me for contributing to the "crap" often published in that paper. Of course I refused to notice such yipping. (Truth is, I sent back hot letters, explaining myself and accusing the letter writers of not reading what I had written and of being morons besides and what's the use of writing op-ed pieces if those who read them are morons and why don't you just take your moron self down to the local hazardous waste disposal plant and turn yourself in and if I was a moron like you, buddy, I'd just shut the hell up and . . . oh my.)

4   Frankie Tinkle, "mother of three" and lifelong resident, quoted in the *San Francisco Chronicle,* August 12, 1993, p. A17.

5   Tony Serra, San Francisco attorney and Nesler's lawyer, quoted in the *San Francisco Chronicle,* August 13, 1993, p. A18.

6   A few months later, another malefactor, this time a bank robber, tried the same strategy—"The Lord specifically commanded me to rob the banks so that's what I did"—with the same results. See *Los Angeles Times,* October 30, 1993, p. B3.

7   According to the *Los Angeles Times* (September 10, 1993, p. A32), Nesler blurted out this accusation during the sanity phase of her trial, charging that psychiatrists covered up for a probation officer who molested her when she was fourteen, the cover-up being arranged, she yelled, "because he's a state senator." She named no names, but state senator Patrick Johnston issued a statement acknowledging he had been Nesler's probation officer and denying the allegation.

8   See John Crewdson, *By Silence Betrayed: Sexual Abuse of Children in America* (Boston: Little, Brown, 1988), p. 157; Mary A. Fischer, "McMartin," *Los Angeles Magazine,* October 1989, pp. 128–29.

9   "The Dark Tunnels of McMartin," *Journal of Psychohistory* 21 (1994): 412.

10   See my *Child-Loving: The Erotic Child and Victorian Culture* (New York: Routledge, 1992), pp. 341–58; Richard Wexler, *Wounded Innocents: The Real Victims of the War against Child Abuse* (Buffalo: Prometheus Books, 1990), pp. 148–49; and *Los Angeles Times,* March 16, 1994, pp. A1, A2.

11   This is a reconstruction, I admit, but it's not nearly as far from accurate as you are thinking. The underwear grilling did, in fact, go on for a very long time,

sustained by Buckey's bemused candor and Ms. Ferrero's unremitting snideness, which managed to suggest that there really was a point to the line of questioning.

12   "McMartin Molestation Case Leaves Legacy for Preschools," CNN *Newshour*, March 23, 1994, transcript 562, segment 3.

13   *Los Angeles Times*, July 27, 1994, p. A10.

14   Mary A. Fischer, "Instant Karma: McMartin 10 Years After," *Los Angeles*, October 1993, p. 56.

15   Quoted in *Los Angeles Times*, January 13, 1995, p. F33. In an irony that may have been unintentional, the Manns assigned the central role of Raymond Buckey to former Hollywood pedophile pinup Henry Thomas, who even gets a brief nude scene. It's as if the star from *E.T.* were now transporting his erotic innocence directly to this Gothic victim part. It is worth pointing out that the film, even with it's obligatory (remember this is an Oliver Stone project) attack on THE MEDIA, still inspired violent reactions. Lead prosecutors sputtered and sloshed — "fantasies, distortions, inaccuracies, and major omissions" — and those involved with the defense gloated. Peggy Ann Buckey, Ray's sister, said that maybe the movie would quiet things down, that because of it "this would never be repeated," a moving but probably futile sentiment (see *Los Angeles Times*, May 22, 1995, p. B3; *Time*, May 22, 1995, pp. 69–70).

16   It may matter in rousing skepticism, of course, but the skepticism is limited to the same playing field. It also matters to the Buckeys, some of whom feel vindicated, they say, and to the predictably furious folks on the other side. It also mattered to the Manns, whose house in Hollywood was burned down during the filming in what investigators said was arson (see *Los Angeles Times*, May 22, 1995, pp. B1, B3). Perhaps Virginia McMartin Buckey, the feisty founder of the school, received some measure of satisfaction from the movie too; she certainly did from a slander suit she won against one of the parents: "I wanted him to shut up." He did. She died in December 1995, not long after the movie was aired (*Los Angeles Times*, December 19, 1995, pp. B1, B10).

17   Walter Urban, defense attorney, in an interview published in David Hechler, *The Battle and the Backlash: The Child Sexual Abuse War* (Lexington, Mass.: Heath, 1988), p. 329.

18   Ibid.

19   *Los Angeles Times*, April 16, 1995, pp. B1, B4.

20   Fischer, "Instant Karma," p. 53.

21   Dominick Dunne, "Menendez Justice," *Vanity Fair*, March 1994, p. 111. Other details are drawn from this article, from television news coverage and Court TV, and from accounts in the *Los Angeles Times*.

22   Used for the CBS miniseries *Menendez: A Killing in Beverly Hills*, shown mid-May 1994.

23   Transcript from *The Donahue Show*, February 2, 1994, p. 9; concerning the statements of Ms. Judy Zamos, identified as "Jury Alternate in Lyle's Trial."

Notes to Chapter Seven   331

24 *Los Angeles Times,* April 18, 1996, p. B1.

25 *Los Angeles Times,* March 2, 1994, p. B3.

26 *Los Angeles Times,* April 21, 1994, p. B2.

27 *Los Angeles Times,* December 26, 1993, pp. J1, J4.

28 *Los Angeles Times,* January 29, 1994, pp. B1, B3.

29 *Boulder Daily Camera,* October 23, 1993, p. 1C; *Colorado Daily,* October 20, 1993, pp. 1, 7.

30 See *Time,* November 13, 1995, pp. 89–90; *Newsweek,* May 8, 1995, pp. 58–60; *Los Angeles Times,* December 12, 1995, p. A11.

31 *Morning Journal,* May 20, 1994, p. 5.

32 April 5, 1994, pp. 71–73.

33 *Courage to Heal,* p. 94.

34 Pp. 345–47.

8. Accusing the Stars: Perversion among the Prominent

1 To be more accurate, the three surviving sisters, in a book entitled *Family Secrets,* pawed over in a *People* special article, October 16, 1995, pp. 176–77.

2 A friend who read this said innate sexiness was not a quality she associated with Woody Allen and doubted anybody but me did. She said I should find better examples, as everyone shares her view. I can only say that I don't and that all any of us can do is attend to personal sensations in these matters. Maybe it's a gender thing, though I doubt it; maybe she (and those agreeing with her) are simply not as richly and readily responsive as I.

3 Richard Berendzen, with Laura Palmer, *Come Here: A Man Overcomes the Tragic Aftermath of Childhood Sexual Abuse* (New York: Villard Books, 1993), p. 84.

4 Ibid., p. 135.

5 Ibid., pp. 64, 7.

6 Ibid., pp. 8, 12–21, 9.

7 Ibid., p. 190.

8 Ibid., pp. 270, 192.

9 *Los Angeles Times,* March 27, 1996, p. A19.

10 *Los Angeles Times,* June 9, 1994, pp. B1, B4.

11 *Los Angeles Times,* March 31, 1994, pp. A3, A23.

12 Avoiding the God problem, but taking on gay morality head-on, Howard B. Anderson, of the L.A. Area Boy Scout Council, wrote to the *Los Angeles Times* (February 19, 1995, p. M4) saying the Boy Scouts did *not* think gays were immoral, that the Scouts simply had a duty to "reflect the values of the parents" and not forget "the impact of a role model on pre-adolescents and adolescents." Nobody, he said, was being in the least "judgmental."

13 *Toledo Blade,* September 5, 1993, page not indicated by my slapdash friend.

14 See Philip Jenkins, *Pedophiles and Priests: Anatomy of a Contemporary Crisis* (New York: Oxford University Press, 1996), for an analysis of the reasons why

the focus has been on priests, the hyperbole involved, the inflation of the numbers, and the way these contemporary moral panics come in waves.

15   CNN joined hands with *America Undercover* on these numbers, the latter saying, by way of Richard Sipe ("former priest and author") that three thousand was "a bare minimum" estimate of priest-molesters.

16   In order: *USA Today*, December 7, 1993, p. 3A; *Los Angeles Times*, December 11, 1993, p. A31; Kenneth Woodward, religion editor of *Newsweek*, on *Sonya Live*, November 15, 1993.

17   *Los Angeles Times*, March 1, 1994, p. A17.

18   *Los Angeles Times*, June 2, 1995, pp. B1, B3.

19   *Los Angeles Times*, November 1, 1996, p. B4.

20   *Los Angeles Times*, January 19, 1996, p. B10.

21   Quoted in *Newsweek*, August 31, 1992, p. 56.

22   Ibid., p. 53.

23   August 31, 1992, p. 57.

24   The material in the paragraph comes from the *Village Voice*, November 9, 1993, p. 18.

25   Reported in Alan Dershowitz, *The Abuse Excuse and Other Cop-outs, Sob Stories, and Evasions of Responsibility* (Boston: Little, Brown, 1994), p. 131.

26   *Los Angeles Times*, March 16, 1993, p. A6.

27   Adam Gopnik, "The Outsider," *New Yorker*, October 25, 1993, pp. 86–93.

28   *Los Angeles Times*, February 20, 1995, p. F2.

29   Maureen Dowd, "Auteur as Spin Doctor," *New York Times*, October 1, 1995; *Time*, July 17, 1995, p. 14.

30   Christopher Anderson, *Michael Jackson Unauthorized* (New York: Simon and Schuster, 1994), p. 227.

31   Ibid., pp. 231, 250, 254, 257.

32   Ibid., p. 82.

33   More has come since—a child, another marriage—but who can keep up?

34   La Toya was later obliged to admit on NBC's *Today* that she had no evidence whatever that her brother had molested young boys (*Los Angeles Times*, December 10, 1993, p. F26).

35   Anderson, *Michael Jackson Unauthorized*, p. 331.

36   *Los Angeles Times*, February 2, 1994, p. B6.

37   Anderson, *Michael Jackson Unauthorized*, p. 14.

38   *Enquirer*, July 11, 1995, p. 12; *Newsweek*, August 28, 1995, p. 59; *Esquire*, January 1996, p. 53.

39   Quoted in Randy Taraborelli, *Michael Jackson: The Magic and the Madness* (New York: Birch Lane, 1991), p. 21. In the Diane Sawyer interview (June 14, 1995) cited earlier, there is a taped interview of Michael's father responding, with a sneer, to statements that the boy was so terrified of the father and of fouling up in performances that he vomited often before and after: "If he did 'gurgitate, he 'gurgitated all the way to the bank."

40 Anderson, *Michael Jackson Unauthorized*, pp. 106, 122.

41 J. D. Salinger, *The Catcher in the Rye* (Boston: Little, Brown, 1951), pp. 224–25.

9. Recovered Memory

1   Twain, quoted in Elizabeth Loftus and Katherine Ketcham, *Witness for the Defense* (New York: St. Martin's Press, 1991), p. 31; Robbe-Grillet quoted in *Mirabella*, December 1993, p. 43.

2   In order, Ellen Bass and Laura Davis, *The Courage to Heal: A Guide for Women Survivors of Child Sexual Abuse*, rev. ed. (New York: HarperCollins, 1992), p. 22; Renee Fredrickson, *Repressed Memories: A Journey to Recovery from Sexual Abuse* (New York: Simon and Schuster, 1992), pp. 167, 14, 171; Beverly Engel, *The Right to Innocence: Healing the Trauma of Childhood Sexual Abuse* (New York: Ivy Books, 1990), p. 2; E. Sue Blume, *Secret Survivors*, quoted in Elizabeth Loftus and Katherine Ketcham, *The Myth of Repressed Memory* (New York: St. Martin's Press, 1994), pp. 142, 144; and Mike Lew, *Victims No Longer: Men Recovering from Incest and Other Sexual Child Abuse* (New York: HarperCollins, 1990), p. 69.

3   For Bradshaw, see Loftus and Ketcham, *The Myth of Repressed Memory* pp. 152–53; Fredrickson, *Repressed Memories*, pp. 48–51. There are sixty-three items in Fredrickson's list.

4   Bass and Davis, *Courage to Heal*, p. 14.

5   *Remembering Satan* (New York: Knopf, 1994), p. 80.

6   See *Los Angeles Times*, November 29, 1993, pp. A28–A29, which reports that twenty-three states have removed statutes of limitations in civil cases since 1988 in order to "cope with the wave of suits citing recovered memories."

7   Michael Yapko, *Suggestions of Abuse: True and False Memories of Childhood Sexual Trauma* (New York: Simon and Schuster, 1994), p. 157; Lenore Terr, *Unchained Memories: True Stories of Traumatic Memories Lost and Found* (New York: HarperCollins, 1994), p. 11.

8   Quoted in *Lingua Franca*, July–August 1994, p. 26. See also Crews's two-part article, "The Revenge of the Repressed," *New York Review of Books*, November 17 and December 1, 1994, pp. 54–60, 49–58.

9   Quoted in Wright, *Remembering Satan*, p. 160.

10 Peter Gay, *Freud: A Life for Our Time* (New York: Norton, 1988), p. 751. The examples are also Gay's.

11 "The Universality of Incest," *Journal of Psychohistory* 19 (1991): 127–28.

12 *Time*, November 29, 1993, p. 51. Janet Malcolm quotes the brilliant Adam Phillips (*On Flirtation*) on this point: "Psychoanalytic history often gets trapped in the morally stupefying world of blaming. Instead of trying to discover facts about Freud's life that will finally validate or invalidate psychoanalysis, we should figure out what he was trying to do, how he came to do it—and what he didn't realize he was doing—in order to work out whether we think psychoanalysis is worth having: whether it produces the kind of life stories we go for. Proving

that Freud did not always behave well is not the best way of doing this" (*New York Times Book Review*, November 6, 1994, p. 11).

13 *Time*, November 29, 1993, pp. 52–59, 56. *Time* is not alone, of course. *Newsweek* suggests that someday we may think of Freud as "an old joke that everybody gets, but no one can remember how important it once was" (December 18, 1995, p. 62). For an intelligent, wry update on the attack, see Sarah Boxer, "Flogging Freud," *The New York Times Book Review* (August 10, 1997), pp. 12, 14.

14 Ibid., pp. 55, 52.

15 *Repressed Memories*, p. 31.

16 Franklin was released July 3, 1996. See *Los Angeles Times*, July 4, 1996, p. A31. Also, for earlier developments in the unraveling: November 21, 1995, p. A3; December 25, 1995, pp. A1, A38–A39; July 3, 1996, pp. A1, A20–A21.

17 March 1994, pp. 76–87.

18 *Larry King Live*, October 29, 1991.

19 *Psychology Today*, January–February 1996, p. 52.

20 See Rose's *The Making of Memory* (New York: Doubleday, 1992); and his review of recent books on recovered memory in the *New York Times Book Review*, February 26, 1995, p. 20.

21 Elizabeth Loftus and Katherine Ketcham, *The Myth of Recovered Memory: False Memory and Allegations of Sexual Abuse* (New York: St. Martin's Press, 1994), p. 3; *Newsweek*, September 26, 1994, p. 68.

22 July 17, 1995, p. 47.

23 Rose, *The Making of Memory*, p. 104.

10. The Backlash . . .

1 David Hechler, *The Battle and the Backlash: The Child Abuse Sex War* (Lexington, Mass.: Heath, 1988), p. 65.

2 *Rocking the Cradle of Sexual Politics: What Happened When Women Said Incest* (Reading, Mass.: Addison-Wesley, 1994), p. 10.

3 Richard Ofshe and Ethan Watters, *Making Monsters: False Memories, Psychotherapy, and Sexual Hysteria* (New York: Charles Scribner's Sons, 1994), p. 79; World Wide Web page on "False Memory Syndrome," August 15, 1996: http://iquest.com/-fitz/fmsf/about FMS.html.

4 And by me too, you're thinking I should be saying; but you'll follow the argument better if you repress such cynicism for now; recover it later if you feel you must.

5 Jill Waterman et al., *Behind the Playground Walls: Sexual Abuse in Preschools* (New York: Guilford Press, 1993), p. 270.

6 June 2, 1994.

7 William Cash, "An American Tradition," *Spectator*, September 11, 1993, pp. 16–17.

8 *New York Times Book Review*, January 3, 1993.

9 *New York Review of Books*, December 1, 1994, pp. 49–50.

10 *New York Review of Books*, November 17, 1994, p. 59.

11 *Newsweek*, June 12, 1995, p. 30; *Los Angeles Times*, June 12, 1995, p. A17.

12 *Los Angeles Times*, June 14, 1995, pp. A1, A24–A25.

13 Jeanne Bishop, letter to *New Yorker*, November 7, 1994, p. 22. Related to blaming the parents is the tendency to hold parents responsible, sometimes criminally so, for the activities of their children. In a Michigan case in which parents were fined for the misconduct of their sixteen-year-old son, even *Time* thought the verdict "alarming to any parent who has ever come up against the intransigence, sneakiness or willfulness of a child—which is to say, just about every parent of an adolescent." All the same, in 1995 alone, ten states, *Time* says, and any number of communities enacted sanctions against parents (May 20, 1996, p. 50).

14 *Los Angeles Times*, December 12, 1995, p. E7.

15 November–December 1994, p. 94.

16 According to the *NRCCSA* (*National Resource Center on Child Sexual Abuse*) *News*, a New Jersey Supreme Court ruling in 1993 makes it inevitable that defense attorneys will request "taint hearings" in child-molesting cases. Such hearings will be required "to determine whether defective interviewing rendered the children's statements so unreliable that they should be barred from testifying" (March–April 1995, p. 3).

17 *Los Angeles Times*, May 22, 1994, p. A26.

18 The books treated in this section are Richard Wexler, *Wounded Innocents* (Buffalo: Prometheus Books, 1990); Richard A. Gardner, *True and False Accusations of Child Sex Abuse* (Creeskill, N.J.: Creative Therapeutics, 1992); Michael D. Yapko, *Suggestions of Abuse: True and False Memory of Childhood Sexual Trauma* (New York: Simon and Schuster, 1994); Alan M. Dershowitz, *The Abuse Excuse and Other Cop-outs, Sob Stories, and Evasions of Responsibility* (Boston: Little, Brown, 1994); Robert A. Baker, *Hidden Memories: Voices and Visions from Within* (Buffalo: Prometheus Books, 1992); Elizabeth Loftus and Katherine Ketcham, *The Myth of Repressed Memory: False Memory and Allegations of Sexual Abuse* (New York: St. Martin's Press, 1994); and Richard Ofshe and Ethan Watters, *Making Monsters: False Memories, Psychotherapy, and Sexual Hysteria* (New York: Charles Scribner's Sons, 1994). Page numbers are given in the text.

19 Quoted in Louise Armstrong, *Kiss Daddy Goodnight: Ten Years Later* (New York: Pocket Books, 1987), p. 145.

20 By Joseph E. Grinch and Kimberly A. Grinch (Lake Oswego, Ore.: Recollex, 1997).

21 Richard Rose on CNN *Newsday*, May 14, 1994, transcript 700; Dershowitz, *The Abuse Excuse*, p. 27.

22 On CNN *Crossfire*, March 1, 1994, transcript 1039.

23 Christopher Bagley and Kathleen King, *Child Sexual Abuse: The Search for Healing* (London: Tavistock/Routledge, 1990), p. 92.

24 Katy Butler, "Did Daddy Really Do It?" [review of Loftus and Ofshe books], *Los Angeles Times Book Review*, February 5, 1995, p. 11.

25 Letter to *Los Angeles Times*, December 16, 1993, p. 10.

26 Sandra L. Bloom, "Hearing the Survivor's Voice: Sundering the Wall of Denial," *Journal of Psychohistory* 21 (1994): 467–75; Robert B. Rockwell, "One Psychiatrist's View of Satanic Ritual Abuse" and "Insidious Deception," both in *Journal of Psychohistory* 21 (1994): 450; 22 (1995): 323; E. Sue Blume, letter to *New York Times Book Review*, quoted in Ofshe and Watters, *Making Monsters*, p. 200; quoted in Nieltje Gedney, "A European Response to the Backlash Movement," *Journal of Psychohistory* 22 (1995): 265.

27 *Victims No Longer: Men Recovering from Incest and Other Sexual Child Abuse* (New York: HarperCollins, 1990), p. xv.

28 There are some awful things in Armstrong's books, and one sometimes gets the impression of a splendid intelligence running on a narrow-gauge track, as, for instance, when her pedestrian abuse of Freud descends to nyah-nyah phrases like "Freudulent 'science.'" It's as if she carefully keeps herself uninformed on what might complicate her opinions or challenge her prefabricated thesis. But it's not often "as if" she were a brilliant person masking as a dolt, and the power of her analysis is unmistakable.

29 Armstrong, *Rocking the Cradle of Sexual Politics* (Reading, Mass.: Addison-Wesley, 1994), pp. 4, 264.

30 Ibid., pp. 36, 209.

31 Armstrong, *Kiss Daddy*, p. x.

32 Armstrong, *Rocking the Cradle*, p. 26.

33 *Unchained Memories: True Stories of Traumatic Memories Lost and Found* (New York: HarperCollins, 1994), p. 162.

11. Other Stories, Other Kids

1 Adam Phillips, *On Kissing, Tickling, and Being Bored: Psychoanalytic Essays on the Unexamined Life* (Cambridge: Harvard University Press, 1993), p. 26.

2 Trans. and ed. James Strachey (New York: Norton, 1963), p. 236.

3 *Los Angeles Times*, February 17, 1995, p. E8.

4 June 20, 1994, p. 65.

5 Quoted in *Los Angeles Times*, January 18, 1995, p. E2.

6 OK, it's not Dickens saying this but some character in *The Haunted Man* (1859), but it amounts to the same thing for my purposes—or I can say it does.

7 Ros Coward, "Innocent Pleasure," *New Statesman & Society* 3 (April 13, 1990): 12; Diane H. Schetky and Arthur H. Green, *Child Sexual Abuse: A Handbook for Health Care and Legal Professionals* (New York: Brunner/Mazel, 1988), p. 15.

8 Coward, "Innocent Pleasure," p. 12. See also Noelle Oxenhandler, "The Eros of Parenthood," *New Yorker*, February 19, 1996, pp. 47–49.

9 All this is covered in a short half page on p. 277; but the intelligent honesty displayed by Bass and Davis here is clear.

10 Charles Dickens, *Great Expectations*, chap. 57.

11 This nonsense was the basis for a solemn editorial in the *Los Angeles Times*,

March 3, 1995, p. B6. The witlessness displayed is an index of our eagerness to believe that children think only what we think. Asked if contemporary morals are declining among the young, the young cross their fingers behind their back and say, "Yes sir!" And, wonder of wonders, we swallow it.

12 *Time*, June 20, 1994, p. 22.

13 The Samuelson op-ed piece appeared May 9, 1994, p. 73; the "Kids Growing Up Scared" special ran January 10, 1994, pp. 43–48, with the quote used here on p. 44.

Appendix

1 And once "Margaret" on *Dennis the Menace*.

2 Not many months after the conference, the papers carried news of the early death from "natural causes" of Tommy Retig, Provost's precursor on *Lassie*. Retig, dead at fifty-four, had not adjusted well to life after stardom: "a troubled life filled with failure to land adult roles. He also faced arrests and convictions for growing marijuana and importing cocaine, bankruptcy, divorce, and a string of jobs. . . . Retig remained a staunch advocate of recreational drug use throughout his adult life" (*Los Angeles Times*, February 17, 1996, p. A22).

3 And it's a sudden, unexpected out-the-door, loved one minute and despised the next. Shelley Fabares, another ex-star from *Mickey Mouse* and *Donna Reed* (now on *Coach*), said, "It was like, I went to bed on Tuesday having worked since I was 3. I got up on Wednesday morning and didn't work for four years" (*Los Angeles Times*, "TV Time," July 28, 1996, p. 5).

4 Quoted in Paul Petersen, "Kids and the Law" (1997 World Wide Web posting: http://www.minorcon.org/kidslaw.frm.html).

5 From *The Wonder Years*, a successful television series. Savage is one of the success stories, still working in television movies, theater, and the like while attending Stanford and majoring in English. Smart kid.

6 A good turnout, but nothing unusual. A "national talent search" to find a boy to play Beaver Cleaver in a film based on the television series drew a thousand kids to Universal Studios in one day and more than five thousand nationwide. One man who flew his son to Los Angeles from Mesa, Arizona, said, "We just always called Aaron 'The Beaver' at home . . . so when he heard about this on the radio, we had to come out and take a chance." Good thinking.

Index

Barr, Jerry, 2–3, 29
Barr, Roseanne. *See* Roseanne
Barr, Stephanie, 2–3
Barrie, J. M., 113, 144, 237
Barrymore, Drew, 160
Baskin, Roberta, 219
Bass, Ellen, 71, 168, 208, 244, 271–72, 278, 291, 309 n.6, 334 n.2
Baxter, Dolph (pseud.), 32, 37, 43–44, 47
Baxter, Mary (pseud.), 29, 31–50, 218
Baxter, Philip (pseud.), 39–40, 47
Beauty contests: and children, 103–4, 319 n.90
Bennett, William, 268; on caning, 149; on Hollywood, 266
Berendzen, Richard, 215–18
Bergmann, Martin, 142
Berlin: molestation rate in, 78
Bernadin, Joseph (cardinal), 223
Besharov, Douglas J., 79, 324 n.17
Best Kept Secret, The: Sexual Abuse of Children, 246
Between the Acts, 279
Big, 70
Big Brothers/Big Sisters, 220–21
Birkin, Andrew, 314 n.31, 322 n.17
Bishop, Jeanne, 266
Black Beauty (film), 123
Black, Lucas, 132
Blackboard Jungle (film), 159
Blake, William, 53
Bleak House, 291
Bless the Beasts and Children (film), 122
Blinn, William, 300
Bloom, Allan, 269
Bloom, Sandra L., 275
Blue Lagoon, The (film), 126
Blume, E. Sue, 275–76, 334 n.2
"Body, The," 70
Bomba, 63
Bono, Sonny, 118
Bonsall, Brian, 159
Boone, Pat, 283
Boop, Betty, 18–19
Borden, Lizzie, 222
Boston Globe, 146

Boy Scouts. *See* Scout leaders
Boys of St. Vincent, The (film), 221
Bradshaw, John, 70–71, 243
Branch Davidians, 16
Brandeis, Louis (Justice), 165
Brazil: street children in, 85
Break the Silence, 80
Breaking the Silence, 2–5, 76–78, 82
Briand, Ludwig, 126
Brontë, Charlotte, 57
Brothers, Joyce, Dr., 81–82, 97, 316 n.37
Brown, Blair, 159
Brown, Buster, 19, 63
Brown, Eric, 127
Brown, Kelly, 83–84
Brown, Randy, 83–84
Brown, Raymond, 184–85
Brown, Tom, 57
Brownmiller, Susan, 265
Buchanan, Patrick, 193, 224
Buckey, Raymond, 195–202, 209–10
Bugsy Malone (film), 126
Bullock, Sandra, 19, 105
Bullough, Vern L., 13, 171, 311 n.21
Butler, Samuel (the elder), 143
Buttermaker, Coach, 289

California: Dana Point, 219–20; Jamestown, 193–95; Manhattan Beach, 196–97; Petaluma, 100, 181; Picom Rivera, 201; San Diego, 221, 263–64; San Mateo, 93; Santa Catalina, 220; South Pasadena, 206; Universal City, 297; and war on teen sex, 185; and youth crime, 154
California Department of Justice, 168–69
California Social Services Committee on Child Abuse, 177
California State Committee on Credentials, 40, 49
California, Wrightwood: and the Baxter trial, 42–44
Campbell, Billy, 207
Caning: of Michael Fay, 147–51
Carnegie Corporation, The, 108
Carnegie-Mellon University: cyberporn

study, 170; teenage pregnancy study,
185–86
Carradine, Keith, 126
Carroll, Lewis, 70, 113, 126, 133, 141, 144,
237
Castration, 11, 91; chemical versions of,
90, 95
Caulfield, Holden, 95, 112–13, 237, 289
Cavett, Dick, 224
CBS, 80
Center for Missing and Exploited Children, 78
Champ, The (film), 134
Chapin, Billy, 129
Chapin, Lauren, 302–3
Charlotte (N.C.) Observer, 90, 207
Child (magazine), 56, 69, 99, 142; on
modesty, 314 n.2
Child, the: and abduction, 20; and accusations of molestation, 12, 16, 30–50;
and the adolescent, 18–19, 31–32, 151;
and anti-molestation education, 96–
98, 101; in beauty contests, 103–4,
319 n.90; and boundless love, 72; in
cinema, 114–37; and class, 20, 63–67;
as construction, 14–21, 52–53; and
construction of sexuality, 52–72; and
constructions of "the cute," 112–37;
defining the parent, 68–69, 142, 286;
demonizing, 151–60; as empty figure,
15, 18–20, 53–54, 193; and eroticism,
13–14, 17–20, 53–54, 282–83, 286–88,
311 n.21; being exposed, 74–109; and
fashion, 104–5; and gender, 20; and
happiness, 281–83; and Horatio Alger,
64–67; and inability, 208; and independence, 67–69; our indifference to,
160–64; and innocence, 15–16, 53–
54; and latency, 15–16, 55–56, 58;
and memory, 240–41; as molesters,
151–53; and naughtiness, 63–64; and
nostalgia, 24–25, 70–72, 240–41,
282; and no-touch, 108; photographs
of, 105–6; being protected, 74–109,
282–83; and purity, 15–16; and race,
20; and resentment, 53, 67, 140–64;
respecting, 136–37; and Romantic

idealization, 7, 14–15, 53–54, 59–63,
70–72, 281–82; and safety, 293–94;
and savagery, 57–63; spanking of,
145–51, 159, 292; as species, 67; as
subjects of hysterical stories, 166–
90; testimony of, 208–9; and women,
16–17
Child abuse, 13, 107–9, 160–64; emotional, 107–9, 160; neglect, 80, 107–9,
160, 180
Child abuse, physical, 80, 107–9, 160,
180; and murder, 80–81, 162–66
Child abuse, sexual: and accommodation syndrome, 81, 208–9; accusations
of, 89; and automatic guilt, 10; child
perpetrators of, 151–53; as criminals, 153–56; on the decline, 13; and
the Dutroux case, 86–87; educating
children on, 96–102; as epidemic, 9–
10, 244; expansion of, 78–79; and
false allegations, 81, 268–69; and the
Gothic, 10–13, 30–31, 94, 194, 221,
252, 264, 273, 283–84; and inflated
statistics, 78–80, 102, 252; and intention, 79; and memory, 22–24, 216–17,
240–58; and Michael Jackson, 229–
37; myth of sudden enlightenment,
77–78; and myths of stranger abduction, 78, 180–85; in other countries,
85–86; and our relish for sensation,
86–88; and parents, 75; and prominent people, 214–37; punishment
of, 91–94; reality of, 7–8, 249; and
silence, 3–5, 76–78, 82; a small problem, 13, 80; stories of, 7, 9–10, 20–22,
205–7; and symptoms, 10, 101; and
trials, 20, 30–50, 192–212; as unfathomable, 88–89; and Woody Allen,
224–29; worse than murder, 16–17
Child actors, 297–307
Child molesters: as aliens, 173–75; and
the backlash, 260–78; and castration,
11, 90–91, 95; children as, 151–53;
and the clergy, 221–24; defining and
locating, 82–85, 88–89; hysterical
stories of, 166–90, 205–7; and the
Gothic, 11–13, 30–31, 94, 194, 221,

Safer, Morley, 2
Samuelson, Robert, 293
San Francisco Examiner, 93–94
San Gabriel Civic Opera, 37
Sarandon, Susan, 126, 134
Satanic abuse, 175–80
Satanic Panic, 176
Saturday Night Live, 116
Satyricon, 145
Savage, and the child, 57–63
Savannah Smiles (film), 132–34
Save the Children, 88, 161
Sawyer, Diane, 102, 234–35, 333 n.39
Sawyer, Tom, 17, 144
Scalia, Antonin (justice), 161
Scandal: as opportunity, 26–27
Scapegoating, 7, 11
Scardino, Hal, 135
Scared Silent, 81, 151
Schmidt, David, 148
Schroder, Ricky, 17, 19, 322 n.18
Schwartz, Lloyd, 300
Scott, Sir Walter, 1
Scout leaders: and child sex abuse,
     219–21
"Scream" (Michael Jackson single), 234
Screen Actors Guild (SAG), 297, 299, 303
Searching for Bobby Fisher (film), 136
Second Best (film), 136
Sex education, 96
Sex Respect (sex education program), 96
Sexual child abuse. *See* Child abuse,
     sexual
Sexuality: construction of, 52–53; and
     the modern child, 52–72
Sexual predators. *See* Child molesters
Shalala, Donna, 79–80, 309 n.4
Shane (film), 114, 135–36
Shields, Brooke, 104, 124–26, 127, 236
*Shifting the Burden of Proof: Suing Child
     Sex Abusers,* 274
Shot in the Heart, 285
Showalter, Elaine, 326 n.1
Silence. *See* Breaking the Silence
Silverstone, Alicia, 18–19
Simon, Paul (senator), 78

Singapore: and Michael Fay caning,
     147–50
Sinyard, Neil, 157–58, 325 n.51
Sith, Kate, 228
60 Minutes, 2, 309 n.1
Sleepers (film), 188–90
Sleepless in Seattle (film), 124
Sling Blade (film), 132
Smith, Donna, 253–54
Smith, Liz, 228
Smith, Margaret, 176–77
Smith, Roger, 283
Solutions, 280–95
Spanking, 292; and eroticism, 145–51;
     statistics on, 145–46
Spellman (Cardinal), 124
Spielberg, Steven, 136–37
Spock, Benjamin (Dr.), 146
Stadler, Matthew, 115
Stand by Me, 70, 122–23, 128
Stern (German paper), 87
Stevens, Wallace, 191
Stone, Oliver: and HBO McMartin movie,
     200; on the media, 186
Stone, Sharon, 103
Stories: and the backlash, 260–78; and
     the Baxter trial, 30–50; and brutal
     simplicity of, 201–2; and child mo-
     lesting, 7, 9–10, 22–24, 94, 205–7,
     250–51; and child-molesting trials,
     192–212; of children and crime, 152–
     56; and comedy, 284, 286–95; as
     defining cultures, 1, 7; desire for, 7;
     destructive power of, 108–9; and
     double-speak, 20–21, 25; and entice-
     ment, 129–30; of exposure, 102–8;
     function of, 6–7; and the Gothic, 11–
     13, 20, 30–31, 94, 273; and the happy
     child, 281–83; and high-profile cases,
     214–37; and humanism, 290–91; and
     hysteria, 166–90; and memory, 22–24,
     241–42, 252–57; and movie children,
     115; new versions of, 24–27, 280–
     95; open-ended quality of, 260–61;
     of protection, 95–102; and recov-
     ered memory, 216–17; of resentment,

156–64; and scapegoating, 7; being trapped by, 24–27, 31–32, 40–50; and truth, 1, 40; of unprotected children, 100–1

Suggestions of Abuse, 269–70

Summit, Roland, 196, 275

Swift, Tom, 57

Symptoms: and recovered memory, 242–43, 268; of sexual child abuse, 10, 101

Taraborelli, Randy, 333 n.39

Tarzan, 63

Tavris, Carol, 264–65, 275–76

Taxi Driver (film), 127

Taylor, Elizabeth, 105; and Michael Jackson, 231, 237

Taylor, John, 253

Teacher (film), 127

Teachers: and sexual child abuse, 30–50, 218–19

Teenage pregnancy, 185–86, 325 n.50

Temple, Shirley, 17, 19, 104, 112–13, 140; and appeal to adults, 114–15, 118–21; and cult of the adorable, 322 n.15; and earnings, 302–3; emptiness of, 120; as model for later variants, 115

Tennyson, Alfred, 139

Terr, Lenore, 245, 277–78

Texas, Houston, 207

Therapists: attacks on, 266–70, 272

This Boy's Life (film), 128

Thomas, Clarence (supreme court justice), 92

Thomas, Danny, 300

Thomas, Henry, 136, 331 n.15

Thomas, Lord Denham, 191

Thornton, Billy Bob, 132

Three-Strikes Laws, 91

Throwaways, 80, 180

Thurber, James, 217

Thurmond, Strom (senator), 168

Tiger Bay (film), 132

Time, 72, 75, 151, 162; and the backlash, 266; and the Dutroux case, 87–88; on erotic fashions for kids, 104; and

explanations of pedophilia, 88–89; on Freud, 249; on Gary Gilmore, 285; on internet dangers, 95, 170; on memory, 257; on Michael Fay caning, 147–48; on spanking, 146; on Woody/Mia, 226–27, 229; on youth crime, 154

Toledo Blade, 220

Tom Jones, 34, 36, 46

Touchstone, 261

Trials: child molesting and spectacle, 20, 30–50, 192–212; children's testimony in, 208–12

True and False Accusations of Child Sexual Abuse, 268–69

Truffaut, François, 62

Twain, Mark, 237, 239

Twilight Zone, The (TV series), 298

Twist, Oliver, 54, 290–91

UNICEF, 160–61

United States Advisory Board on Child Abuse and Neglect, 76

United States Department of Health and Human Services, 78–79

United States Department of Justice, 80

United States Office of Human Development Services, 161

United States Senate: hearings on "Child Pornography and Pedophilia," 172

United States Supreme Court, 92; on children and Constitutional rights, 161; on spanking, 145

Universal Studios, 297

University of California, Davis: study on Satanic ritual abuse, 179

University of Colorado, 206

University of Southern California Police Seminar, 172–73

Unspeakable Acts (film), 200–201

Urban, Walter, 331 n.17

USA Today, 146, 153

Vice-Versa (film), 70

Victim role, 10, 12

Victims No Longer, 71

James R. Kincaid is the Aerol Arnold Professor of
English at the University of Southern California. He
is the author and editor of numerous books including
Annoying the Victorians and *Child-Loving: The Erotic
Child and Victorian Culture*.

Library of Congress Cataloging-in-Publication Data
Kincaid, James R.
Erotic innocence: the culture of child molesting/
by James R. Kincaid.
Includes bibliographical references and index.
ISBN 0-8223-2177-7 (cloth: alk. paper).
ISBN 0-8223-2193-9 (pbk.: alk. paper)
1. Child sexual abuse. I. Title.
HV6570.K545 1998   362.76—dc21   97–41074 CIP